Case Studies in Knowledge Management

Murray E. Jennex
San Diego State University, USA

Acquisitions Editor: Renée Davies
Development Editor: Kristin Roth
Senior Managing Editor: Amanda Appicello
Managing Editor: Jennifer Neidig
Copy Editor: Joyce Li
Typesetter: Jennifer Neidig
Cover Design: Lisa Tosheff
Printed at: Integrated Book Technology

Published in the United States of America by
Idea Group Publishing (an imprint of Idea Group Inc.)
701 E. Chocolate Avenue, Suite 200
Hershey PA 17033
Tel: 717-533-8845
Fax: 717-533-8661
E-mail: cust@idea-group.com
Web site: http://www.idea-group.com

and in the United Kingdom by
Idea Group Publishing (an imprint of Idea Group Inc.)
3 Henrietta Street
Covent Garden
London WC2E 8LU
Tel: 44 20 7240 0856
Fax: 44 20 7379 3313
Web site: http://www.eurospan.co.uk

Library of Congress Cataloging-in-Publication Data

Case studies in knowledge management / Murray Jennex, editor.
p. cm.
Includes bibliographical references and index.
ISBN 1-59140-351-0 (hardcover) -- ISBN 1-59140-352-9 (softcover) -- ISBN 1-59140-353-7 (ebook)
1. Knowledge management--Case studies. I. Jennex, Murray, 1956-
HD30.2.C378 2005
658.4'038--dc22
2005004515

British Cataloguing in Publication Data
A Cataloguing in Publication record for this book is available from the British Library.

Case Studies in Knowledge Management

Table of Contents

Section III:
Knowledge Management Strategy

Section IV:
Knowledge Management in Support of Projects

Section V:
Knowledge Management is Support of Knowledge Transfer

Preface

Knowledge Management (KM) has been growing in importance and popularity as a research topic since the mid 1990s. This is sufficient time for many organizations to implement KM initiatives and KM systems (KMS). This book presents twenty cases investigating the implementation of KM in a number of business and industry settings and a variety of global settings. The purpose of this book is to fill a deficiency that I've observed while teaching KM. KM is being taught in specialized courses and as a topic included in Decision Support Systems (DSS), Enterprise Information Systems (EIS), and Management Information Systems (MIS) issues courses. The deficiency I've observed is in moving discussions of KM from a focus on theory to the more practical focus of how to implement KM to help organizations improve their performance. Existing course materials do include some short cases and/or vignettes discussing KM in business settings, but I haven't found any source that has multiple, detailed teaching cases. This book is meant to fill that void.

The cases contained in this book are presented as teaching cases. All have discussion questions and are written in a style that students can easily read and understand. Also, additional sources and support materials are included where appropriate. The book includes cases from many different countries in an attempt to appeal to as wide an audience as possible. Cases are included from Australia, Austria, Bahrain, China, Egypt, Germany, Great Britain, Hong Kong, India, New Zealand, and the United States. Additionally, a variety of business situations are presented including banking, consulting, engineering, government agencies, manufacturing, military, project management, software development, and public utilities. Also, several different related processes and technologies are discussed. Related processes include organizational learning (OL) and organizational memory (OM). Technologies include Customer Relationship Management (CRM), Enterprise Resource Planning (ERP), Data Warehousing, networking, and Intranets. Finally, several issues are addressed including knowledge capture, knowledge sharing, knowledge transfer, knowledge representation, organizational culture, management support, KM/KMS success, KM sustainability, retaining worker knowledge, creating learning organizations, and management support.

WHAT IS KM?

There are many definitions of KM but this book combines the KM and OM literature to define KM as the process of selectively applying knowledge from previous experiences of decision-making to current and future decision making activities with the express purpose of improving the organization's effectiveness. This definition allows us to define the goals of KM as:

- Identify Critical Knowledge
- Acquire Critical Knowledge in a Knowledge Base or Organizational Memory
- Share the stored Knowledge
- Apply the Knowledge to appropriate situations
- Determine the effectiveness of using the applied knowledge
- Adjust Knowledge use to improve effectiveness

WHY OM AND OL?

Why is OM, and OL included in a book on knowledge management? Jennex and Olfman (2002) found that the three areas are related and have an impact on organizational effectiveness. KM and OM are observed to be manifestations of the same process in different organizations. User organizations 'do' knowledge management; they identify key knowledge artifacts for retention and establish processes for capturing it. OM is what IT support organizations 'do'; they provide the infrastructure and support for storing, searching, and retrieving knowledge artifacts. OL results when users utilize captured knowledge. That OL may not always have a positive effect is examined by the monitoring of organizational effectiveness. Effectiveness can improve, get worse, or

Figure 1. The KM/OM/OL Model (Jennex & Olfman, 2002)

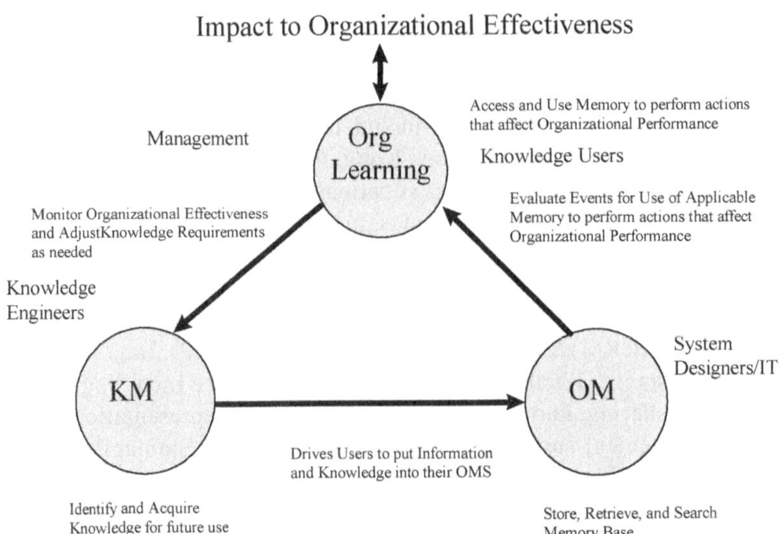

remain the same. How effectiveness changes influences the feedback provided to the organization using the knowledge.

WHAT IS A KMS?

The cases in this book address the implementation of Knowledge Management Systems (KMS). However, KMS is a term that does not have a consensus definition. Yes, we know what the initials KMS stand for and we have an understanding of what a system is. The IPO model: Inputs, Processes, Outputs, defines a basic system that when we add feedback, is a fair description of a KMS in a learning organization. We get further insight into what an information system is from Alter (1999) who defines an information system as humans or machines limited to processing information by performing six types of operations: capturing, transmitting, storing, retrieving, manipulating, and displaying. This is further refined by Churchman (1979, p. 29) who defines a system as "a set of parts coordinated to accomplish a set of goals;" and that there are five basic considerations for determining the meaning of a system:

- system objectives, including performance measures
- system environment
- system resources
- system components, their activities, goals and measures of performance
- system management.

Churchman (1979) also noted that systems are always part of a larger system and that the environment surrounding the system is outside the system's control, but influences how the system performs. These definitions are useful but don't fully describe a KMS. Reviewing the literature provides definitions that range from purely technical to something that includes organizational issues. These definitions are summarized below.

Alavi and Leidner (2001, p. 114) defined a KMS as "IT-based systems developed to support and enhance the organizational processes of knowledge creation, storage/retrieval, transfer, and application." They observed that not all KM initiatives will implement an IT solution, but they support IT as an enabler of KM. Maier (2002) expanded on the IT concept for the KMS by calling it an ICT (Information and Communication Technology) system that supported the functions of knowledge creation, construction, identification, capturing, acquisition, selection, valuation, organization, linking, structuring, formalization, visualization, distribution, retention, maintenance, refinement, evolution, accessing, search, and application. Stein and Zwass (1995) define an Organizational Memory Information System (OMIS) as the processes and IT components necessary to capture, store, and apply knowledge created in the past on decisions currently being made. Jennex and Olfman (2004) expanded this definition by incorporating the OMIS into the KMS and adding strategy and service components to the KMS.

Additionally, we have different ways of classifying the KMS and/or KMS technologies where KMS technologies are the specific IT/ICT tools being implemented in the KMS. Alavi and Leidner (2001) classify the KMS/KMS tools based on the Knowledge Life Cycle stage being predominantly supported. This model has 4 stages, knowledge creation, knowledge storage/retrieval, knowledge transfer, and knowledge application and it is expected that the KMS will use technologies specific to supporting the stage for which the KMS was created to support. Marwick (2001) classifies the KMS/KMS tools by the mode of Nonaka's (1994) SECI model (Socialization, Externalization, Combination, and Internalization) being implemented. Borghoff and Pareschi (1998) classify the KMS/KMS tools using their Knowledge Management Architecture. This architecture has 4 classes of components: repositories and libraries, knowledge worker communities, knowledge cartography/mapping, and knowledge flows; with classification being based on the predominant architecture component being supported. Hahn and Subramani (2001) classify the KMS/KMS tools by the source of the knowledge being supported: structured artifact, structured individual, unstructured artifact, or unstructured individual. Binney (2001) classifies the KMS/KMS tools using the Knowledge Spectrum. The Knowledge Spectrum represents the ranges of purposes a KMS can have and include: transactional KM, analytical KM, asset management KM, process-based KM, developmental KM, and innovation and creation KM. Binney (2001) does not limit a KMS/KMS tool to a single portion of the Knowledge Spectrum and allows for multi-purpose KMS/KMS tools. Zack (1999) classifies KMS/KMS tools as either Integrative or Interactive. Integrative KMS/KMS tools support the transfer of explicit knowledge using some form of repository and support. Interactive KMS/KMS tools support the transfer of tacit knowledge by facilitating communication between the knowledge source and the knowledge user. Jennex and Olfman (2004) classify the KMS/KMS tools by the type of users being supported. Users are separated into two groups based on the amount of common context of understanding they have with each other resulting in classifications of: process/task based KMS/KMS tools or generic/infrastructure KMS/KMS tools.

While I tend to favor a more holistic/Churchmanian view of systems and the KMS and like to classify the KMS by the amount of context needed by the users to effectively use knowledge, others are equally happy with these other KMS definitions and classification schemes. It is not the point of this book to settle the debate; in fact, many of the enclosed cases use definitions different than the holistic. KM is a young discipline and it will have multiple definitions of key terms for a while as we go through growing pains in establishing our definitions. That is okay, but for us to mature we need to settle on some of our fundamental definitions. Defining a KMS is one of those fundamental definitions we need to agree on. This is needed for our practitioners, and to some degree, our researchers. Practitioners need to speak a common language to each other and to their clients. The KMS is one of those concepts that clients expect us to understand. It is hoped that the cases in this book, when taken as a whole, provide support for the holistic definition as the KMS discussed are varied in their components and purpose.

ORGANIZATION OF SECTIONS

This book is organized into seven sections, each dedicated to an area of KM research. The following paragraphs describe these sections.

Section 1 looks at using KM in support of OL and contains two cases. The first case is from Lynne P. Cooper, Rebecca L. Nash, Tu-Anh T. Phan, and Teresa R. Bailey and describes a KMS used in the United States' Jet Propulsion Laboratory to help new employees learn about the organizational culture. The second case is from Brigette McGregor-MacDonald and describes the KMS used in Marsh, Inc. to help employees learn and pass on their knowledge to other employees. Both cases look at key issues and discuss the importance of management support in sustaining the KM effort.

Section 2 explores using KM to support the retention of organizational knowledge in organizations where the work forces are in transition. Hani Abdel-Aziz, and Khaled Wahba discuss the use of OM to capture knowledge in an Egyptian Professional Services company that had a high rate of employee turnover. Gail Corbitt discusses the issues affecting knowledge loss and the creation of two financial divisions when HP split into HP and Agilent. These papers find that the processes used to capture knowledge are critical. Additionally, issues such as corporate culture, technical infrastructure, and training are discussed

Section 3 discusses the importance of a KM strategy in the implementation of a KM initiative. Afsoun Hatami and Robert D. Galliers look at the long term impacts of strategy on the success of an OM system used to support decision making. Suzanne Zyngier, Frada Burstein, and Judy McKay discuss the use of corporate governance as a method of implementing KM strategy in Australia's Science and Technology Development Organization. Summer E. Bartczak and Ellen C. England discuss the issues involved in developing a KM strategy for the United States' Air Force Material Command's KM initiative. These cases also explore the impact of leadership and the use of a strategic framework in the development of a KM strategy.

Section 4 discusses the use of KM in the support of projects and project management. Elayne Coakes, Anton Bradburn, and Cathy Blake, discuss the use of KM to capture and use best practices in the British construction firm Taylor Woodrow to improve project performance. Jill Owen and Frada Burstein look at where knowledge resides in an Australian consulting firm and how the firm uses this knowledge to improve project performance. Both cases discuss the importance of understanding knowledge transfer dynamics to improve the flow of knowledge within a project team.

Section 5 discusses KM in support of knowledge transfer. Zhang Li, Tian Yezhuang, and Li Ping, discuss the dynamics of using a Enterprise Resource Planning system to capture and transfer knowledge in a Chinese manufacturing firm. Thomas Hahn, Bernhard Schmiedinger, and Elisabeth Stephan look at the use of communities of practice and other techniques to improve the transfer of knowledge in and between Austrian small and medium sized manufacturing firms. Florian Bayer, Rafael Enparantza, Ronald Maier, Franz Obermair, and Bernhard Schmiedinger discuss the use of Know Com to facilitate the decentralized control of the flow of knowledge between small and medium sized German die and mould makers.

Section 6 discusses a variety of issues associated with the implementation of KM and a KMS. Yogesh Anand, David J. Pauleen, and Sally Dexter discuss the development and sustainability of the KM initiative in the New Zealand Reserve Bank. Colin White and David Croasdell discuss issues in representing knowledge in Enterprise Resource Planning Systems at Nestle USA, Colgate-Palmolive, Xerox, and Chevron-Texaco. Minwir Al-Shammari discusses issues in using a Data Warehouse and a Customer Relationship Management system to capture and transfer knowledge in a Middle Eastern telecommunications company. Ivy Chan and Patrick Y.K. Chau explore why a KM initiative failed in a Hong Kong manufacturing and export firm. Nikhil Mehta and Anju Mehta discuss issues faced by India's Infosys Technologies, Limited. Eliot Rich and Peter Duchessi discuss the issues involved in sustaining the KM initiative at the United States' System Management Solutions International.

Section 7 discusses how to determine KM outcomes. A.N. Dwivedi, Rajeev K. Bali, and R.N.G. Naguib discuss a general KM framework for the British healthcare industry and how to manage KM successfully. Murray E. Jennex discusses how the use of knowledge can impact individual and organizational productivity.

REFERENCES

Alavi, M.& Leidner, D.E. (2001). Review: Knowledge management and knowledge management systems: Conceptual foundations and research issues. *MIS Quarterly, 25*(1), 107-136.

Alter, S. (1999). A general, yet useful theory of information systems. *Communications of the Association for Information Systems, 1*(13).

Binney, D. (2001). The knowledge management spectrum: Understanding the KM landscape. *The Journal of Knowledge Management, 5*(1), 33-42.

Borghoff, U.M. & Pareschi, R. (1998). *Information technology for knowledge management.* Berlin: Springer-Verlag.

Churchman, C. W. (1979). *The systems approach* (revised and updated). New York: Dell Publishing.

Hahn, J. & Subramani, M.R. (2000). A framework of knowledge management systems: Issues and challenges for theory and practice. *Proceedings of the Twenty-first International Conference on Information Systems, Association for Information Systems*, (pp. 302-312).

Jennex, M.E., Croasdell, D., Olfman, L. & Morrison, J. (2005). Knowledge management, organizational memory, and organizational learning at the Hawaii International Conference on System Sciences. *International Journal of Knowledge Management, 1*(1), 1-7.

Jennex, M. E. & Olfman, L. (2004). Modeling knowledge management success. *Conference on Information Science and Technology Management, CISTM.*

Maier, R. (2002). *Knowledge management systems: Information and communication technologies for knowledge management.* Berlin: Springer-Verlag.

Marwick, A.D. (2001). Knowledge management technology. *IBM Systems Journal, 40*(4), 814-830.

Nonaka, I. (1994). A dynamic theory of organizational knowledge creation. *Organization Science*, (5)1, 14-37.

Stein, E.W. & Zwass, V. (1995). Actualizing organizational memory with information systems. *Information Systems Research, 6*(2), 85-117.

Zack, M.H. (1999). Managing codified knowledge. *Sloan Management Review, 40*(4), 45-58.

Section I

Knowledge Management in Support of Organizational Learning

Chapter I

Learning from Simple Systems: The Case of JPL 101

Lynne P. Cooper, Jet Propulsion Laboratory, USA

Rebecca L. Nash, Jet Propulsion Laboratory, USA

Tu-Anh T. Phan, Jet Propulsion Laboratory, USA

Teresa R. Bailey, Jet Propulsion Laboratory, USA

EXECUTIVE SUMMARY

This chapter describes the development and operation of a knowledge system to support learning of organizational knowledge at the Jet Propulsion Laboratory (JPL). It describes in detail requirements generation, implementation, and rollout of the system and presents results from performance and usage data collected over 19 weeks of operation. Although the underlying technology was relatively straightforward, the development process had to address concerns from multiple stakeholders, support a broad user base, and incorporate a cost-effective approach to knowledge validation. These, in turn, impacted requirements, design, and maintenance of the system and how it was deployed within the organization. This case demonstrates that a relatively "simple" system can effectively support learning or organizational knowledge, while still presenting a variety of challenges during the implementation process.

BACKGROUND

The Jet Propulsion Laboratory (JPL) is a federally funded research and development center (FFRDC) operated for the National Aeronautics and Space Administration (NASA) by the California Institute of Technology (Caltech). JPL's history dates to the

1930s and Caltech's pioneering work in rocket propulsion. After two decades of support to the Army, JPL was transferred to NASA in December 1958. JPL brought with it experience in building and flying spacecraft, an extensive background in solid and liquid rocket propulsion systems, guidance, control, systems integration, broad testing capability, and expertise in telecommunications using low-power spacecraft transmitters and very sensitive Earth-based antennas and receivers.

Following the success of Sputnik, JPL developed the first U.S. satellite, Explorer 1. In the 1960s, JPL began to conceive and execute robotic spacecraft to explore other worlds. Ranger and Surveyor missions were launched to the moon, and Mariner missions visited Mercury, Venus, and Mars. JPL has since achieved stunning successes with an armada of missions such as Voyager, Galileo, Magellan, Deep Space 1, and Mars Pathfinder. It also had to deal with highly publicized failures such as the Mars Climate Orbiter and Mars Polar Lander missions. JPL is currently operating several missions (e.g., Cassini mission to Saturn, the Stardust comet sample return, Spitzer space observatory, and the twin Mars Exploration Rovers, Spirit and Opportunity), with many new missions in various stages of development.

As a major national research and development (R&D) laboratory, JPL's mission is

1. to explore our own and neighboring planetary systems;
2. to search for life outside the Earth's confine;
3. to further our understanding of the origins and evolution of the universe and the laws that govern it;
4. to make critical measurements to understand our home planet and help protect its environment;
5. to apply JPL's unique skills to address problems of national significance and security;
6. to enable a virtual presence throughout the solar system by creating the Interplanetary Network; and
7. to inspire the next generation of explorers.

In pursuit of this mission, JPL has a rich program of technology development, science, and mission development (the three "value-adding" processes of the Laboratory).

To enable the mission of the Laboratory, JPL boasts an extensive infrastructure of research, fabrication, test and design facilities and tools. Employees make use of a robust and extensive intranet, serviced by high-speed networks, internal and public access portals, and a multitude of Web-based systems, for example, to support accounting, human resources, document management, and internal communications functions. Hundreds of thousands of Web pages are published by individuals, teams, and organizations, and are accessible through directory and search utilities.

JPL covers 177 acres north of Pasadena, California. The university-like campus is home to about 5,500 employees and on-site contractors. Nearly three quarters of the workforce are involved in R&D activities in support of the three value-adding processes. Of the R&D personnel, roughly one third have PhDs, and an additional one third have master's or professional degrees. JPL has an annual operating budget of approximately $1.4 billion. Additional information about JPL can be found at www.jpl.nasa.gov.

SETTING THE STAGE

The system described in this article, JPL 101, is a series of Web-accessible quizzes built upon a database of general organizational knowledge, which is encoded as questions and has answers annotated with connections to related information and resources. JPL 101 was conceived of by the Knowledge Capture (KC) team, a subset of JPL's Knowledge Management (KM) project. This four-person team consisted of a librarian, two Web and database system designers, and an engineer who alternated between KM-related projects and working on Mars missions.

The motivation for the system was twofold. First, there was a growing concern by KC team members that the KM project in general was isolated from the value-adding processes that formed the mainstream work of the Laboratory. This isolation was believed to lead to products and services that did not fully address users' needs.

The second motivation was a desire to share valuable knowledge gained through a previous knowledge capture task. Prior to his retirement in fall 2001, the Deputy Director of the Laboratory agreed to do a series of retrospective interviews. During his tenure, JPL went through a decade of sweeping changes that fundamentally altered the way JPL conducted business. The primary purpose of the interviews was to collect information for the incoming deputy director who was new to the organization. However, it was felt that the insights gained during the interviews were of potential value to the greater Laboratory population. In particular, discussion about stakeholder relations and the interplay between NASA, Caltech, and JPL served to make sense of the changes that occurred throughout the 1990s.

This combination of motives led to the concept for JPL 101. It was felt that by calling attention to work related to the value-adding processes, the system could help improve the connection of the KM team to the rest of the Laboratory. In addition, by incorporating information gained through the interviews with the deputy director, valuable insights into stakeholder issues and basic operations could be shared with the Laboratory population.

Although inspired by events local to the KC team, the circumstances correspond to a broader organizational issue. To perform the planetary exploration mission and "do what no one has done before," large numbers of technical and professional disciplines must be integrated to support innovation (the value-adding process). In addition, infrastructure and support services are required to perform routine organizational functions (the enabling processes). While cross-functional project teams have become a common approach to integrating multidisciplinary knowledge in support of product development (Brown & Eisenhardt, 1995), less attention has been paid to bridging gaps between value-adding and enabling processes.

In established firms, emergent knowledge processes (EKPs) (Markus, Majchrzak, & Gasser, 2002), such as product development, take place within the context of the organization's bureaucracy. The clash between those tasked with operating the bureaucracy and those who must work within it can be viewed as another flavor of "thought world." Dougherty (1992) describes thought world differences between members from the marketing, engineering, and manufacturing functions in new product development teams. Areas such as human resources, contracting, accounting, and information technology also draw from different professional disciplines, focus on different critical issues, and use different approaches to define and solve problems. While cross-functional teams serve to bridge thought worlds by creating a shared vision of a successful, marketable product, there are few resources (e.g., mission statements) that are effective at providing the same sort of actionable focus for the organization as a whole.

Thought world-related problems, such as conflict and miscommunication, can be mitigated by helping people to learn about other domains and to recognize and exploit differences (Dougherty, 1992). Knowledge management systems (KMS) have the potential to support this type of learning. Knowledge-based approaches have been used to support transfer of best practices (Markus, 2001), knowledge reuse for innovation (Majchrzak, Cooper, & Neece, 2004), identifying experts, and a variety of business processes (Davenport, Jarvenpaa, & Beers, 1996).

Therefore, JPL 101 was envisioned as an educational resource for Laboratory personnel, and a way to assist them in exploring the abundance of electronic and other resources available to them. The orienting question that guided development was "How do you help people to make sense of the 'big picture' given that direct work-related exposure may be minimal (or nonexistent)?"

CASE DESCRIPTION

This case describes the 11-month evolution of JPL 101 from initial concept to fully operational system. There were three distinct stages: (1) *beta test* of initial concept, (2) *feasibility analysis* for use as a contest, and (3) *implementation*. Each of these phases is addressed in the following sections.

Beta Test

The goal of the beta test phase was to quickly assess whether it was worth pursuing implementation. Due to the structure of the KM project, there was flexibility to explore interesting concepts, but implementation required explicit approval and sponsorship by the KM project. From the very beginning, JPL 101 was conceived of as a quiz. The name was chosen as a tongue-in-cheek reference to beginners' classes in college to emphasize the educational nature of the resource, and to convey that much of the content is basic material that employees should know. The quiz metaphor seemed like a natural approach in an organization that values education as highly as JPL does.

The beta test version consisted of a paper prototype. Over the course of one week, the team brainstormed questions; experimented with different formats, difficulty, and wording of questions; and had much fun creating wrong answers. The resulting 81 questions were divided into three roughly equal groups. Participants were given the three sets of questions in different orders to make sure that all the test questions would have at least a subset of the group looking at them. Timed tests were then conducted where people worked their way through the quizzes. As expected, there were the occasional chuckles as people viewed the more humorous entries.

Reaction to the quiz from the KM project team was generally positive but skeptical as to the potential value of the system. While this beta testing did not garner enthusiastic support from the KM project, it did provide feedback used to determine the rough size of the quiz, appropriate mix of questions, and what constituted a reasonable level of difficulty for the questions.

Beta testing of content provided insight into the types of questions that had the potential to be controversial — primarily those that asked about absolutes such as "firsts," "only," or "bests." This led to standards for structuring a "good" question and guidelines for a reasonable amount of material to include in the answer.

Following the internal beta test, organizations within JPL that were perceived as potential stakeholders of the eventual system — Internal Communications, Human Resources, and the Ethics Office — were contacted. Additionally, a shortened, improved set of questions was tested as a demonstration model on actual work groups from the team's home organizations. The response was overwhelmingly enthusiastic. People were anxious to share the information with their colleagues, contribute questions and answers, and considered it both valuable and fun. Everyone, including people who had been with the organization for a number of decades, indicated that they learned something either through the questions or the supporting information given in the answers. In addition to encouraging proceeding with development, people also began suggesting questions that they thought would be good to include.

The beta test phase ended in a surprising way with the serendipitous opportunity to show one of the Laboratory's highest-ranking executives the paper prototype. He was instantly interested in the concept, brought his staff members in to have them take the quiz, and formulated the idea of using the JPL 101 concept as a Laboratory-wide contest as part of the 40th anniversary of planetary exploration being celebrated that year. Given this level of advocacy, the go-ahead from the KM project was quickly granted and immediately began our second phase of development, the feasibility analysis of using JPL 101 for a contest.

By the end of the beta test phase, the following was achieved:

- Confirmation that the basic concept was sound and likely to be positively received by the Laboratory population
- A cadre of stakeholders interested in seeing the system implemented
- A clear understanding of what constituted a well-formulated question: clear, concise, and simple structure; cautious use of absolutes; and humorous wording
- A practical approach to ensure correctness of the question by either triangulating an answer (two-sources to confirm) or verification through an unimpeachable source
- A requirement from the Knowledge Management project that the system encourage employees to explore the JPL intranet

Feasibility Assessment

The direction to evaluate if and how JPL 101 could be used to support a Laboratory-wide contest led to a detailed requirements analysis and resulting design decisions described in the following. At the same time, the team was also involved in a separate effort investigating how to capture decision rationale. It was decided to test some of ideas from that effort internally using informal decision-mapping techniques to capture the requirements generation process. These decision maps form the basis for the following discussion.

Answering the question "Is a contest feasible?" first required answering a set of key questions, as shown in Figure 1. An assessment was conducted by methodically working through each of these questions, identifying additional constraints, and

Figure 1. High level decision map

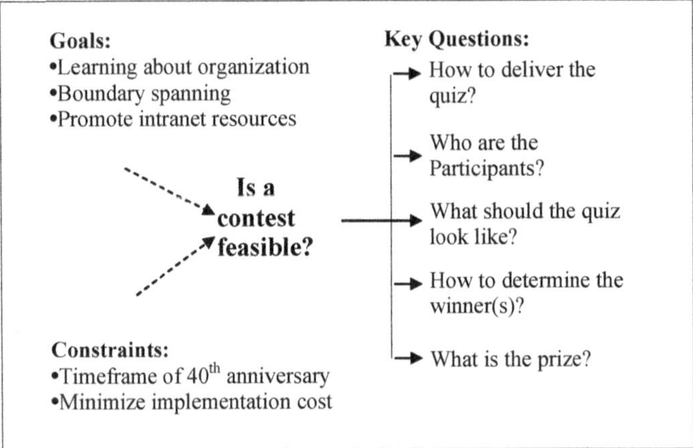

incorporating stakeholder concerns. The decision maps were used to track open issues, options, assumptions, information sources, and resulting requirements and design decisions. Even for a simple system such as JPL 101, the decision map quickly became a tangled web of interactions and information that did not easily fit into single categories. The decision maps presented in the following sections are simplified for illustration purposes.

How Do You Deliver the Quiz?

This turned out to be the easiest question to answer. Two potential methods were considered as shown in Figure 2. The first was to use a paper system, by sending a hard copy to all participants. This option was quickly eliminated as too burdensome due to the need for hand scoring of the quizzes, no ability to time-tag responses, and the reproduction and mailing costs. This option also was contrary to the KM requirement to promote exploration of the intranet.

The second option was to use a Web-based delivery mechanism via the JPL internal intranet. In addition to being the area of expertise for our team members, this option eliminated the negatives from the first option and contributed to a reasonable definition of our participants. After making this decision, the team immediately began prototyping activities so that we would have a system to experiment on during the rest of the assessment period.

Who are the Participants?

The delivery mechanism decision effectively limited participation to those who had routine access to the JPL intranet. Four categories of potential participants were identified based on the derived requirement that participants have a JPL-issued badge and identification number: current JPL employees, current JPL contractors, JPL retirees, and others resident at JPL but not falling into the previous categories. From within these categories, several issues were identified:

Figure 2. Delivery mechanism decision map

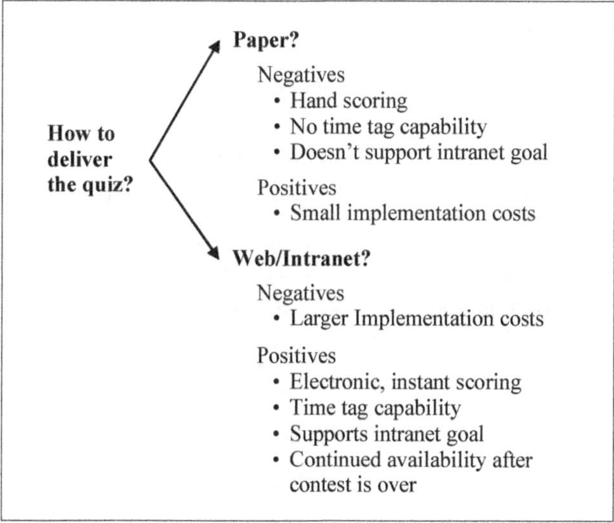

1. **Timekeeping constraints:** How much time could people in the individual categories commit to participating before we needed to provide them with an account code? This was resolved through the Ethics Office and resulted in a requirement that each individual quiz takes 15 minutes or less. Also, our Ethics Office confirmed that JPL personnel could participate, but that the Human Resources department would have to determine whether contractors could participate.
2. **Contractor constraints:** Could contractors participate, and if so, were there any timekeeping constraints, and were they eligible for prizes? These issues remained open during the feasibility analysis.
3. **Retiree participation:** Would we actively work to enable retiree participation, and if so, were they eligible for prizes? It was decided that our system should not *preclude* participation from retirees as long as they had intranet access (we would *not* provide external access) and they had a JPL badge. However, they would not be eligible for prizes.

As shown in Figure 3, these decisions led to the following:

- System must be capable of supporting an upper bound of 8,000 participants.
- The individual quizzes must be sized to keep participation under 15 minutes.
- Participants must have a current JPL badge and intranet access.
- Only current JPL employees are eligible for prizes.

What Should the Quiz Look Like?

Beta testing determined how to construct good individual questions. The next set of decisions addressed how to construct the quizzes. Figure 4 shows the decision map for the quiz design. In addition to requirements to keep participation under 15 minutes

Figure 3. Participation decision map

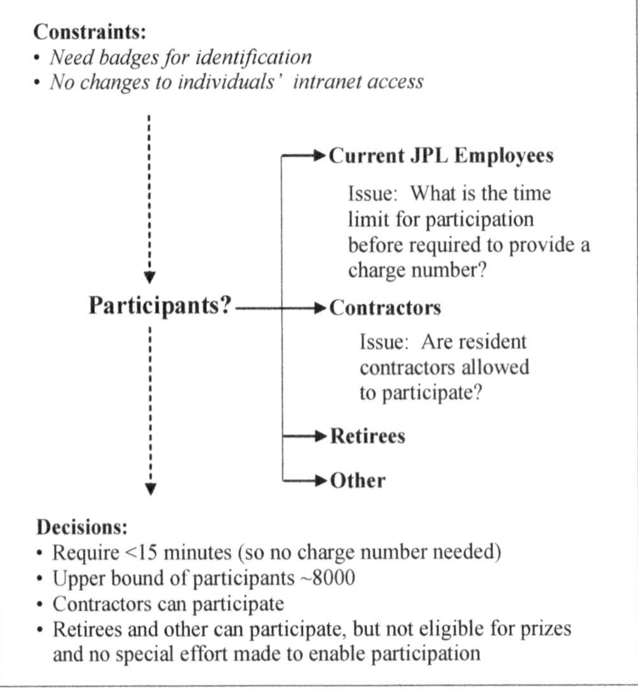

and be able to differentiate 8,000 participants, specific goals that we set for the system were as follows:

- Make the quizzes challenging but not burdensome
- Ensure that the number of questions we have to generate is reasonable
- Have a broad mix of questions that include some aspect from all areas of the Laboratory community

The driving factor in the quiz design was the need to differentiate 8,000 participants to determine the winner(s). We knew that there was limited project support for this effort and therefore felt that we would have resources to reliably develop only 100 to 120 questions. This is too small a number of questions to be able to distinguish the number of potential participants solely based on score, so we determined that a time component was also needed.

Several options were considered for incorporating a time-based component to the score. Our executive advocate had suggested a "fastest finger" approach where whoever got the most right in the shortest time would win. This approach, however, brought to bear issues of network latency (which is a function of the number of users) and would require that the system time tag all quizzes, leading to concerns about server load.

A technically feasible approach to the quiz design was not possible until we answered the question of how to determine the winner. However, it was determined that

Figure 4. Quiz design decision map

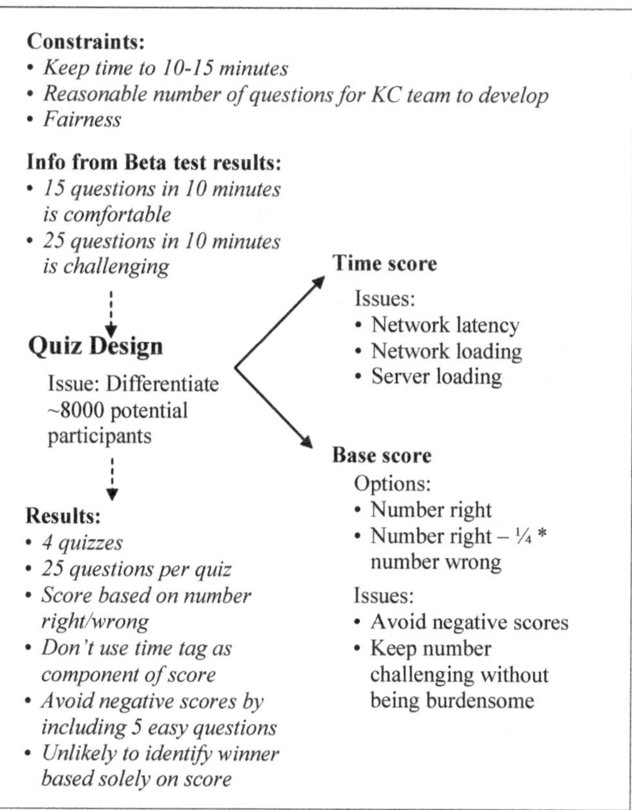

we were looking at a four-week contest, consisting of four quizzes at 25 questions each, and that it was highly unlikely that we would be able to identify a single winner based on this design.

How Do You Determine the Winner?

One way to work around the inability to reliably create a single winner is to create multiple categories of winners. We assumed that it would be harder for newer employees than more experienced employees, and that different categories of employees would shine in different subject areas. Based on these assumptions, participants would be grouped based on number of years of tenure, with three categories of under five years, five to 20 years, and more than 20 years, driven by the demographics of the Laboratory and a desire for fair groupings.

A multitiered approach was chosen, with weekly results feeding into identification of grand winners. The weekly results would be based on a score computed as the number of right answers minus a fraction of the number of wrong answers, similar to the Scholastic Aptitude Tests (SATs). Options for handling ties, which were highly likely on a weekly basis, were a tie-breaker quiz, drawing names from the pool of highest scores, or simply

Figure 5. Winner determination decision map

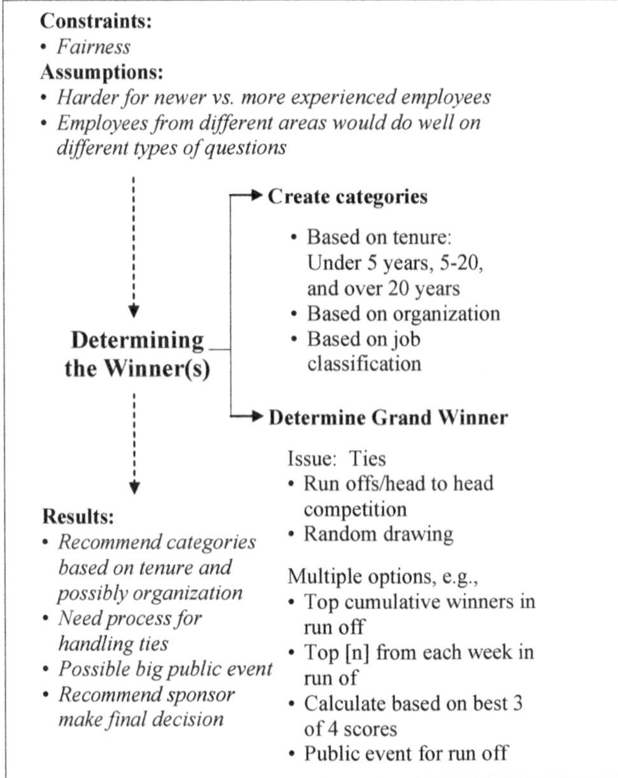

accepting multiple winners. The best choice for these options would depend on whether prizes were given at the weekly level. One consequence of our scoring scheme, which was chosen to increase differentiation, is that it would be possible to actually obtain a negative score. To reduce this possibility, we decided to include at least five easy questions per quiz.

The multiweek format also led to multiple options for determining the grand winners, as shown in Figure 5. These options, based on cumulative results, imply that winners participate each week, which in turn raises issues of fairness (because people may be on travel or vacation), and could result in a drop in participation due to people feeling that they were out of the running.

Inherent in the determination of winners is the ability to identify the participants and associate them with their results. The multiweek format meant that we also needed to correlate participation by the same individuals across weeks. Therefore, our system had to

- have a method to handle ties;
- ensure a fair opportunity for participation;
- provide a fair and culturally acceptable method for determining winners;

Figure 6. Prize decision map

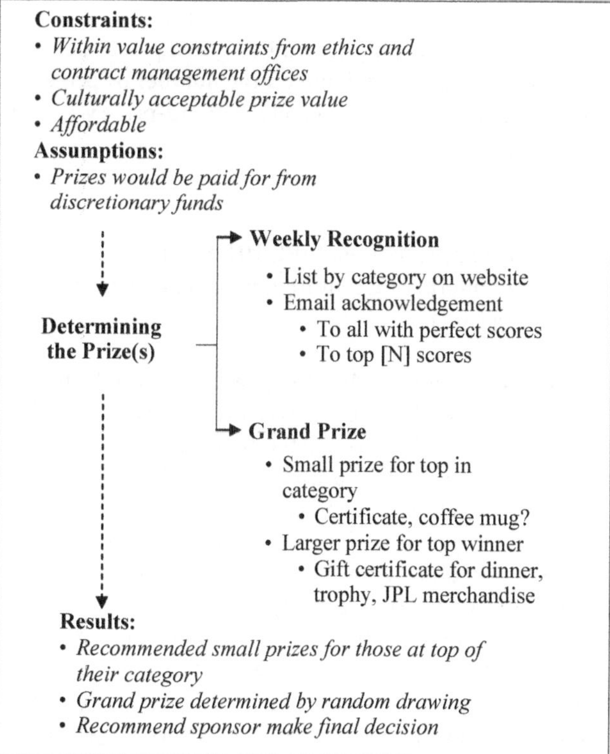

- provide a method for differentiating between different categories of participants;
- have the technical capability to implement a scoring scheme based on both score and time;
- have a reasonable approach to addressing attempts to "game" the system; and
- reduce the probability of negative scores.

What is the Prize?

Due to JPL's status as an FFRDC, there were a number of constraints on the prizes. While the Ethics Office confirmed that it was all right to give prizes, our Contracts Management Office ruled that prizes were an "unallowable" cost based on JPL's contract with NASA, and therefore would have to be paid for from discretionary funds and remain under a specified value. Our executive-level advocate said that his office would provide or obtain the discretionary funds to cover the costs of the prizes. Figure 6 provides an overview of our decision process for determining prizes.

Because the structure of the contest was two tiered with weekly quizzes leading to a grand prize winner, we looked at a combination approach. For weekly winners, a number of ties were expected. Rather than a prize, we evaluated different recognition mechanisms, for example, a system-generated e-mail for those obtaining a perfect score, or those with the top scores. Alternatively, we considered listing the top scores by category on a Web site.

The prize options included merchandise from the JPL gift shop, trophies, or certificates, with the possibility of a higher-valued grand prize such as a gift certificate for dinner. We decided to leave the decision on the number of prizes to award, how to acknowledge weekly winners, and how to select the grand-prize winner up to the contest sponsor.

Summary

Despite the relatively simple nature of JPL 101, the decision space quickly became complicated with multiple interacting requirements and constraints. Management was presented the following options:

Option 1: Use the JPL 101 quiz for a Laboratory-wide contest. Winners in each category would be chosen based on best score over the four weeks of the contest. Token prizes, as permitted, would be given to the finalists, with the ultimate grand-prize winner(s) chosen from a random drawing of the finalists. This option required additional software development and coordination across multiple departments, but had the potential to generate significant interest and participation. Additional details would be worked out with the internal contest sponsor.

Option 2: Proceed with JPL 101 as originally conceived without the contest element. This option required minimal software development, kept the focus on the content and therefore the goals of the KM project to promote intranet capabilities, and was considered less risky. However, it would not benefit from the executive-level attention and did not have prize incentives as a way of gaining interest.

After several months of debate, cost considerations won out, and Option 2 was chosen.

Implementation

JPL 101 is a Web-accessible database of general organizational knowledge. Knowledge is encoded as questions, answers, and connections to related information and resources (see Cooper, 2003a for a detailed discussion of the use of the quiz interface). The system is organized into quizzes each containing five to 10 multiple-choice and matching questions. The deployment of the system took place over 12 weeks, after which it entered steady-state operation. During each of the first 12 weeks, a new quiz was added. Following the 12-week initial deployment of the content, the system provided access to the full set of past quizzes.

The implementation of JPL 101 was relatively simple, with a minimal amount of user functions. Due to rapidly dwindling support from the KM project, low maintenance costs were essential and the questions and answers needed to be robust with regard to obsolescence. In addition to question and answer fields, the JPL 101 database also included administrative fields for identifying the category, originator, quiz, and validation date for each question.

During the initial 12-week deployment, the entry page for JPL 101 featured a direct link to the current week's quiz. Access to previous quizzes, background information, and feedback mechanisms were provided through pull-down menus. After the 12-week deployment period, the entry page provided a direct link to the list of previous quizzes as well as the menu-accessible items.

Design Considerations

JPL 101 was designed based on the assumptions that the general JPL population had access to a computer, was able to effectively use a Web interface, and would find the use of a quiz-based model for the knowledge acceptable. The first two are reasonable assumptions given the proliferation of Web-based institutional applications for general exchange of information, support of business and administrative functions, and organizational communications. The third assumption was validated during preliminary beta testing of the concept.

Based on the assessment of the organization and with guidance from the Ethics, Human Resources, and Internal Communications offices, several constraints were incorporated into the design process. First, the overall set of quizzes were made representative of concerns across the wide range of disciplines in the Laboratory so that no group would feel "ignored" in the process and to ensure that the thought-world issues were addressed. Second, in order to avoid potential problems with time-keeping rules, the quizzes were kept short. Third, we had to ensure that people could participate at their convenience, and that pragmatics, such as individuals being on travel, would not limit participation. Fourth, since participation would be voluntary, there had to be motivations to use the system. Fifth, the goal of the system was learning, therefore it was critical that there were mechanisms for assessing whether people actually benefited from the system. Finally, it was important that people *not* feel that they were being graded or assessed in any way. Therefore it was necessary to ensure that participants could take the quizzes without fear of violating their privacy. This limited the type of performance and participation data that could be collected.

Content

The heart of JPL 101 is the content. The content categories were carefully chosen to emphasize areas important to the Laboratory, essentially representing the different thought worlds. Table 1 provides a description of the different categories, the rationale for including them, and an example of each.

Over the course of the 12 weeks, a total of 66 questions were presented. Each question went through a rigorous quality check to ensure accuracy and that it met the standards for a well-formulated question. The distribution of questions across categories is also provided in Table 1.

Two areas received special attention in developing the questions: JPL Basics and Stakeholders. The 21 questions in the Basics category covered material ranging from how to get help with computer problems to knowledge on new institutional resources and local restaurants available after hours. This is the type of knowledge that generally does not receive high visibility, but contributes to the overall work environment. The Stakeholder category consisted of 10 questions that covered the multiple constituencies to which JPL is responsible. Because JPL is a National Laboratory operated for NASA by the Caltech, there is a wide spectrum of stakeholders who influence the operations of the Laboratory. Understanding the nature of these stakeholder relationships and the various legal,

Table 1. JPL 101 question categories

Area	Description	Rationale	Example
Basics (n=22)	General knowledge about how JPL operates at and below the level of published procedures	Make it easier for employees to learn about things that make it easier to get their job done (and correct misconceptions)	What is the number to call if you're having computer hardware or software-related problems? (A: x4-HELP)
History (n=6)	Knowledge of key accomplishments and of individuals who contributed greatly to the Lab	Establish a connection to the past and share accomplishments that contribute to a sense of pride.	Who was the director of GALCIT, and co-founder of JPL? (A: Theodore von Kármán)
Missions (n=10)	Knowledge about missions, which are the primary product of the Laboratory and the focus of our work	Share the excitement of space exploration, which is the reason for existence for the Lab	What is the name of the rover that explored the surface of Mars in 1997? (A: Sojourner)
Product Developmen t (n=9)	Knowledge about how the Laboratory builds and operates space missions and instruments	The three JPL core processes represent the reason the Lab exists: our mission of space exploration. All work at the Laboratory contributes either directly to one of these three areas, or is responsible for supporting these processes.	Where could you go at JPL to evaluate your spacecraft under environmental conditions that are similar to those found in space? (A: 25-foot Space Simulator)
Science (n=5)	Knowledge about key scientific principles of importance in space exploration		What is the most active volcanic body currently known in the solar system? (A: Jupiter's moon, Io)
Technology (n=4)	Knowledge about the development of technology of importance in space exploration		What is the name of the substance nicknamed "frozen smoke"? (A: Aerogel)
Stakeholders (n=10)	Knowledge about external entities that impact or are impacted by JPL	JPL is answerable to multiple constituencies and is often highly constrained in the way it can operate. It is critical for JPL personnel to understand these factors and how they impact their work.	Who is the President of Caltech? (A: Dr. David Baltimore)

contractual, and public trust concerns of the Laboratory is important for efficient operation.

PERFORMANCE ASSESSMENT

Two primary methods were used for collecting performance, participation, and user data: background collection of usage statistics and quiz answers, and user participation in the form of e-mail feedback, an online survey, and an online form to submit comments. The background data collection was performed using a commercial monitoring package associated with the Web server. It provided information such as hit rates, IP addresses, number of unique visitors, amount of time spent on site, and time distributions of users.

In addition, the quiz database recorded the answers submitted each time someone took a quiz.

The online survey was used to collect basic organizational demographics (tenure, organizational unit, job category, and whether a manager or not) and responses to two questions: "Did you learn anything from the questions?" and "Did you learn anything from the answers?" Taking the survey was voluntary, as was responding to the demographic questions. The second anonymous response method was an online feedback form. Users could submit comments, problems, feedback, and candidate questions for the system. While most users decided to remain anonymous, some made the effort to include their names and contact information. Finally, the e-mail based feedback form was available to contact the development team directly. This was not anonymous and was the least-used form of feedback.

Results

JPL 101 premiered on January 13, 2003, and ran for 12 weeks ending its initial deployment on April 6. It remains in operation, although new content is not currently being developed. Results are presented based on analysis of the data collected during the initial 12 weeks, and extending through Week 19 of operations relative to the following: design considerations, usage, motivation for use, learning results, and general reaction.

Design Considerations

Background usage and database data were analyzed to assess how well the design considerations were met. Background usage data indicated success in meeting the participation time goals of the system. The average time spent in the system each workday ranged from 2:01 minutes to 8:21 minutes, with the mean being 3:53, which are within the limits recommended by JPL Ethics and Human Resources offices.

A second consideration was that the quizzes needed to be challenging but not too hard. Figure 7 shows the average quiz scores for the 12 quizzes, based on data from the entire operational period. With the exceptions of weeks five and eight, the average quiz scores stayed between 70% and 90%, meeting the goal.

Figure 7. Average quiz score per quiz

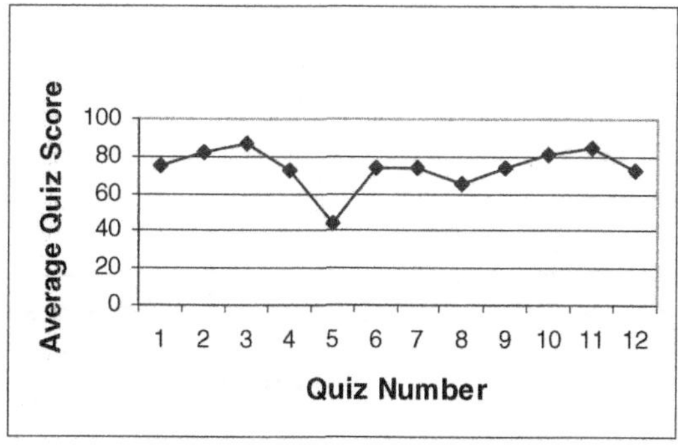

Additionally, there was a concern with question quality. Because the JPL culture is such that participants would readily point out any errors in the questions, evaluation of question quality was based on the number of corrections required. Two inputs regarding the accuracy of questions were received, one of which resulted in a minor change (attributing an additional source for information in an answer). Given the volume of material in 66 questions plus all the associated ancillary information, two minor comments were well within the range for acceptable performance.

Participation

Ultimately, a measure of success for a system is the number of people who use it. Given that this is a voluntary-use resource and not required for anyone's job, participation statistics are critical for gauging overall success. Background usage statistics were collected including hit rates and unique visitors based on IP addresses, modified to filter out members of the development team and automated Web crawlers. During the 19 weeks of operation covered in this study, a total of 2,144 employees participated, roughly 40% of the Laboratory population. Figure 8 shows the usage statistics over time for the 19 weeks.

In addition to reaching a large audience, the goal was to reach a broad audience. Although privacy and user-burden concerns prevented automatic collection of organizational demographics on general participants, a voluntary survey instrument was used to collect some data. Five hundred and thirty-three surveys were received over the course of 19 weeks, representing a participation rate of just under 25%. The organizational tenure for participants ranged from brand new (zero years) to a maximum of 47 years, with an average of 15.3 years and a standard deviation of 10.5 years. Users spanned the entire Laboratory, with participation concentrated most heavily in the Technical and Administrative divisions, where the majority of Laboratory personnel are assigned. Participants were distributed across technical, administrative, and science disciplines, and included both managers and nonmanagers. Taken in total, the data collected via the online survey indicates a broad and substantial audience.

Figure 8. Participation by week, annotated to show key communication activities

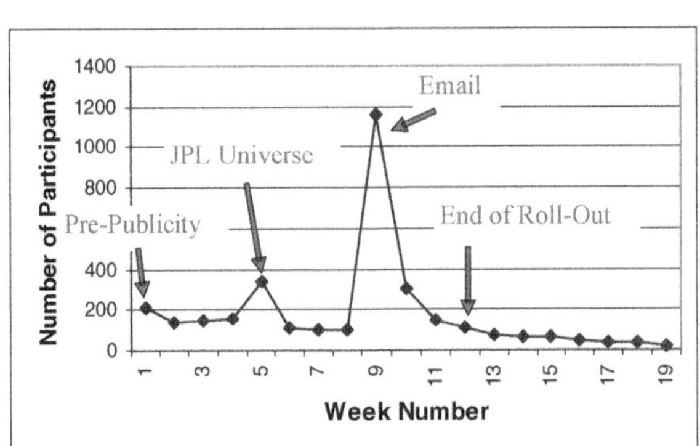

Impact of Communication Mechanisms

Because JPL 101 is a voluntary-use system, providing general rather than job-specific knowledge, a number of institutional communication mechanisms were employed to let people know this resource existed. These mechanisms were as follows:

- **JPL Universe:** a traditional, biweekly organizational "newspaper" distributed to personnel through interoffice mail. There was a multicolumn story about JPL 101 plus a sample quiz the week before rollout.
- **Cafeteria Monitors:** closed-circuit television screens in the cafeterias that broadcast announcements. Consisted of "teaser" questions — shorter versions of quiz questions, plus the URL for the site — for three days prior to rollout.
- **Daily Planet:** electronic daily "newspaper" for JPL personnel. Accessible via intranet. Publicity was via an a small graphic posted on the sidebar of the page that linked to JPL 101, starting the first day of rollout and continuing through the 12-week rollout period. In addition, a short informational article was placed in center column "news item" area during Week 5 of rollout.
- **Inside JPL Portal:** Web portal that provides central access to JPL Web space for internal users. A link to JPL 101 was included in sections for new employees and institutional knowledge management during the first week.
- **This Week:** electronically distributed (e-mail announcement with link to Web page) weekly newsletter that highlights personnel announcements, organizational changes, and upcoming talks and events. A one-paragraph blurb about JPL 101 plus access information was included several times throughout the 12-week rollout.
- **All.Personnel e-mail:** a tightly controlled list that sends e-mail to the entire Laboratory population. A single all.personnel e-mail was sent during Week 9.

Publicity for JPL 101 began 1 week prior to its rollout. Prerelease publicity included an article in the *JPL Universe* and announcements on the JPL monitors. In partnership with the Internal Communications Office, the primary entry point for JPL 101 was the *Daily Planet*. Unfortunately higher priority events limited entry to a single sidebar icon during the initial weeks. This icon remained until the end of the initial 12-week run. Later during the first week, access was added via the Inside JPL portal. These links continued throughout the entire period.

The impact of each of these devices can be seen in the usage statistics shown in Figure 8. The first spike in the graph occurs during Week 5 and corresponds to the publication of the *Daily Planet* article. Additionally, a smaller increase, not visible in the weekly statistics but present in the daily statistics, occurred when links were added to the Inside JPL portal. The most prominent feature of the graph, however, is the gigantic spike that occurs during Week 9. This corresponds to the sending of the all.personnel e-mail publicizing JPL 101. This spike is due almost entirely to the *day* that the e-mail was sent.

Learning Results

The primary goal of the system was individual learning. Success was assessed in attaining this goal in two ways. The first, and most direct way, was to use the survey to simply ask participants if they learned anything. Almost 90% of the survey respondents indicated that they had learned something from either the questions, the answers, or both. Preliminary analysis found small but significant negative correlations ($p < .01$) between tenure and learning, and being a manager and learning. No other relationships were found.

The second approach to evaluating learning was to look at the quiz response data. Figure 7 shows the average scores for each of the 12 quizzes. These data indicate that on average, people missed one to two questions per quiz, indicating that a learning opportunity existed. Detailed analysis of individual questions shows that the number of respondents getting a specific question right varied from a low of 33% to one question where everyone who answered got it right.

There was also interest in how well people performed across the different categories of questions and in what questions were skipped. Table 2 provides a summary of the performance in each of the categories. Inspection of Table 2 data indicates that JPL personnel performed well on questions relating to the three value-adding processes, slightly below average on Basics, History, and Missions, and significantly below average on Stakeholder questions. While JPL 101 is not intended as a diagnostic system for organizational knowledge, these results suggest a gap in knowledge about stakeholders that should be remedied. Inspection of the data on questions that were skipped clearly showed that matching-type questions were skipped more often than multiple-choice question, with all five matching questions placing within the bottom-six response rates.

Other

Feedback via e-mail and through the online form was overwhelmingly positive. (The sole negative comment received via any of the feedback mechanisms was a complaint about the use of the all.personnel e-mail.) For example, one respondent wrote, "This is great and I love it! I learned more about JPL in the past few weeks just by taking these quizzes then the three years I have been here. Thank you." Several constructive comments were made about how to improve the system. Respondents were pleased with the quiz-type presentation, and one suggested that "JPL 101 is the paradigm that should be used for all training and knowledge dissemination at JPL."

One area of disappointment was the lack of suggestions for questions. During beta testing for JPL 101, one of the most surprising results was the level of excitement individuals had over the idea of the quiz, and their desire to contribute questions and make suggestions for material. Because of this response, the feedback form in the system included a field specifically for submitting potential questions. Only three suggestions were received, resulting in two new questions.

Summary

In summary, the variety of data collected during the 19 weeks of operation for JPL 101 provided valuable information used to assess overall performance and success of the system. The following section discusses these results and the potential learning to be gained from them.

Table 2. Summary of performance across question categories

Category	Number of Questions	Average % Skipped	Average % Right
Basics	2.2	2.1	73.2
History	6	1.7	70.9
Missions	10	1.4	75.6
Product Development	9	0.8	83.5
Science	5	0.8	85.2
Stakeholders	10	1.5	66.0
Technology	4	0.6	85.1
Total/Average	66	1.3	77.1

CURRENT CHALLENGES/PROBLEMS FACING THE ORGANIZATION

JPL 101 was a small effort created to share special information and promote intraorganizational appreciation for the different areas that need to work together to accomplish the JPL mission. When JPL controls spacecraft en route to other planets, small forces applied in the right direction at the right time are the difference between reaching the destination and missing by hundreds of kilometers. The JPL 101 effort was viewed in a similar light.

The motivating factors for the creation of JPL 101 represent common themes in organizations, for example, getting different parts of the organization to work together effectively, communicating culture and values to new employees, addressing stakeholder concerns, aligning infrastructure and support functions with value-adding processes. As with many KM systems, the effects of the knowledge conveyed through JPL 101 cannot be measured directly (Cooper, 2003b). Conditions before and after remain virtually indistinguishable. The differences, if any, have been small and below the surface, for example, less frustration when following a policy, a little more respect for others doing their jobs, and a greater sense of community. By having a positive individual impact, we expect to have a positive organizational impact, as suggested by Jennex and Olfman (2002). While we cannot measure it, the net result of JPL 101 was that nearly half the employees learned something new that is relevant to the organization. And that, in turn, should have a positive effect on the organization.

As noted by Kuchinke (1995), "organizations have in fact little control over *whether* learning takes place, but they do have potentially substantial amounts of control over the *kind* of learning that occurs within their bounds" (p. 309). In this respect, JPL 101 provides a learning opportunity where the content, by its mere presence, indicates a degree of organizational importance and the system serves as an intervention aimed at reducing thought-world differences between personnel.

The deployment of JPL 101 also led to gaining new insights into the development and use of knowledge management-type systems at JPL. First, fun worked. The use of humor and clever construction of questions and answers did not diminish the fundamental value of the content, but instead contributed to user satisfaction.

Second, there were remarkable differences in the effectiveness of different institutional communications channels, as evidenced by the usage data. While one must be cautious about extrapolating from a small number of experiences, the data for JPL 101 imply that specific channels are more effective in motivating participation than others. In this case, the all.personnel e-mail (which was short and clearly indicated that participation would take a small time investment with high potential for payoff) resulted in orders of magnitude increases in participation.

Third, the differences in successful response rates for different question categories do provide a level of diagnostic information regarding gaps in individual knowledge about the organization. The particularly low scores in the stakeholder category reinforced the concern about general awareness of stakeholder issues. This information could be used to modify communication and training activities to place special emphasis on areas with subpar performance.

Fourth, the feedback responses were overwhelmingly positive, particularly with respect to the quiz interface. Given the JPL culture, it was felt that this was a good approach (Cooper, 2003a), but there was surprise at the level of enthusiasm and with the degree of frustration expressed regarding other online training interfaces. This result indicates that modifications to existing training approaches may be warranted.

Finally, the future value of a KMS is dependent upon continued support. Management support (e.g., funding) for JPL 101 stopped immediately after the initial 12-week deployment. No new content has been developed and updating of the current content is on a volunteer basis. This was anticipated and the questions were designed to minimize obsolescence and the system incorporated mechanisms to make content maintenance easy (e.g., on the order of minutes to update questions or answer content). It is the sense of ownership felt by the development team coupled with the intentionally low-maintenance design that keeps this system operational.

JPL 101 has been in operation for over 18 months. During that time, only five questions became obsolete due to reorganizations and personnel reassignments. However, the content included in the answers to those questions provided links that would take the participants to the correct information. Usage levels have dropped to less than 20 users per month, but there are both new and repeat users, with new employees accounting for about one third of the participants. Online survey responses continue to show that well above 90% of respondents feel they have learned something as a result of participating.

The factors motivating the development of JPL 101 still exist in the current environment, and will probably continue to exist for the foreseeable future. Organizations must continuously work to facilitate understanding and respect across the different components of the organization. The potential impact of JPL 101 during its initial 12-week deployment was enhanced by having large numbers of employees from across the organization learning and thinking about the same things at the same time. The potential now has changed somewhat as small numbers of individuals access the system in an ad hoc fashion, reducing the "shared-experience" aspect. The system does, however, provide a means of reinforcing previous learning for repeat visitors, and can help new employees begin the acculturation process. Even the obsolete questions serve a purpose by capturing a snapshot of the organization and key personnel as they had existed during an important period in JPL's history. While the current organizational climate is not conducive to continuing development of JPL 101, we are confident that future opportunities will exist to extend the system.

FURTHER READING

The following Web sites provide additional information about JPL, NASA, and the NASA Knowledge Management team:

http://www.jpl.nasa.gov
http://www.nasa.gov
http://km.nasa.gov

In addition to the references provided in this chapter, we recommend the following books and articles:

Argyris, C. (1999). *On organizational learning* (2nd ed.). Malden, MA: Blackwell Business.

Huber, G.P. (1991). Organizational learning: The contributing processes and the literatures. *Organization Science, 2*(1), 88-115.

Senge, P., Kleiner, A., Roberts, C. Ross, R., & Smith, B. (1994). *The fifth discipline fieldbook: Strategies and tools for building a learning organization.* New York: Currency Doubleday.

ACKNOWLEDGMENTS

The work described in this article was carried out at the Jet Propulsion Laboratory, California Institute of Technology, under contract with the National Aeronautics and Space Administration. We would like to acknowledge the contributions of Eric Ramirez in the implementation and administration of JPL 101, and offer special thanks to Barbara Amago, Winston Gin, Cara Cheung, Sanjoy Moorthy, and Angela McGahan for their contributions. An earlier version of this chapter was presented at the 37th Hawaii International Conference on Systems Sciences – 2004.

REFERENCES

Brown, S.L., & Eisenhardt, K.M. (1995). Product development: Past research, present findings, and future directions. *Academy of Management Review, 20*(2), 343-378.

Cooper, L.P. (2003a). The power of a question: A case study of two organizational knowledge capture systems. *Proceedings of the 36th Annual Hawaii International Conference on System Sciences.*

Cooper, L.P. (2003b). A research agenda to reduce risk in new product development through knowledge management: A practitioner perspective. *Journal of Engineering and Technology Management, 20*, 117-140.

Davenport, T.H., Jarvenpaa, S.L., & Beers, M.C. (1996). Improving knowledge work processes. *Sloan Management Review,* Summer, 53-65.

Dougherty, D. (1992). Interpretative barriers to successful product innovation in large firms. *Organization Science, 3*(2), 179-202.

Jennex, M.E., & Olfman, L. (2002). Organizational memory/knowledge effects on productivity, a longitudinal study. *Proceedings of the 35th Annual Hawaii International Conference on System Sciences.*

Kuchinke, K.P. (1995). Managing learning for performance. *Human Resource Development Quarterly, 6,* 307-316.

Majchrzak, A., Cooper, L., & Neece, O. (2004). Knowledge reuse for innovation. *Management Science, 50*(2), 174-188.

Markus, M.L. (2001). Toward a theory of knowledge reuse: Types of knowledge reuse situations and factors in reuse success. *Journal of Management Information Systems, 18*(1), 57-93.

Markus, M.L., Majchrzak, A., & Gasser, L.A. (2002). Design theory for systems that support emergent knowledge processes. *MIS Quarterly, 26*(3), 179-212.

Chapter II

A Knowledge Management Case Study in Developing, Documenting, and Distributing Learning

Brigette McGregor-MacDonald, Marsh Inc., UK

EXECUTIVE SUMMARY

This case study reflects the work of a global organization in its knowledge management efforts to sustain and transfer learning from a global leadership development curriculum. It focuses on the Knowledge Management (KM) solution developed to support employees to sustain their learning, to enable them to share their insights and experiences with others, and thus increase organizational capability. The paper is written to illustrate an example of a large organization's efforts to engage employees to share their learning from a management programme across geographical and cultural boundaries.

INTRODUCTION

This case study reflects the work of a global organization in its knowledge management efforts to sustain and transfer learning from a global leadership development curriculum. It focuses on the Knowledge Management (KM) solution developed to support employees to sustain their learning, to enable them to share their insights and experiences with others, and thus increase organizational capability. The paper is written to illustrate an example of a large organization's efforts to engage employees to share their learning from a management programme across geographical and cultural boundaries.

Georgensen (1982) estimates that learners retain approximately 10% of material covered in a tutor-led workshop when back at the workplace. The KM strategy in this project was to support high-performing, high-potential employees to retain a greater proportion of the tutor-led learning and experience. This in turn increases organizational capability by transferring the learning to colleagues and delivers a greater return on investment to the business.

A key challenge of the KM strategy was to effectively manipulate existing KM platforms within the business and research and propose the use of additional ones.

The issue was to make best use of the current multiple resources in the organization, acknowledging that not one of them was totally suited to meet the needs across the globe. The Learning and Development team worked to find a solution with either a range of existing platforms or, as a result of research and testing of new technologies, a new KM platform to support the strategy.

There are a number of cultural challenges associated with implementing effective KM across a global organization with presence in over 100 countries, with different levels of technology sophistication, language, and experience. Revenue-generating business demands mean implementing an effective KM strategy with "learning" content as another challenge entirely. For example, time spent documenting personal reflections from learning and on-the-job experiences, and reading others' reflections from learning and on-the-job experiences struggles to compete with business opportunities that deliver an immediate bottom-line return.

The nature of the insurance industry is relationship based. Interaction has historically been, and still is, predominantly face-to-face or over the telephone. As Nixon (2000) confirms, many other industries have found implementing effective technology-based KM solutions with only face-to-PC interaction is a cultural and pragmatic challenge. In their everyday role, brokers prefer to pick up the phone and talk to someone or go to see them versus logging on to a computer, entering a password they need to have remembered and change regularly to maintain security protocols. The Lloyds of London broking environment, established in 1688, reinforces the face-to-face relationship-based culture. Experience of working with an internal client group to support employees to use the system suggests that if the Internet connection is slow or a password is typed incorrectly thus denying access, users will pick up the phone before trying again, or worse, will avoid the system in future.

BACKGROUND

The Organisation

Marsh Inc. is the world's leading risk and insurance services firm. Its aim is "[t]o create and deliver risk solutions and services that make our clients more successful." Founded in 1871, it has grown into a global enterprise with 400 owned-and-operated offices and 42,000 colleagues, who serve clients in more than 100 countries. Marsh's annual revenues are $6.9 billion, and the company meets client needs in two principal categories:

- Risk Management, insurance-broking, and programme-management services are provided for businesses, public entities, professional services organisations, private clients, and associations under the Marsh name.
- Reinsurance-broking, risk and financing modeling, and associated advisory services are provided to insurance and reinsurance companies, principally under the Guy Carpenter name.

The organisation is made up of distinct divisions with specialist knowledge. One of the key business drivers for the future is to maintain and develop the specific knowledge within each of these divisions, while sharing more learning and experiences across the business, particularly to reduce "reinvention of the wheel" comments across divisions and geographies.

SETTING THE STAGE

Knowledge Management Platforms in Learning

Newman (1991) defines KM as "the collection of processes that govern the creation, dissemination, and utilization of knowledge." The cascade and consistent communication of corporate goals and performance management is pivotal to business success, learning interventions, and employees' personal development. In 2000, Marsh made a fundamental shift in the mechanism used to cascade company strategy across the globe. Local performance management tools, processes, and procedures were replaced with one common approach to aligning goals and consistently measuring performance with the Balanced Scorecard.[1]

At the beginning of 2001, there was no common, pan-European technology platform specifically targeting learning and the consistent documentation of learning in Marsh. E-mail provision was the one common tool and platform across the globe. The company had a variety of software to support the creation and application of databases and had the capability to share databases across geographies, through shared network drives, Internet-based secure "filing" programmes, Microsoft Access and Lotus Notes programmes. Few employees were aware of the range of these capabilities and even fewer were aware of how to manipulate such tools.

In 2001, the firm implemented a global learning management system with specific, pan-European capabilities including e-learning, registration for tutor-led learning, and an online lending library with books, CDs, tapes, videos, and computer-based training (CBT). The system also provided the capability to record for each learner what learning they had accessed and to allow an "approver" path for line manager involvement and alignment to learning. Usage statistics have increased from 11% of the total European population in 2001 to more than 28% in 2004.

In 2002, the organisation launched a company-wide portal, an interactive client and colleague platform to source information about Marsh to both external and internal requestors. The portal is intended to ultimately replace local country-specific intranet sites. The learning management system is now operating effectively from this medium. Local intranets are still in operation across Europe providing more specific local information to employees with the portal offering a platform that spans the entire region and links to colleagues and learning in the United States.

The business is using a number of communication tools to promote cost-effective knowledge sharing, the most common being an interactive, Internet-based tool Webex™, used alongside the telephone for conference calls to share presentations, documents, and access to specialised software. This tool allows Internet dialogue over the course of a meeting and has "ownership" rights for a person or persons to own a presentation document and to be able to make adjustments online in real time with feedback from the conference call participants. This tool can also be used with external clients and has been particularly useful in sharing across boundaries as all colleagues have a desktop computer and access to a phone.

CASE DESCRIPTION

This paper will specifically focus on the KM strategy implemented for the European implementation of a global leadership programme. The programme is one of three core programmes in a Global Leadership Development Curriculum and targets high-performing, high-potential colleagues with people management responsibility. It is a three-day off-site event. Titled "Managing Essentials," it was launched in the spring of 2002. The business used an external provider to deliver across the globe with a core team of dynamic and experienced facilitators. This strategic decision enabled consistency of message, delivery, language, and experience.

The audience for the programme is diverse in years within the organisation and in the industry, time in a management role, geography, and first language. In Europe alone, the target population of colleagues to attend the programme in the first 18 months was close to 500 (50% from the United Kingdom and 50% from continental Europe). Results from employee surveys and dialogue on the programme demonstrated the need to create ownership and responsibility for change at this level. The Learning and Development (L&D) network of colleagues managing the programme at the local level across the globe is also diverse. Technology has played a key role in communicating across geographies with both the delegate and the L&D communities by way of the telephone, Internet, e-mail, various global software platforms, and even camera.

The ultimate KM strategy for Managing Essentials is to improve organisational capability and capacity.[2] Underpinning this are four main goals:

1. For delegates of the programme to sustain their learning of best-practice management tools and techniques
2. For delegates to sustain the pan-European colleague network from the programme
3. For delegates to share their learning and lessons learned from implementation with other colleagues
4. To demonstrate a measurable return on investment against the learning intervention

Next is an account of what actions have been taken to address each element of the strategy and the observed outcomes to date. Georgensen's (1982) hypothesis of learning retention was a key factor in the design of the strategy with pre- and postcontact with delegates at progressive intervals to reinforce the learning. For this reason, the material that follows identifies the cycle stage of the actions taken to the programme (pre, during, or post).

Sustaining the Learning

Pre Event

High-performing, high-potential colleagues were the target audience for Managing Essentials because this population was generally known to be more capable and willing to cascade learning, lead by example, and to therefore impact the majority of colleagues as a result of their experience on the event. To ensure appropriate employees with this skill set were exposed to the learning, employees could not self-register for the programme but had to be nominated by a senior colleague in their business.

To combat cultural issues that historically reinforced silos within the business and across geographies, Managing Essentials is delivered at a pan-European level as opposed to local country level. Nominations are managed by the Programme Manager through the database to ensure a 50/50 split of participants from the UK and continental Europe. The deliberate mix of delegates on each event, sharing and cascading knowledge and breaking down business segment and geographical boundaries, has been recognised by delegates as a core strength of the programme.

During the Event

Every delegate received a hard copy binder of materials covering the learning models and references from the three-day event and supplementary reading materials and references. The facilitators referred delegates to their binders throughout the programme and ensured key action points were documented in the binder to encourage participants to refer back to it and use it when back at the office.

On approximately 60% of the conference calls held with delegates post event, at least one employee referred to his/her frequently returning to the binder to remind him/her of his/her learning. Many claimed to keep their binder on their desk where it could be easily referred to.

Post Event

The Marsh internal Learning and Development team developed a sustainability timetable post programme using a variety of KM tools. A summary of activity is noted in Table 1.

Months three, six, and 12 of the postprogramme plan were proposed in first quarter 2003, but have not yet been fully implemented. Europe has consistently implemented up to the three-week stage in this timeline and has sporadically implemented the six-week and onwards activities.

Each of the KM tools and practices used in the above timeline has its pros and cons. The objective of using this range of tools and methods is to provide an overall synergy to all the learners involved, appreciating different learning styles. The feedback the team has had is that the facilitated conference call is useful for reminding delegates of their

Table 1.

Within two weeks	Take time to reflect and think Receive group photo of delegates Commence three to six month challenge
Two weeks	Receive the following information by e-mail: • E-mail distribution list along with ideas on how to use it, that is, "What I have learned this month" • Copy of the APT² (see *Transferring Learning Across the Organisation*) model previously completed on-site • Copy of Excel spreadsheet with all delegates' background pre work • Excel spreadsheet with names of all participants on the programme across Europe since spring 2002 Receive an additional e-mail directing delegates to specific e-learning materials to reinforce key learning points, accessible through the global learning management system Attend conference call with other delegates (recorded and transcribed for later reference)
Three weeks	Receive an A5 colour laminate for their desk with key models and messages from the three-day event
Six weeks	Receive notification of bimonthly Webex™ calls to share feedback on three to six month challenges
Three months	Line managers of participants receive online questionnaire to complete on noticeable changes in participants' performance since attendance on the programme
Six months	Attend video conference with delegates to reinforce the network
Annually	Attend a central conference of delegates to review content and lessons learned on implementation, and facilitated discussions around transfer of learning and knowledge management

learning and bringing the "community" back together again. The conference call does not, however, lend itself to support those colleagues who speak English as a second language and the transcript of the call, while a valuable record of verbatim comments and stories, is detailed and time consuming to analyse at a later date.

As the networking opportunity of the event holds such great wealth for the participants and lends itself to the transfer of knowledge both to the network after the event and to their colleagues back in the office, a digital photo is now taken on site on the last day of the programme and circulated to the delegates approximately two weeks afterwards via e-mail. For those people who learn more effectively in a group and through visual stimulus (as opposed to audio or kinesthetic), the photo provides a reminder of the experience and the learning.

The A5 laminate needs no translation, it's colourful, and delegates do not need to actually "do" anything with it other than hang it somewhere prominent on their desk as a reminder. When walking around the offices, these laminates are becoming more and more visible with the numbers of colleagues attending the programme. This is a simple way to cascade the message as yet other colleagues ask questions about the laminate on the desk and the explanation cascades the learning.

The central conference would provide value to the delegates and the organisation, but taking more than 250 colleagues out of the business for a day and bringing them to a central location has financial and work flow implications. A compromise suggested by the participants has been to hold local country conferences. This is something the team considered implementing in fourth quarter, 2004.

Three years after implementation, the learning management system the business has implemented globally is becoming a powerful tool. European colleagues are beginning to embrace the tool although they are just scratching the surface to use it to its full functionality. Employees have been forced to become familiar with the system and to register for learning events through this medium where previously they called through to a learning team to manually register for events. Many, however, are not using the personal learning history, assigning a mentor, or reporting functionality of the system. The second e-mail sent at the two-week stage post programme (above) targeting the high-performing, high-potential employees, enforces strategic organisational goals of employing more blended learning, promoting the learning management system, e-learning, sustained learning, and the use of technology as a learning tool.

Transferring the Learning Across the Organisation

During the Event

Key learning from best-practice networks of learning professionals in the United Kingdom led to the discovery of Unilever's[3] Transfer of Learning tool known as APT^2 (Acquire, Practice, Transfer to Job and Transfer to Colleagues). This tool has been consistently utilized at the end of each of the three days in the Managing Essentials programme. Delegates identify and publicly document what learning they have acquired, how they will practice that learning (in a safe environment where they can afford to make mistakes), how they will transfer the learning to the job, and how they will transfer the learning to colleagues. At the end of each day, this is recorded by each participant on post-it notes and posted on flip charts, where it stays over the duration of the programme. Delegates can add to it as required over the three days. After the event, the data are recorded electronically by the programme management team for redistribution to delegates by e-mail, primarily providing an aid to sustain the learning but also to remind and share with the group how everyone committed to transfer the learning. Feedback on this process has been that it is a useful reminder of the programme content as everyone records what key learning they have acquired each day, and a generator of ideas of how to implement the learning. This record is also used as a tool to describe to senior leaders what key learning the participants are taking away from the programme and what they are committing to do back in the office on their return.

One of the richest sources of knowledge transfer and sustainability is storytelling. The power of the true story, the real experience of someone in the room or someone the participants know as a colleague has an impact few, if any, other mediums can match. Participants in the programme, like many others in the financial services industry, are rarely satisfied with theories. They need proof, not simply of how something has worked but of how something has worked in their environment under the same pressures they work under. The external providers Marsh work with to deliver the learning are insightful in the way they share their stories and experiences to emphasise and reinforce learning points. A key aspect of the KM strategy has become to collect, collate, and share participant stories across the relevant geographies, where a colleague can be named for their success at making a difference — not only for the what, but also the how — after attending the programme. The KM strategy reflects this as participants are asked to attend conference calls post programme and to share a story of their learning and implementation back at the office.

The stories from the conference calls are cascaded (with employee permission) back to the external providers who facilitate the programme. The external facilitators also elicit stories from participants over each three-day event, record the story and the source, and then use these stories at future events. For delegates experiencing later programmes, this makes the experience tailored when they hear the external facilitators referencing known employees and their real experiences with the material. One example of such a story was that of a woman who consistently used four key questions with her team in monthly one-to-one meetings. She had read a number of texts and had experimented with a variety of tools to develop her people to be proactive, show initiative, and involve her when appropriate. She shared these four questions on the programme and her experiences in asking them of her team; how they first reacted, how they reacted over the short term, and how they react today. As a result of her story and the reaction of the group on the programme, her story and the questions are now included as part of the learning event. A testament to the KM efforts is the fact that on recent programmes in Europe, delegates have brought this story to the workshop, having heard it from other colleagues or seen it practiced.

Demonstrating Return on Investment

Pre Event

At the launch of the first programme, all nominations were collected through e-mail. The team relied on e-mail to communicate the new programme and to connect with the target population. Lists of nominators, nominees, and delegate information were initially collated by a central team on a programme-by-programme basis on spreadsheets. Over time, as management information reporting was required, a more functional database was developed allowing easy access to all details of attendees from across Europe by country, business unit, programme attended, and nominator. The ease, speed, and flexibility of reporting available in this database has increased efficiency and accuracy in the information reported. For example, one leader in the business asked for a report of all the colleagues in his/her business unit who had attended the programme over a given time period. The leader used the list to ask all those colleagues who had attended to make a formal presentation in a full office meeting to share their knowledge. The learning management system has now been successfully implemented throughout the majority of Europe and options are currently being generated to maximise this facility in the nomination of participants, ensuring cross-business unit and cross-geography participants on each programme.

A three to six month Business Challenge is a key part of the prework for participants. The Business Challenge was devised together with the external provider delivering the workshop and the global Learning Team. The Challenge is agreed upon with the local line manager and brought to the event to share, discuss, and create an action plan. The Challenge meets a number of the KM strategy criteria in that it aligns the individual and his/her manager to a business output of his/her learning and demonstrating a return on investment measurement (subject to the goal being specific, measurable, achievable, realistic, and timed).

The Business Challenges are one example of thread being sewn between many of the delegates as discussion is generated when delegates realize many have the same or a very similar Challenge, albeit in a different business unit or geography. Connecting cross-function and cross-geographical border issues and people continues to be a focus for discussion around the return on investment for the event. The postprogramme conference calls have begun to identify business opportunities across divisions in the organization and direct revenue-generating projects as a result of the network established and promoted at the event. It is hoped that in time these trends and successes will be recorded by delegates on an Internet-based platform for any employee to see, learn from, and follow.

The networking and quick understanding of the knowledge and business representation in the room is a fundamental quick win of the curriculum and the platform on which further learning will be maintained and shared. Feedback after the first few programmes in 2002 alluded to the struggle to get to know everyone and how they contributed over the three-day event. As a result, Europe implemented an additional prework assignment named Background Information. Each participant was asked to complete a brief electronic proforma prior to the event documenting his/her name, office location, business unit, three to six month Business Challenge, time of service with the company, greatest achievement while at Marsh, and what they do on a Sunday afternoon. These data are e-mailed to the Programme Manager to be collated into a simple spreadsheet and circulated to delegates at the beginning of Day 1 of the event to help people know and remember colleagues they meet and learn from. This document is also circulated after the workshop by e-mail, along with an e-mail distribution list to encourage the network to sustain and grow.

Post Event

Marsh Europe invested in a questionnaire distributed to a random selection of colleagues who had attended the programme. These questionnaires were sent out to delegates six to eight months post event through an online Web-based interview tool allowing the results to be recorded electronically and transferred into a database for future reference. The outcome of the questionnaires was verbatim comments leading to a number of conclusions about the event itself, the impact of efforts to sustain learning, and the needs for KM tools.

The feedback identifies that while colleagues felt that the programme gave them much material to enrich their personal effectiveness, few were able to make the connection to how the learning had impacted the organisation. The Business Challenge template has been revised in the third year of delivery of the programme to include a specific question to the delegate of the hard-dollar value of the business challenge they hope to complete as a result of their learning. These documents are signed before each delegate leaves the event and sent to a central global team to collate. The next step proposed in this process, with a high-man-hour intervention, is to go back to each delegate three to six months after the programme to reconcile proposed dollar return with actual return to clearly demonstrate a tangible bottom-line impact. One particular Business Challenge has estimated a return equal to the financial value of delivering one Managing Essentials event for 30 employees.

It has been agreed to investigate the development of a leadership "portal" which would also enable colleagues across Europe to interact, share learning and lessons learned to a greater proportion of delegates with the tool targeting all those who have attended Managing Essentials, rather than those who attend each individual programme.

KM Across the Learning and Development Community

The global Learning and Development network has been investigating KM opportunities to enhance and ensure consistency in the role of colleagues increasingly involved in managing this programme around the globe. Through the programme's life of just more than two years, colleagues in different geographies have approached its implementation in slightly different ways, all sharing their experiences with the global Programme Manager based in New York. The global Learning network is now looking to use a specific database functionality through the cross-company e-mail system to communicate with each other, store documentation, and to share tasks.

The decision to use this particular database came after consideration of a number of internal options, including a Microsoft® Access database, use of an intranet, and use of technology known as E-Room. None of the above media allowed an economical, easy global access and storage of documents along with online interactive communication through electronic discussion boards. The Access database would be difficult to share and update across the globe on each regional internal network. Ensuring secure access to the intranet site to restrict access to only L&D colleagues would come with comparatively high expense on a direct cost basis and the "one more log-on and password" toll to colleagues in using it. The E-Room facility offered the closest match as a type of online filing cabinet where information could be stored, e-mails could be sent and access levels could be dictated; unfortunately, this option was prohibitively expensive for the number of users anticipated over the foreseeable future.

While the chosen database is not the most visually stimulating platform, the challenges of the other options make it the most practical and economical solution.

CONCLUSIONS

The KM strategy for a core Leadership Development programme in Europe is to sustain learning for colleagues who attend, cascade learning to others, and demonstrate return on investment from the event. While the organization had a number of KM tools available in various geographies, these were mainly used to manage day-to-day business knowledge. Sharing of learning materials and experiences was a relatively new concept in the organization. The existing tools have been flexed to implement a structured programme of interventions to increase organizational capacity through this sharing of knowledge. There is now a set of tools and practices in place to reinforce and cascade the learning across Europe aligned to the organizational culture using a variety of mediums including, but not limited to, the PC. These tools and practices are being shared in the internal learning community across the globe. The foundations of the strategy are in place and are being executed. It is too early to confirm the long-term success of this solution, but feedback to date suggests the strategy is supporting sustainable KM and breaking down geographical and business silos to improve organizational capacity.

Epilogue and Lessons Learned

The same external partners continue to deliver the three-day learning event across the globe. The challenge over recent months has been to maintain the organisations' commitment and energy to the KM strategy. Priorities in the business are regularly reviewed to ensure effective investment is appropriately placed where it can maximize return. The KM strategy has provided a measurement tool in the Business Challenges, although the financial implication of the Challenges has only recently been recorded and realized. Attendance on postprogramme conference calls is lower over the last eight months than what it was 12 months ago. In Europe, the number of colleagues comfortable with a three-day learning event in English outside of the United Kingdom is diminishing. Over this time, the organization has developed a more pan-European business, uniting colleagues from across Europe in an increasing number of projects. Delegates and learning professionals in the business are now pushing the KM strategy to deliver a global, Web-based interactive tool to share stories, post documents, and caretake the learning community. Lessons learned include:

- KM across a large organization with diversity across geographies, languages, and regional, local, and office cultures requires persistence, creativity, and ownership from the audience. Knowledge must be easy to access, relevant to the day job, and seen as an added value to individuals personally and professionally, and to individual and team performance.
- This programme benefited from transparent senior leader involvement and commitment. Senior leaders gave their time to be present at the three-day event and their endorsement to the KM strategy post event. Without this support, which included a time and a direct financial cost, the learning and therefore KM strategy would not be implemented.
- Stories from colleagues, peers, and senior leaders are rich, credible, and effective tools in transferring and sustaining learning, both for the storyteller and for the listener.
- Upon implementation of the Managing Essentials programme, the KM was necessarily owned by the L&D team. This meant a small number of people brainstorming on ideas to develop the strategy. Now that the programme is embedded, known and branded as a success, the L&D team can now hand this responsibility over to the end users who have already attended the programme. This will generate a wealth of more ideas immediately relevant to the business, hand in hand with ownership of those KM processes.
- Blend the KM activity with a variety of media to match learning styles in the audience. After a learning event, keep any KM intervention 60 minutes or less for two reasons: the delegate is more likely to clear time to attend in his/her diary, and the facilitator is more likely to retain the attention span of all attendees.
- Keep the key messages short and simple to allow easy, quick, and frequent reinforcement. The Managing Essentials learning event has approximately 10 key, high-level statements. While each delegate usually chooses between one and three of these messages to focus on first when back at the office, the programme manager refers to a variety of the 10 whenever communicating to the group.
- In this case, the external delivery partners' style, delivery method, and connection with the delegates have a significant impact on the effectiveness of the KM. On conference calls after the programme, delegates make consistent reference to the humor and personal teaching "stories" of the facilitators when reflecting on the event. The three-day event is, however, a relatively short intervention in the overall strategy. Coupled with the dynamic facilitation, the role of the programme manager is important in reinforcing the key messages. Over the life of this case, the

programme manager's job was to know and reinforce the relevant stories to share with delegates and to be a central source of connection between delegates to encourage the learning networks to continue.

- KM projects require significant resources. Organizations looking to build KM as an organizational capability need to expect it to take time. As this case demonstrates, KM is evolving from a technology-based field to one of business efficiency through the effective communication of common key messages. After working on the sustainability and KM for this single learning event for two years, this company has introduced a number of tools and processes that have impacted success. There is still, however, much to do to achieve behavioral change in managers across the business as a result of the learning event.

REFERENCES

Georgenson, D.L. (1982). The problem of transfer calls for partnership. *Training and Development Journal, 36*(10), 75-78.

Kaplan, R., & Norton, D. (1992). The Balanced Scorecard—Measures that drive performance. *Harvard Business Review, 70*(1), 71-79.

Newman, B. (1991). From the introduction to "An open discussion of knowledge management." Retrieved from *www.km-forum.org/what_is.htm*

Nixon, N.M. (2000). *Common knowledge: How companies thrive by sharing what they know*. Boston: Harvard Business School Press.

ENDNOTES

1 Kaplan & Norton (1992).

2 The programme is just one aspect of the effort to increase organisational capability and capacity.

3 Unilever, USA – "APT² is Unilever's expression of its learning organisation. The company uses APT² to educate employees on the difference between 'training' and 'learning,' promote the many forms of learning outside the classroom, and actively engage its workforce in recycling knowledge for sustained competitive advantage."—Karen Pacent, Unilever

Section II

Knowledge Management in Support of Retaining Organizational Knowledge

Chapter III

A Case Study on Assessing the Readiness of Professional Services Company to Build an Organizational Memory Information System

Hani Abdel-Aziz, Cairo University, Egypt

Khaled Wahba, Cairo University, Egypt

EXECUTIVE SUMMARY

The information system (IS), which supports capturing, gathering, and distribution of knowledge, is one component of organizational memory; and it is defined as an organizational memory information system (OMIS). The professional services (PS) division of an IT company, "CITE,"[1] in Egypt was suffering from knowledge loss due to a high turnover rate. The objective of this case is to highlight the factors that could help "CITE" to develop an efficient OMIS service. Data were collected from the internal structure of the PS division, where all employees were interviewed in order to come up with the appropriate factors that need improvement. Based on the Organizational Memory Information System Success Model developed by Jennex, Olfman, and Pituma (1998), the research highlighted key issues that should be taken into consideration when developing an OMIS for the PS division of "CITE." The main findings that were affecting the development of an efficient OMIS were mainly training, management of OMIS, communication, technology, and corporate culture.

INTRODUCTION

The information system (IS), which supports capturing, gathering, and distribution of knowledge, is one component of the organizational memory; and it is defined as an organizational memory information system (OMIS). The professional services (PS) division of an IT Company "CITE"[2] in Egypt was suffering from knowledge loss due to a high turnover rate. The objective of this case is to highlight the factors that could help "CITE" to develop an efficient OMIS service. Data were collected from the internal structure of the PS division, where all employees were interviewed in order to come up with the appropriate factors that need improvement. Based on the Organizational Memory Information System Success Model developed by Jennex, Olfman, and Pituma (1998), the research highlighted key issues that should be taken into consideration when developing an OMIS for the PS division of "CITE." The main findings that were affecting the development of an efficient OMIS were mainly training, management of OMIS, communication, technology, and corporate culture.

Putting those factors into consideration, the PS division of "CITE" should consider different issues in order to successfully build an OMIS. "CITE" should consider switching to a centralized model in the way it manages knowledge, to develop specialized training programs for its employees on how to efficiently use the existing IS, to develop rewarding programs for tacit knowledge sharing among its members, to develop a communication mechanism between the users of the OMIS and the team responsible to build and develop the content of that IS, and finally to enhance the existing OMIS technical resources especially in terms of search and retrieval capabilities.

This paper proceeds as follows. In the next sections, theories included in the research will be briefly discussed, as well as an in-depth analysis of the model used in the research. Next, the findings will be highlighted. After, the final recommendations, based on the findings and their interpretation, will be outlined.

BACKGROUND

"CITE" is one of the main players in the IT market worldwide, with a large portfolio of products and services, including hardware (servers, workstations, and storage), software (Internet and desktop applications), and services (support services and professional services). For the purpose of this paper, our main focus will be on the professional services (PS) side of "CITE's" different activities.

On the global level, IT services are generally divided into hardware/software support services, systems integration services, IT consulting services, processing services, IT training and education services, application development and outsourcing services, and network integration and management services.

The term "professional services (PS)" in IT does not have one specific definition, as PS might include one or more of the services mentioned above. However, for most of the IT companies, the term "PS" is used to cover two main types of services, which are systems integration and IT consulting.

On the global level, systems integration services constitute 18% of the global IT services market, while the consulting services constitute 5% of that market. Thus the PS segment — as defined above — represent 23% of the global IT services market. In 2000, the PS market reached approximately $97 billion, while the global IT market size was approximately $2.1 trillion and the IT services size was around $429 billion (American Chamber of Commerce, 2002).

Between 1999 and 2002, the global IT market's average growth rate was 9%, while the IT services segment was growing at a rate of 11.1% during the same period (American Chamber of Commerce, 2002).

In 2000, the total IT market in Egypt was valued at $730 million, indicating a 17% increase from 1999. In 2004, the IT market in Egypt is expected to reach $1.3 billion. The IT services segment was valued at $210 million in 2000, representing 28% of the total market size, where consulting services reached $29 million and integration services reached $36 million. Thus the PS segment represents 30% of the local IT services market and 8% of the local IT market. The PS segment is expected to reach $135 million by 2004, with an average annual growth rate of 22% (American Chamber of Commerce, 2002).

Based on the high growth rate of the Egyptian IT market, "CITE" decided in 1997 to have a direct presence in the country. Therefore, "CITE" established an integrated business operation in Egypt that covers its complete portfolio of products and services, and where PS was one of the main units that started with a PS manager and nine PS consultants focusing on complex IT solutions architecture and implementation such as Internet solutions (service providers, security, etc.), high-availability solutions (clustering, disaster recovery, etc.), and data management solutions (centralized storage solutions and backup solutions in multivendor environments, etc.). From 1997 to 2000, the PS division was able to successfully deliver more than 60 PS projects per year, while generating average revenue of $1.6 million per year. The operation in Egypt is part of a larger regional operation in Dubai, United Arab Emirates (UAE), where the same model is adopted in other countries in the region.

SETTING THE STAGE

In general, the PS industry, which includes systems integration services, legal, accounting, and tax consulting, is knowledge intensive. What PS firms sell clients is their knowledge and its application to specific client problems. A major justification for large PS firms' investment in knowledge management is that it gives them the capability to offer clients the benefits of the whole firm's experience, not just that of a particular client team. This is only possible through the effective creation, diffusion, and use of professional knowledge.

PS knowledge is as complex and difficult to manage as any other knowledge domain of interest to organizations, and effective management of PS knowledge means meeting a variety of challenges. There are multiple types of PS knowledge, including market intelligence, best practices, methodologies, tips and tricks, and discussion around specific engagements. PS knowledge is embodied in professionals — a mixed blessing. While professionals are knowledge workers who are probably relatively comfortable creating, sharing, and using knowledge, they do have constraints. Most are extremely busy; their productivity is measured in terms of billable hours. So they have little slack time to contribute to or use knowledge repositories.

Trying to implement a knowledge management system of any scale without technology is extremely difficult, but the technology itself does not make the knowledge management system work; it can facilitate and enable connections and communications but it will not make them happen. Most knowledge management experts will acknowledge that technology contributes about 15% of the solution for knowledge-enabled enterprise. However, this is a very important 15%, a point easily demonstrated by trying to implement a knowledge management program without IT. The right technology to create infrastructure and provide facilitating access to people with information is critical for success. It is not in itself sufficient, however (Gamble & Blackwell, 2001).

An intranet can empower sharing efforts by integrating databases and information sources to provide a kind of one-stop for information. The intranet will lower communication costs related to the printing, mailing, and processing of documents. It can improve productivity by making information more widely and quickly accessible. It can facilitate higher team productivity by creating a collaborative working environment, allow for rapid implementation of solutions as a result of open protocol standards, and with the right kind of support, make transparent the use of knowledge base in terms of business objectives. In order to achieve any of these benefits, it is very important to ensure that a strategy for managing content has been implemented (Stenmark, 2002).

CASE DESCRIPTION

The PS division of "CITE" started providing services to the company's local customer base in 1997. At that time, PS division staff members included nine consultants focusing mainly on the Internet solutions, high-availability solutions, and data management (storage/backup) solutions areas. From 1997 to early 2000, the average number of projects implemented by the PS division, per year, was between 60 to 70 projects, with an average of seven projects per consultant per year. These projects were always delivered on time and with high quality according to the Acceptance Reports signed by the customers.

By midyear 2000, and after the exponential growth in the IT market in Egypt, the company started facing a high turnover rate; seven consultants left the company because they were offered more senior positions in other companies or because they have decided to start their own private business. While the departed employees have been replaced and the total number of employees has even increased, the revenues have been flat, the number of successfully delivered projects has been flat, the number of incomplete projects has been increasing, and the customer satisfaction level has been decreasing.

According to the preliminary data gathered and through informal interviews, the problem was not only the high turnover rate but the real problem was *the consequences behind this turnover rate, and its increasing value with elapsed time*. The main identifiable problem was the loss of knowledge, where knowledge dissipation did affect the revenues of the company and its image in the local market. Those losses in knowledge caused by high turnover rate have put "CITE" into a risky situation compared to its local competitors.

Today, PS members consist of 12 consultants. However, the reports received from customers show many negative symptoms, including flat number of projects delivered per year (no increase since the second quarter of 2001), late implementation of projects, low quality of solutions, and poor qualification of the customers' requirements. In addition, the PS division is showing flat revenues since the first quarter of 2001 (revenues have not exceeded $1.6 million since first quarter 2001).

The PS division was relying on its IS to provide all new PS team members with the required knowledge and to play its role in supporting the organizational memory. But the high turnover rate has clearly led to a loss of knowledge and seriously affected the company's knowledge base. "CITE" had to find a solution for its IS to better support its organization memory.

After conducting an internal survey, the PS management found that most of the failed projects' implementations were multivendor integration projects that were handled by the new team members. According to the PS management, the new members should already have the right level of skills — for the company's own products — to do their job at the right level especially when they have all been given extensive training on the company's products. In addition, the company offers them the necessary IS tools to perform at the right level. The main tools offered by the company are based on technologies such as access to the Internet, access to PS portal service, access to PS intranet, and e-mail. The PS management was relying on its IS to provide all new PS team members with the required knowledge and to play its role in supporting organizational memory. From a knowledge management perspective, the above-mentioned IS technologies represent the tools required to build and to deal with "CITE's" organizational memory. However, it is becoming clear that the high turnover rate had clearly led to a loss of knowledge and had seriously affected the company's knowledge base, while the company's IS did not play its expected role in minimizing the leakage of knowledge.

As there are multiple types of PS knowledge (including best practices, methodologies, tips and tricks, and discussion on specific engagements) and as the structure of a PS knowledge initiative must accommodate these multiple types, in the next sections of this case study, we will analyze "CITE's" success in implementing its organizational memory information system (OMIS), based on the OMIS Success Model as defined by Jennex, Olfman, and Pituma (1998). In essence, an OMIS is viewed as a component of organizational memory. An OMIS is defined as "a system that functions to provide a means by which knowledge from the past is brought to bear on present activities, thus resulting in increased levels of effectiveness for the organization" (Stein & Zwass, 1995).

The theoretical framework used in the case study is mainly using the model developed by Jennex, Olfman, and Pituma for organizational memory information success (Jennex, Olfman, & Pituma, 1998) to build an OMIS.

Organizational Memory

The notion of organizational memory (OM) has been around for more than a quarter of a century, and many definitions have been proposed. The knowledge in the minds of individual workers is also considered a part of OM. Stein and Zwass define it as "the means by which organizational knowledge is transferred from the past to present" (Stein & Zwass, 1995). Most often, OM definitions focus on the persistence of knowledge in an organization, independently of how this persistence is achieved. Therefore, the knowledge in the minds of individual workers is also considered as part of the corporate memory (Heijst, Spek, & Kruizinga, 1996).

Although, OM has been defined by many authors, there is no one agreed-upon definition. Some authors view it as abstract and supported by concrete/physical memory aids such as databases (Walsh & Unggson, 1991). Others view it as concrete and including computerized records and files (Huber, 1991; Jennex, Olfman, & Pituma, 1998). Stein and Zwass (1995) define it as "the means by which organizational knowledge is transferred from the past to present." In essence, they view an OMIS as a component of OM. The main function of a corporate memory is to improve the competitiveness of the organization by improving the way in which it manages its knowledge. The knowledge assets and the learning capacity of an organization are viewed as the main source of competitive advantage (Davenport & Prusak, 1998).

Organizational Memory Information System

This section describes the OMIS Success Model, which was developed by Jennex, Olfman, and Pituma (1998). The purpose of this section is to specify a model for measuring the effectiveness of "CITE's" OMIS.

Based on the OMIS definition by Stein and Zwass (1995), the model presented here provides an explanation as to why an OMIS increases organizational effectiveness. In essence, it allows measurement of a system that is thought to be an OMIS. If the system in question increases organizational effectiveness, then it would be considered an OMIS given that it provides a means of bringing past knowledge to bear on present activities (Jennex, Olfman, & Pituma, 1998).

OMIS Success Model by Jennex, Olfman, and Pituma

Based on the OMIS Success Model by Jennex, Olfman, and Pituma (1998), Figure 1 illustrates the adopted model in this case study, which is a block-recursive one that includes five blocks.

System Quality

The first block of the model defines the system quality in terms of the characteristics of the OMIS. System quality describes how good the system is in terms of its operational characteristics. The system quality block contains three constructs: (1) the technical capabilities of the organization, (2) the form of the OMIS, and (3) the level of the OMIS. Technical resources define the capability of an organization to develop and maintain an OMIS. These include aspects such as the amount of past experience already gained in developing and maintaining an OMIS, the amount of technical expertise used to develop and maintain the OMIS, the type of hardware used to run the OMIS, and the competence of the users.

Technical resources will impact both the level and form of the OMIS. The level of the OMIS refers to its ability to bring past information to bear upon current activities. The form of OMIS refers to the extent to which it is computerized and integrated. In addition, the form of the OMIS should impact its level. Given the effectiveness of IT to provide timely information, it is expected that a more fully computerized and integrated system will provide a more sophisticated capability to retrieve past information. This

Figure 1. OMIS success model

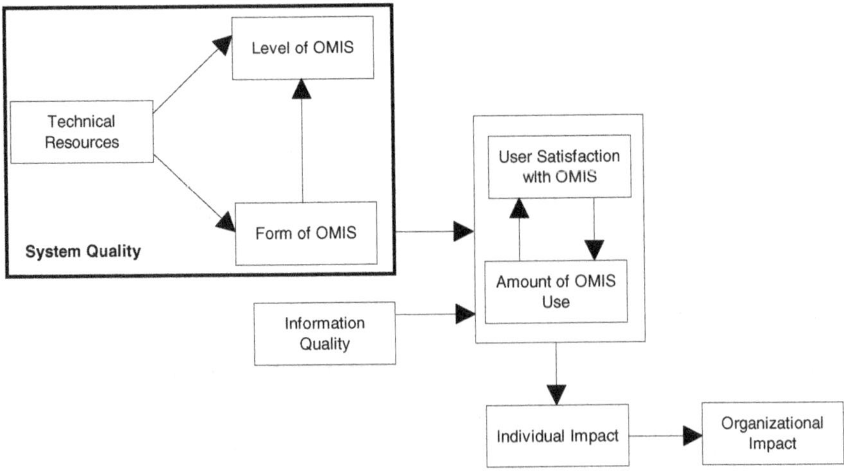

Source: Jennex, Olfman, & Pituma (1998)

block shows that the level of the OMIS is the final measurement of its capabilities in terms of system quality, and can be used as a surrogate measure of the block in terms of its effects on the system usage block.

Information Quality

Information quality defines how good the system is in terms of its output. Factors in this category span a broad range from importance, relevance, usefulness, and informativeness to clarity, content, accuracy, and completeness. Information quality affects the system usage block.

Success Measures in Terms of Usage

Information use refers to the utilization of the outputs of the system. This construct is most applicable as a success measure when the use of a system is voluntary. User satisfaction is a construct that measures perceptions of the system by users. It is considered a good surrogate for measuring system success when use of the system is required, and therefore amount of use would be equal regardless of the effectiveness of the system.

However, it is evident that both of these constructs provide feedback to each other, especially where use is voluntary. Use will influence user satisfaction either positively or negatively, and user satisfaction will influence use. A more satisfied user might be expected to increase usage. This block leads to individual impact, and therefore a combination of the two constructs can be used as a surrogate measure of the block.

Individual and Organizational Impact

An individual's use of a system will produce an impact on that person's performance in the workplace. In addition, an individual "impact" could also be an indication that an IS has given the user a better understanding of the decision context, has improved his or her decision-making productivity, has produced a change in user activity, or has changed the decision maker's perception of the importance or usefulness of the IS.

Each individual impact will in turn have an effect on the performance of the whole organization. However, organizational impacts are typically not the summation of individual impacts, so the association between individual and organizational impacts is often difficult to draw.

CURRENT CHALLENGES FACING "CITE"

Data collected have been qualitative, and most of the questions have been open ended with some close-ended type of questionnaire finally put together to collect qualitative data as previously mentioned. The data collection method used has been structured interviews, "face to face," with all 14 employees in the company, including the 12 PS consultants and the two employees in the IS support team. It should be noted that, before conducting the interview with the 12 PS consultants, each of them had been given a clear definition of the term "OMIS" in terms of functions, resources, and tools. The main assumption we used is that the slowdown in IT industry at that time on the international and local levels, and the related increase in job insecurity, do not negatively impact the employees' use of the OMIS in terms of sharing knowledge.

As for the interview questions, they have targeted the following areas: the existing setup and how it supports the OMIS, the main issues that hinder the implementation of a successful OMIS, and the main areas that need improvement. The interview questions have targeted each of the factors stated in the above section, where each of the factors with its main points has been put into questions targeting answers that should clarify how the model could be applied, as well as the main points needed to be covered in the implementation phase. The role of the questions is to highlight the main factors in relating all those points all together, combined with the Jennex, Olfman, and Pituma OMIS Success Model, which had finally led to a realizable framework towards the implementation of a successful OMIS. On the other hand, and as this case study is qualitative, the findings will be directly resulting from the questionnaires' answers. This means that we have to assume that all interviewed employees had given honest answers without any intentional bias. The main limitation of this case study is that we are only qualifying the "computer documents" form of OMIS by focusing on intranet, e-mail, and portal services. The other two forms of OMIS (paper documents and self-memory) are not covered. Also, other means of knowledge diffusion and transfer (such as direct contacts between people and communities of practice) are not covered. On the other hand, cultural issues related to knowledge management and organizational memory are not analyzed.

After conducting the interviews with all the staff members of the PS division of "CITE," a successful implementation of an OMIS is affected by multiple factors. The following factors have been identified.

Training

Training is important to the success of an OMIS. Training has never been managed in the right way from an OMIS perspective. It was shown that new staff members have always relied on themselves in developing the necessary skills and knowledge on how to efficiently use the OMIS. On the other hand, all employees have never been trained on how to share knowledge by making it available to colleagues.

Management of OMIS

Management of the OMIS is a crucial factor. There is a clear problem in the management of the OMIS, as there is no single owner of that task. Due to its nature, several applications do constitute the OMIS. Each of these applications has its owner. Also, content is not centrally managed, which leads to inconsistency problems. Another clear OMIS management problem is the lack of content in some specific areas such as integration with other vendors' products. Due to the current decentralized management aspect of the OMIS, this subject has never been approached. In addition, "CITE" has not determined strategy that defines what exactly should be made available in the knowledge base, nor its location or how it is to be acquired.

Communication

Communication is one of the negative issues towards the success of "CITE's" OMIS. One aspect is determined, that is, the lack of communication between the owners of the different Web sites from one side and the PS consultants delivering services to customers in the field on the other side. The incompleteness and poor content in some areas, such as integration services, has a negative effect on the overall performance of the PS organization.

Technology

Technology has an important role in the success of an OMIS. Information search and retrieval is an important aspect of any OMIS. However, "CITE's" search and retrieval system is good only in performing basic search, as it lacks a high level of search granularity.

Corporate Culture

"CITE's" corporate culture is encouraging all staff to use the OMIS, but it is not rewarding or acknowledging personal initiatives of knowledge sharing. In other words, explicit knowledge is shared because it is published on the local intranet Web sites or because it is made available through the company's portal; but the company has no defined strategy or any type of mechanism that encourages its employees to share their personal tacit knowledge. Therefore, the key issue is to instill a corporate-wide culture that encourages and rewards knowledge sharing.

RECOMMENDATIONS

As a solution to "CITE's" problem of a lack of OMIS effectiveness, several actions have been recommended:

Create a Chief Knowledge Officer Position

As shown, the decentralized management style of "CITE" led to different knowledge management problems that are due to the lack of company strategy on what knowledge should be made available, its location, and how it is acquired. Also, other reported problems were due to how to interact and deal with knowledge, how to efficiently use the OMIS, and what are the most relevant technologies to adopt in order to implement an efficient OMIS. To solve these problems, an owner must be responsible to coordinate all related activities. Therefore, a chief knowledge officer (CKO) has to be hired with a main business objective to set a company strategy for knowledge management in general, and also to be responsible of the implementation of that strategy by implementing an efficient OMIS.

Develop Specialized Training Programs on OMIS

In order to push new members of the PS team to use the OMIS efficiently, a specialized training program has to be developed and then delivered to all new hires. Also, in order to guarantee that the previous generations of PS consultants are efficiently using the OMIS, all old members of the PS team have to be given refreshment training and update training on how to better use the OMIS and its new versions, if any.

Shift the Corporate Culture

One of the main problems facing "CITE" is the incompleteness of available information regarding the integration with other vendors' products. A good portion of such knowledge is a tacit one that employees develop over time through their experience gained in complex installation. Therefore, it is becoming very crucial to instill a culture that encourages knowledge sharing. A formal infrastructure is needed to make knowledge sharing flourish, where "CITE" must redefine its business processes to foster a new corporate culture. Also, "CITE" must have people who can make sense of knowledge sharing and apply it.

"CITE's" top management must create an environment that encourages employees to continuously share what they know. The centerpiece of that environment is interactive learning, which occurs either through work experience or communication with fellow practitioners. The key to interactive learning is the give and take that occurs when employees share knowledge. A lack of time is a major obstacle to this process, and "CITE" must find ways for it PS consultants to share what they know. We recommend that "CITE" makes knowledge sharing part of the performance reviews, and builds rewards into the compensation and benefits plans of its employees. In addition, "CITE" should also publicize employees' efforts, praise their participation and give special titles to those who actively transfer knowledge. In other words, "CITE" has to reward and recognize—formally and informally—the PS consultants who spend a lot of time helping each other and contributing to the corporate knowledge base.

Develop a Communication Mechanism Between the PS Consultants and the Content Owners

It was shown that the lack of communication between the content users (the PS consultants) and the content owners (the owners of the different Web sites) leads to problems related to information relevance, completeness, importance, and richness. The owners of the Web sites must be informed about what exactly the Web sites' users need, and how and when information should be published. Presently, there is no defined mechanism for the users to communicate with the sites' owners. Therefore, such mechanism should be put in place. One possible solution is to use e-mail surveys.

Enhance the Existing OMIS Technical Resources

It was shown that the limited features of the existing search and retrieval system have led to the dissatisfaction of the PS team, especially the new team members. Therefore, it is becoming important to enhance the level of search granularity by implementing new and advanced search and retrieval techniques, such as PQR (prompt query refinement), that assist the user in interactively refining the query until a satisfactory set of focused and relevant documents is returned.

REFERENCES

Alavi, M., & Leidner, D. (1999, January). Knowledge management systems: Emerging views and practices from the Field. *Proceedings of the 32nd Annual Hawaii International Conference on System Sciences.*

American Chamber of Commerce. (2002). *Information technology in Egypt.* Cairo: The American Chamber of Commerce in Egypt, Business Studies and Analysis Center.

Argyris, C. (1998). Teaching smart people how to learn. *Harvard Business Review on Knowledge Management.*

Arsham, H. (2002). Questionnaire design and surveys sampling. Retrieved from *http://ubmail.ubalt.edu/~harsham/stat-data/oper330Surveys.htm*

Atwood, M. (2002, January). Organizational memory systems: Challenges for information technology. *Proc. of the 35th Annual Hawaii International Conference on System Sciences.*

Brown, J. (1998). Research that reinvents the corporation. *Harvard Business Review on Knowledge Management.*

Conklin, E. (1996). Capturing organizational memory. Retrieved from *http://touchstone.com/*

Davenport, T., & Prusak, L. (1998). *Working knowledge. How organizations manage what they know.* Cambridge, MA: Harvard Business School Press.

Davenport, T., & Smith, D. (2001). *Managing knowledge in professional service firms. The knowledge management yearbook 2000-2001.* Butterworth Heinemann.

DeLone, W., & McLean, E. (1992). Information systems success: The quest for the dependent variable. *Information Systems Research, 3*, 60-95.

Drucker, P. (1998). The coming new organization. *Harvard Business Review on Knowledge Management.*

Gamble, P., & Blackwell, J. (2001). *Knowledge management. A state of the art guide.* Kogan Page.

Gravin, D. (1998). Building a learning organization. *Harvard Business Review on Knowledge Management.*

Hansen, M., Nohira, N., & Tierney, T. (2001). *What's your strategy for managing knowledge? The knowledge management yearbook 2000-2001.* Butterworth Heinemann.

Heijst, G., Spek, R., & Kruizinga, E. (1996). *Organizing corporate memories.* CIBIT.

Jennex, M. (2000). Using an intranet to manage knowledge for a virtual project team. In *Internet-based organizational memory and knowledge management.* Hershey, PA: Idea Group.

Jennex, M. (2001). Internet support for knowledge management/organizational memory systems. *Issues and Trends of IT Management in Contemporary Organizations.*

Jennex, M., & Olfma, L. (2002). Organizational memory/knowledge effects on productivity, a longitudinal study. *Proceedings of the 35th Annual Hawaii International Conference on System Sciences.*

Jennex, M., Olfman, L., & Pituma, P. (1998, January). An organizational memory information systems success model: An extension of DeLone and McLean's I/S success model. *Proceedings of the 31st Annual Hawaii International Conference on System Sciences.*

Kinni, T. (2001). With an eye to the past: Transmitting the corporate memory. *The knowledge management yearbook 2000-2001.* Butterworth Heinemann.

Kleiner, A., & Roth, G. (1998). How to make experience your company's best teacher. *Harvard Business Review on Knowledge Management.*

Laupase, R., & Fink, D. (2001). Converting consultant's tacit knowledge to organisational explicit knowledge: Case studies of management consulting firms. *Issues and Trends of IT Management in Contemporary Organizations.*

Leonard, D., & Straus, S. (1998). Putting your company's whole brain to work. *Harvard Business Review on Knowledge Management.*

Mack, R., Ravin, Y., & Byrd, R. (2001). Knowledge portals and the emerging digital knowledge workplace. *IBM Systems Journal, 40,* 925-955.

Marwick, A. (2001). Knowledge management technology. *IBM Systems Journal, 40,* 4.

Mitchell, H. (2001). Technology and knowledge management: Is technology just an enabler? *Issues and Trends of IT Management in Contemporary Organizations.*

Newell, S., & Scarbrough, H. (1999, January). Intranets and knowledge management: Complex processes and ironic Outcomes. *Proceedings of the 32nd Annual Hawaii International Conference on System Sciences.*

Nonaka, I. (1998). The knowledge-creating company. *Harvard Business Review on Knowledge Management.*

Quinn, J., Anderson, P., & Finkelstein, S. (1998). Managing professional intellect. Making the most of the best. *Harvard Business Review on Knowledge Management.*

Rotaba, Z. (2002). *Building corporate memory for an IT company in Egypt.* Unpublished master's thesis, Maastricht School of Management, Maastricht, The Netherlands.

Roth, G., & Kleiner, A. (2001). Developing organizational memory through learning histories. *The Knowledge Management Yearbook 2000-2001.* Butterworth Heinemann.

Stein, E., & Zwass, V. (1995). Actualizing organizational memory with information systems. *Information Systems Research, 6,* 85-117.

Stenmark, D. (2002, January). Information vs. knowledge: The role of intranets in knowledge management. *Proceedings of the 35th Annual Hawaii International Conference on System Sciences.*

Stephenson, M., & Davies, T. (2001). Technology support for sustainable innovation. *The Knowledge Management Yearbook 2000-2001.* Butterworth Heinemann.

Wah, L. (2001). Making knowledge stick. *The Knowledge Management Yearbook 2000-2001*. Butterworth Heinemann.

ENDNOTE

[1] For confidentiality reasons, the name "CITE" has been given instead of the original name of the company under study.

APPENDIX

Interview Question

System Quality

Technical Resources

(To: IS support team)

1. What is the type and capacity of your networking infrastructure, and what is its degree of availability?
2. What is the type and capacity of your hardware servers and desktop clients, and what is their degree of availability?
3. What are the types of software solutions and software packages used to implement your OMIS?
4. What tools are used to capture and gather knowledge?
5. How is knowledge captured and gathered?
6. How are documents analyzed (in terms of text analysis and feature extraction)?
7. How is knowledge categorized?
8. What tools are used for knowledge distribution, sharing, and collaboration?
9. Have the users had training on how to use the organizational memory?

The Level of OMIS

(To: PS consultants)

1. Is the search and retrieval easy?
2. Can search and retrieval be done online?
3. Are search queries easy to structure and communicate?
4. What is the speed at which information can be retrieved?
5. What is the degree of completeness of the search function?
6. Does the OMIS provide a mechanism to discuss work-related issues and to archive these discussions? How?

(To: IS support team)

1. Is the knowledge for corporate memory collected actively or passively (e.g., do you have someone dedicated to maintain the knowledge base)? How?
2. Is the knowledge in the organizational memory distributed actively or passively? How?

The Form of OMIS

(To: IS support team)

1. Can all types of data be accessed from the same desktop environment?
2. Can the OMIS be remotely accessed?
3. Are the different hardware systems (servers and storage) compatible?
4. Are the software systems compatible?
5. How much of the accessible information is online?
6. How much of the accessible information is available through a single interface?
7. Do you think you have a coherent logical knowledge base structure?
8. Is the data consistent through the different subsystems?
9. What is the number of distinct subsystems searched to retrieve the desired information?

Information Quality

(To: PS consultants)

1. Do you think the OMIS provides you with important knowledge? Why?
2. Do you think the OMIS provides you with the relevant knowledge for your business needs (tools, best practices, methodologies, competition, etc.)? Why?
3. Do you think the OMIS provides you with useful knowledge for your business needs? Why?
4. Do you need to use sources other than OMIS to get complete answers to your inquiries? Why?
5. Is the provided information rich in terms of content? How?
6. Does the OMIS provide you with links to experts (knowledge map, who knows what, expertise directory, or skill database)? How?

(To: IS support team)

1. Is the content reviewed on an ongoing basis?
2. Do you have a strategy determining what information should be in the knowledge base, where it is located, and how it is to be acquired?
3. What are the resources dedicated to the revisions and/or entry of information?

Use

(To: PS consultants)

1. What is the number of tasks performed through OMIS?
2. What is your actual daily use of the system?
3. How many application packages do you use?
4. What is the level of sophistication of usage?
5. How many times per day do you use each component of the system?
6. What is the duration, in minutes, per access of each component?
7. What is the frequency of use (e.g., hourly, daily, etc.)?
8. Do you perceive any short-term job benefit from using the OMIS? Why?
9. Do you perceive any long-term job benefit from using the OMIS? Why?
10. Do you think your company culture supports the use of OMIS?

Impact

(To: PS consultants)

1. What is the number of PS projects you completed in the past 12 months?
2. How many of them have you delivered at the right time?
3. What is the amount of projects/work that had to be repeated in the past 12 months?
4. How many projects have been implemented right the first time?
5. What was the degree of complexity of the projects assigned to you?
6. What was the degree of quality (in terms of completeness, accuracy, and documentation) of the proposed solutions?
7. What was the degree of customer satisfaction?
8. How do you perceive your company's performance (in terms of professional services) relative to its competitors?
9. How do you perceive your company's performance (in terms of professional services) relative to its business plans?

Chapter IV

Rebuilding Core Competencies When a Company Splits: A Case Study of Assessing and Rebuilding Expertise

Gail Corbitt, California State University, Chico, USA

EXECUTIVE SUMMARY

In 1999, Hewlett Packard announced the split of its company into two smaller companies, HP and Agilent. As a result, the financial work, processes, and systems needed to be cloned in both new organizations at the same time people, assets, and transactions were becoming separate and distinct. The focus of this case study is on how the core competencies associated with the split were defined, identified, and transferred to all employees who needed to have them. The results of an internal and external literature search are included along with survey results. Results indicate that the purposes of and processes used for data collection concerning core competencies within an organization are critical to their usefulness.

INTRODUCTION

When most companies were looking for other organizations with which to merge and/or to acquire, Hewlett Packard (HP) was deciding to split its large company into two smaller firms, HP and Agilent. The company set up a new strategic objective to make the two newly created financial organizations fully functional by cloning the systems and core competencies needed to support those systems within a year. The project had two major components: (1) to identify needed core competencies in each worldwide organization and (2) to complete a transfer of this core knowledge to those who needed it. This paper describes the company scenario that existed in 1999, the processes used to define and identify core competencies, and finally how the knowledge transfer was organized and executed.

SETTING THE STAGE

In 1999 when HP announced that it was splitting the company by spinning off the test and measurement groups from the computer technology groups, it became the largest company to ever announce a split. Employees wore T-shirts that said "Split Happens" and the financial organization was faced with a daunting task of how to take the work, processes, and systems done by one global organization to create two global organizations that could operate autonomously after the split was finalized a year later. The company had to make many decisions quickly and really had only six months to accomplish cloning systems, moving employees into separate locations, and replicating the core competencies needed to run two separate organizations.

The task was complicated by the fact that the company decided to let employees throughout the world decide for whom they wanted to work, HP or Agilent. The split became official in June 2000 when the stock was finally distributed between the two companies (Fast 50, 2004), but by the end of October 1999 all employees of the Global Financial Services area had to choose for which company they wanted to work. (A total count of employees is not available but it involved over 1,000 people worldwide, about half of whom were on the technology/systems side of the financial organizations.) The focus of this case study is on the technology and business process side of the organization chart and excludes the customer service groups.

It was decided that as part of the split, both organizations would be staffed from the original presplit HP group of employees, and for the most part, the company honored employee choices. This choosing by the employees created an interesting situation. Depending on where employees decided to go, the expertise needed to run the systems and/or business processes was potentially lopsided. In fact, this is exactly what happened. For example, nearly everyone who had expertise in accounts receivable decided to stay with HP, leaving a void in Agilent. At the same time, nearly all the general ledger systems people decided to go with Agilent, leaving a void in HP.[1] The biggest challenge was in Europe, where all but a handful of employees decided to stay with HP, forcing Agilent to hire college graduates to fill systems positions in Belgium as the company was reorganizing.

As a result of the split and the way the staffing was decided, the company had some interesting questions arise. What are the core competencies needed to run the systems in the global financial organizations worldwide? Once the core competencies are defined, where are the voids and holes in expertise in each new organization? Finally, what can be done to correct the deficiencies in the shortest possible time? In short, what knowledge transfer is needed where and to/for whom? A new strategic objective was set for 1999-2000 that basically stated that the financial systems and the knowledge needed to support and sustain the systems would be cloned in each organization by June 1, 2000, and that the two separate organizations would be fully functional and autonomous by the end of October 2000. In October 1999, the list of roughly 125 distinct systems (with many variations) was relatively straightforward, but the "knowledge" or core competencies needed to run these systems was basically unknown.

As employees transitioned from one organization into two, three distinct groups needing knowledge emerged:

1. New employees hired to fill gaps left by exiting or transferred personnel (such as in the case of Agilent in Europe).
2. Current employees who were hired to do job A but were now doing job B because of changes in organizational structure and/or requirements.
3. Current employees who were left in a reduced skill area where only one or two people remained who had the knowledge needed to do the job(s).

The last group did not appear to have immediate needs and generally had no plans to hire immediately, but left the company vulnerable if one person decided to leave the organization in the near future. A strategy of creating backup personnel in key areas was generally thought to be important to this process.

Within this context, the project to meet the strategic objective had the following major activities: (1) to determine and articulate a method to determine the core competencies; (2) to design a way to capture, access, and update the expertise that made up the core competency "knowledge" base; and (3) to articulate a way to keep the data current in the future. The challenges were (1) to determine how to meet the needs of these three groups who have potentially different gaps in knowledge in the two emerging organizations and (2) to figure out ways to define, store, and access the needed "knowledge" so that existing people can tap into the expertise as they need it to keep doing their jobs.

BACKGROUND

As this project emerged, a literature search (both internal and external to the organization) was conducted in order to determine the state of the art of developing knowledge transfer programs and/or building (or rebuilding) core competencies. It was soon clear that there are several directions that a person in this field can take and that the intended purpose of any study in this area can affect the outcomes. For example, the internal search uncovered a group within HP who had conducted what was called a core competency study the year before (1998) to identify those critical skills, abilities, and knowledge that were needed by employees who were considered to be the best in a particular job group. On the surface this looked like what was needed for the task at hand, but the researcher soon discovered that the purpose of "the core competency" study was to further develop existing employees. As a result, the skills, abilities, and knowledge included such things as "interpersonal sensitivity," "managerial self-image," and the "ability to be self-assured." While these are clearly important, they are not core competency skills that are candidates for knowledge transfer with the purpose of rebuilding two "weakened" organizations due to transferring personnel.

Since the internal search for solutions did not reveal anything helpful to the purposes at hand, an external, more academic search was conducted. This search revealed that "knowledge" has many contexts and it is not a simple term to define. In a study by Croasdell, Jennex, Yu, Christianson, Chakradea, and Makum (2003), the study of knowledge is examined from the perspectives of artifacts and processes. The authors looked at work across the disciplines of knowledge management (KM), organizational memory (OM), and organizational learning (OL). In addition to describing the differences between data, information, and knowledge, the authors also examine work in the areas of understanding and learning.

While there are many papers that address the differences in these concepts in more detail, knowledge in general is thought to have a minimum of two components: (1) information ("know what") and (2) "know how" (von Hippel, 1988). Within the context of discovering the core competencies within an organization, information is a skill or ability that can be transferred from one person to another without loss of integrity. "Know how," on the other hand, is the "accumulated practical skill or expertise that allows one to do something smoothly and efficiently" (von Hippel, 1988). If this is the minimum that knowledge entails, then the full dimension of knowledge includes the information (know what) and "know how" components, as well as the understanding (know why) and creative (care why) dimensions (Kogut & Zander, 1992). In the context of the Croasdell et al. study (2003), knowledge includes artifacts of information (know what) that can be captured in a database as well as the "meaning based on personal interpretation" (p. 3). For purposes of cloning expertise within the corporate setting at hand, however, knowledge also needs to include "understanding" or knowing when to use the information in the proper context.

In other words, the first step in the HP scenario was to define what was meant by core competency skills, knowledge, and/or abilities. At the time, one path in the literature focused on knowledge creation where a core competency was defined as those things that lead to innovation within the firm or organization (Nonaka, 1994). Knowledge creation had two main components: explicit or codifiable knowledge, and tacit knowledge that is individual and/or context based. The explicit knowledge is similar to the artifacts and the "know what" component discussed previously. Tacit knowledge is the notion that explicit knowledge takes on different meanings and uses depending on the person who accesses and then uses the explicit skill, ability, or knowledge. This is similar to the "know how" and understanding components. In fact, building core competencies within this line of thinking acknowledges that both informal and formal sharing of knowledge can build new tacit components. From this work, one can conclude that in order to identify and rebuild core competencies at HP and Agilent, it is important to start with the individual and keep individuals (experts) associated with identified skills, abilities, and knowledge. The knowledge base is dynamic as more ways to use the information are uncovered over time.

Another interesting path within the KM literature at the time was the notion of "distributed cognition" discussed by Boland, Tenkasi, and Te'eni (1994), which is how to get knowledge shared within an organizational community. This is the second part of the HP strategic objective related to knowledge transfer. Distributed cognition is the process of exchanging information in an autonomous environment such that those sharing can enhance their own levels of understanding of their own situation and that of others. At HP, once we knew what we meant by core competencies, certainly we needed to figure out an efficient way to share the knowledge with everyone who had a need to know in both organizations. Again, the sharing of knowledge is person based and the autonomous sharing includes such things as company intranets where individuals add to the "information base" in order to help others better understand company situations. This seemed valuable to the HP situation because in several of these studies, the HP intranet was used as one of the best examples of information sharing and was a model for how to do knowledge transfer. In addition, the company intranet was also cloned in Agilent.

Clearly the HP intranet is an incredible source of information with over a terabyte of data moving across the intracompany network daily. While the intranet meets the criteria (as defined by Boland, Tenkasi, and Te'eni, 1994) of ownership, easy travel, and multiplicity, it is also subject to lack of validity of content, anonymous owners, and indeterminacy where interpretations of what is out there for public consumption are unknown, incomplete, and often imprecise. A knowledge system that can support distributed cognition needs to be oriented toward individuals who can not only add to or help build the knowledge base with explicit information and knowledge, but who can also reflect on the interpretations that are possible (Boland, Tenkasi, & Te'eni, 1994).

There is also a group of studies that fall into the organizational memory category that assumes that what the organization knows can somehow be remembered and maintained for future use. One study looked at this body of research and concluded that the term "organizational memory" had become overworked and may need to be revisited within the context of the individual (Ackerman & Halverson, 1999). Instead of focusing on the content or remembering the results (known facts or things on the intranet) along a particular line of inquiry, the process of how the facts were uncovered may be equally important.

Finally, there were a number of articles that discussed knowledge management and repository management of knowledge and information (Croasdell et al., 2003; Davenport, 1998). Building the KM systems, generally happens two ways: (1) a system in which the artifacts accompany the person, process, and context (termed project-based by Croasdell et al.) and (2) a system where the "knowledge" is not associated with a specific person within a context. While these studies did not help define what was meant by core competencies in the HP case, they were helpful in deciding how the data need to be kept and shared within the organization. Many of the studies in this category focused on issues involving methods to capture or create, maintain, categorize, and diffuse knowledge throughout the organization. Since time was of the essence, building a huge infrastructure to house everything needed to run the 125 systems was not feasible.

In summary, existing research from external sources helped to define some guiding principles and definitions. First, knowledge has an information component that can be easily transferred (once it is identified) and even stored in a database, but the "know how" and/or understanding components of knowledge are more at the heart of a company's core competencies. For purposes of this project, knowledge is defined most simply as information, skills, and abilities *in use* within the corporation. While information can be tracked, captured, and defined, knowledge is created and may be organized by different individuals in different ways. Managing this knowledge, therefore, has an autonomous characteristic to it that is housed within and, therefore, needs to be owned by individuals. In this respect, the management of knowledge at the individual level becomes the basis for what was called an "expertise database."

Second, it is clear from the definition of knowledge or core competencies that in order to both identify core competencies and develop a knowledge transfer program within a short time frame, one must enlist the support and trust of individuals who both have and need core competency skills, abilities, and knowledge. Thus while the content including understanding is what is needed to keep the organization functioning, the process used to identify what core competencies are and who has/needs them may be equally important. Time was short for this project and yet high-quality information was critical to the success of the respective organizations. We absolutely had to know what skills, abilities, and knowledge were critical to the organizations. In addition, the trick was to enlist the help of those who had knowledge to help train and get those who needed knowledge up to speed as quickly as possible. All of this took place at a time when everyone felt overworked and there was a great deal of uncertainty in the environment of both organizations.

CASE DESCRIPTION

Having said that support (implying participation) and trust of employees are important, the first mandate from management in the needs assessment part of the study was to use a "fast and good enough" approach. In other words, the researcher needed to identify the core competency needs related to knowledge transfer, keeping in mind the organizational goals of expediency, needing a high level of detail, and using a method that requires the least amount of individual employee time. After looking into several methods that included one-on-one interviewing by the researcher, it was determined that electronic focus group meetings were the most expedient with the highest level of needed detail. While individual groups by job group within the company were desired, time permitted only a job family approach. Because the skills needed by the two new organizations were believed to be the same since the business processes and systems were being cloned, there was no need to do separate groups for each company as long as ranking the items could be done within each company.

Initially, the focus groups were designed to be the end-all for needs assessment. The organizational structure of the target audience consisted of functional areas such as vendor payables, accounts receivable, assets, tax, and general ledger. Based on a previous study of needed skills, abilities, and knowledge of employees, job families were identified. For the target group of the current study, there were four job families within which all jobs were grouped: (1) systems developers, (2) process engineers, (3) SAP implementers, and (4) production systems (and applications) support personnel. (The prior study was done in 1998 for the purpose of identifying skills, abilities, and knowledge needed to advance in one's job. After reviewing the items identified in the 1998 study it was determined that the purpose was sufficiently different and that the skills from one study could not be used for identifying candidates for knowledge transfer. A comparison of the data appearing in Table 2 in the Results section confirms the accuracy of this assumption.)

GroupSystems (an electronic meeting software system) was used to capture detailed lists of core competencies across functional areas within job families. In other words, four sessions were conducted by job family. Managers were asked to send a representative group of employees to each session. Representative employees were defined as experts or those who are more than adequate at performing their job.

Using the GroupSystems tools, participants developed a list of core skills and abilities needed to perform their jobs. The list was then prioritized by importance and then each skill was rated by accessibility in the new organization. The idea was that after the two ratings, the most important items that were the least accessible appeared at the top of the list. Participants then commented on the items in the prioritized list by identifying how best to address the gap in skill and/or ability. The same process was used to develop a commented prioritized list of knowledge and/or information items. These procedures were repeated for each of the four job families. At the end of each four-hour session, the details of each session were recorded using the computer-assisted tools in GroupSystems. Microsoft Word files of all the items, ratings, and comments were compiled, compared, and then consolidated in an Access database.

Due to time constraints and competing projects, however, the groups were smaller than desired and not every functional area was represented. For example, for the systems development group people from accounts receivable were not represented in the focus group. Other problems with the focus group approach included a bias toward the Americas since these groups were done in Colorado, and a small number of people from each company. In one group all but one representative was from Agilent, so there was only one representative for all of HP, which naturally made the results biased.

Nonetheless, 231 unique core competency skills were identified during the focus group sessions that were then used as the basis for questionnaires for each job family. Skills, abilities, and knowledge were all grouped into one list since the distinction is purely academic for the study's purpose; however surveys contained items that were most related to each job family. On each survey, an employee was asked to rate the criticality of each skill where critical is defined as a skill that is important and is also in short supply within the new organization.

At the time the questionnaires were developed, it was believed that two rating scales were needed, one for importance and one for availability or accessibility (similar to those used in the focus group sessions). The survey instruments were very long, however, because some of the skills lists had over 100 items on them. By having employees rate each item on two scales, it was believed that the response rate would be too low to be useful, so accuracy was sacrificed for expediency. (Competing projects such as Y2K, the split of the company's systems, and year-end close still limited the time of employees.) As added incentive to complete the survey, employees were given a free lunch chit for a completed survey. In addition to the rating of the items developed from the focus groups, respondents were asked to add missing items to the list and identify those items for which they considered themselves an expert. By cross-referencing the self-reported experts with the identified experts in the focus groups, we had a more validated list of experts than we had by using only self-reported experts.

Data were tracked and recorded by respondent so that experts can be readily identified. The Access database was updated by entering data from each completed questionnaire. Appendix A contains the database tables that were used to capture and analyze the data.

Table 1. Response rate by location

	SAP Implementers	Process Engineers	Production and System Support	Systems Developers
Atlanta				
Total Sent*	12	15	15	11
Total Return	6	10	6	6
% Returned	50%	67.7%	40%	54.5%
Colorado Springs				
Total Sent	33	26	30	16
Total Return	21	7	10	7
% Returned	63.6%	26.9%	33.3%	43.8%

**Total Sent for Atlanta is an estimate because questionnaires were hand delivered and the actual count could be off by a few in each case.*

Survey Results

Table 1 shows the response rate of the questionnaires for both Colorado Springs and Atlanta. The organizations of WWFS (World Wide Financial Services) for HP and the GFS (Global Financial Services) for Agilent both have employees in Colorado and Atlanta. Separate needs assessments were canceled for Europe and Asia Pacific in the interest of completing the knowledge transfer activity in a timely manner. While questionnaires were distributed via interoffice mail in Colorado, they were hand delivered in a meeting environment in Atlanta.

In addition to the respondent analysis, Table 2 is included to show that skills, abilities, and knowledge considered to be core competencies are not the same as those skill, abilities, and knowledge needed to advance in one's career. This difference suggests that the way the questions are worded and the purposes of the data can produce vastly different results. The list of items developed from the focus groups was validated with the managers and is believed to be accurate for current core competency assessment. All managers agreed with the content of the list and, except for the addition of 15 items added during the survey portion of the study, the list did not change in content from the original list developed by the focus groups.

The ranking of the items by criticality, however, did vary from the ratings made by focus group participants. Since the detailed data are not important to the results of the expertise database and are company specific, the rankings are not reported in this study.

In addition to the analysis of the skills by type, there were five levels of skills identified. Levels were determined by comparing topics from the list to topics suggested for new hire versus basic ability training. These levels vary by intended audience and have been assigned arbitrary levels that roughly correspond to the order that the knowledge transfer should take place. Note that these levels are most significant to the training aspect of knowledge transfer but can also be applied to documentation, Web-based material, and mentoring. (Interestingly, at a corporate meeting held in February 2000, three other groups within HP had conducted similar studies and all identified four to five levels of knowledge transfer. While the topic content did vary from one organization to another, the definition of levels and the inclusion of core competency at

Table 2. Comparison of competency job skills by type of study

Core competency skills, abilities, and knowledge needed for career advancement

	Technical	Nontechnical	Total
Corporate specific	4 (3.9%)	10 (9.7%)	14 (13.6%)
Noncorporate	18 (17.5%)	71 (68.9%)	89 (86.4%)
Total	22 (21.4%)	81 (78.6%)	103 (100%)

Core competency skills, abilities, and knowledge needed to rebuild company

	Technical	Nontechnical	Total
Corporate specific	50 (20.7%)	44 (18.3%)	94 (39%)
Noncorporate	105 (43.6%)	42 (17.4%)	147 (61%)
Total	155 (64.3%)	86 (35.7%)	241 (100%)*

**Five skills were not classified.*

a level above new hire basics were consistent across all four parts of the corporation. This leads to at least some degree of internal validity to this approach.)

Level 1: New Hire Training (done by the Personnel Department)

The topics covered at this level apply to all new employees to the organization, thereby eliminating internal hires or internal transfers to new jobs. The topics covered include the following:

- Company history and policy
- Company culture
- Standards of business conduct/misconduct/corrective action

Level 2: Team-Specific Overview (done by team leader or manager)

The first day on the job after the employee completes the I-9 paperwork (U.S.-specific activity) and is processed by security, the manager makes arrangements to meet the new employee and give him/her a site tour. The manager also introduces him/her to a mentor who is typically a coworker or another member of the team. Additional topics covered by the manager at this time include things such as parking "rules," emergency/evacuation procedures, payroll-related procedures such as time sheets/cards, scheduling time off, and so forth, and performance evaluation process and expectations. (None of the items in the study were identified as core competencies at this level but it was decided to include those things on the manager's checklist for new employees in the final write-up. This seems to give a more complete picture of all the needed knowledge transfer for all groups of employees.)

Level 3: New Hire Boot Camp/Orientation (new hires only)

The New Hire Boot Camp is a highly modular training system that accommodates both internal hires, someone hired within the HP/Agilent organization, and external hires. The Boot Camp was designed as a direct result of the needs assessment as it became clear that new hires had different knowledge needs from existing employees. In transitioning organizations, there were many new hires. An external hire is someone hired from outside the current HP or Agilent organization who is new to the HP or Agilent culture, such as all the college hires who were brought into the Brussels Agilent organization. (In addition, internal hires are people who have worked for HP or Agilent before, but are new to the Financial Services Organization [FSO] or someone who transferred from another FSO department. In general, the assumption for internal new hires is that they are new to the FSO. Employees who transfer within the FSO do not generally need the level 3 topics at all.) Given that internal hires are new to the FSO, topics appropriate for all new hire boot camp participants that were identified as core competencies include the following:

- Overview of all the business processes used by the WWFS and GFS
- Business control knowledge
- Overview of the system platforms and the relationship between systems and business processes
- Audio conferencing
- Working in a global organization

Topics identified as core competencies that external hires need and that most internal hires do not need include the following:

- Orientation to the intranet and use of Portico[2]
- System security measures
- Voice-mail system skills and uses

Level 4: Core Competency Topics (potentially all audiences can use)

Level 4 topics are those topics that have a broad-based audience that extend beyond the individual work group or department. All of the topics in this level are topics that were identified in the initial needs assessment as needing ongoing knowledge transfer by at least five people. (Needing ongoing knowledge transfer was determined by those items that were ranked as critical [seven or higher] by at least five people or ranked as at least a five by 10 or more people.) These topics are generally not site specific but may contain modules that are unique for different geographies. A modular approach is used in developing the topics so that when courses are put together for a training, knowledge transfer participants can pick the modules that are most appropriate to their needs. Since each module is stand alone in its composition but may have prerequisite knowledge contained in other modules, participation in a particular module can happen with no information loss as long as the participant has the prerequisite knowledge. For example, a person who has used SAP can skip the overview to SAP and still take the modules relating to OSS (online support services) or Basis (systems administration components).

In addition to training, an expertise database was built as part of this project and contains relevant Web addresses (URLs) for basic as well as advanced information for many of the level 4 and 5 topics. The corporate intranet is a vast source of information, but even with the Portico/Sherlock search engine, finding relevant and timely information is difficult. As part of the needs assessment, experts in each knowledge or skill area have been identified, and relevant URLs are added to the database as the topics are explored and updated by the experts. This is a documentation knowledge transfer component and is an evolving component that can sustain knowledge transfer over time. The general design of the database is included as Appendix A and the needs assessment is the primary source for populating the database tables. In addition, as training needs were validated and developed, additional experts were identified and added to the database. Further uses of the data are discussed in more detail in the succeeding section of this chapter.

When the training was offered, two to three times as many people signed up for the training than expected. This high show-up rate tends to validate that the core competencies identified at this level are, in fact, key skills needed to rebuild the organizations. By the time the training was completed in June 2000, over 120 people had received the core competency training.

Level 5: Core Competency Team-Specific Topics

Level 5 topics are those that are department or work-group specific that generally do not cross departmental lines. Generally, the knowledge transfer for these skills are accomplished through a job-specific class attended by only one to two people, individual mentoring, or job shadowing. No topics in this category are identified here but each manager is encouraged to work with their employees to identify the employee's unique needs. The expertise database acts as a list of resources for knowledge transfer in the case of mentoring or documentation. In addition, the experts can give relevant sources for more information including good training courses. For the most part, the needs assessment data are used to develop the information needed by managers. The skills identified at this level matched those identified in the needs assessment data but were ranked as critical by fewer than five people in the survey.

In this way the survey data became the foundation for an expertise database to which focus group and survey participants wanted to have access. In addition, the skill areas were used to identify gaps in expertise needed in each company and, therefore, became the basis for an extensive knowledge transfer project. The identified experts were used as a resource list to help develop core competency training. In addition, experts who could be called on to help with the knowledge transfer were associated with each skill area. These areas were in turn used to associate URLs in the vast intranet used by HP/Agilent to synthesize information and expertise by topic area. Experts were assigned Web pages to update and maintain that contained tips and tricks, answered the most frequently asked questions, and had current information needed by colleagues in the organization. This model meets the criteria of a distributed cognition model described by Boland, Tenkasi, and Te'eni (1994), and the individual autonomous criteria described by Kogut and Zander (1988).

CURRENT CHALLENGES/PROBLEMS FACING THE ORGANIZATION

Like most case studies, this research has limited applicability to other situations. The fact that three other groups within HP did a similar study with similar conclusions is interesting but is still bound by the corporate environment of one organizational culture. Furthermore, the expertise database built from survey and focus group data is incomplete at the present time due to time constraints and the omission of those who did not respond to the survey. There are some topics that have no identified experts.

On the other hand, there have been several situations in which the data in the database can be useful if complete. For example, managers who want to build teams with a balanced mix of skills and expertise want to consult the database for team selection. Another request came in to identify experts in each company for topics that have scarce resources in one company or the other. At some point the data in the database need to be complete by calling the people who did not respond to the survey. Having the experts identify the most important Web sites for information about each topic is of undisputed value to the company.

Since knowledge and expertise are person bound, and people change jobs and situations within the company, the process used to identify the experts is also of value. This study showed that small groups of employees can identify both the critical core competency areas within an organization and can identify experts for topics. In this case, 90% of all topics and 100% of the topics considered critical were identified by the small focus groups even though a full survey was conducted. The data from the focus groups included identification of whom to contact for expertise on each topic, and these data were more complete (i.e., more topics had identified experts) than self-identification of expertise in topics. A similar focus group approach can be repeated as business needs change, and over time the expertise database can be updated. In other words, there is some evidence in this study that identifying topics and knowing who to call are possibly necessary and sufficient for knowledge transfer within an organization.

As corporations rely on virtual global teams to accomplish work, the need to easily identify experts in critical skill areas may become more important. As company intranets grow with little attention to deleting invalid or outdated pages, the need to have someone identify the most relevant URLs may become more important as well. Too much information at a person's fingertips may be as great a problem as a lack of information.

EPILOGUE

Shortly after this study was well underway, HP decided to upgrade the SAP system to 4.5. This was a technical upgrade, so new functionality was not added to the system. There were expectations by employees that the new version had desired new features. It was clear that greater understanding of SAP was needed by many employees in the organizations. After June 2000, HP entered into an agreement with SAP to use enterprise solutions for all new development efforts in the GFO — if new functions were needed and SAP had a solution, the SAP solution was the HP solution. Agilent, on the other hand, decided to switch its ERP system to Oracle.

To my knowledge the expertise database was never maintained after about July 2000. Owners were assigned Web pages and a general cleanup of the intranet in the new HP was nearly complete by August 2000. To my knowledge the expertise database met original expectations for getting the knowledge transfer complete but proved to be a low priority after the split was complete. In addition, the computer industry took a huge downturn in 2001, the stock price in both companies fell and layoffs were commonplace throughout HP.

REFERENCES

Ackerman, M.S., & Halverson, C. (1999, January). Organizational memory: Processes, boundary objects, and trajectories. *Proceedings of HICSS 1999,* Maui, HI.

Boland, R.J., Tenkasi, R., & Te'eni, D. (1994). Designing information technology to support distributed cognition. *Organization Science, 5*(3), 456-475.

Croasdell, D.T., Jennex, M., Yu, Z., Christianson, T., Chakradea, M., & Makdum, W. (2003, January). A meta-analysis of methodologies for research in knowledge management, organizational learning, and organizational memory: Five years at HICSS. *Proceedings of HICSS-36,* Kona, HI.

Davenport, T. (1998). Some principles of knowledge management. Retrieved from *www.itmweb.com/essay538.htm#KM/HP*

Fast 50. (2004). Retrieved from *www.fastcompany.com/fast50-04/profile/?barnholt1419*

Kogut, B., & Zander, U. (1992). Knowledge of the firm, combinative capabilities, and the replication of technology. *Organization Science, 3*(5), 383-397.

Nonaka, I. (1994). A dynamic theory of organizational knowledge creation. *Organization Science, 5*(1), 14-37.

Von Hippel, E. (1988). *The sources of innovation.* Cambridge, MA: MIT Press.

ENDNOTES

1 These are used as representative examples, but may not be the actual unit names.

2 Portico is the HP search engine used on the company intranet.

APPENDIX A: DATABASE SCHEMA

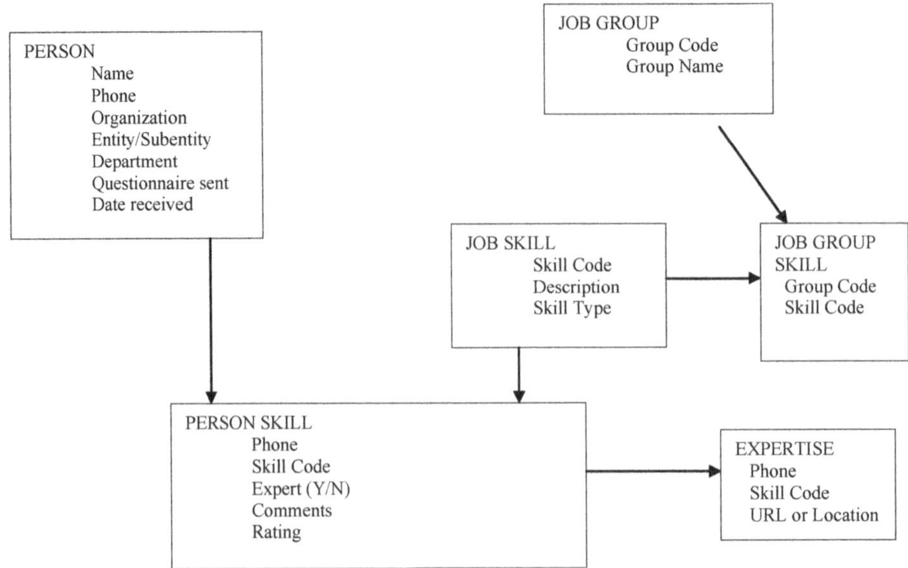

Section III

Knowledge Management Strategy

Chapter V

Exploring the Impacts of Knowledge (Re)Use and Organizational Memory on the Effectiveness of Strategic Decisions: A Longitudinal Case Study

Afsoun Hatami, London School of Economics, UK

Robert D. Galliers, Bentley College, USA

EXECUTIVE SUMMARY

This chapter introduces the impacts of knowledge management (KM) and organizational memory (OM) on strategic decision making. Close consideration and treatment of OM as part of a KM strategy are suggested as a central issue to the effectiveness of strategic decision making. This chapter uses the modified version of McLean's Information System (IS) Success Model by Jennex and Olfman (2002) as a lens to examine the impact of knowledge strategy and technological resources, along with the impact of individuals and members from wider organizational context on decision-making processes. These components are then analyzed within Galliers' (2002) IS Strategy Framework of emergent and deliberate strategizing. Furthermore, this chapter highlights the intermingled approaches to organizational KM practices that are due to the contextual nature of knowledge and the human need for social interaction. Results from our exploratory and continuing longitudinal study have clearly shown the significance of culture and human-driven knowledge requirements along side the use of an ERP system as part of an OMS. The authors account for the intersubjectivity of the concept and claim that organizations relying on acquired knowledge from past experiences on average make higher-quality decisions on business strategies for better future performance.

INTRODUCTION

The impact of globalization, ICT innovations and market integrations continue to change competitive business environments, making knowledge and expertise primary sources for competitive advantage, at least in knowledge-intensive industries. In addition, rapid technological change affects dramatically the nature and pace of firms' competitive moves (e.g., Ball, 2002). The knowledge-based view of the firm perspective conceptualizes firms as bearers of tacit, social, and path-dependent organizational knowledge (Hitt et al., 1999). In competitive environments, the manner in which corporations learn from past performances and manage knowledge impacts future decisions. The extent to which advanced ICTs play a supportive or impeding role in the knowledge strategy of a firm depends not only on the knowledge infrastructure of a company, but also on the attitude of decision makers towards knowledge sharing, creation, and use, as well as the technology itself. Related topics in literature concern the strategic games decision makers play (e.g., Brindle, 1999), technological discontinuities (Tushman & Andersen, 1986), and hypercompetition (D'Aveni, 1994).

The literature on IS and strategy places emphasis on either the "hard" or the "soft" approaches to managing knowledge and organizational memory. The former assumes that knowledge can be captured and stored in the organization's structure and technological systems, such as knowledge management systems (KMS). The softer approaches view organizations as social systems and claim that knowledge is embedded within human minds, with growing attention to social networks and organizational culture, that is, "knowledge worker" (Drucker, 1995), "social capital" (Davenport, 1998), and so forth. We will present that organizational effectiveness arises from a complex interplay between deliberate decisions and ongoing actions, rather than one or the other. Knowledge exploitation and exploration can be a powerful force when employed in tandem (Huang, Chen, & Frolick, 2002; Galliers, 2002). Thus, decisions (deliberate or emergent) play a part in determining the strategic direction of the firm (compare Mintzberg & Waters, 1983). For future frameworks to become more useful in practice, there is a balance between these two extremes that needs to be struck.

In the light of the IS Success Model, this paper argues that effective decision making depends on the use of quality information, including systems that capture lessons learned from past decisions and performances. Thus, it is assumed that organizational effectiveness depends, in part at least, on effective decision making based on the effective management and use of knowledge and OM. How much of which type of knowledge and resources are used by top management teams and boards during strategic analysis and choice remains a topic that requires further investigation.

LITERATURE REVIEW

Related to the issue of globalization and ICTs is the institutional context (e.g., Oliver, 1997). In attempting to explain variations in firm performance, Oliver (1997) extended the resource-based view on the firm to incorporate the institutional perspective, where substreams emerged. The research substreams have focused on specific types of resources inside a firm, three of which are tacit knowledge, strategic leadership, and decision making (Hitt & Tyler, 1991).

Knowledge Management and Organizational Memory for Organizational Effectiveness

Knowledge Management

Modern conceptions of knowledge stem from the philosopher Michael Polanyi (1966) and have been applied to business and knowledge management by the Japanese management scholar Ikujiro Nonaka (1994). The latter suggests that tacit and explicit knowledge are important, while the former's emphasis is on tacit knowledge. However, Western firms have focused largely on managing explicit knowledge (Grover & Davenport, 2001).

Explicit knowledge is by definition codified data and as such can be processed by modern ICT and stored for future retrieval. So far, the primary interest has been in the information technology (IT) paradigm of Knowledge Management (Haldin-Herrgard, 2000; Walsham, 2001). However, the knowledge that differentiates companies from one another is mostly tacit in nature and embedded within human minds, processes, relationships, services, and products. The conversion of the tacit into explicit knowledge — a process of externalization according to Nonaka and Takeuchi (1995) — allows knowledge to be codified, stored, and disseminated throughout the organization, facilitating organizational learning and knowledge creation. This process has to take place within a specific knowing context for organizations to create a memory base that can be leveraged to build upon past experiences as opposed to having to reinvent the wheel.

However, converting tacit knowledge from the human memory and processes into organizational memory is a challenging task to master (Gold, Mahotra, & Segars, 2001). The difficulty arises due to the intangible nature of tacit knowledge, which is personal, intuitive, and embedded within intangible resources. There is a well-established critique of technically led Knowledge Management practices, which involve codification strategies directed at making tacit knowledge explicit. Critics argue that tacit knowledge is embedded in contexts of social action and objectifying and storing it in repositories takes away its inherent value (Marshall & Brady, 2001).

Hence, a critical concern for practitioners remains how to institutionalize individual tacit knowledge to secure the intangible assets that otherwise would remain hidden (Zack, 1999; Augie & Vendelo, 1999, as quoted in Haldin-Herrgard, 2000). An integrated approach to Knowledge Management and Organizational Memory is seen as a means of squaring the circle between operational efficiency and organizational effectiveness (Baird & Cross, 2000).

Organizational Memory

The concept of Organizational Memory is concerned with how to collect, store, and provide access to experience, skills, and know-how. Effective use of this knowledge depends on the selective use of memory. This is a critical consideration if organizations are to benefit from the use of knowledge to impact organizational effectiveness. Indeed, interactions between all organizational dimensions are a requirement: technological, sociotechnical and socioemotional, cognitive, processes, strategies, cultural, and structural issues.

Knowledge strategy is highly contextual and depends on the purpose of its reuse, for example, projects, processes, relationships, and know-how. A critical enabling factor is to create a knowledge-sharing organizational context by building a strong organizational knowledge infrastructure supported by knowledge networks and technologies (Galliers, 2002).

Exploitation of organizational knowledge for effective decision making requires an integrated interactive approach, whereby ICT may act as powerful facilitators. Dynamics of technology implementation focus on content and processes of knowledge integration. Organizational Memory systems may provide to be useful depending on the type of knowledge (re)used and the organizational context. Externalization and diffusion of tacit knowledge have different requirements for knowledge repositories depending on the reuser and the purpose of knowledge reuse (Markus, 2001). Hence, architectural requirements for building a knowledge infrastructure, that is, repositories, should only be regarded as enabler of a greater context of a knowledge-sharing culture.

In the hypercompetitive global context, where learning, innovation, and speed matter the most, strategy and decision making are becoming inseparable. Throughout this paper, we try to emphasize that despite the emergent advanced ICT for managing knowledge, Organizational Memory and Organizational Learning are social processes and effectiveness is achieved through a synergistic integration of a congruent knowledge infrastructure, culture, and technological resources (Galliers, 2002). This research accounts for the impact of emerging technologies for OMS/KMS as well as their interaction with tacit knowledge and managerial discretion.

Role of Organizational Learning and Leadership in Strategic Decision Making

Strategic Decision Making

Strategic decision making is characterized as a complex, unstructured, nonlinear, and fragmented process often based on conflicting information (Green, Amason, & Mooney, 1999), which is influenced by the input of individual biases, negotiation, and political games (Bennett, 1998). Information and knowledge upon which decisions are based come partly from individuals' memory and from Organizational Memory. Organizational Memory systems may serve as repositories of data, information, and knowledge, which are retrieved and used to build upon and make new decisions.

In the context of using knowledge in social processes, humans have different approaches to making decisions. Some lean more towards the rational positivistic approach of weighing facts, and others have the tendency for a more normative approach.

The latter involves relying primarily on experience-based tacit knowledge, subjective judgments, intuition, and "gut feeling" as opposed to hard data. Although there is a tendency to view both as intermingled and complementary, the debate on rationality versus relativism in the literature argues as to which sources are tapped by top managers to make sense of complex and uncertain situations in making strategic business decisions. In the light of Organizational Memory, this has considerable implications on the knowledge strategy, Organizational Memory structure, and systems.

Organizational Learning

New perspectives on learning and innovation arise from the knowledge-based view of the firm. For example, "absorptive capacity" (Cohen & Levinthal, 1990) refers to the ability of a firm to recognize the value of new, external information, and to use it for commercial value. Lei, Hitt, and Bettis (1996) suggest that competencies that lead to competitive advantage have dynamic qualities and create value only through continuous development. Increasingly, more executives are becoming aware of the potential benefits of KM and KMS for continuous organizational learning and retaining the lessons learned.

KM strategy involves the fostering of a LO. The concept of the LO is based on the work of Argyris (Argyris & Schon, 1978) and Senge (1990). Senge (1990) discusses the concept of generative learning, which is about adaptive learning and coping with accelerating pace of change. He introduces a view on leadership based on vision, which is to facilitate generative learning.

Mintzberg (1973) argues that strategy is less a rational plan arrived at the abstract than an emergent phenomenon. Furthermore, decision makers should continually learn about shifting business conditions and balance what is desired and what is feasible. Accordingly, the key is not getting the "right" strategy but fostering strategic thinking, whereby it is important to achieve insight into the nature of the complexity and to formulate concepts and worldviews for coping with it.

Impact of Systems Thinking on Decision Making and KM/OM

Organizational Learning theorists (e.g., Senge, 1990) emphasize the systems perspective in attempting to explain the element of tacitness (i.e., tacit knowledge and hidden assumptions) as the underlying currents of decision making and strategy formulation, especially where there is a lack of explicitness in terms of quantitative support for further analysis. This argument may provide one part of the explanation of why difference in knowledge reuse may have different impact on the effectiveness of decisions.

When confronted with a situation, the decision maker recalls memories of past performance and experiences that seem most relevant. This recollection acts as a reference and consciously or unconsciously influences current perception of the problem situation and hence subsequent behavior (i.e., decisions made, style of communication, and approaches to similar challenges). Here, OMS may serve as a powerful tool to make selective choices on remembering past lessons learned. Since context shapes human perception to a great extent, the way the initial tacit-to-tacit knowledge is communicated into the explicit determines how understanding is gained of the problems situation.

Strategic Leadership

Strategic leadership (Finkelstein & Hambrick, 1996) is seen as a unique resource in the knowledge-based view of the firm. Strategic decision theory describes the role of top executives as organizing, coordinating, commanding, and controlling agents (Fayol, 1949). This stream of literature views the strategic choice of executives based on their cognitions and values. From this stream, the concept of "managerial discretion" emerges, which is linked with personal characteristics and organizational and environmental factors (Finkelstein & Hambrick, 1996).

Mintzberg (1973) classified managerial roles into interpersonal, informational, and decisional. The premise is that decision maker's personal frame of reference, experiences, education, functional background, and other personal attributes have significant effects on their decisions and actions. In regards to managerial discretion in decisions about strategic assets, Amit and Schoemaker (1990) highlight forces that influence the decision-making task under uncertainty, complexity, and conflict. They refer to psychological theorists (Kahneman, Slovic, & Tversky, 1982) who suggest that discretionary managerial decisions are affected by a range of cognitive biases toward the handling of uncertainty and complexity, and that shape the strategic direction of multinational companies in the global markets.

These have significant implications on the manner OM is tapped for knowledge reuse to make more effective decisions. Emphasis on the contextual nature of organizational decision making has been made by Mintzberg (1978), Isenberg (1987), and Mintzberg and Waters (1983) to further highlight the role of the firm's implicit or tacit knowledge acquired throughout its history, and of which it is not explicitly aware. They (also Hamel & Prahalad, 1989) look at intentional choices and tacit forces within organizations.

Agor (1986) and Scharmer (2001) claim that decision makers often rely on intuition when there is a high level of uncertainty, such as when facts are limited, ambiguous or incongruent with events, when variables are not scientifically predictable, when time is limited, when several alternatives seem plausible, and when the cost of failure is large. Recognizing the value of experienced-based intuition in decision environments, situational factors compel managers to focus more on this ability (Agor, 1986; Behling & Eckel, 1991; Wally & Baum, 1994). An interesting question remains what impact OM/OMS may have on identifying and integrating knowledge into strategic decisions.

The Role of Technology

Leveraging knowledge effectively has become a key organizational capability. The central issue to most companies is how to effectively capture, share, retain, and reuse the knowledge that already exists within the organization. In an attempt to capture and convert tacit knowledge, organizations have tended to rely on technological solutions to create an institutional memory for knowledge networks. OMIS have received considerable attention in IS development and management. Such systems are a tangible conceptualization of the concept of knowledge, combining the attributes of culture, history, business process, and human memory. Integrated systems can facilitate a major step in capturing knowledge assets.

Emerging ICT may provide powerful support for enabling both face-to-face and virtual human interaction and participation (Rolland et al., 2000). Most of these solutions have been object-oriented methods for modeling organization memory (Wang, 1999). Memory systems include social networks, knowledge centers, and various computer-based programs (Olivera, 2000). The promised benefits of using memory systems are to improve business performance by tapping into resources that contain acquired knowledge from past experiences and use this to make more knowledgeable analysis and wiser decisions.

Technology that supports collaboration is rapidly placed in the hands of users and represents a tool for building relationships and facilitating the exchange of ideas. Decision support systems (DSS), for example, involve online analytical processing of capturing the structure of the real-world data in the form of multidimensional tables (MIS) and statistical systems specialists (West & Hess, 2002). Manipulation and presentation of such information through graphical displays provide valuable support to the decision maker. Data modeling, symbolic modeling, and "what if" analysis are phases of DSS (Koutsoukis et al., 1999). The role of these technologies in organizational memory is to convert and store expertise into databases, build a collective corporate memory that permeates processes, products, and services in digital networks, and to facilitate its diffusion among users (Hackbarth & Grover, 1999).

Digital systems also have gained considerable criticism concerning the limits of codification strategies (Walsham, 2001). Such criticism focuses on a lack of interpretative conceptualization of intersubjective understanding of tacit knowledge and its embeddedness in contexts of social action (Marshall & Brady, 2001). Communication is a complex and multidimensional process, and tacit knowledge can be shared most effectively in the real world (as opposed to virtual) to achieve an interpretation and mutual understanding (Walsham, 2001).

Given that knowledge is highly context specific while experience is both time and context sensitive (perceptions in a specific time under certain conditions), the downside to ICT-based organizational memory is that once the tacit knowledge from the past has been simplified and converted, users do not tend to question the underlying assumptions of the coded knowledge anymore once it is retrieved for future references. Hence, there may be a risk to misinterpretation and misperception of the data coded. While it is clearly inefficient to reinvent the wheel every time a decision is made, the ever-changing environment requires a more critical view on information and knowledge and a more open-minded approach to consider issues anew as opposed to relying on past memory. In this case, ICT-based knowledge repositories may pose limits, biases, and rigidities to flexible and critical thinking.

On the one hand, adopting technological solutions facilitate greater control over intangible assets, speed, and efficiency. On the other hand, attempting to objectify and codify the tacit into IS or KMS may take away the dynamics of the "tacitness" once it is locked into systems. How useful will that knowledge be once it is transformed? Are ICT systems capable of capturing and diffusing the tacit value of knowledge? What are some of the sociotechnical consequences?

In practice, the application and impact of OMIS as part of a KM strategy remains a challenge. First, it is important to identify where crucial forms of memory reside before a deliberate attempt to develop OM. But is this at all possible? Not all knowledge and experience are necessarily valuable or worth being remembered and reused.

To know which knowledge would contribute to the company's competitiveness, the first task is to strategically identify business-specific knowledge: that which differentiates the company from its competitors. Depending on the source, purpose, and (re)users, the management of different types of expertise requires different cultural and technological requirements, and that is highly contextual. In addition, we should recall that tacit knowledge is both "sticky" and difficult to identify.

THEORETICAL FRAMEWORK

The modified version of McLean's IS Success Model by Jennex (2002) is applied in our case study at a multinational firm. Furthermore, the components of the model are being analyzed within Galliers' (2002) IS Strategy Framework to account for the emergent versus deliberate strategic application of knowledge in OM.

The IS Success Model

According to the model (Figure 1), the knowledge network infrastructure comprises two main blocks: systems quality emphasizing technical resources in terms of form and level of OMS, and information quality, emphasizing the particular knowledge strategy or process in terms of richness and linkages of information and knowledge for use. The IS Success Model is seen as a good fit with the research aim because it accounts for both technical and nontechnical issues of a knowledge strategy. The research seeks to find whether both approaches, the use of human tacit knowledge and systems and tools, as well as the use of emergent and deliberate KM are required for a synergistic reuse of knowledge and OM. The empirical study will identify any OM/KM infrastructure of the company and examine the extent to which managers use knowledge and memory as indicated in the IS Success Model and how their approach shapes decisions.

Figure 1. OM/KS modified IS success model

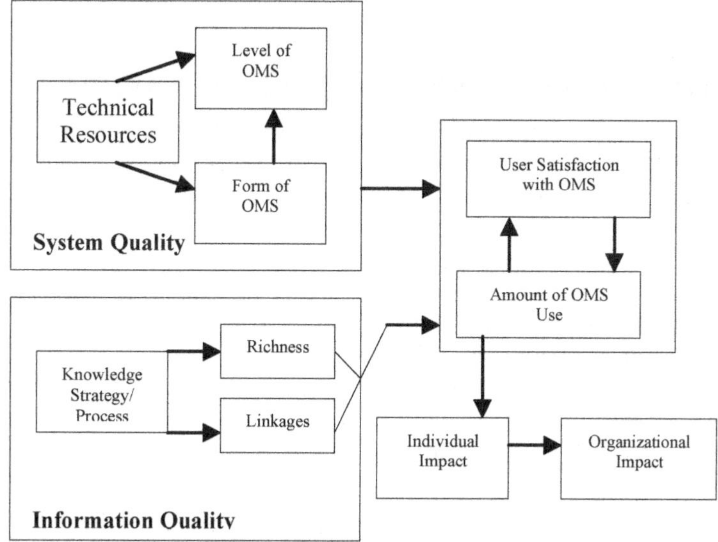

Source: Adopted from Jennex & Olfman (2002)

The contribution of this study is to show that despite the sophistication of technological resources, the reuse of knowledge is a human process and the degree to which it may contribute to organizational effectiveness primarily depends on users.

METHODOLOGY

Organizational KM is a multiparadigmatic discipline that requires various theoretical perspectives and methodologies (Hitt & Tyler, 1999) for a richer understanding. The underlying belief behind this research views the world as multidimensional, with dynamic and complex relationships based partly on sociopolitical influences in the social system. Recognizing the dynamics and complex nature of large high-performing enterprises, the case study requires drawing upon multiple theories and paradigms to seek a richer understanding.

This research uses an exploratory case study on OK/OM and KMS/OMS usage in the context of management's strategic decision making. Empirical data is being gathered through 27 semistructured interviews with four senior managers (including the CEO) and 25 directors and managers at various levels during 1999. Nine follow-up interviews were completed at the beginning of 2001 to obtain the longitudinal understanding of the case. One of the researchers who spent three months on site benefited not only from the opportunity for unlimited document research, but also from observing meetings and interactions between the researched. It is realized that observation is useful in understanding the behavior of human agencies in their natural social system and to make sense of the world of intersubjectively created meanings among the agencies (Lee, 1991).

The personalized responses from interviews and observations provide us with enough unbiased raw data to interpret reality in terms of what it means to the people and to make sense of the phenomena under investigation — namely, how knowledge is being used for effective decision making and why this is so.

DISCUSSIONS OF THE FINDINGS

A case study is conducted in company "Innovative Chemical Limited" (ICL). ICL is one of the leading chemical specialists in Europe, and has a strong presence in providing customized compound to the pharmaceutical industry. ICL has more than 6,000 employees globally and is headquartered in the UK. Overseas offices, such as those in the United States, Malaysia, and India, are primarily responsible for sales activities and low-cost production of standard products. ICL is structured hierarchically, and is comprised of 14 divisions, such as central administration, research and development (R&D), manufacturing, engineering, sales, and logistics. According to four directors, prior to 1995, ICL was growing at a rather steady pace. Continuously growing demand started in late 1994 has triggered a series of expansion, in particular in ICL's manufacturing, engineering, and R&D capacity. More than 1,000 jobs were created as a result of such expansions.

Growing orders in 1995 and 1996 have also led to an increasing number of delays and complaints from its customers. Directors of manufacturing, engineering, and logistics commonly recalled that ICL was in a stage of dysfunction and chaos, as the business process and management system were not adequate to cope with the growing demand.

Also, it was noted by the general manager that the lack of information integration has made the management of information and resources remarkably inefficient. The decision to implement an enterprise resource planning (ERP) system, SAP R3, in late 1997 by an international IT consultancy giant, was believed to be an effective solution to streamline ICL's business processes and improve its information management capability. Even though the implementation was lengthy, costly, and problematic, the joint effort of ICL and the consultant team did manage to get the new ERP system running in June 2000 across all sites around the globe.

KM, one of the ERP modules implemented, was believed by the management as a systematic approach to mobilize, utilize, and exchange knowledge dispersed in ICL. According to the IT director, the KM module is able to produce very comprehensive reports based on information generated from ERP. Also, the information is dimensionalized and correlated in a new way that was not feasible when the sheer amount of legacy systems was run in isolation. The human resources (HR) director argued that the KM module is a very effective way of capturing best practices and disseminating knowledge throughout ICL.

While some directors, such as finance, quality, IT, and HR, found the new system incredibly useful, many other directors, such as engineering, manufacturing, and logistics, claimed that they did not find the system directly relevant to their work. As observed in ICL, many directors did not stay in their offices long. Rather, most of their work was carried out in the meeting rooms, shop floor, testing laboratory, or warehouse. As the manufacturing director noted:

It is wonderful to have systems like R3, expensive though. It is useful, but not for me though. In a typical day, I will spend most of my time talking to people. We are not in a business where everything can be done by shutting your office door.

This is because many decisions related to activities, such as production, scheduling, and resource allocation, were made based on the agreements reached between divisional heads. Also, according to the manufacturing director, his role, like many other directors involved in the production process, was to plan and make decisions based on the input from the line managers in their own division, rather than solely based on information generated from ERP. As one of the sales managers indicated:

We are not in the commodity market where your margin is pretty much fixed. If one customer comes along and wants the product in three days and is willing to pay three times of the market-going rate, you know you are getting more value out of what you would have normally made. In the custom-built market, manufacturing product that fits customers' specification is paramount, and being able to get your products delivered at short notice is clearly our niche.

The impact of ERP on organizational memory was found to vary from division to division, in particular influenced by the location where knowledge is created and embedded. For instance, in the production-related divisions, knowledge was generated within the divisional boundary and integrated based on the task requirement. The dispersion of knowledge and the need for cross-functional knowledge integration has pinpointed the shortfall of using ERP. This is particularly apparent when such functionally specific knowledge is not codified in the new system. Information generated and managed by ERP did provide useful reference, such as inventory level, input, and output, for decision makers across ICL. However, it is evident that the diversified nature of organizational memory cannot be fully comprehended by ERP alone. In particular, even though the management of divisional information can be centralized, knowledge sharing across divisions can only be enabled through the establishment of social network (Nahapiet & Ghoshal, 1998). As recalled from one of the conversations with the managing director, all senior managers and directors, with the exception of two, have been working for ICL for more than 25 years. This is evident in the strong collaborative culture observed in the production-related divisions. Hence, even though ERP can be a useful tool to capture and share best practices generated within ICL, organizational learning, based on Huber's (1991) conceptualization of knowledge acquisition, distribution, and interpretation, still relies on the social interaction of organizational members to apply, negotiate, and refine the organizational knowledge.

Furthermore, it is found in the case study that the way in which managers perceive the usefulness of ERP in relation to their decision making is largely influenced by the decision strategy (either deliberate or emergent). Findings from the case study suggest that the differentiation between deliberate and emergent strategies can best be conceptualized as a continuum. In other words, managers do adopt both strategies, according to the task that they perform. When the decision requires a high degree of dependency on others' input, the decision strategy seems to shift toward the emergent end, while the decision that requires a lower dependency appears to be more deliberate.

In addition to the strategy deployed or favored by the decision makers, the way in which prior knowledge is used also shows its influence on the effectiveness of decision making. For instance, when knowledge is dispersed across and embedded in various divisions, integration of knowledge between different stakeholders to collectively form a decision is found to be paramount. This is particularly apparent in the production-related divisions where expertise is high, yet interdependence is also high. Under such circumstances, the decision-making process can only be enabled through the sharing and integration of knowledge across different divisions through efficient means. As evident in the case study, even though the implementation of ERP has made information flow freely across divisional boundaries, it does not show that the social relationships that are vital for knowledge sharing and integration can be automatically improved. Hence, the implementation of ERP system can be interpreted as a radical change in ICL's OMS. It is crucial to be aware that the new system does not necessarily alter the social system through which knowledge is generated and used.

Referring to the IS success model, our findings indicate that technical resources can be drastically improved through the adoption of new technologies, in this case ERP. Nevertheless, the way in which knowledge is generated, utilized, and managed for decision making will largely depend on how the social system facilitates or prohibits the linkage between different divisions to generate integrated knowledge. This model is particularly useful in explaining why the understanding of the technical and social dimensions of IS is extremely vital in illustrating the interplay between the use of ICT and knowledge and its effect on decision making.

LIMITATIONS AND BIASES

One challenge on the part of the researchers has been to be aware of managerial biases and recognize strategic games being played out during the decision-making process. The fact that individuals tend to give their own perspective creates biases and different interpretations of an event in its context. This has theoretical, methodological, and practical implications for the arguments outlined here and requires a multiparadigm approach to research.

Some biases are inherent to the nature of the topic. The theoretical challenge is that the tacit, intangible, and socially unconscious nature is never completely observed and objectified by either participants or observers. The intangible element may never be completely accessible and the tacit may never be made completely explicit. Hence, people cannot step out of their worlds or objectify them in a supreme action of reflection (McCarthy, c. 2001).

CONCLUSIONS

In the context of global competition, a key to success is the ability to capture organizational learning, to effectively reuse the knowledge through efficient means, and to synthesize these into a more intelligent problem recognition, strategic analysis, and choices in strategic decisions.

The IS literature deals little with the role of knowledge in strategizing and decision making that accounts for the interaction of technical and nontechnical knowledge resources and how these influence organizational learning. We are continuously examining what knowledge strategies and technological resources are used by decision makers to expand and tap into their organization's memory in order to make more intelligent business decisions.

A very useful model is the revised IS Success Model (Jennex, 2002), which we are using in our longitudinal case study. By including our findings on an ongoing basis, we attempt to continuously enhance the literature and contribute to a richer understanding of how information and knowledge are reused and leveraged by means of knowledge strategies and OM systems. As seen in the case study, managers preferred to rely on their experience-based knowledge and practice managerial discretion to a self-satisfying extent. Technological resources and knowledge processes were used in an intermingled manner. The level as well as the form of the technology is highly dependent on the nature of data, information, knowledge, context, and urgency of the managerial decision. OM systems may serve as repositories of data, information, and knowledge, which are retrieved by users. However, the extent to which this has a strategic impact only depends on the context in which the knowledge is used within its cultural setting. Hence, architectural requirements for building knowledge infrastructures, the ERP system in our case, should only be regarded as an enabler of a greater context of a knowledge-sharing culture. We have also observed that the knowledge strategy used as part of the organizational learning process is highly contextual and the richness and linkages to other processes depend on the purpose of its reuse. We were able to confirm that OM and OL are deeply embedded social processes, and organizational effectiveness is achieved through a synergistic integration of a knowledge-sharing culture and technological resources (Galliers, 2002).

It is our intention to continue to work in the area of how different knowledge strategies and emerging technologies may serve executives in decision making and strategy development. Future research along these lines may serve toward bringing some of the issues into the dialogue of academic research and managerial practices.

ACKNOWLEDGMENTS

The authors would like to express their gratitude to Professor Jimmy Huang for the insightful conversations and his contribution to the data in the case study.

REFERENCES

Agor, W. (1986). *The logic of intuitive decision making: A research-based approach for top management.* New York: Quorum.

Amit, R., & Schoemaker, P.J.H. (1993). Strategic assets and organizational rent. *Strategic Management Journal, 14*(1), 33-47.

Argyris, C., & Schon, D. (1978). *Organisational learning: A theory of action perspective.* Addison-Wesley.

Baird, L., & Cross, R. (2000). Technology is not enough: Improving performance by building organizational memory. *Sloan Management Review, 41*(3), 69-78.

Ball, M.K. (2002). Knowledge management: Intelligence for today's business world. *KM World, 11*(3), S14-S15.

Barnard, C. (1938). *The function of the executive.* Cambridge, MA: Harvard University Press.

Behling, O., & Eckel, N. (1991). Making sense out of intuition. *Academy of Management Executive, 5*(1), 46-54.

Bennett, R.H. (1998). The importance of tacit knowledge in strategic deliberations and decisions. *Management Decision, 36*(9), 589-597.

Bowman, C., & Daniels, K. (1995). The influence of functional experience on perception of strategic priorities. *British Journal of Management, 6*(3), 157-168.

Brindle, M. (1999). Games decision makers play. *Management Decision, 37*(8), 604-612.

Cohen, W.M., & Levinthal, D.A. (1990). Absorptive capacity: A new perspective on learning and innovation. *Administrative Science Quarterly, 35*, 128-152.

D'Aveni, R. (1994). *Hyper-competition.* New York: Free Press.

Davenport, T.H., & Prusak, L. (1998). *Working knowledge.* Boston: Harvard Business School Press.

Drucker, P. (1995). *The post-capitalist executive. Managing in a time of great change.* New York: Penguin.

Dunford, R. (2000). Key challenges in the search for the effective management of knowledge in management consulting firms. *Journal of Knowledge Management, 4*(4), 295-302.

Earl, M.J. (1989). *Management strategies for information technology.* London: Prentice Hall.

Earl, M.J. (1993). Experiences in strategic information systems planning. *MIS Quarterly, 17*(1), 1-24.

Eisenhardt, E. (1986). Speed and strategic choice: How managers accelerate decision making. *California Management Review.*

Eisenhardt, K.M. (1989a). Agency theory: An assessment and review. *Academy of Management Review, 14*, 57-74.

Eisenhardt, K.M. (1989b). Making fast strategic decisions in high-velocity environments. *Academy of Management Journal, 32*, 543-576.

Fikelstein, S., & Hambrick, D.C. (1990). Top management tenure and organizational outcomes: The moderating role of managerial discretion. *Administrative Science Quarterly, 35*, 84-503.

Finkelstein, S., & Hambrick, D.C. (1996). *Strategic leadership: Top executives and their effects on organizations*. Minneapolis/St. Paul, MN: West Publishing Company.

Foyal, H. (1949). *General and industrial management*. New York: Pitman.

Galliers, R.D. (2001). *Rethinking information systems strategy: Towards an inclusive strategic framework for business information systems management*. (Working paper). London: Department of Information Systems, London School of Economics.

Galliers, R.D., & Baets, W.R.J. (Eds.). (1998). *Information technology and organisational transformation. Innovation for the 21st century organisation*. Chichester, UK: Wiley.

Galliers, R.D., & Leidner, D.E. (2002). *Strategic information management*. Butterworth-Heinemann.

Galliers, R.D., & Newell, S. (1998). *Back to the future. From knowledge management to data management* (Working Paper 92). London: Department of Information Systems, London School of Economics.

Gold, A.H., Malhotra, A., & Segars, A.H. (2001). Knowledge management: An organizational capabilities perspective. *Journal of Management Information Systems, 18*(1), 185-214.

Gomez-Mejia, L. (1997). Cultural diversity and the performance of multinational firms. *Journal of International Business Studies, 28*, 309-336.

Green, G., Amason, A.C., & Mooney, A.C. (1999). The effects of past performance on top management team conflict in strategic decision making. *International Journal of Conflict Management, 10*(4), 340-359.

Grover, V., & Davenport, T.H. (2001). General perspectives on knowledge management: Fostering a research agenda. *Journal of Management Information Systems, 18*(1), 5-21.

Habermas, J. (1984). *The theory of communicative action, 1, Reason and the rationalization of society*. London: Heinemann Education.

Hackbarth, G., & Grover, V. (1999). The knowledge repository: Organizational memory information systems. *16*(3), 21-30.

Haldin-Herrgard, T. (2000). Difficulties in diffusion of tacit knowledge in organizations. *Journal of Intellectual Capital, 1*(4), 357-365.

Hambrick, D.C., & Mason, P.A. (1984). Upper echelons: The organization as a reflection of its managers. *Academy of Management Review, 9*, 193-206.

Hamel, G. (2000). Knowledge strategy. *Excellence, 17*(7).

Hamel, G., & Prahalad, C.K. (1989). Strategic intent. *Harvard Business Review, 89*(3), 63-76.

Hatten, K., & Rosenthal, S.R. (2001). Why and how to systemize performance management. *Journal of Organizational Excellence, 20*(4), 59-73.

Hendersen, A., & Fredrickson, J. (1996). Information-processing demands as a determinant of CEO compensation. *Academy of Management Journal, 39*, 575-606.

Hitt, M.A., & Tyler, B. (1991). Strategic decision models: Integrating different perspectives. *Strategic Management Journal, 12*, 327-352.

Hodgkinson, G.P., & Johnson, G. (1994). Exploring the mental models of competitive strategists: The case for a processual approach. *Journal of Management Studies, 31*(4), 525-552.

Hoskisson, R.E., Hitt, M.A., Wan, W.P., & Yiu, D. (1999). Theory and research in strategic management: Swings of a pendulum. *Journal of Management, 25*(3), 417-446.

Huang, Z., Chen, L., & Frolick, M.N. (2002). Integrating Web-based data into a data warehouse. *Information Systems Management, 19*(1), 23-34.

Huber, G. (1991). Organizational learning: The contributing processes and the literatures. *Organization Science, 2*, 88-115.

Huff, A.S. (1982). Industry influence on strategy reformulation. *Strategic Management Journal, 3*, 119-131.

Hughes, B. (1995). Why do managers need myths? *Executive Development, 8*(7).

Isenberg, D.J. (1987). The tactics of strategic opportunism. *Harvard Business Review, 65*(2), 92-97.

Jennex, M.E., & Olfman, L. (2002,). Organizational memory/knowledge effects on productivity, a longitudinal study. *Proceedings of the 35th Annual Hawaii International Conference on System Sciences*, HI.

Jennex, M.E., Olfman, L., Pituma P., & Yong-Tae, P. (1998, January). An Organizational Memory Information Systems Success Model: An extension of DeLone and McLean's I/S Success Model. *Proceedings of the 31st Annual Hawaii International Conference on System Sciences*, HI.

Jensen, M.C., & Murphy, K.J. (1990). Performance pay and top management incentives. *Journal of Political Economy, 98*, 225-264.

Kahneman, D., Slovic, P., & Tversky, A. (1982). *Judgment under uncertainty: Heuristics and biases*. Cambridge, UK: Cambridge University Press.

Knickerbocker, F. (1973). *Oligopolistic reaction and multinational enterprise*. Boston: Harvard Business School Press.

Lei, D., Hitt, M.A., & Bettis, R.A. (1996). Dynamic core competences through meta-learning and strategic contest. *Journal of Management, 22*, 549-569.

Long, D.W., & Fahey, L. (2000). Diagnosing cultural barriers to knowledge management. *Academy of Management Executive, 14*(2), 113-127.

Markus, M.L. (2001). Toward a theory of knowledge reuse situations and factors in reuse success. *Journal of Management Information Systems, 18*(1), 57-93.

Marshall, N., & Brady, T. (2001). Knowledge management and the politics of knowledge: Illustration from complex products and systems. *European Journal of Information Systems, 10*(2), 99-112.

Marwick, A.D. (2001). Knowledge management technology. *IBM Systems Journal, 40*(4), 814-830.

McCarthy, G.E. (c. 2001). *Objectivity and the silence of reason: Weber, Habermas, and the methodological disputes in German sociology*. New Brunswick, NJ: Transaction Publishers.

Mintzberg, H. (1978). Patterns in strategy formation. *Management Science, 24*, 934-948.

Mintzberg, H., & Waters, J.A. (1983). The mind of the strategist(s). In S. Srivasta (Ed.), *The executive mind* (pp. 58-83). San Francisco: Jossey-Bass.

Nahapiet, J., & Ghoshal, S. (1998). Social capital, intellectual capital, and the organizational advantage. *Academy of Management Review, 23*, 242.

Nonaka, I. (1994). A dynamic theory of organizational knowledge. *Organization Science, 5*(1), 13-37.

Oliver, C. (1997). Sustainable competitive advantage: Combining institutional and resource-based views. *Strategic Management Journal, 18*, 697-713.

Olivera, F. (2000). Memory systems in organizations: An empirical investigation of mechanisms for knowledge collection, storage and access. *Journal of Management Studies, 37*(6), 811-832.

Polanyi, M. (1966). *The tacit dimension.* London: Routledge & Kegan Paul.

Porter, M. (1980). *Competitive strategy.* New York: Free Press.

Porter, M.E. (2001). Strategy and the Internet. *Harvard Business Review, 79*(3), 63-78.

Porter, M.E., & Millar, V.E. (1984). How information gives you competitive advantage. *Harvard Business Review, 62*(4), 149-160.

Prusak, L. (1996). The knowledge advantage. *Strategy and Leadership,* March-April.

Quinn, J. (1992). *Intelligent enterprise: A knowledge and service based paradigm for industry.* New York: Free Press.

Quinn, J.B. (1980). *Strategies for change: Logical incrementalism.* Homewood, : Irwin.

Sanders, W.G., & Carpenter, M.A. (1998). Internationalization and firm governance: The roles of CEO compensation, top team compensation, and board structure. *Academy of Management Journal, 41*(2), 158-178.

Scharmer, C.O. (2001). Self-transcending knowledge: Sensing and organizing around emerging opportunities. *Journal of Knowledge Management, 5*(2), 137-151.

Schoemaker, P.H. (1990). Strategy, complexity and economic rent. *Management Science, 10*, 1178-1192.

Selznick, P. (1957). *Leadership in administration: A sociological interpretation.* New York: Harper & Row.

Senge, P. (1990a). *The fifth discipline. The art and practice of the learning organisation.* New York: Doubleday/Currency.

Senge, P. (1990b). The leader's new work: Building learning organizations. *Sloan Management Review,* Fall, 7-23.

Simeon, R. (2001). Top team characteristics and the business strategies on Japanese firms. *Corporate Governance, 1*(2), 4-12.

Simon, H.A. (1979). *Models of thought.* New Haven, CT: Yale University Press.

Spender, J.C. (1989). *Industry recipes: An enquiry into the nature and sources of managerial judgement.* Oxford: Blackwell.

Thompson, J. (1967). *Organizations in action.* New York: McGraw-Hill.

Tushman, M.L., & Andersen, P. (1986). Technological discontinuities and organizational environments. *Administrative Science Quarterly, 31*, 439-465.

Tversky, A., & Kahneman (1981). The framing of decision and the psychology oaf choice. *Science, 211*, 453-458.

Wally, S., & Baum, R. (1994). Personal and structural determinants of the pace of strategic decision-making. *Academy of Management Journal, 37*, 932-956.

Walsham, G. (2001). Knowledge management: The benefits and limitations of computer systems. *European Management Journal, 19*(6), 599-608.

Wang, S. (1999). Organizational memory information systems: A domain analysis in the object-oriented paradigm. *Information Resources Management Journal, 12*(2), 26-35.

Weick, K. (1995). *Sensemaking in organizations.* Thousand Oaks, CA: Sage.

West, L.A. Jr., & Hess, T.J. (2002). Metadata as a knowledge management tool: Supporting intelligent agent and end user access to spatial data. *Decision Support Systems, 32*(3), 247-264.

Williamson, O.E. (1964). *The economics of discretionary behavior: Managerial objectives in a theory of the firm.* Englewood Cliffs, NJ: Prentice-Hall.

Woods, E. (2001). Knowledge management and peer-to-peer computing: Making connections. *KM World, 10*(9), 6-8.

Chapter VI

Governance of Strategies to Manage Organizational Knowledge: A Mechanism to Oversee Knowledge Needs

Suzanne Zyngier, Monash University, Australia

Frada Burstein, Monash University, Australia

Judy McKay, Swinburne University of Technology, Australia

EXECUTIVE SUMMARY

This chapter introduces the theory and model of governance as a means of implementing knowledge management strategies in large organizations. It draws on case study research into the governance of knowledge management strategy implementation in a major scientific research and development facility. It suggests that the implementation of strategy through such a framework operates to ensure the delivery of anticipated benefits in an authorized and regulated manner. Furthermore, the authors hope that an understanding of the theoretical underpinnings of internal governance processes will not only inform researchers of a better design for studying knowledge management systems, but will also assist in the understanding of risks and the role of evaluation and review in the implementation of those strategies.

INTRODUCTION

To date, research has examined different understandings of the concept of knowledge management (KM) and from this, a multiplicity of approaches to implement strategies have been derived. This case study contributes new research that examines the role of governance in the effective delivery of strategies to manage organizational knowledge. This case study looks at the implementation of a KM strategy and in particular examines the mechanisms that are employed to oversee and control the development and implementation of strategies to manage knowledge. KM processes comprise the methods employed in the acquisition, distribution, and utilization of knowledge in the organization. Organizational knowledge is present in explicit (codified) and tacit (abstract) forms and as such differing strategies are required in order to deploy it effectively.

A strategy is a plan or tactic for the implementation of the management of organizational knowledge. KM governance does not design the strategy to manage organizational knowledge. Governance manages risk to ensure the delivery of anticipated benefits in an ongoing process that must be quality assured, be fiscally viable, meet goals and strategic objectives, and must be responsive to changing requirements of organization and of staff (Farrar, 2001). A governance mechanism directs, monitors, and controls how this function is fulfilled and gauges success as reflected in the timeliness of service delivery and the satisfaction levels of the internal stakeholders and also, potentially, of external stakeholders. A governance body will therefore work with those who design and implement the strategy but does not function to operationalize that strategy.

Recent international corporate scandals — including Barings Bank in the UK, Enron in the United States, and HIH in Australia, to name only a few — have highlighted the importance of governance in organizations. Corporate governance is predicated on the clear collective mental picture of the board of directors of the future of the company, and clear understanding of the mission of the company and a strategy or vision of means to achieve this. Specific legal or statutory duties are imposed on directors and other officers of companies (Francis, 1997). These include a duty to act honestly, to exercise care and diligence, and to not make improper use of information. The particular background, qualifications, and management responsibilities of the director are taken into account under law when evaluating the director's compliance with the duty of care and diligence. Usually, the constitution of the organization will state the duties of the directors. The directors are responsible to the shareholders for the profitability or otherwise of the company. Additionally the task of the board in Australia is "to ensure corporate learning, renewal, evolution and succession" (Francis, 1997, p. 78).

In this case study, governance refers to governance that in "its narrower and most usual sense refers to corporations and to systems of accountability by those in control" (Farrar, 2001, p. 3). Organizational governance therefore requires knowledge of trends in industry and of competitors, technology, the economy, and the social environment. Governance requires the examination of the company's structure, vitality, adaptability, intellectual assets, and potential. Governance explores scenarios and strengthens and evolves the organizational management and organizational succession. Governance is the implementation of authority through a framework that ensures delivery of anticipated or predicted benefits of a service or process, in an authorized and regulated manner.

The governance process provides a context for the analysis of the ongoing development of strategies to manage organizational knowledge and the evaluation of the effectiveness of those strategies. Analysis of these strategies includes the evaluation of the effectiveness of those strategies. KM governance is comprised of the processes and principles that act as a framework to exercise authority that ensures the effectiveness of strategies to manage organizational knowledge. In this case study, we will describe the nature of the organization including size, spatial distribution, and resources available. We further discuss the organizational structure, nature of staffing, and the mode of operation, giving insight and perspective on how these attributes impact strategic planning and approach to KM. We describe the development of the current KM strategy including a review of prior strategies and the motivating factors in the evolution of the governance model of KM leadership. We specifically examine the understanding of and strategies for the capture and dissemination of explicit knowledge and those employed to harness and share tacit knowledge. Outcomes and current challenges that face the organization are discussed in order to gain a closer understanding of the governance of information and knowledge management and its operation at the Science and Technology Development Organization (STDO).

We investigated how strategies to implement knowledge transfer are governed or regulated at the STDO in Australia. The STDO is a research and development organization with widely distributed staff working together across multiple sites. The breadth and depth of research conducted by the STDO relies on sharing knowledge for innovation. These factors underpin their organizational knowledge strategy and denote this organization as an interesting case to examine. Specifically, the KM strategy meets the needs for the creation, dissemination, and utilization of knowledge to fulfill organizational objectives. The range of governance functions included a formal structure that both informs and is informed by the KM strategy. This research sought to answer the following questions:

1. What are the governance mechanisms invoked to guide the implementation and ongoing management of KM strategies?
2. Does the structure of an organization appear to impact the development, implementation, and governance of a KM strategy?

ABOUT THE CASE: UNDERSTANDING THE ORGANIZATION

The STDO was established in 1974 through the merger of the Australian "Operations" Scientific Service, the Services in-house Research and Development (R&D) units and the Science Branch of the Department of "Operations." These were located in Melbourne and in Adelaide. It is now an independently operating concern within the Australian Department of "Operations" but operationally autonomous of it. The mission of the STDO is to ensure the expert, independent, and innovative application of science and technology to Australia and to Australian national interests.

SIZE, DISTRIBUTION, AND RESOURCES

Since the establishment of the STDO, many new smaller research facilities have been created in other locations to enlarge research scope and consequential geographic distribution of the organization. The STDO is currently a multisite organization with a corporate office at "Operations" headquarters in Canberra, and three research laboratories known as Research Areas (RA): Platforms Sciences Laboratory, headquartered at Fisherman's Bend in Melbourne, and Systems Sciences Laboratory and Information Sciences Laboratory, both headquartered at Edinburgh in Adelaide. STDO also maintains research facilities in Canberra, Sydney, Rockingham (near Perth), at Scottsdale in Tasmania, and at Innisfail in northern Queensland. In July 2002, STDO reorganized its laboratory structure around three core businesses. These are technological platforms (material sciences, structures, propulsion, and aerodynamics), electronic systems (systems technologies and military operations in the air, land, and sea environments), and information systems (development of intelligence, surveillance, and similar systems).

The STDO is engaged in a range of research and development activities for its customers. These are the Australian "Operations" Staff, Australian Customs, security organizations, and other parts of the Department of "Operations." These organizations commission the majority of STDO research and development activity. The STDO further complements this with its own initiatives to position Australia so that it is in a position to exploit future developments in technology. As such, most of this research is solely funded by the Department of "Operations"; however, it also engages in collaborative research arrangements with industry, universities, and other research institutions.

The Australian Government through the Department of "Operations" allocates the annual budget of the STDO. The allocation in the year 2001-2002 was approximately $275 million. The Australian Government sees the STDO as having a dual role in contributing to Australian defense capabilities and also adding to Australia's national wealth. The total "Operations" budget for 2002–2003 was $14.3 billion; of this, the total STDO budget was $263.8 million. In 2001–2002, the STDO spent approximately $25.1 million (or 9.1% of its budget) sourcing research, development, and technical support from industry and other research and development organizations. These investments took the form of collaborative and commercial actions. STDO-developed technology has also been assigned to industry under numerous licence agreements.

STAFFING AND STRUCTURE

The STDO employs approximately 2,100 people of whom 75% are research active and are supported by the other 25% of the staff. Of this staff, over 600 have a PhD. In this environment, innovation is the prime focus and sharing of knowledge to facilitate innovation is essential. Therefore, the breadth and depth of research with the need for sharing and innovation across multiple sites make this organization an interesting case to examine for the management of knowledge.

The current structure of the organization is a federal structure where each core business or division operates as a self-sufficient entity responsible and reporting to STDO headquarters in Canberra. The chief "Operations" scientist is the equivalent of the chief executive officer and is ultimately responsible to and for the entire organization. The

Figure 1. STDO corporate structure

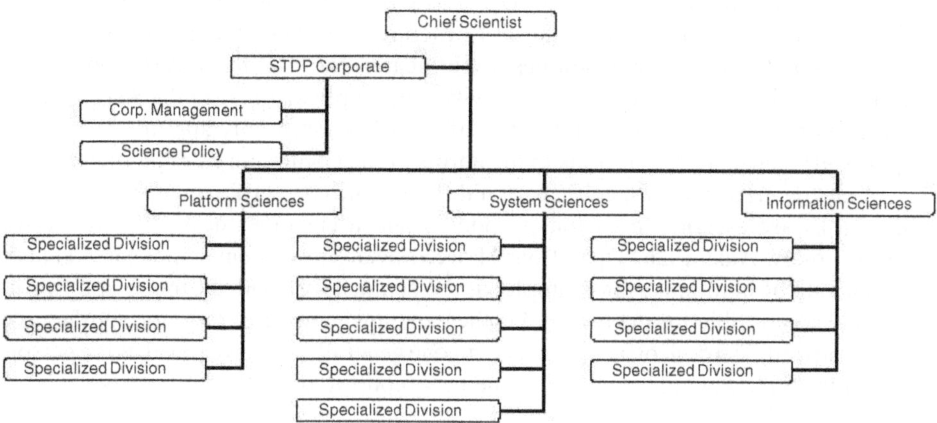

corporate structure is shown in Figure 1. There are three silos of research operations. These are shown in the corporate structure as the Science Laboratories and are known within the STDO as an RA. A chief officer or research leader is in charge of each operating division. Each silo has several operating divisions known as Research Area Capabilities (RACs). Each of these RACs conducts independent research activity. Each reports on its research and is financially responsible to the director of its RA. Each research activity is a separate entity contributing to the aims and objectives of the organization as a whole, but without duplication of activity between divisions.

Within the head office the Policy division and the Corporate Management division provide policy advice and support and corporate management services to the whole organization. These include operations such as human resources and information technology (IT) planning which are centralized.

MANAGEMENT PHILOSOPHY

The prevailing management philosophy in the Department of "Operations," and therefore in the STDO, is derived from its departmental environment and from the public service environment. Both the Australian Public Service and the "Operations" staff are strongly hierarchal with a clear command and control character. Additionally, since 2000 there have been a series of structures and processes within the organization that have guided management and corporate governance within the Australian Public Service. These include statutory accountability and accountability for public monies together with a new imperative of communication with stakeholders. Further, the governance structures in the Public Service give a balance of both power and authority to the organization's governing body, which includes the chairperson, nonexecutive governing body members, and executive management. External reporting requirements now include annual reporting, the use of relevant accounting standards, commitment to performance measures, and external audit.

Work Structure

The research conducted by the STDO is structured on a task or project basis. Thus each research undertaking is within the task structure. This task structure is how funding is achieved and is also how resources are allocated for staffing, travel, conference attendance, and other research-related activity. This applies to 75% of the STDO that is involved in research. The remaining 25% of STDO is essentially administration and support staff whose work conforms to the norms of the Commonwealth public service.

A customer, usually a specific part of the "Operations" staff, commissions STDO tasks. Tasks are assigned a customer sponsor and a customer desk officer. STDO positions follow Australian "Operations" Force ranks. The customer sponsor is generally someone of high rank, for example, at the senior level. The customer sponsor is ultimately responsible for the task and is the person who gives permission for the task to move forward. The desk officer, who is someone generally at a lower level, is the person to whom the STDO people working on the task report to on a day-to-day basis.

SETTING THE STAGE

The STDO is a single dispersed national enterprise, which was purposively selected as a knowledge-intensive organization according to its large size and its reputation for pursuing KM strategies. The aim of this research was to investigate governance mechanisms invoked to guide the implementation and ongoing management of KM strategies. The research methodology comprised the interpretation of qualitative data collected in seven one-hour in-depth, one-on-one interviews with respondents within the STDO.

Because the interviewees were selected on advice from the STDO staff, there could have been some sample bias; however, the sample conformed to parameters that were established by the authors and these were implemented in conjunction with staff at the STDO. It was a purposive sample of both members of the Information Management and Knowledge Management Governance Board and of those responsible for the implementation of the KM strategy. The interviews were semistructured and in-depth, each lasting approximately one hour. The interview questions canvassed the following themes:

1. The organizational philosophy of KM
2. The history and implementation of the KM strategy
3. The process and allocation of responsibility for KM
4. The organizational structures that support and govern the initiative

Of the seven people interviewed for this case study, six were members of the Information and Knowledge Management Governance Board; the seventh informant worked on research for the tacit knowledge element of the KM task. All informants were permanent, tenured members of staff employed in the STDO and had postgraduate qualifications. The STDO does not employ contract staff, although it does engage consultants to provide advice in areas outside of the scientific research realm.

CASE DESCRIPTION

The STDO Informants revealed a number of factors that led to the development of their strategy to manage organizational knowledge. These included the following:

1. **The external impacts of KM activity in the Department of "Operations."** The Department of "Operations" had previously appointed a senior officer as a chief knowledge officer (CKO) who had commissioned the STDO to conduct a preliminary study into the state of KM in defense as a research task. Simultaneously, the STDO was part of a major "Operations" change management program which resulted in STDO officers designing a change program with a number of strategies. One of those seven strategies related to KM.
2. **The serendipitous impact of KM research commissioned by the Department of "Operations" that had been carried out by the STDO was an influence on their own activity.** The results of this research were influential in the STDO recognizing a need to articulate and implement its own KM strategy. "STDO had therefore registered some skills in or at least conducted research into knowledge management and this was then picked up by STDO" (Informant 6). Thus the STDO developed a knowledge base of its own in KM which was subsequently pursued by the STDO as an impetus toward what was seen as a worthwhile and productive activity in harnessing its knowledge resources.
3. **The anticipated threat of knowledge loss due to the age profile of senior researchers within the organization.** The third motivation for the implementation of a strategy to manage organizational knowledge was the average age of the researchers. "In the STDO the average age of the workers — most of them come here just after they finish their PhD and then stay for life.... They just won't retire. Our average age in some divisions was above 60 for the top-two levels" (Informant 2). Many staff have been employed for a very long time and much of their knowledge is locked in their memories, has changed as they progressed up the bureaucracy, and may be published in long-forgotten documents. "And we've got piles of stuff and they say, 'You know, back in '64 you wrote a paper on thermonuclear dynamics' and they go, 'Yeah, I know the one' — what happens when that person retires? So there were some real issues in access to information that were tied to succession planning" (Informant 2). Thus the threat of high-level knowledge loss through employment attrition is very real for this organization.
4. **The impact of government in challenging the management practices and organizational arrangements in the public service.** Control mechanisms presently in place for a public sector with devolved authority and enhanced responsibility are now manifest in internal control, responsibility for risk management, internal audit and audit committees, responsibility for budgeting, for financial management, and for staffing (Barrett & Sotiropoulos, 2001). These factors appear to be borne out in the structures and control mechanisms at the STDO.

The STDO is an R&D organization. It sees itself as a knowledge producer. This knowledge is produced in explicit forms as documented research in its raw form, research papers, and knowledge embedded in technology that is produced. The concept of knowledge that underpins its KM strategy incorporates both explicit and tacit knowledge.

The mode of managing and leveraging knowledge in the STDO is within the scientific tradition of building on what is known in order to create and innovate. Scientific knowledge is grounded in building evidence based on prior knowledge. The tradition of publishing new knowledge in scientific journals and reports has created a ready supply of explicated knowledge that can be leveraged through the management of knowledge resources. This was acknowledged by staff who told us that "unless we've got access to what's happened before, you can't have scientific excellence; unless people were reinforced — you know — innovation; taking on ideas; standing by; changing our transfer mode and teamwork" (Informant 2).

This demonstrates several attributes. These are as follows:

- Acknowledgment of the importance of excellence in research practice
- Understanding that knowledge and innovation are substantially built on what was known before
- Understanding that without proper record, an organization will risk recreating work already done

Tacit knowledge is also implied through this statement about the importance of the STDO's attitude to cooperation and teamwork in knowledge creation and innovation. This underlies its approach to the transfer of tacit forms of knowledge based on experience and the capacity to extrapolate form prior knowledge to reach a new and different conclusion. Teams and cooperative work practices facilitate knowledge production from the interaction between individuals sharing what they know.

Prior Systems: Explicit Knowledge Capitalization

Prior to the development of the KM strategy in 2000 and the subsequent formation of the Information and Knowledge Management (IMKM) Board in 2002, there were two systems for handling explicit knowledge:

1. The Library and Information Services who delivered both traditional and online information management service
2. The Registries who sought to manage the internal documents of the STDO

While the Library and Information Services are still maintained as a core STDO service that is delivered at each STDO location, the Registries are no longer considered as core and it is believed by some that "our systems really have broken down from the days when we used to have registry files and people would file things ... there were rigorous rules for how one handled different kinds of correspondence.... You know, there was minutes and there was letters, if you had a significant phone call you had to write that down. All these things got put on files and there were rules for how all that worked and everyone understood the rules and it was almost like every registry file told a story. If you got involved in a story and you were asked to do something, the first thing you would do was find a file and start reading and that's when you knew what you needed to do or the background to what you've been asked to do and that I think was a very powerful thing" (Informant 6).

The structures that controlled the management of one form of explicit organizational knowledge — the client file — have been substantially abandoned since 1994. Client files were controlled by a manual registry system that controlled correspondence, minutes, letters, and records of significant phone calls as well as notes on the R&D of the work task. There had been documented rules for these processes that were understood by all staff. The registry files were a first reference point when a researcher was engaged in a project. The registry files could provide context for the project, of previous projects and background on the relevant client. It would also provide a detailed record of all the transactions between the client and the STDO, and of the progress of the item of research.

Problems

Running the Registries was abandoned, as this was not seen as core function to the STDO. The distribution of PCs to all staff and the concomitant decentralization of word processing functions was one of the major factors leading to the loss of the Registries and of the key role that they played in the STDO. The PCs were distributed without document management protocols, but with a local hard drive that permitted the saving of documents that can and cannot be readily traced, tracked, or shared. Work done as research-in-progress documents that were formerly lodged with the Registries can now be put into the bottom drawer with only a final research report being given to the client. It is commonly suggested that the very nature of a research culture is one that promotes sharing through collaborative work or by publishing. However, one individual commented that both "styles of working that were increasingly forcing organizations to be outcome focused, and being personally accountable were completely at odds with a system that says 'let's share information as a group'" (Informant 1). No other mechanisms were available to knowledge workers at the STDO to support the transfer of explicit knowledge for their work purposes.

Prior Systems: Tacit Knowledge Transfer

Prior to the development and implementation of the KM strategy, there was one system in place to share knowledge. This was done through the establishment of research hubs. These hubs of people connected both virtually and physically across the organization were created by the STDO to provide a forum for the exchange of knowledge in the various fields of research as well as to facilitate the coordination of research divisions. Four research hubs were created. These were the Radio Frequency Hub (1996), the Opto-electronics Hub (1996), the Human Factors Hub (1998), and the Simulation Hub (2001). These objectives were and still are to facilitate the coordination of research across the STDO divisions to develop and maintain scientific excellence. Additionally, these hubs are open to researchers who are associated with but not necessarily employed by the STDO. This has been done deliberately with the aim of enhancing interaction between researchers at the STDO and universities, industry, and the CSIRO. It is acknowledged at the STDO that there is a high degree of employment mobility of its work force among these entities. Therefore, this was a means of knowledge transfer, of retaining knowledge of former employees, and of leveraging the knowledge of coresearchers.

Problems

These hubs were led and formed on an ad hoc basis. There were no coordinated mechanisms to support the hubs or their leaders either in a physical or virtual environment. No other mechanisms were available to knowledge workers at the STDO to support the transfer of tacit knowledge for their work tasks.

Leading KM at the STDO

KM leadership focus must be based on the development of an organizational culture respecting knowledge and sharing, on the KM infrastructure and support system, and on encouragement for KM line supervisors (Bollinger & Smith, 2001). It is the leader who manages the process of vision creation (Amidon & Macnamara, 2003). It is also the responsibility of the leader to see the articulation of that vision both within and outside the organization. At the STDO, there is no named position of CKO, and no single person is in charge of the implementation of the KM strategy. Strength of leadership is evident in the STDO. It is structured according to the same hierarchical control and command model as its "Operations" parent. This leadership tradition adds complexity to the layers of culture at the STDO where, as noted above, the organizational information transfer structure operates on a federal model in its decision making in research matters. Davenport and Prusak (1997) defined the federal model as being based on consensus and negotiation in the organization's management and reporting structures with a remote central structure and a high level of local autonomy. In the case of the STDO "the culture … once you get down to the working level, was to question because that's what scientists do. So if you were too 'directive' they simply won't accept that" (Informant 6).

The role of chief knowledge strategist has been assigned to the person with the role of FASSP who is the head of the Sciences Policy division as shown in Figure 1. The chief knowledge strategist is not a knowledge leader or a knowledge champion in the accepted sense (O'Dell, Hasanali, Hubert, Lopez, Odem, & Raybourn, 2000) but demonstrates the qualities of leadership however these attributes are nominated in the position description according to the requirements of the organizational strategic plan. Further, the chief knowledge strategist does not devise or implement the strategy but has responsibility to the organization that knowledge is leveraged to meet the aims and mission of the organization.

Before the governance structure was established, KM operated as a number of separate activities implemented through the independent initiatives of the Library and Resource Centre simultaneously with the activity of the hubs. These activities were dependent on the availability of ad hoc funding for discrete projects and did not attempt to function as a single strategy throughout the organization. As such, there was limited fiscal responsibility and no management of the risks and obstacles to the strategy. Figure 2 illustrates the ad hoc existence of the individual but unrelated KM initiatives that were in place at that time.

How Did the KM Governance Structure Arise?

The strategy crew was developed in 2000 as an outcome of a strategic retreat that was attended by the director of each laboratory together with the headquarters branch heads. At the retreat, the directors identified key areas where the STDO was particularly vulnerable. One of the 12 critical success factors identified was KM — expressed specifically in those terms. Headquarters management understood that the issue was not fundamentality a problem only about information but was an issue about both process and information. "Hence we have the information governance board so that people were aware of what was going on. It's easy to lose track of all the bits and pieces" (Informant 2).

The STDO conducted its own research into the implementation of Information Management and Knowledge Management strategy implementations. They found that

Figure 2. Position of KM (2000) at the STDO prior to the development of governance mechanisms

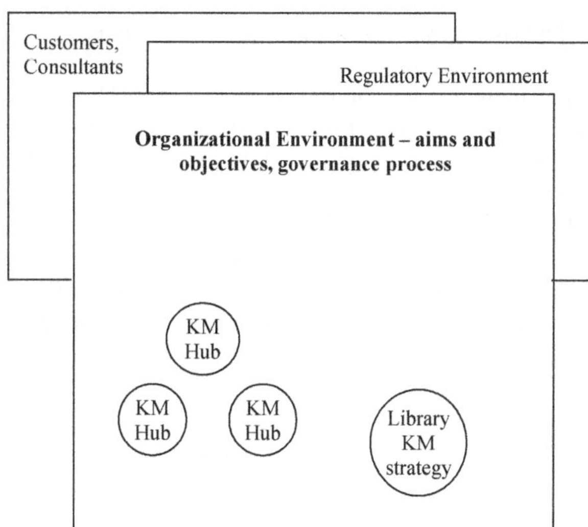

when a strategy was implemented using an individual working and engaging with other individuals, that is, a one-to-one model, the strategy usually failed. When a strategy is implemented using an individual working with and engaging groups, that is, a one-to-many model, the strategy usually failed. However, they found that when the initiative was implemented within an organization by a group of people engaging other groups, that is, it is implemented as a many-to-many model, then the initiative usually succeeded. As a consequence "the strategy crew became convinced that if we had a single champion, it would fail. We needed multiple [KM] stakeholders across the organization and we decided that it wasn't just the knowledge management that would fail … any of these change strategies would fail if they only had one particular champion" (Informant 2). Thus a strategy was developed with multiple champions who were responsible for presenting the strategies back to their peers.

Development of the Governance Process

The STDO strategic plan specifies the goal of corporate governance and information management to make sure that information users can access relevant knowledge resources; accordingly, the chief knowledge strategist has sought to enable these activities. He saw the contributions of elements of KM coming from a number of different sections within the organization.

- The understanding of and contribution to the management of tacit knowledge came from neural networks research which sought to establish an effective model for tacit knowledge transfer.

- The understanding and control of explicit knowledge came from library, information management and document workers who had previously been working in this field.
- The contribution of information architecture through the Information Technology and Systems department was a headquarters-based concern. The importance of the active involvement of the Information Technology and Systems department was particularly pertinent in the context of need for STDO KM conformity to an enterprise-wide architecture within the STDO where it must comply with the architecture of its parent organization, the Department of "Operations."
- Further, these elements required financial resources to develop an overall IMKM design and plan to create the delivery of an electronic library service, to improve the intranet, and to develop a knowledge improvement program. Governance was the mechanism that could implement authority over the IMKM plan and provide the framework to ensure delivery of expected benefits in an authorized and regulated manner.

Mechanisms were also needed to evaluate the effectiveness of the strategy. Informants indicated that the need for governance was recognized and triggered from two directions:

1. The "issue came up of 'do these people need money?' Well suddenly that forces you to think about policy" (Informant 1). This indicates an awareness and responsibility for the concern that if money is being spent by the organization, then governance of expenditure is required. As acknowledged earlier, the Australian Public Service was operating within a new context of governance and accountability that in particular focused on authorized, regulated, and effective use of public monies.
2. STDO's own research found that the issue of governance to ensure fiscal and managerial accountability emerged as the underlying factor inhibiting most of the cultural and infrastructure management of a KM strategy. "In particular, divided management responsibility and an attitude of 'it's someone else's problem' were a common theme" (Informant 3).

Of particular interest is the juxtaposition of accountability and divided management responsibility as shown in these two statements. It can be concluded that the structure of governance of the KM strategy evolved due to external forces and from the insight and leadership shown. The IMKM Governing Board was formed with key stakeholders who represented the interests of multiple areas of management and of the interests of the researchers in the organization. This composition of the board was felt to give real opportunity for issues to be resolved. "It meant that for the first time ever [they] weren't coming together to argue about who should get what money. They weren't coming together to see who should get the lead of what program. They were coming together to work at strategic objectives. One of which was knowledge management. So it was treated as being part of a whole rather than being a sideline. Because they were all working on a range of items we were very careful not to fragment the technology planning from the people initiatives, from the various areas. And although they were people with interest they weren't necessarily the people who had ownership of that process. And that sort of reinforced the many people interested but a particular person was the owner of changing the process" (Informant 1).

Figure 3. KM structure (2003) at the STDO since the development of governance mechanisms

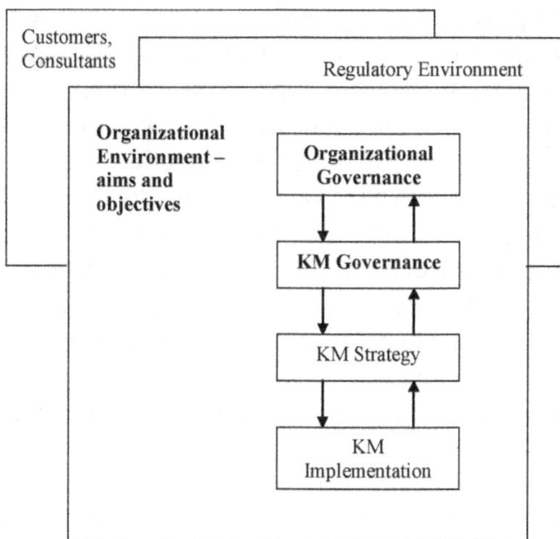

Figure 3 illustrates the dual relationship between the organizational governance structure and the IMKM Board governance function. The organizational governance process established policy that put the control and development of knowledge as a priority the outcomes of this policy are reported back by the IMKM Board governance process. The IMKM Board establishes the policies for and controls over KM strategy development. Strategy is developed and implementation managed. The outcomes of strategy implementation are reviewed and evaluated and then reported back to the IMKM Board for further action.

Impact of Governance on KM Strategy Implementation

The Strategic Plan of the STDO clearly describes the key focus or vision for the organization. Knowledge improvement is clearly enunciated as a focus within the Strategic Plan. The IMKM Plan is the vehicle to achieve this goal at the STDO and it comprised seven core elements. The STDO has developed a description for the purpose of each core element, documentation of the goal for each and the required activities.

These are

- Corporate Governance and Information Management;
- Client Program;
- External Relations;
- Strategic Positioning;
- People;
- Resource Management; and
- Information Systems Infrastructure.

The goal of Corporate Governance and Information Management was to ensure that the users of information could get access to the information they require to do their research, their task, or their job. The activities that are seen as achieving these goals are to improve information governance, to develop an overall architecture and an IMKM Plan, to create the digital delivery of library services, to improve the intranet, and to develop a knowledge improvement program.

The goal of the Client Program was to ensure that the STDO has the right information for and from its clients to support research programs, further providing a coordinated approach to support the organization's activities. The activities that are seen to achieve these goals are the improvement of the programmatic aspects of the Management Information System (including both hardware and software issues) and to develop STDO research programs to support the organization's activities and research programs.

The goal of the External Relations aspect of the plan was to leverage the STDO information capability to undertake interactions between STDO and external, nonclient agencies. The activities planned to achieve this are through improving current Internet publishing, to further investigate external KM relationships with similar research and development agencies, and to extended the international defense research document repository (scheduled for 2005-2006).

The goal of the Strategic Positioning is to improve the information management capability required to adapt STDO for the future. This is seen as being achievable through the implementation of an automated Balanced Scorecard (scheduled for over the next four years).

The goal of the People facet of the plan was to ensure that STDO managers have the information tools to effectively manage people, to support strategic people initiatives, and to support workforce planning and full-time employee management.

The goal of Resource Management is to continuously improve STDO resource management information systems by improving the financial aspects of management information systems and to maximize the take up of defense resource information systems tools.

The goal of Information Systems Infrastructure planning was to improve the quality of STDO networks and information systems. There are a number of activities that are planned to achieve this. These are the use of a better-coordinated approach to information systems planning, the implementation of a Document and Records Management (next phase in the next two years), and through continued input into the "Operations" Applications Register. The "Operations" Applications Register is a register of hardware and software owned and operated in the Department of "Operations" and its wholly owned operations.

The components of the IMKM Plan were divided up into tasks with individuals charged with the achievement of the goals of each task according to the tacit or explicit nature of the knowledge resources being harnessed. As described earlier, this task format is standard work practice for the STDO in its R&D work for the "Operations" staff.

Managing Tacit Knowledge Transfer

The organization has also developed a research task to specifically address tacit knowledge. This dates from 2002 and is ongoing. This tacit knowledge transfer is recognized organizationally as "the really hard stuff, individual bench-scientist experiences and things like that" (Informant 5). Progress to date has comprised a great deal of reading about the theoretical aspects of KM and its application to R&D environment of the STDO. This has included exhaustive examination of KM case studies of similar institutions as well as more generalist implementations.

Current activity includes the pilot and broad distribution of a survey to all staff into the knowledge-sharing practices of both individual researchers and support staff. This forms an audit of tacit knowledge transfer and adds to the organizational knowledge map. The aspects of tacit knowledge-sharing practices that are being examined through over 300 variables comprehensively include the cultural issues affecting KM. They also canvass frequency and mode of communication (e-mail, phone, interactive chat sessions, or in person) and whether this is with internal and/or external contacts. This task relates to the use of communication through professional reading activities that are expected at the STDO as part of maintaining currency of knowledge. They seek to establish the quantity of the information that is found on the Web, in academic literature, and that is verbally or even physically passed on to others as relevant and useful. They seek to establish use patterns of the STDO's library resources and services and the STDO intranet. This will produce a pattern of individual information needs and preferences reflecting both reliance on tacit and, in part, on explicit resources.

Another facet of tacit knowledge sharing that is being examined is that of the role of informal communities within the STDO. This is described as the relationships with a group of people whom individuals can turn to when they have questions or problems within technical, professional, or research work in the STDO. Initial research by the STDO found that "they [researchers] sourced most of their information through networking and their colleagues" (Informant 6). As well as providing technical/professional or research help, internal KM research seeks to audit whether the informal networks include those who help each other work in the organization, by describing their own experiences of activities in the organization, giving advice and suggestions for how to gain promotion and perhaps how do work within STDO's administrative structures.

An important activity that has a long history in the STDO, and is now incorporated into the IMKM plan, are the practice hubs that are actually examples of communities of practice. These were created between 1996 and 2001 for the exchange of information and views in the various disciplines. The other priority was to make possible the gathering of research work across STDO divisions, to support scientific excellence, and to develop the interaction between researchers at STDO and their equivalents at other R&D institutions and universities. Membership of the hubs is voluntary and is built on the technology interests of research staff within the following fields: Radio Frequency, Opto-electronics, Human Factors, and Simulation Activity. Each hub has defined a number of subordinate foci. The four STDO research hubs are overseen but not claimed by the IMKM Governing Board as their own. This is a conscious decision because "at a whole lot of levels we were doing knowledge management, but just not calling it that. That was also an expectation issue — there was no point in going and grabbing something. I mean if I put out a knowledge management plan that included the hubs . . . if [we were] wandering around checking up on what the hub's doing as secretary of the Information Governance Board, people would say, 'Why were you doing that? That's my core business'" (Informant 1).

The third facet of the management of tacit knowledge is through the knowledge improvement plan. Some projects that are currently being investigated for this strategy include a Science Excellence Forum, a STDO Yellow Pages, and an alumni involvement program for retired researchers (Hackett, 2000). One of the motivations for the alumni proposal is succession planning for the management and utilization of corporate and individual memory. The STDO currently has a mentoring program that works toward this purpose; however, the demographics of the workforce, as described earlier, show this as an imperative. Storytelling (Snowden, 2002) has been identified as another means of sharing tacit knowledge; however, this element of the strategy is yet to be implemented.

Another strategy is Pathways, a five-year program to support the integration of new employees into the organization. It focuses on organizational memory (Spender, 1996; Walsh & Ungson, 1991) and encompasses an understanding of the organization as a whole, an understanding of the Australian Public Service, and in particular, of the Department of "Operations." Additionally, professional development through continuing education, mentoring, skills enhancement, and career planning are important. The program also supports both individual and team development and management. This program has the additional purpose of fostering organizational culture. The STDO has initiated a separate program called Smartways with the intention of soliciting responses for knowledge transfer and other systems improvements in the organization. This was also a mode of increasing levels of trust — specifically seen by the strategists as a people and cultural issue in the capture and sharing of knowledge.

Managing Explicit Knowledge Transfer

The management of explicit knowledge is well understood at the STDO comprising internal reports in paper and electronic formats, material on the STDO intranet, library and information centre resources, document management, and record keeping functions. This is further enhanced by databases created for active participation in research cooperation with equivalent international entities.

The initial parts of the IMKM plan implemented were projects to manage explicit knowledge that had been identified as being the "low-hanging fruit" — clearly required and easily achievable. These were in the main activities that the library staff had identified that were not being handled very well in STDO but that could be achieved with the support of resources. The library and information service staff was clearly placed to understand and manage the explicit knowledge — the traditional database and paper-based resources. However, the one of the key issues in this domain was making available and the management of the life cycle of internal publications — technical reports and published papers. This was well supported by staff and researchers who were enthusiastic for proactive management of the information produced as part of their research. An additional aspect of the plan was to implement a means of establishing a complete record of all external publishing in journals and conferences. This external publishing ultimately may also be available to the public through the organization's Internet site.

Another project being activated was the proposed new development of a document and record management system. No system has replaced the Registries since they were abandoned in 1998. Observed outcome has been that "over the years ... all our correspondence was [by] e-mail and the whole thing has fallen down and no one anymore takes the time to put anything on a registry file and we don't have the proper corporate systems to create virtual files either" (Informant 7). Problematically, the issue of budgeting for the implementation of a new document and record management system has been an obstacle. This was particularly pertinent in the context of conformity to an enterprise-wide architecture, where the STDO must comply with the architecture of the Department of "Operations" of which it is a part. Building document and record management system would be an automated means of explicit KM at significant points in the business process.

Of these initiatives to manage explicit knowledge, the last development was the STDO news online being posted on the intranet. It was the most direct way of apprising the organization as a whole of the research being conducted in all RAs and RACs. The outcome has been to keep individuals informed of all research activity. This permits cross-fertilization and leveraging of knowledge through the development of cross-disciplinary research.

OUTCOMES TO DATE

Respondents reported 15 benefits of implementing the governance of the KM strategy. They can be divided into risk management benefits, strategic benefits, and financial benefits.

Risk Management Through Governance

1. Management roles and responsibilities have been allocated.
2. Enterprise information architecture strategy has been instigated to standardize the approach to KM and to conform with the Department of "Operations."
3. A number of new electronic repositories have been established. These include internal publications, material published externally, and material created for the cooperative international research program. All were created with an extensive, controlled thesaurus of metadata.
4. There has been an overall increase in usage of all electronic repositories by the staff; metrics were taken of usage before the implementation of the strategy in 2001 and have been compared with usage patterns in October 2003.
5. The intranet has been redesigned to improve use and access to it. There is now a uniform design of the intranet across all STDO locations.
6. STDO news is now online.
7. A five-year induction program for new staff has been created to foster the organizational culture and transfer of the way "we do things around here."
8. Resource planning for the KM strategy has been enabled.
9. An organizational learning project in the form of a continuing education initiative has been put into effect.
10. Specifications for a document and records management system have been developed.
11. Further enhancement of hubs that are now responsible to the IMKM Board for their proactive functioning. In return, they are now funded by the IMKM Board and facilitated in their activity.
12. Specifications for an organizational yellow pages have been developed.

Strategic Benefits of Governance

1. Everyone at the STDO is now actively engaged in thinking about KM.
2. Individually and collectively, people are now looking at their own knowledge domain and beginning to realize that the information they are collecting might be useful to others.
3. Individually and collectively, people are now looking at their expertise — that it too might be useful to others — and they are willing to look at sharing or making that tacit knowledge available to others.

Financial Benefits Through Governance

The governance mechanisms applied to the planning, development, and implementation of the KM strategy at the STDO have ensured that

1. KM strategy is fiscally viable through its alignment with and support of organizational strategy;
2. KM is subject to evaluation and measurement through internal research mechanisms; and
3. KM is recognized as making a contribution to knowledge retention and knowledge sharing.

INFERENCES DRAWN

The governance of the KM strategy at the STDO is designed and structured to meet the needs for the creation, dissemination, and utilization of knowledge to fulfill organizational objectives. This is being achieved through the harnessing of explicit knowledge and information resources and the leveraging of tacit knowledge resources. In this case study organization, the role of governance to coordinate and manage risks through the IMKM Board is met by a number of responsible individuals who represent different sectors of the organization both in skills and in their interest and motivation for achieving an effective outcome.

The IMKM Board governs the strategy, which is a formal structure that both informs and is informed by the KM strategy. Governance manages risks of the KM strategy to ensure the delivery of anticipated benefits of quality assurance of the strategy, fiscal viability, developing and meeting strategic KM goals and objectives, and to be proactive and reactive to changing requirements of the STDO management and staff. Through its regular meetings and distribution of responsibilities to board members, governance directs, monitors, and controls how the KM strategy is implemented and gauges success as reflected in the timeliness of service delivery and the satisfaction of stakeholders. This is an exemplar of the need for an organization-wide perspective for the implementation of a strategy to manage organizational knowledge, and the capacity for governance to sustain and advance the effective implementation of a strategy to manage organizational knowledge.

CURRENT CHALLENGES FACING THE ORGANIZATION

This case study has looked at the implementation of a KM strategy in the STDO and has examined the governance mechanisms as a context for the analysis of the ongoing development of KM strategies and the evaluation of the effectiveness of those strategies. KM governance is specifically the implementation of authority that comprises the processes and principles that act as a framework to exercise authority that ensures the effectiveness of strategies to manage organizational knowledge.

The rationale behind the methods employed in the acquisition, distribution, and utilization of both explicit and tacit forms of knowledge have been described and analyzed. The strategy is not owned and championed by a single person or department; it is owned by staff and it is both responsive and responsible to staff and management.

The main challenge faced by the STDO is that of the limited resources for the KM strategy in an organizational environment where more must be done with less. The STDO is realistic in its next steps to further implement this strategy. It plans to audit and map previously untracked tacit resources. It plans to implement the document and record management system, to implement the organizational yellow pages, to create an alumni program, to look to embed best practice to minimize knowledge loss, and to create a Web-based bulletin board to facilitate internal communication so as not overload the e-mail system. The more challenging issue being looked at is that of the transfer of complex knowledge that lies between the organization and other organizations. This has been recognized and is seen as being a long-term proposal requiring in-depth research and discussion.

The STDO plans to look at the strategy as it develops — to evaluate what works and what does not. It will adjust and realign the strategy according to the success or otherwise of its initiatives. It is empowered both organizationally and geographically by the representative nature of the IMKM Governance Board. It is willing and able to take time to look at its actions and to evaluate and revise strategies according to both its successes and its failures.

EPILOGUE

This case study has demonstrated the role of governance in the effective delivery of a KM strategy. Governance processes operate to implement authority through a framework to ensure the delivery of anticipated benefits in an authorized and regulated manner. This supports enhanced decision making through effective control of organizational knowledge. The governance framework centralizes the processes to measure progress, review implementation, and manage the risks of KM. Governance processes confront the cultural issues, the structural obstacles, and other relevant issues as they arise during the implementation and ongoing operation of that strategy. The management of these risks assists in the resolution of such issues and, in turn, strengthens the strategies to manage knowledge that an organization employs.

LESSONS LEARNED

1. KM governance must be constructed as a formal structure that is representative of stakeholder interests and that both informs and is informed by the KM strategy. The participation of a number of key stakeholders in the IMKM Board ensured commitment of all those parties to the process, to policy development, and to the eventual implementation of strategies developed.
2. In managing risk, the governance mechanism ensures the delivery of anticipated benefits on KM in an ongoing process that is quality assured, fiscally viable, meets goals and strategic objectives, and is responsive to changing requirements of organization and staff. Through the establishment of the IMKM governance board, the STDO was able to harness existing knowledge-sharing practices and to evaluate, extend, and strengthen them specifically to target both tacit and explicit knowledge sharing activities. It, therefore, meets organizational needs for the creation, dissemination, and utilization of knowledge.
3. Governance processes control and confirm the fiscal accountability of a KM strategy. By requiring measurement of outcomes against aims and objectives that could be proved at the highest level of organizational governance, KM governance processes confirmed the organizational value of expenditure on knowledge management for the STDO.
4. In an organizational environment of the limited resources for the KM strategy, the IMKM Board is able to devise policies that are in accord with organizational aims and objectives, and report these back at the highest level of organizational control. In implementing KM governance processes, STDO was able to prioritize its future steps of strategy implementation and at the same time demonstrate the worth of its activity to the organization as a whole.

FURTHER READING

Earl, M.J., & Scott, I.A. (1999). What is a chief knowledge officer? *Sloan Management Review, 40*(2), 29.

Holsapple, C.W., & Joshi, K.D. (2002). Knowledge management: A threefold framework. *The Information Society,* (18), 47-64.

IT Governance Institute, & COBIT Steering Committee. (2000). *COBIT framework* (3rd ed.). Rolling Meadows, IL: IT Governance Institute.

Kelleher, D., & Levene, S. (2001). *Knowledge management: A guide to good practice.* London: British Standards Association.

Oxbrow, N., & Hart, C. (2003). *The knowledge proposition.* London: TFPL.

Wiig, K.M. (1997). Knowledge management: An introduction and perspective. *Journal of Knowledge Management, 1*(1), 6-14.

Zyngier, S., Burstein, F., & McKay, J. (2004,). Knowledge management governance: A multifaceted approach to organizational decision and innovation support. Paper presented at the *2004 IFIP International Conference on Decision Support Systems (DSS2004), Decision Support in an Uncertain World,* Prato, Italy.

REFERENCES

Amidon, D.M., & Macnamara, D. (2003). The 7 C's of knowledge leadership: Innovating our future. In C.W. Holsapple (Ed.), *Handbook on knowledge management 1: Knowledge matters* (Vol. 1, pp. 539-551). Berlin: Springer-Verlag.

Barrett, P., & Sotiropoulos, G. (2001). Corporate governance in the public sector context. Retrieved December 12, 2003, from *http://www.anao.gov.au/WebSite.nsf/Publications/4A256AE90015F69B4A256A330018550F*

Bollinger, A.S., & Smith, R.D. (2001). Managing organizational knowledge as a strategic asset. *Journal of Knowledge Management, 5*(1), 8-18.

Davenport, T.H., & Prusak, L. (1997). *Information ecology: Mastering the information and knowledge environment.* New York: Oxford University Press.

Farrar, J. (2001). *Corporate governance in Australia and New Zealand.* South Melbourne, Australia: Oxford University Press.

Francis, I. (1997). *Future direction: The power of the competitive board.* South Melbourne, Australia: FT Pitman.

Hackett, B. (2000). *Beyond knowledge management: New ways to work and learn.* (Research Report No. 1261-00-RR). New York: The Conference Board.

Husted, K., & Michailova, S. (2002). Diagnosing and fighting knowledge-sharing hostility. *Organizational Dynamics, 31*(1), 60-73.

O'Dell, C., Hasanali, F., Hubert, C., Lopez, K., Odem, P., & Raybourn, C. (2000). Successful KM implementation: A study of best-practice organizations. In C. Holsapple (Ed.), *Handbook on knowledge management 2: Knowledge directions* (Vol. 2, pp. 411-443). Berlin: Springer-Verlag.

Snowden, D. (2002). The new simplicity; Context, narrative and content. *Knowledge Management Journal, July/August*, 11-17.

Spender, J.C. (1996). Organizational knowledge, learning and memory: Three concepts in search of a theory. *Journal of Organizational Change Management, 9*(1), 63-78.

Walsh, J.P., & Ungson, G.R. (1991). Organizational memory. *Academy of Management Review, 16*(1), 57-91.

Chapter VII

Challenges in Developing a Knowledge Management Strategy for the Air Force Material Command*

Summer E. Bartczak, Air Force Institute of Technology, USA

Ellen C. England, Air Force Institute of Technology, USA

EXECUTIVE SUMMARY

It is widely acknowledged that an organizational knowledge management strategy is a desired precursor to the development of specific knowledge management (KM) initiatives. The development of such a strategy is often difficult in the face of a lack of organizational understanding about KM and other organizational constraints. This case study describes the issues involved in developing a new KM strategy for the Air Force Material Command (AFMC). It centers around the AFMC KM program manager, Randy Adkins, and his challenges in developing the future KM strategy direction for the AFMC enterprise. The case study begins with a description of the history of the AFMC KM program and the existing KM system, but then focuses primarily on issues to be considered in future strategy development, such as maintaining top leadership support and understanding, conflict with the IT organization, funding cuts, future KM system configuration needs, and outsourcing of KM. The intent of this case study is to demonstrate, using Randy Adkins and AFMC as an example, many common issues that can be encountered as leaders struggle to develop viable KM strategies.

BACKGROUND

The Air Force Material Command

The Air Force Material Command (AFMC) is one of the Air Force's nine major commands (Figure 1). It is headquartered at Wright-Patterson Air Force Base in Dayton, Ohio, and employs 85,000 military and civilian employees across the globe. The primary mission of AFMC is to "develop, acquire, and sustain the aerospace power needed to defend the United States and its interests... today and tomorrow" (HQ AFMC PA, 2001a). As such, it has cradle-to-grave oversight for the Air Force's aircraft, missiles, and munitions (HQ AFMC PA, 2001a). Key mission essential tasks supported by AFMC include product support, supply management, and depot maintenance (see Appendix 1 for a further breakdown).

According to the AFMC Public Affairs Fact Sheet (HQ AFMC PA, 2001a), AFMC fulfills its responsibilities through organizations that serve as product centers, research laboratories, test centers, air logistic centers for maintenance, and specialized centers (Figure 2). Weapon systems, such as aircraft and missiles, are developed and acquired through four product centers, using science and technology from the research laboratories. These weapon systems are then tested at AFMC's two test centers and are serviced and repaired at its three air logistics maintenance depots. The command's specialized centers perform various other development and logistics functions. Eventually, aircraft and missiles are "retired" to its Aircraft Maintenance and Regeneration Center in Tucson, Arizona.

AFMC's central governing organization, Headquarters (HQ) AFMC (Figure 3), consists of all the functional areas that provide support for command organizations. The Directorate of Requirements (DR)—the focus of this case study—is the command's focal point for policies, processes, and resources that support the product and information services mission (HQ AFMC PA, 2001b) and is the home of AFMC's Knowledge Management program which has the official name, Air Force Knowledge Management (AFKM).

SETTING THE STAGE

Evolution of KM in AFMC

In the early 1990s, the U.S. Department of Defense (DoD) recognized the need to streamline its acquisition process. As a result, the Air Force (AF) created a System Program Office (SPO) to develop technology solutions to help achieve that end. One such technology solution was called the AF Acquisition Model. Initially, this information system included an online repository of all acquisition regulations, step-by-step processes for conducting acquisitions, and miscellaneous help information such as points of contact and lessons learned. Although the technology used was immature, this digital repository was a first of its kind in the military and an idea quickly copied by the other services.

After its initial success, the SPO proposed the same idea to the Office of the Under Secretary of Defense for Acquisition Technology for possible implementation across the

Figure 1. U.S. Air Force major commands

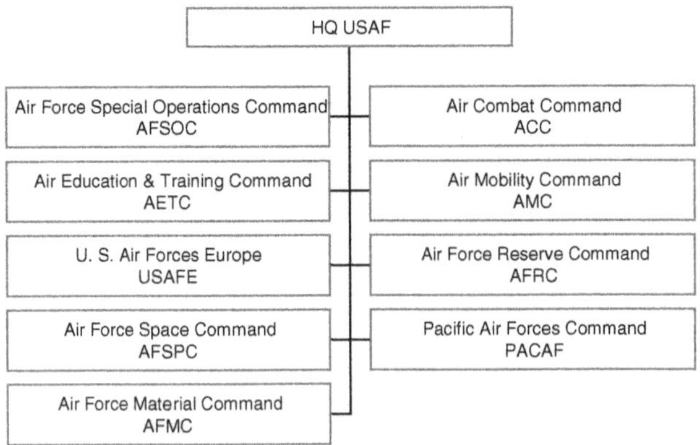

DoD. The proposal was approved in 1998 and the resulting effort became known as the Defense Acquisition Deskbook program. Now, as a DoD-level project, the program (and the accompanying information system) was to be managed and developed by an interservice Joint Program Office. As such, major Deskbook activities were transferred to the Joint Program Office and AFMC/DR personnel were assigned the remaining task of keeping the AF's Deskbook documents that resided on the system updated and current. Although the Joint Program Office retained oversight responsibility for the Deskbook program, a yearly funding stream of $1.5 million remained to support AFMC/DR's portion of the effort. Of this $1.5 million budget, only $500,000 was committed to maintenance of the Deskbook program. As such, AFMC/DR found itself asking, "What can we do with an extra million dollars?"

The answer came quickly in the form of an AF Inspection Agency study that identified a need for an overarching "lessons learned" program for the AF. While the need was AF-wide, the AFMC/DR Deskbook Team decided to use its own expertise and excess funding from the Deskbook program to address the problem for the AF. As a result, it produced a formal requirement to develop an information system-based AF Lessons Learned pilot program. Using the AFMC Deskbook system design as a foundation, the Deskbook Team added additional capabilities that allowed the capture and dissemination of "lessons learned" information.

While researching and developing the Lessons Learned pilot program, the Deskbook Team decided that the new business concept touted as "KM" captured the essence of

Figure 2. Air Force Material Command organization

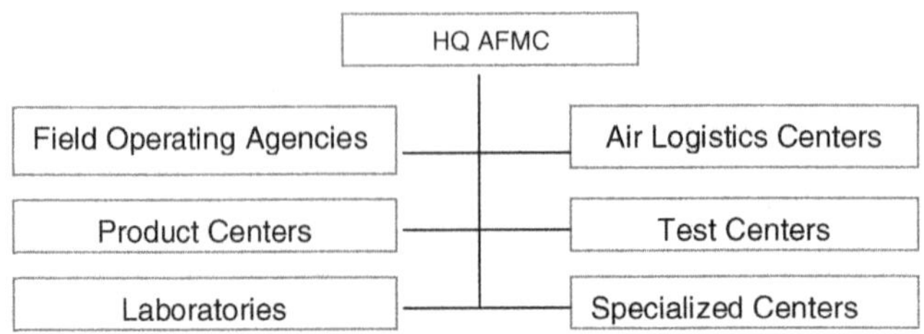

Figure 3. HQ AFMC organization and directorates

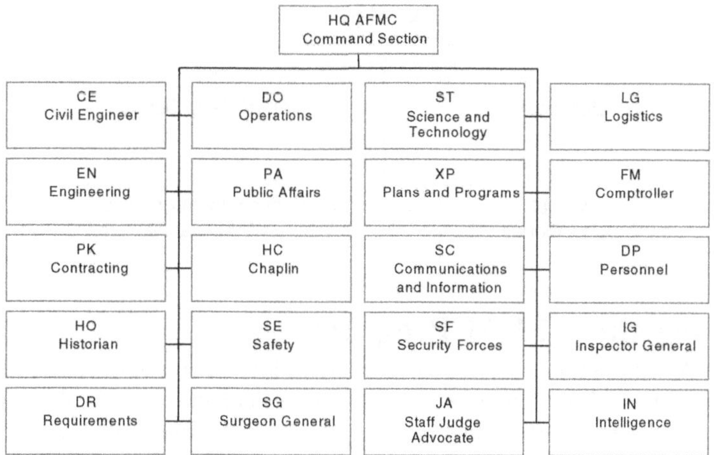

what they were doing. The Team's understanding of KM was that it should be used to enhance organizational performance by explicitly designing and implementing tools, processes, systems, structures, and cultures to improve the creation, sharing, and use of knowledge that was critical for decision making. With this understanding, the Team felt that the goals of KM and the goals of the Deskbook and Lessons Learned projects were consistent. The Team also strategized that if it labeled its efforts as KM, it was possible the Team could receive more leadership support and funding. From that point forward, AFMC/DR Deskbook Team approached its projects and proposals from a KM perspective.

In addition to the Deskbook and Lessons Learned projects, the AFMC/DR Deskbook Team had also developed Web-based acquisition training to educate the acquisition workforce in lieu of sending them to classroom training. Randy Adkins, a civil service employee with 20 years of experience in various positions at Headquarters AFMC, was in charge of the development of this Web-based training program. At the same time, Robert Mulcahy, the deputy director of AFMC/DR, expressed concern with the impending retirement-driven talent drain that was soon to affect his organization as well as all of the AFMC enterprise. Previous studies both inside and outside the AF indicated that more than 50% of the AF's civilian acquisition personnel would be eligible to retire by 2005 (Cho, Jerrell, & Landay, 2000). Unless this issue was immediately addressed, Mulcahy knew that the acquisition workforce would lack the talent, leadership, and diversity needed to succeed in the new millennium. In searching for a solution, he recognized the value of KM concepts as they applied to his organization. He soon became a KM champion and pushed for a merger of the Deskbook, Lessons Learned, and Web-based training programs. He felt these programs, and the information systems that comprised their foundation, were synergistic and could be used in tandem to help capture and disseminate the knowledge of the rapidly retiring civilian workforce. In early 1999, Mulcahy turned to Adkins to spearhead the consolidation which would result in a new combined effort called the AF Knowledge Management (AFKM) program. Together, he believed they could bring KM to AFMC.

Figure 4. AFKM system components

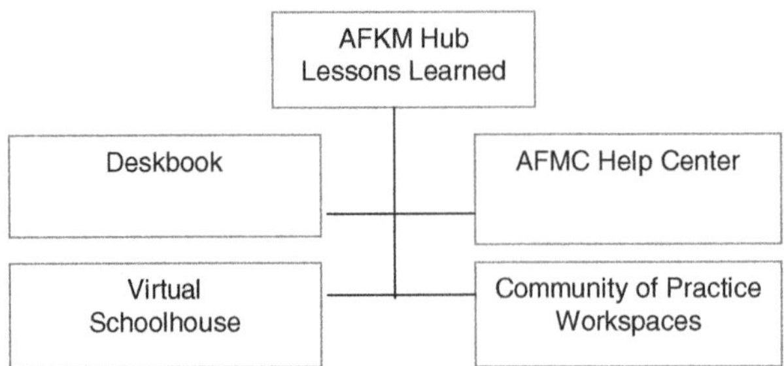

Developing the AFKM Program

Randy Adkins worked tirelessly to educate himself on KM and to develop an overarching strategic direction for the many existing elements of the AFKM program and AFKM system. His initial efforts in developing the AFKM program were aimed primarily at applying commercial KM processes and technologies to solve specific business problems. In doing so, his focus was on identifying, capturing, and leveraging knowledge and expertise within the organization. The ultimate goal of the AFKM program was to design information system solutions so that AFMC users could share information and knowledge and, at the same time, create a supportive, collaborative, and information- and knowledge-sharing culture (HQ AFMC/DRI, 2001).

The AFKM "System"

Under Adkins' direction, the Deskbook Team, deemed the AFKM System Development Team 1999, continued to grow the Web-based system beyond its original three components (Lessons Learned database, DoD Acquisition Deskbook, and Web-based training). The AFKM System Development Team structure is shown in Appendix 2. By mid 2000, the AFKM system was comprised of five basic components (Figure 4) — the Lessons Learned database, the AFMC portion of the DoD Acquisition Deskbook, the AFMC Virtual Schoolhouse (Web-based training), the AFMC Help Center module, and a Community of Practice (CoP) collaboration workspace module.

The AFKM home page (Figure 5) described the functionality of the AFKM system as follows:

Air Force Knowledge Management is the place to go to find out what you need and to share what you know. . . . [It] applies commercial knowledge management concepts and technologies to address AF business problems. It includes: collaborative workspaces for communities of practice, high-value Internet links, Internet-based learning technology to provide training via the Web, and a repository of lessons learned, best practices, and other bits of usable knowledge. The objective is to make our jobs easier and to enhance job performance by integrating organizational lessons learned, community wisdom, training and collaborative technology to support current and future projects. (AFKM Home Page, 2001)

The AFKM system was designed to be used as a portal. The main portal entry point is the AFKM Hub (or AFKM home page) which includes access to Lessons Learned, DoD

Figure 5. AFKM home page

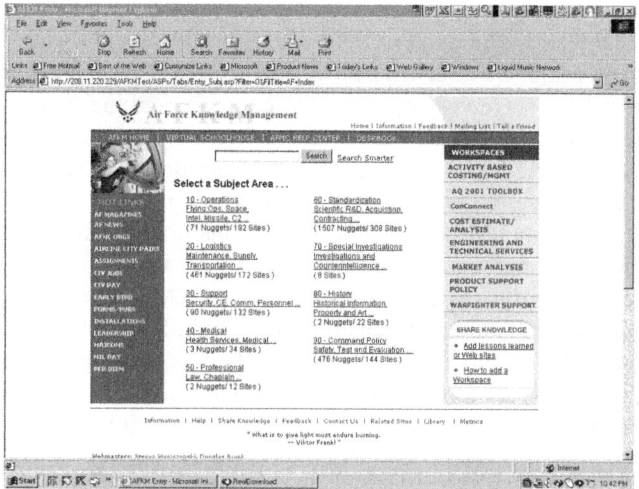

Acquisition Deskbook, AFMC Help Center, Virtual Schoolhouse, and CoP workspaces. The AFKM Hub evolved from the original Lessons Learned Web site and now serves as the access point to a range of knowledge and information resources. The DoD Acquisition Deskbook provides a variety of documents describing the laws, directives, policies, and regulations related to DoD acquisitions. The AFMC Help Center provides an English-language search engine for both AFMC and other customers to find information or documents that may reside on any of the many AFMC Web sites. The Virtual Schoolhouse delivers over 20 online courses for AF acquisition training. And finally, the CoP workspaces allow for information exchange, collaboration, and problem solving. The specific functions of each of these portal components is further described in Appendix 3.

CASE DESCRIPTION

It wasn't long after Adkins had taken charge of the AFKM program that he realized it was approaching a crossroads. Specifically, a strategic vision and plan for the future of the program and underlying system was lacking. With strong leadership support and sufficient funding, the AFKM program and system had grown; however, there were now a variety of emerging issues that had to be considered in any future KM strategy development. Some of these key issues are discussed.

Leadership Support

As the deputy director of AFMC/DR, Robert Mulcahy had been a staunch supporter and champion of AFMC's KM efforts. It was his vision that had brought the program together under Adkins. He knew the value of creating the AFKM program and understood the benefits it could bring to AFMC, the AF, and the DoD. Mulcahy had protected and given support to the AFKM System Development Team so that it could expand and explore new opportunities. He believed all of AFMC, not just the headquarters organization, could benefit from KM. Mulcahy was a key reason the AFKM program was successful.

Upon Mulcahy's departure to a new job in early 2000, David Franke was appointed as his replacement. Major General Michael Wiedemer had also become the new Director of Requirements. Both were very open to KM concepts and the AFKM program, but neither was as educated or enthused about KM as Mulcahy had been. Franke, to whom Adkins primarily reported, was not sure that KM should be a centerpiece of AFMC strategy. Franke saw the primary benefits of KM as coming from the building "of" and participation "in" communities of practice. While encouraging Adkins and the AFKM Team to continue their pursuits, he did not have a firm vision for KM or the AFKM program in the future. He was also not sure that AFKM could compete with other programs for additional resources given all the other AFMC priorities. All in all, it was Adkins' assessment that Franke simply didn't see KM as needing emphasis above and beyond other programs. As a result, Adkins predicted that he might have increased difficulty getting the backing and exposure for AFKM that it needed to compete with other AFMC programs for scarce resources.

Conflict with AFMC's IT Organization

Dealing with the headquarters' information technology (IT) organization, referred to as the Directorate of Communications and Information, was a continual challenge. This organization saw many conflicts between its responsibilities and the direction being pursued by the AFKM System Development Team. The Directorate saw its role as providing technology solutions; AFKM was also providing technology solutions. Although the conflict had not escalated to an intolerable level, Adkins noted that his Team and the IT folks "just didn't talk anymore."

Within HQ AFMC, the Directorate of Communications and Information had primary responsibility for command, control, communications, computer, and information (C4I) issues and execution. As such, it possessed sole authority for policy, procedures, and standards with respect to C4I systems and programs. As the AFKM System Development Team expanded its efforts, a conflict had arisen regarding collaboration software tools. The IT organization had mandated and implemented LiveLink® software as the only authorized collaboration tool. This action not only conflicted with the AFKM System Development Team's work on CoP workspaces, but appeared to be, in the Team's estimation, a much more sophisticated collaboration tool than was needed by the average customer. Based on the AFKM Team's in-depth experience, Adkins had tried to convince the IT folks that an AFMC-wide LiveLink® implementation would be a waste of money at this point. Although Adkins had hoped to work with the IT organization on KM issues, this "disagreement" had driven them farther apart. Adkins stated:

We've had numerous discussions, but we have never been able to partner. So they're off getting everybody to do LiveLink®, trying to force everybody to do LiveLink®. I'm off trying just to get people stuff to help them do their jobs better.

Knowledge of the conflict with the IT organization was not limited to the HQ either. When asked by Adkins about his experience with LiveLink®, one of his CoP customers had remarked, "I will tell you . . . you are on the radar warning receiver. They know you're out there and you are a huge threat to them."

Although Adkins had been able to continue the AFKM efforts, he knew the conflict with the IT organization, regarding LiveLink® and other information system issues, was not going away. Since both organizations claimed a role in providing and establishing KM systems, disputes would be ongoing. While Adkins and his Team had a wealth of KM knowledge and system development expertise, the IT organization was still the authorized policy maker. If conflicts continued, the AFKM program and system risked being changed, dismantled, or simply "taken over." This, too, was something that weighed heavily on Adkins' mind.

Funding Cuts

It was Adkins' understanding that a $600,000 budget cut was in the offing for 2001. Such a cut would force him to make hard choices that would affect the AFKM program's future. In practical terms, the budget cut would require Adkins to let go of six AFKM System Development Team contractor personnel. If cuts did come to pass, he knew he would have to reassess, reprioritize, and reorganize the current AFKM system development workload distribution.

Adkins was also worried about the impact on AFKM system customers. From its inception, the AFKM program had attempted to serve a wide range of customers. Whether it was supporting DoD-wide efforts such as Deskbook, AFMC internal efforts such as the Help Center, or outside command efforts such as the Engineering and Technical Services CoP for Air Combat Command, the AFKM System Development Team had eagerly built new applications. While some of the projects had been fully funded by the requesting customers, many had been accomplished on an as-can-pay basis or without funding support at all. Adkins knew that without AFKM program funding assistance, some customers would never be able to get their KM efforts off the ground. With the budget cuts looming, customer support practices would have to be reevaluated as well.

AFKM System Usage Concerns

Despite rave reviews about the usefulness of the AFKM system from customers, Adkins was disturbed by low use, or "hit" rates. Simple system access metrics showed that, although use continued to rise, it was only a small portion of what it could or should be. To counter this phenomenon, Adkins and the AFKM System Development Team attempted to improve awareness with a series of road shows. They traveled to many AFMC bases to market the AFKM system's many capabilities. While this effort had increased usage somewhat, overall AFKM usage was still low. From a macro view, Adkins understood that KM and the AFKM system tools were still in their infancy. However, the low usage statistics did not help the AFKM System Development Team justify the benefit or the budget. Adkins was glad that his superiors had supported the Team's efforts on intuition and common sense; however, he also understood that he could be asked at any time to measure the true impact and return on investment. Remarking about the necessity of good metrics, Adkins said, "we had a budget drill not too long ago where I lost a little bit of money and some people . . . that reinforced the fact that I needed better metrics." In preparation of such requests, Adkins needed to seriously consider how he could improve results.

Lack of Understanding about KM

Adkins constantly encountered a lack of knowledge about KM. Few individuals, at any level across AFMC, had much idea of what KM was all about. Adding to the confusion was the fact that there seemed to be no accepted standard definition for KM. While it was easy to communicate the importance of individual KM applications, such as lessons learned databases, document repositories, and electronic yellow pages for experts, it was much more difficult to explain the more comprehensive KM concepts. This made it hard to get people interested in the purpose and goals of the AFKM program. Adkins realized that "learning about KM" took time, but also understood that ignorance by those whom he relied on for support could threaten the AFKM program's survival before it really had a chance to prove itself on a large scale. Again, any strategy for the future of AFKM had to address an education element.

Technological Challenges

The AFKM System Development Team was facing technological challenges even though it was very skilled in responding to the fast-paced changes in technology. In the past, it had Web enabled all of its products, making extensive use of technologies such as HTML, java script, active server pages, and so forth. After the Deskbook, Lessons Learned, and Help Center products achieved stability, the Team continued development efforts and had found a niche in developing CoP workspaces for customers. The Team became so efficient in developing workspaces that it could hand over a "CoP in a box" with a few minor customer-specific tweaks in only a few days' time. Instead of providing content, as it had done with Deskbook and Lessons Learned systems, the Team now simply provided the software framework and the customer became responsible for adding the information and knowledge. Actually, the CoP workspace component had been an important addition to the AFKM system as it had resulted in immediate benefits to various customers and helped to spread the word about the AFMC KM efforts. Adkins believed that continued development of CoPs might, in time, provide a central focus for the AFKM System Development Team's development efforts.

Along with this development, however, another technological challenge had arisen with the development of the AF portal. The new AF portal was to be, by decree, the de facto "single access point" for all AF information and knowledge. This raised a key question of how to design future AFKM system applications. Adkins acknowledged that his team was still heavily involved in the "technology piece" of building CoPs, but saw that the capabilities of the AF portal might eventually change that. Because the AF portal offered some "community" features, he saw the technical nature of the AFKM Team's work on CoPs possibly changing. As such, he now had to consider yet another host of issues such as how should AFKM products tie in to the AF portal? How could the AFKM Team take advantage of AF portal capabilities? Would the AFMC-centered KM system lose its identity and mission with the establishment of the AF portal? Would the AF Portal provide new collaboration tools that would conflict or supersede those developed by the team at AFMC? These questions, again, made a clear future strategy very difficult for Adkins to envision.

The AFKM Name

Another issue for consideration in AFKM strategy development involved the AFKM name. When the AFKM Team began the Deskbook and Lessons Learned initiatives, there were no other known KM programs in the AF. This situation, combined with the fact that the Lessons Learned tool was originally designed to serve the entire AF, gave cause for the Team to label the program "AF" KM instead of "AFMC" KM. As time passed, however, KM initiatives began popping up across the service and the "AF" KM label seemed suddenly inappropriate. A representative from the AF chief information officer's office, who was heading the AF-wide KM movement, had even called Adkins to insist that his program's name be changed to avoid confusion with what would become the real AF-wide KM program.

Adkins realized this was not a simple name change from "AFKM" to "AFMC KM" — it had significant implications for his organization. On the positive side, Adkins thought a name change might actually be a good thing. With other KM initiatives surfacing throughout the AF and with the advent of the AF portal, he had found that the title "AFKM" was no longer descriptive of what his Team was providing. His thoughts were that the specific AFMC KM system and products had to be identifiable, especially now that they would be "buried" behind the AF portal. He used the following example:

And so, if I was Joe Blow out there at Ogden Air Logistics Center and I open the [AF] Portal and I happen to see this link [AFKM Hub], I wouldn't click on it . . . because I don't have any idea [of what it is] unless I happened to have that wonderful briefing we gave them.

On the negative side, Adkins knew a name change wasn't that simple. In addition to generating confusion among existing customers, a name change could signal a reduction in program scope and applicability, which might ultimately impact leadership support at the highest levels and funding.

Outsourcing AFKM Strategy

Since the initial collection of programs and systems (e.g., Deskbook and Lessons Learned) had been brought under the AFKM umbrella, Adkins had lacked a coherent strategy to guide future developments. Although most of the previous work of the AFKM Team had been technology-oriented, Adkins realized that a more comprehensive KM strategy that also addressed people and cultural issues was needed. So far, most AFKM program and system development priorities had been opportunistically selected depending on funding source and visibility potential, but were not consistent with an overall objective or strategy. However, with so many issues developing that could ultimately impact AFKM's existence, Adkins realized that a strategic vision, and ultimately an implementation road map, were needed to guide future AFKM developments and to help him make "hard decisions."

Not confident that he or the existing AFKM System Development Team had the expertise or time to develop a comprehensive strategic plan and roadmap on their own, Adkins contracted to AeroCorp[2] to lead the development. Although AeroCorp contractor personnel had composed a portion of the AFKM System Development Team all along, Adkins had only recently selected them as the primary contractor due to their growing

KM expertise. To their credit, AeroCorp, with more than 5,000 employees nationwide, had successfully completed other government KM projects since 1997. In outsourcing to AeroCorp, Adkins justified his decision by saying,

We find AeroCorp provides unique benefits to the government and is the best value for the technical services required. AeroCorp rates are competitive with the other contractors reviewed; AeroCorp is a highly regarded supporter of KM at the OSD [Office of the Secretary of Defense] level; AeroCorp is the developer of the AFKM Virtual Schoolhouse; and AeroCorp has proven integration expertise. In addition, AeroCorp rated extremely high in the area of customer service and past performance.

Although the final statement of work for the AeroCorp contract reflected a number of specific deliverables (see Appendix 4) that ranged from strategic visioning to deployment plan and execution, Adkins' foremost concern was the development of the AFKM strategic vision and plan (or roadmap). These documents would be key in helping him to decide the future direction of AFKM. With a strategic vision and road map, he would have at least a starting point for decision making.

CURRENT CHALLENGES/PROBLEMS FACING THE ORGANIZATION

Randy Adkins had hoped that by outsourcing the AFKM strategy development to AeroCorp that resolution of major issues associated with the evolution of the AFKM program and system would be addressed. The statement of work outlined that it was AeroCorp's job to do the following (HQ AFMC/DRI, 2000):

1. Help AFMC management define a strategic vision for KM to support the AF acquisition community mission.
2. Integrate the AFKM Lessons Learned database, AFMC Help Center, and the Virtual Schoolhouse into a single dynamic system based on this strategic vision.
3. Provide support to these existing systems throughout the integration effort and ultimately for the integrated AFKM system.

AeroCorp's initial deliverable was to build an AFKM strategic vision and plan within 60 days. According to the statement of work, this plan should incorporate both the cultural and technical aspects of the acquisition environment. The resultant document was to include a road map of how to proceed from the current business environment to the envisioned environment (HQAFMC/DRI, 2000).

Consequences of Outsourcing KM Strategy Development

The first action taken by AeroCorp under the new contract was to conduct both a cultural and technical needs assessment "snapshot" of AFMC with respect to KM. These needs assessments were to provide the "as is" picture of AFMC's environment while providing recommendations for the "to be" vision and the necessary supporting policies and processes. Actual completion of the needs assessments went rather quickly and were presented to Adkins in early 2001. Each report included both specific, one-liner recommendations for transitioning from the "as is" state to the "to be" state, and an additional section provided an even more in-depth description of recommendations of what needed to be done to achieve the "to be" state. These assessments with the final recommendation descriptions are detailed in Appendix 5. On the whole, the assessments were comprehensive and surfaced many technical and cultural issues that had to be addressed if AFMC was to transform itself into a true knowledge-sharing organization. These final reports, however, were not what Adkins had expected the strategic vision and plan document to be. The recommendations captured the complicated nature of the current AFMC environment yet, while providing a good road map for the future, were so broad and involved that it was difficult to determine a starting point. To further compound his disappointment, Adkins also learned that AeroCorp considered completion of the assessment reports as having not only fulfilled deliverable #1, the AFKM Strategic Vision and Plan, but also deliverable #2, the AFKM Integration Recommendations Document. He was baffled.

Although Adkins had not gotten exactly what he expected from AeroCorp, the company was allowed to continue work on the remaining deliverables. Adkins hoped that the subsequent documents would make things clearer. Deliverable #3, the AFKM Integration Blueprint, which AeroCorp referred to as a KM methodology, took much longer to produce than the assessments. Delays resulted, first of all, from the turnover of two AeroCorp program managers during early 2001. The current program manager, Mike Lipka, though very knowledgeable about KM, was relatively new to AeroCorp and had to get up to speed on the AFKM project. The key delay, however, stemmed from the fact that AeroCorp had difficulty developing a concise KM methodology or "blueprint" that could address the enormity of what AFMC needed to do to develop a comprehensive KM program that would help it evolve into a true knowledge-sharing organization.

Although the initial assessment and recommendations documents had stated that a systems engineering approach would be used to design the "integration blueprint," the use of integrated definition (IDEF) process modeling methodology surprised Adkins and Lipka. Neither Adkins, nor his superiors, were familiar with this methodology. Lipka, having not been the program manager when the decision to use IDEF was made, had not seen it applied to KM before. Developed for use in systems engineering, IDEF modeling had been around for quite a few years. Its primary users had been the DoD and other large organizations. IDEF had originated with the AF's Integrated Computer Aided Manufacturing (ICAM) program in the mid 1970s, but had evolved over the past six or seven years to also address modeling enterprise and business areas. As such, it was used for modeling "as is" enterprise processes and defining information requirements for improved planning. On the whole, there were 14 separate methods being developed within the IDEF family for use in business process engineering and reengineering, software process definition and improvement, and software development and maintenance areas. It provided a multitude of viewpoints required to describe business area processes and software life-cycle processes and activities. As such, it stood that IDEF could be appropriate for modeling an enterprise approach to KM and subsequent KM systems development, but it did not appear to be a really usable methodology for the average customer. After seeing the initial draft of the high-level IDEF model (Figure 6), neither Adkins nor Lipka were satisfied. Lipka expressed his opinion thus: "I think we have too much methodology for what we need . . . I think it's [been] a little overengineered."

Figure 6. AeroCorp's proposed KM blueprint (IDEF model)

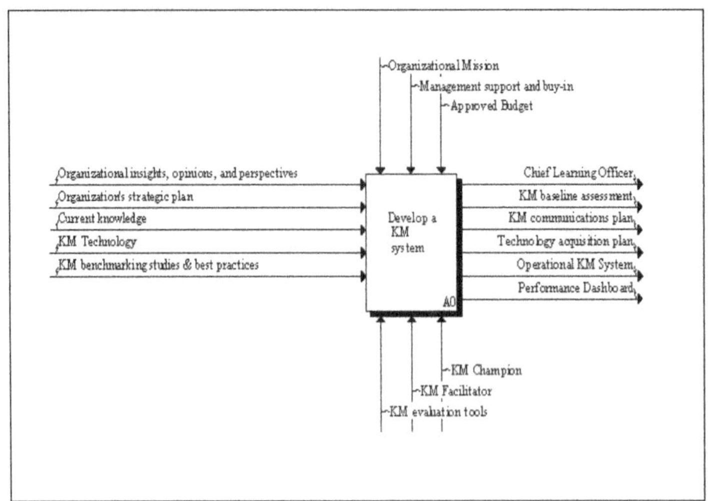

No one was more frustrated, however, than Adkins. After almost a year of working with AeroCorp and waiting patiently for a strategic vision and plan he could really use to press forward, what he had now was a cultural and technical needs assessment, some recommendations for transitioning AFMC into a knowledge-sharing organization, and a road map (or methodology) for doing so that was too unfamiliar and complicated for him or others to practically implement. And faced with the impending budget cut, it did not appear that AeroCorp would have the opportunity to make needed changes. Adkins knew, however, as the AFKM program lead he was still responsible for the strategic direction and success of the AFKM program. He was unsure exactly what to do next, but he knew the responsibility for a solution was his alone. He began to ponder the facts and options. Would he ever get a document from AeroCorp that would provide a KM strategy and vision for AFMC? Had he made a mistake in outsourcing AFKM strategy development? If not, would there be time and money for AeroCorp to prepare something that was more practical? What parts of the needs assessments and strategic plan were usable? In absence of a clear KM strategy for AFMC, what was the right direction for his AFKM Team to take? How did the AFKM effort now fit (technically and conceptually) into the evolving AF-level KM approach? Would his AFKM program and Team survive? At this point, Adkins had no good answers. The only thing he knew for sure was that there had been and would continue to be many challenges in bringing KM to AFMC, but it was he, if anyone, who still had the opportunity to make it a reality.

REFERENCES

AFKM Home Page. (2001). Information Page. Retrieved August 7, 2001, from *https://afkm.wpafb.af.mil/ASPs/Tabs/Entry_Subject.asp* [only accessible from .mil domains]

Cho, G., Jerrell, H., & Landay, W. (2000). *Program management 2000: Know the way how knowledge management can improve DoD acquisition.* Fort Belvoir: Defense Systems Management College.

HQ AFMC/DRI. (2000). *Statement of work.* Wright-Patterson AFB, OH: Air Force Knowledge Management Integration and Support.

HQ AFMC PA. (2001a). Air Force Material Command fact sheet. Retrieved October 17, 2001, from *www.afmc-pub.wpafb.af.mil/HQ-AFMC/PA/fact_sheet/afmcfact.htm*

HQ AFMC PA. (2001b). HQ AFMC/DR home page. Retrieved October 17, 2001, from *https://afkm.wpafb.af.mil/ASPs/Tabs/Entry_Subject.asp* [only accessible from .mil domains]

ENDNOTES

* The views expressed in this case study are those of the authors and do not necessarily reflect the official policy or position of the Air Force, the Department of Defense, or the U.S. Government.

1 Information for this case, except where stated otherwise, is based on personal interviews conducted in October 2001.

2 Pseudonyms have been used to protect the confidentiality of the contract organizations.

APPENDIX 1

Air Force Material Command

Mission Essential Tasks and Objectives

Tasks	Objectives
Product Support	To provide world-class products and services, delivering dominant aerospace systems and superior life-cycle management.
Information Services	To develop, acquire, integrate, implement, protect, and sustain combat-support information systems for the USAF and DoD customers.
Supply Management	To provide and deliver repairable and consumable items (right product—right place—right time—right price).
Depot Maintenance	To repair systems and spare parts to ensure readiness in peacetime and provide sustainment to combat forces in wartime.
Science and Technology	To develop, demonstrate, and transition affordable advanced technologies to achieve AF core competencies.
Test and Evaluation	To provide timely, accurate, and affordable knowledge and resources to support weapons and systems research, development, and employment.
Information Management	To provide secure, reliable, interoperable communication and information services/access anytime, anywhere, to AFMC customers, partners, and employees.
Installations and Support	To provide base support services, property management, and environmental protection at AFMC installations.
Combat Support	To provide the trained and equipped expeditionary combat support forces and capabilities to meet worldwide taskings.

(HQ AFMC PA, 2001a)

APPENDIX 2

AFKM Team and Structure

Throughout the history of the AFKM program, contractors played a key role. Although final authority was always vested in a military officer or civil service employee assigned to AFMC/DR, most programming and technology for the AFKM System came from contractors. The primary contractor for the DoD Acquisition Deskbook development had been Company A.[2] With additional projects, Company B[2] and Company C[2] joined the team. The specific responsibilities and tasks varied from year to year as projects evolved and as the contracts were renewed and renegotiated. The resulting AFKM program organization is shown in Figure 1. AeroCorp was charged with establishing the basic AFKM program by bringing together the existing AFKM Lessons Learned database, AFMC Help Center, and Virtual Schoolhouse. Most of the AFKM System Development Team's work was split between maintaining and updating existing functions and developing new applications. The majority of the new applications focused on building workspaces for CoPs. Each contractor used a number of personnel to work on projects—some personnel worked on AFKM projects exclusively while others came in and out of the projects as necessary. Prior to the 2001 budget cuts, with AeroCorp acting as the lead contractor, 41 personnel had been assigned to the AFKM Team.

Appendix 2 – Figure 1. AFKM Team structure

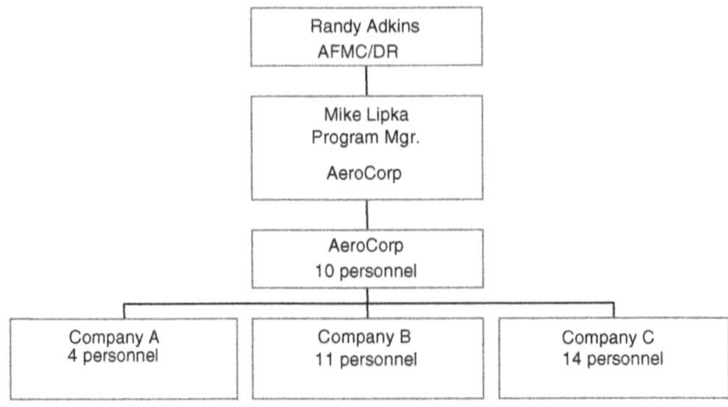

APPENDIX 3

Explanation of AFKM System Components

AFKM Hub. What is now the AFKM Hub was originally the primary Web site for the AF Lessons Learned utility. Although the Web site has evolved, the Lessons Learned are still the centerpiece of the Hub (Figure 1). Lessons Learned have been captured and categorized by subject area and provide valuable knowledge about past processes and events. The AFKM Hub also acts as a portal for all other AFKM components and, as such, it also serves as the default AFKM home page. The AFKM Hub provides a conduit to select relevant information and knowledge resources and provides an avenue for creating a knowledge-sharing organization.

Deskbook. The DoD Acquisition Deskbook (Figure 2) is an automated reference tool that provides the most current acquisition information for all DoD services and agencies. Deskbook simplifies the acquisition process by maintaining a single source of up-to-date reference material on acquisition policy and practices.

AFMC Help Center. The AFMC Help Center (Figure 3) allows AFMC customers to perform a natural language or keyword search of over 130 AFMC Web sites and selected databases. It connects AFMC customers throughout the AF and DoD with the appropriate AFMC information source or point of contact. The search engine used dynamically creates a unique results page separated into four categories:

- ranked list of related Web documents and links
- top-priority major command issues
- bulletin board discussion entries
- contact information for the AFMC command liaisons and topic area points of contact

Appendix 3 – Figure 1. AFKM Hub

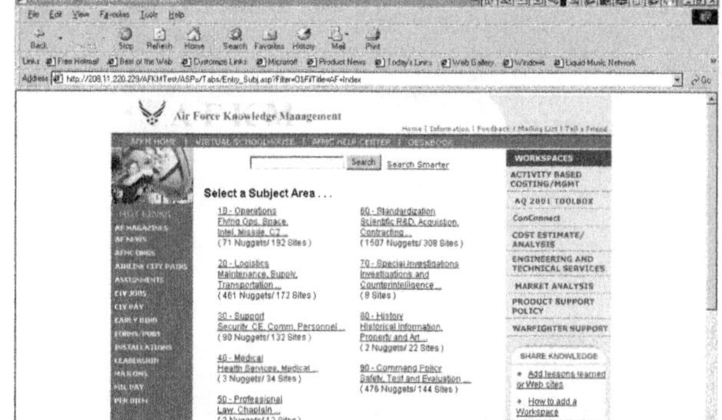

Appendix 3 – Figure 2. DoD Acquisition Deskbook

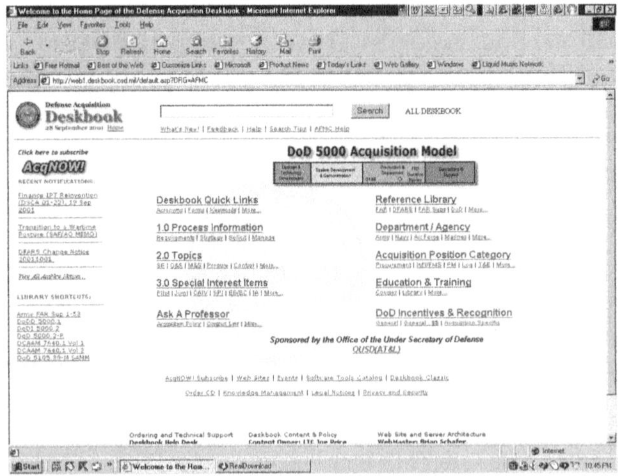

Appendix 3 – Figure 3. AFMC Help Center

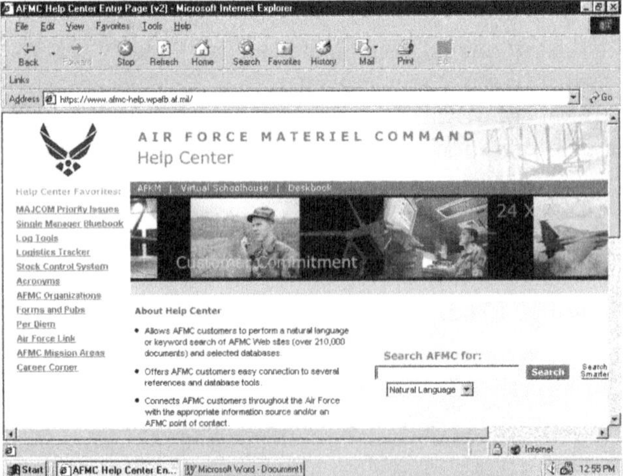

Appendix 3 – Figure 4. Virtual Schoolhouse component

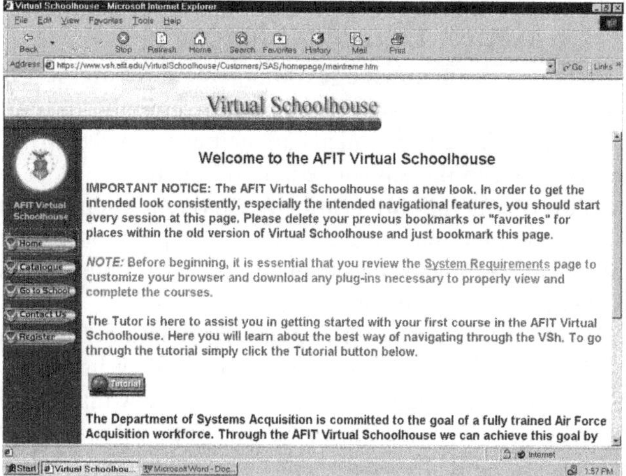

Virtual Schoolhouse. The Virtual Schoolhouse (Figure 4) is a cooperative effort between AFMC/DR and the AF Institute of Technology (AFIT). The Virtual Schoolhouse provides an integrated Web-based learning management system with over 20 online courses. Its purpose is to support the goal of a fully trained AF acquisition workforce.

CoP Workspaces. A CoP is a network of people who share a common goal. CoP workspaces are virtual environments where members of these CoPs can exchange information to complete work tasks and solve problems. Each CoP serves a specific customer set. The AFKM Hub provides workspaces (Figure 5) for a variety of CoPs.

Appendix 3 – Figure 5. CoP Workspaces

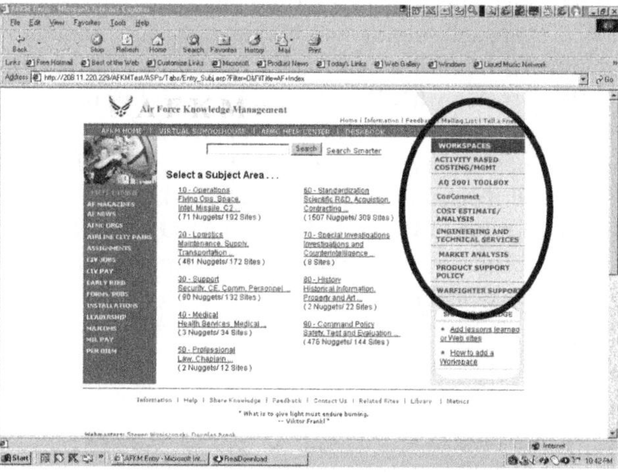

APPENDIX 4

AeroCorp's Contract Deliverables

1. **Deliverable 60 days: AF Knowledge Management Strategic Vision and Plan.** Description: A document that should incorporate both the cultural and technical aspects of the acquisition environment and include a "road map" from the current business environment to the envisioned environment.
2. **Deliverable 120 days: AFKM Integration Recommendations Document.** Description: An integration plan that should define user operational requirements with detailed cultural and technical consequences as well as time and material requirements to implement the recommendations.
3. **Deliverable: AFKM Integration Blueprint.** Description: Based on the approved integration plan, the blueprint document should show how the three existing knowledge management systems will operate in the new integrated environment.
4. **Deliverable: AFKM Integrated Products.** Description: The result of the contractor integrating the three AFKM systems using a phased approach. Each integration effort should provide a working product that can be accessed by the acquisition users in the organizational environment.
5. **Deliverable: AFKM Deployment Plan and Execution.** Description: The plan should support the deployment of the AFKM system. It should identify user support, and release change management support, including training, communications, and measurement, as well as time and material requirements.
6. **Deliverable: Ongoing AFKM Sustainment Support.** Description: Sustainment support should be provided for all AFKM elements. The contractor should provide all the functional and technical support necessary for the maintenance and upkeep of the Lessons Learned, Help Center, and Virtual Schoolhouse components.
7. **Deliverable: Contractor's Progress, Status, and Management Report.** Description: The contractor should use a management and cost-tracking system to support the AFKM effort and ensure technical and funding requirements are accomplished on time and on budget. The contractor should also maintain a continuing dialogue with the government program manager to ensure that schedule and budgetary requirements are met and potential problems are proactively addressed. The contractor will prepare and submit monthly progress and financial reports summarizing the technical accomplishments and expenditures for each task.
8. **Deliverable: Weekly/Monthly Functional Analysis Support Analysis Reports.** Description: The contractor should provide fielded system product support analysis and readiness assessments as directed by HQ AFMC/DR based upon immediate supportability concerns of the command.
9. **Deliverable: 180 Days After Receipt of Order (ARO), Market Research Decision Support Tool.** Description: The contractor should provide a Web-based decision support tool integrated within the Market Research Post Tool.

APPENDIX 5

AeroCorp Cultural and Technical Needs Assessment and Recommendations

Cultural Needs Assessment—Recommendation Descriptions

1. **Design a KM Action Plan that combines the results of the Cultural Needs Assessment with the results of the Technical Needs Assessment.** Data from both assessments will be used to design a "track to action" plan that includes:
   - Methodology and systems engineering
   - Project management procedures
   - Top business technical process needs to streamline for efficiency
2. **Create a KM communications plan with a centralized formulation strategy.** Establish a clear road map so that the big picture can be articulated to all groups; this includes leadership support of the decisions communicated. The communications plan should clearly define why a project is being done and the benefits to the employees. This should support the mission/vision of AFMC in regards to process improvement. Document the strategy and create a plan to achieve the strategy and explain how each project supports the mission/vision. Establish a clear vocabulary for communication of ideas across teams; standardization of vocabulary for communication of ideas across groups is essential. Initiate team-building/communication activities to foster relationships across the organization (dialogue, inquiry vs. advocacy). Balance being a visionary against execution of jobs.
3. **Perform an Organizational Cultural Inventory (OCI) across AFMC.** The OCI expands the point-in-time picture of the AFMC culture collected in this report to include a broader pool. The OCI pinpoints 12 specific types of behavioral norms which focus on behavioral patterns that members believe are required to accommodate the expectations of the organization. Norms are organized into three general clusters that distinguish between constructive cultures, passive/defensive cultures, and aggressive/defensive cultures. In addition to measuring shared behavioral norms, the OCI will also identify the ideal operating culture within an organization, providing an opportunity for quantitative data collection on information about the organization's culture at multiple levels, and add additional confirmation to this qualitative Cultural Needs Assessment. This cultural alignment tool will determine the cultural issues prevalent within AFMC.
4. **Develop a KM transition plan from current practices to the new KM system.** Create a plan of action identifying those items that are helping and hindering AFMC from moving toward their business direction; determine the present state of organization, the desired state, and what must occur during the transition from one to the other. This transition plan should include both internal and external changes within the organization and do the following:
   - Create or incorporate a change management plan that focuses on cultural (and technical) issues within AFMC. A great deal of disillusionment, discouragement, and resistance may need to be overcome. Include a cohesive story of

where the group is going and what it is doing. Consider projects that empower people more with authority and accountability for measurable results.

- Establish clear documentation, which defines roles, responsibilities, and boundaries within AFMC. Create a detailed corporate plan on how business is to be conducted in AFMC and with its customers.
- Establish priorities with specifics that provide needed direction to be executed effectively. Have project contacts to call as subject matter experts. Establish clear transition points of projects between groups. Require that decisions be discussed at the appropriate leadership level prior to being evaluated to upper levels of leadership.
- Identify and change business processes that need to be changed so that business can be run more effectively and efficiently.
- Provide extensive training for all aspects of developed KM protocols.

5. **Create an AFMC knowledge market.** The AFMC knowledge market concept has knowledge "buyers" (seekers of specific knowledge) and "sellers" (suppliers of specific knowledge) who negotiate to reach a mutually satisfactory price for the knowledge exchange. Knowledge "brokers" (people who know who in the organization possesses the information sought) would make connections between buyers and the sellers. Knowledge transactions occur because people expect that knowledge helps them solve problems and succeed in their work. The knowledge market design puts into perspective the sharing culture and provides a framework for formulating actionable steps for building each category within AFMC.
   In addition, the knowledge market will work more efficiently if places are created where people can meet to buy and sell knowledge. Establish "talk rooms" where researchers are expected to spend 20 to 30 minutes casually discussing each other's work. Several organizations have held "knowledge fairs" at which sellers display their expertise for others in the organization. Intranet discussion groups provide an electronic gathering place for people to share knowledge.
6. **Establish a multidisciplined AFMC KM integration team.** This team will work on organizational and KM technical and continuous improvement teams. The initial tasks assigned to the team will be to do the following:

- Organize in such a way that all AFMC interests and disciplines are represented.
- Determine clear and measurable business and technical processes.
- Identify areas where activities overlap and create a business plan which includes management and technical requirements, with metrics to measure the success or failure of the effort. The metric system will be aligned directly with the business case issues and the KM requirements such that it will access and demonstrate incremental progress being made across the AFMC organization.
- Develop a reporting mechanism for continuous improvement item tracking to keep record of items that have been successfully identified (based on data collections) and resolved. Report the findings to AFMC management. Establishment of a clearly defined measurement process will provide the momentum and sustainment of the KM program.

- Foster a workplace that lends itself toward continuous improvement versus policing or auditing of organization information. The ideal workplace would be where peoples' growth and participation occur within the framework of open teamwork, collaboration, and open flow of new ideas. This way, a link exists between the bottom and top of the organization. Address leadership styles and determine which leadership style is appropriate for which situation (situational leadership).

7. **Create a KM Executive Board to oversee KM implementation activities.** The KM Executive Board will include community-wide members whose major role is to define the AFMC KM requirements. Create a KM Executive Board Charter. Start a focused pilot (business case development, lessons learned deployment, strategy, etc.). AFMC leadership needs to know and participate on the Board, chaired by the Deputy AFMC Commander. The AFMC Chief Learning Officer (CLO) should serve as the liaison between the integration team and the KM Executive Board. The responsibilities of the Board should include:

   Endorsing mechanisms for transferring knowledge within the organization, including creating a knowledge map, providing mentoring programs, encouraging job transfers, and holding knowledge fairs.

   7A. Approving the use of Rapid Improvement Teams (RITs) to work complex issues that the community is either unable to agree on a remedy or for which attempted remedies have not worked. The integration team should recommend RIT campaigns as a part of its activities. The CLO would serve as the RIT sponsor and bring RIT recommendations to the KM Executive Board for approval.

8. **Launch a reshaping mission by the AFMC Commander that links the KM strategy to the AFMC Acquisition and Sustainment Strategic Vision and Plan.** The architecture for the KM capability must be explicitly linked to the business processes that are required to implement the AFMC KM Strategic Plan. Without this linkage, one of these two planning elements becomes irrelevant as a guide for achieving AFMC's long-term interests. Establish a task force consisting of representatives from SAF/AQ, AFMC, and each center that will report to the Executive Board. The task force would rely on the collective ideas of many people throughout the AF community, using a number of approaches to obtain input from industry, academia, other federal agencies, members of the acquisition workforce, and employee unions. The task force deliverable should outline initiatives to make it easier and more efficient to manage, reshape the acquisition workforce, and advance the current AFMC program to share best practices within the AFMC acquisition workforce. By documenting the deficiencies in the availability of core knowledge; the effectiveness of knowledge capture, storage, and retrieval systems; and the adequacy of personnel skills and attitudes, AFMC will be able to establish tailored remedies that will provide the most efficient knowledge management capability to its members, partners, and customers. The task force should work in concert with the AFMC internal KM team's objectives.

9. **Establish a rewards and incentive policy for sharing knowledge.** To ensure that such people will share their expertise, AFMC management must make sharing more lucrative than hoarding knowledge. To establish value, evaluation criteria should be established, written, and eventually incorporated in the Human Resources evaluation process so as to provide direct evidence of AFMC employees being rewarded for sharing knowledge. The reward policies should be valuable, such as substantial monetary awards, high recognition, salary increases, or promotions. Such incentives promote a shift in behavior toward nurturing a sharing culture.

Technical Needs Assessment: Recommendation Descriptions

1. **Develop a technology evaluation and approval mechanism that explicitly links requirements for new information technology to process improvements that impact mission accomplishment and customer satisfaction.** As organizations have begun to recognize the value of KM to their future well-being, technology providers have been scrambling to recast their data warehousing, intranet, document management, workflow, and so forth, products and the ultimate KM solution. All of these providers fall short in that KM solutions are not "one size fits all" but, rather, organization specific. Without a business strategy, there is no rational basis to evaluate the various technology solutions and craft a KM toolkit that delivers value to the organization and its customers. Organizational evaluation, then, needs to start with an assessment of the mission and business strategy. Value chain activities (research, develop, test, acquire, deliver, and support) should be used as the first level of indenture for evaluating AFMC's KM system.
2. **Review AFMC Web sites and identify improvements to increase their effectiveness in making knowledge available to the users.** When Web technology was new and viewed as a supplement to accomplishing work, efficiency did not seem very important. Web engineers were more concerned with the eye appeal and user friendliness of the site than whether it provided valuable information. Users readily accepted the fact that they would be directed through several Web sites before accessing any meaningful information. Today, however, the Web is becoming a key work tool for many of AFMC's personnel. For this reason, reduction in search and retrieval time and one-click access to information is no longer an option but a necessity. All AFMC Web sites should be reviewed for their ability to provide value-added knowledge to the workforce.
3. **Establish a working group to reduce redundancy in transactional databases.** Much of the KM literature is focused on collaboration and the extraction of tacit knowledge. However, the foundation of an organization's knowledge and the source of many of its business metrics are found in its rather mundane workhorse transactional data systems. Several of the interviewees for this assessment commented on their inability to trust the data without independent validation. They reported that the same data element could be found in multiple sources with different values. Technology in and of itself cannot fix this problem, but enforcing the rules of good data management can go a long way to establishing trust in the data. Among these rules is assigning responsibility for ensuring the validity of each data element to the maximum possible extent. Each AFMC CoP should form

a working group comprised of its database managers to address issues of data accuracy, replication transparency, and report validity.

4. **Establish a task force to improve the capture of tacit knowledge from CoP designated experts.** Each CoP has its own set of expert and tacit knowledge that should be captured and put in the organization's knowledge repositories. The pervasive dilemma is that expert knowledge is the most difficult to obtain because it is often ill-defined (knowledge holders do not know what they should be contributing) and difficult to provide (experts are usually too busy to provide this knowledge). Every CoP has its novices, apprentices, masters, and gurus. Each of these experience levels has an expectation for the knowledge that is required to perform work. An effective KM system should capture knowledge from the top of the experience pyramid and pass that knowledge down and across the CoP. Learning tools, such as the Virtual Schoolhouse, could provide training to knowledge workers on how to determine what constitutes value-added knowledge. The second important aspect of this recommendation is how to influence the collection of this kind of subjective knowledge. It is important that this not be viewed as an additional duty but as a routine and fundamental part of the job. Performance metrics should include contributions to the knowledge base. Technical equipment (e.g., electronic notes and journals) or personal whiteboards may make it easier to contribute.
5. **Develop a plan for reducing restricted access to data and data repositories.** An effective KM system is open to all participants. Though we are all familiar with the phrase "knowledge is power," many organizations have cultures that treat knowledge as political capital—something to be hoarded and shared only when it is deemed advantageous. If KM is to flourish, that cultural value needs to change from "having knowledge" to "sharing knowledge." Therefore, AFMC should review internally imposed firewalls and password protections to determine those that are needed for security or sensitive data reasons. AFMC should also consider using software that reduces the need for blanket restrictions.
6. **Create a metadata-tagging plan to improve AFMC's ability to search and retrieve stored knowledge.** AFMC currently uses user profile metadata to improve ease of access to Web-enabled search engines. However, user profiles are limited if the desired data files are not also tagged. It is relatively easy to issue a policy that requires all new data files to be appropriately marked. The real question is, "How much of the legacy data can AFMC afford to retroactively tag?" This raises the economic questions of return on investment. AFMC should create a plan that provides the necessary guidelines for tagging data files.
7. **Require each AFMC CoP to develop a collaboration plan.** Knowledge-based activities related to innovation and responsiveness are highly collaborative. The attention that AFMC pays to collaboration can be attributed to its role in leveraging the expertise that is often distributed throughout the organization. Frequently, a CoP—the epitome of a collaborative body—cuts across formal organizational boundaries. A CoP often extends across departments and into other organizations, including customers, allies, partners, and sometimes competitors. The range of collaboration-enabling technology can present a daunting task to the people responsible for selecting the best solution for their organizations. Additionally,

collaboration needs might vary from one CoP to another. AFMC should require each of its formally recognized CoPs to develop a collaboration plan that describes how that community intends to foster collaborative activity and the recommended technology to enable that collaboration.

Section IV

Knowledge Management in Support of Projects

Chapter VIII

Knowledge Management in a Project Climate

Elayne Coakes, University of Westminster, UK

Anton Bradburn, University of Westminster, UK

Cathy Blake, Taylor Woodrow, UK

EXECUTIVE SUMMARY

This case study concerns the company Taylor Woodrow, which is a housing, property, and construction business operating internationally in situations where frontline operations are characterised by project management. Construction projects can sometimes carry substantial risk, and this case examines the role of knowledge management at Taylor Woodrow in minimising the probability of mischance by promoting best practice and lessons learned. The case shows how best practice can be developed through knowledge-sharing facilitated by networks of relationships. Some relationships are external — between the company, its partners, suppliers, and customers. Other relationships are internal — between frontline managers on construction sites and headquarters' staff. The case study indicates how knowledge is collated and distributed for the mutual benefit of all stakeholders.

BACKGROUND

The UK construction industry contributes about 10% of the UK's gross domestic product (GDP) and employed some 1.4 million people in 2001-2002 (DTI, 2002). Construction in the UK is a fragmented trade where there is constant pressure from clients for improvement and innovation in performance. Such is this pressure that the DTI (Department of Trade and Industry, the Government body responsible in the UK) invested £16.5 million in 2002 on a programme of construction-related innovation and research to develop and disseminate information and knowledge.

Taylor Woodrow: General Company Background

Taylor Woodrow is an international housing and development company employing over 7,000 people worldwide. Its primary business is house building, which accounts for more than 95% of its operating profit. The company is the second largest UK-based house builder, delivering 10,000 new homes in the UK, along with around 3,800 new homes in North America, Spain, and Gibraltar each year. The company's UK house-building operation trades mainly under the Bryant Homes brand. In Canada, homes are marketed as Monarch, and in the United States and Spain, directly under the Taylor Woodrow brand.

In the UK, the company currently trades from a network of 11 regional offices, incorporating a central office based in the West Midlands and the construction headquarters in Watford. In addition to housing and commercial property developments, Taylor Woodrow also undertakes Private Finance Initiative (PFI) projects under the UK Government's Private Finance Initiative, mainly in healthcare. The company also undertakes facilities management and specialist engineering consultancy through Taylor Woodrow Construction. This unique skill base of integrated housing, property, and construction expertise ensures that Taylor Woodrow is particularly well equipped to tackle more complex developments, often on brownfield sites in high-profile city centre locations, and up to 30% of the company's construction activity is now in-house support to deliver large and mixed-use housing and commercial projects for the company.

Taylor Woodrow's core market is the UK with 71% of revenue in 2002 (*http://uk.biz.yahoo.com/*, 2003). The remainder of revenue comes from North America (25%), and the rest of the world (mainly Spain and Gibraltar) supplies the remaining 4%. In 2003, turnover was up 7% and profit before tax was up 20% on the previous year (Interim Results Statement, June 30, 2003, available on Web site).

According to the company's Web site (http://www.taylorwoodrow.com/), Taylor Woodrow's vision is to be "the leading developer of living and working environments in the UK and other chosen markets."

The company Web site also details full information about the company's

1. stated culture;
2. principles;
3. objectives;
4. responsibility (to shareholders, customers, people, those with whom they do business, and society);
5. business integrity;
6. health, safety, and environment;
7. community (they seek to be responsible corporate citizens);
8. political activities (they do not support political parties or policies in any form);
9. competition (they support free enterprise);
10. communication (open); and

11. corporate governance (detailing the directors, the board, and other committees, how internal control is carried out, investor relations, and corporate social responsibility policy).

SETTING THE STAGE

Knowledge management began in Taylor Woodrow in 2000 and centred on technical knowledge managed by a team based at the Technology Centre in Leighton Buzzard, UK. The remit of the knowledge manager at Taylor Woodrow was to manage knowledge on a groupwide basis. The main reason that knowledge management was introduced related to the board recognising that Taylor Woodrow needed a systematic process to better manage its substantial technical knowledge base. Hence improving the dissemination of best practice and lessons learned, thus reducing technical risks on its projects. So the knowledge management initiative was an approach to sharing technical excellence and best practice, and to demonstrate added value and business differential to their clients. It was able to demonstrate reduced costs and successful learning on projects to both new and existing clients, which helped maintain client relationships and encouraged repeat business. In 2001-2002 its main emphasis was on defect reduction and producing better buildings for clients, thus KM has been integrated into its construction project processes to add value from which both customers and shareholders benefit.

CASE DESCRIPTION

KM, according to Taylor Woodrow's KM manager "is primarily about people and how they behave and how they solve problems." In order to ensure the initiative is well supported, she felt that one needs to persuade the senior management initially as they are the real influencers of construction project outcomes. The KM process incorporates managers to reduce risks early in the construction process and consider the outcomes of actions, which were taken in previous projects. Enthusiasm for the initiative has come from board level and this is essential to gain support from operational (frontline) managers.

A number of forums have been set up in Taylor Woodrow for design managers, project managers, graduates, and commercial managers, which look at improving processes and sharing knowledge. It would seem that the most important motivator in Taylor Woodrow for participation in these forums and to undertake KM was not only kudos but being able to make improvements to the business. The forums were headed up by senior managers, and to be seen to be actively participating and encouraging improvements at the forums was good for professional development for some participants.

So far, the forums have primarily concentrated on sharing best practice and the Taylor Woodrow KM manager hopes that in the future more project managers will feel able to talk about projects where processes went wrong, how they have learned from the experience, and how they can do better next time. To start the process, Taylor Woodrow has begun to publish a Top Tips bulletin, which anonymises the projects and issues. This particular initiative is similar to a Government scheme, which is called Movement for Innovation, where best practice on construction projects will be captured and disseminated across the industry.

Whilst the KM manager sees herself as a facilitator within the company, Taylor Woodrow has developed and implemented an IT-enabled infostructure called Tayweb for the distribution of organizational knowledge. There are seven main areas that Tayweb supports. These are as follows:

1. One Company – company information;
2. News;
3. People – HR and training;
4. The Way We Work – processes;
5. Knowledge Share;
6. Central Services;
7. Office Zone – information on regional offices.

The Knowledge Share portal of Tayweb can usefully be modelled in terms of a subway metaphor as shown in Figure 1.

This subway operates continuously beneath Taylor Woodrow's business operations supporting the enterprise and its business strategies. In this activity, it is analogous to a computer program constantly running in the background behind other applications. The model, however, only represents the KM system in a single plane, which belies its complexity as it functions in a multidimensional space having a form more like a bowl of spaghetti (Kolind, 1996). The company utilised an eight-step knowledge transfer model (O'Dell, Greyson, & Essaides, 1998) in order to inform the design of its KM system. This involved "focusing on *creating*, *identifying*, *collecting* and *organizing*

Figure 1. Taylor Woodrow's IT-enabled KM system – Tayweb

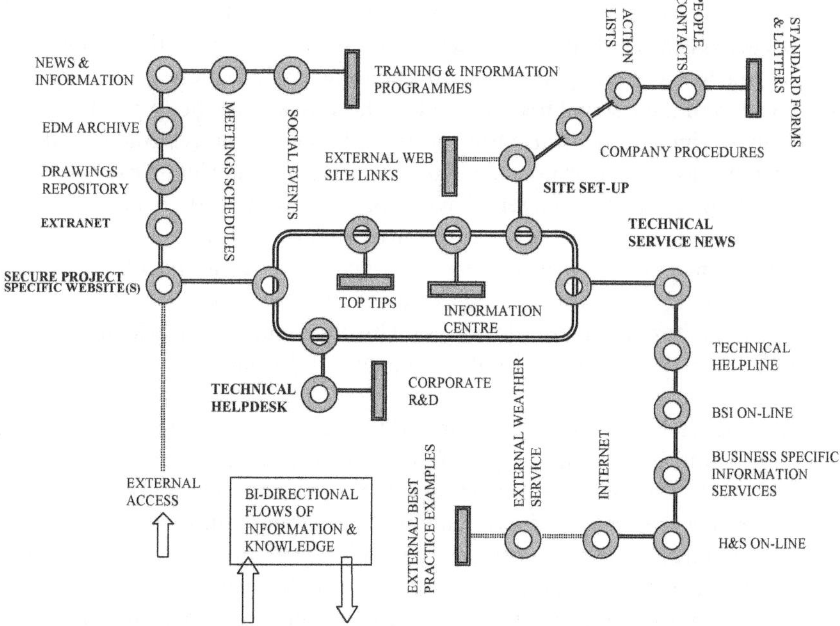

best practices and internal knowledge, in order to understand what [organizations] know and where [the knowledge] is. The process must explicitly address *sharing* and *understanding* of those practices by motivated recipients. Finally, the process involves helping the recipients *adapt* and *apply* those practices to new situations, to create new 'knowledge' and put it into action" (O'Dell et al., 1998).

Tayweb is Taylor Woodrow's intranet, which carries users to any one of seven portals as detailed previously. *Technical Service News* is an electronic, interactive publication summarising the latest technical innovations, legislation, and best practice and is available in the Knowledge Share portal on Tayweb. This provides access to Taylor Woodrow's in-house technical helpline, to online British standards, construction information, online health and safety standards, and provides links to external Web sites for weather information and industry best-practice examples via the Internet. It is also e-mailed on a monthly basis to technical staff.

The Technical Help Desk (THD) is a facility through which the company's Technology Centre offers its specialist technical expertise. Frequent analyses of inquiries to the THD are used to generate Top Tips (technical guidelines), which demonstrate what lessons have been learnt and what innovations have been introduced, both of which constitute new organizational knowledge. In addition, the queries to the THD will also generate seminars and workshops for training purposes (note here that engineers and surveyors who are members of professional bodies such as the Institute of Building and Civil Engineering, or the Institute of Chartered Surveyors, are required by their professional bodies to do a certain number of continual professional development hours per year in order to maintain their qualification).

An important part of the tendering process for projects includes risk assessment and the KM system is a vital source of both technical and historical data that project managers need to access to discover what has been done in the past, and what are the current best practices. In addition, as the managers on construction project sites have laptops issued and the project managers for homes building operate from a regional office with computer access, they will also have access to these technical guidelines. Site general foreman tend not to have computers and so phone for information, their knowledge requirement is part of their social network — they need to know who to phone for help.

Site Setup is primarily an information portal and is an interactive guidance tool the purpose of which is to assist a project manager in setting up a new construction site. At this one-stop shop, project managers have links to external Web sites for other organizations such as the police service, the fire brigade, and the local authority. In addition to the company's own procedures, the site provides a checklist of actions required for sites being newly established as well as a yellow pages of people contacts. There is also a repository of standard forms and business stationery. The intranet also contains organizational structures, what the company's departments do, project profiles, and so forth.

Although Figure 1 shows only one portal through which a secure Web site can be accessed, there could be several. Taylor Woodrow establishes these extranets on a project-specific basis for blue-chip clients such as airports and supermarkets. These are vortals, collaborative project Web sites bounding virtual communities of practice, which are live for the duration of each contract. These vortals confer all the advantages of electronic document management repositories but with additional benefits deriving from Internet access. Each community member has available a directory of teams, a repository of drawings in two and three dimensions continually updated, a document archive including photographs of work in progress, news and information, schedules of meetings, programmes of induction and training, and even listings of social events.

Finally, Tayweb's Knowledge Share portal features a centralised interactive facility, which is available to Taylor Woodrow's entire workforce providing an extensive range of library information services. Here, there are online services such as British standards, health and safety information, and construction information. It also enables users to access a technical library and to order documents.

The perceived returns by Taylor Woodrow from its investment in KM are primarily in terms of the use of best practice and lessons learnt to improve the quality and reduce the defects of their product. In the construction industry, defects can be very costly both in monetary terms and client relationships. Thus KM in this company supports quality management. Measures are now in place for quantifying the return on investment for Taylor Woodrow's KM system and they are being developed to demonstrate added value in monetary terms. The benefits of qualitative outcomes and some assessments of cost savings are collated in Table 1.

Table 1. Returns from knowledge management at Taylor Woodrow

	Technical News Service	Technical Helpdesk	Top Tips	Site Set-Up News	Secure Project Web Sites	Information Centre
Increased Efficiency Of Information Management	Reduction in time spent by senior managers searching for information			Project managers spend less time implementing site set-up procedures	Faster access to information and quicker response times	Offers Taylor Woodrow fast access to knowledge
Permanent Global Availability	24/7 access	24/7 access	24/7 access	24/7 access	Instant global access anytime	24/7 access
Administrative Cost Reduction	Reductions in paperwork	Reductions in paperwork	Reductions in paperwork	Reductions in paperwork	Reduces routine administration	Reductions in paperwork
Access & Response Time Reductions					Faster access to information and quicker response times	
Dissemination Leadtime Reduction	Proactively keeping managers informed of the latest innovations			More time available to concentrate on value added activities		
On-Site Productivity Improvement	Enabling managers to make better informed decisions			Project managers spend less time implementing site set-up procedures		
Savings - examples		1. Investigation of tar macadam defects saves £60,000; 2. Cavity wall ties save £14,000 in stone façade fixture; 3. Design life technology applied to a flat inverted roof saves client £10,800; 4. Re-designed stainless steel wind posts save £20,000.		More time available to concentrate on value added activities	Relatively inexpensive to establish	Enables Taylor Woodrow to work more efficiently

CONCLUSIONS

Over the period we have been studying Taylor Woodrow, the organization has become more aware of the value KM has been able to add to the organization. Increasingly, project staff and management have seen the benefits of communicating their innovations to others in the organization and lessons learnt are being captured in an increasingly systematic way. Taylor Woodrow is able to demonstrate conclusively to its clients that it is a learning organization. KM has a very high significance for the board, which provides specific funding for its development and dissemination.

DISCUSSION

Construction projects embody risk. The larger the project the higher the potential cost penalties. How can risk of this nature be mitigated? Obviously, insuring against risk is one course, but this generates additional costs, as a third party — an insurance company — requires compensation for assuming the construction company's risk. Another way of insuring against risk by reducing the probability of mischance is to leverage knowledge assets within the business.

How then to capture what individuals know and then to distribute this knowledge so that it can be shared throughout an organization? The willingness of individuals to articulate knowledge gained through involvement in work processes may depend on the organization's prevailing cultural paradigm. Some organizational cultures may be resistant to knowledge sharing — others may facilitate it. Sometimes knowledge transfer can be encouraged by incentivising staff in some way. Taylor Woodrow's approach seems to be driven primarily by the self-esteem generated from peer recognition. The company's culture seems to be receptive to KM and has enabled it to become embedded in the organizational fabric.

The importance of ICTs needs to be recognised, but these technologies are only enablers. They are not the key drivers. The critical driver in this instance may be seen as social capital, which comprises sets of relationships and networks underpinning knowledge sharing. Out of knowledge sharing comes learning, and learning at an organizational level delivers a range of business benefits in addition to ensuring that potentially costly errors are not repeated. Some of the Tayweb links signify the importance of these relationships in partnering and collaborations of various kinds not only through the intranet, but also through the various project-specific extranets.

REFERENCES

Bradburn, A., Coakes, E., & Sugden, G. (2002). Searching for linkages between knowledge management, learning organization and organizational culture within large service enterprises in the United Kingdom: What KM practitioners say. In M. Khosrow-Pour (Ed.), *Issues and trends of information technology management in contemporary organizations, IRMA 2002,* Seattle, May, vol. 2 (pp. 928-930). Hershey, PA: Idea Group Publishing.

Department of Trade and Industry (DTI). (2002). *Construction statistics annual 2002 edition.* London: The Stationery Office.

Kolind, L. (1996). The revolution at Oticon: Creating a spaghetti organization. *Research Technology Management, 39*(5), 54.

O'Dell, C., Greyson, C.J., & Essaides, W. (1998). *If only we knew what we know.* New York: Free Press.

Additional Recommended Reading

Kazi, A.S. (2004). *Knowledge management in the construction industry: A socio-technical perspective.* Hershey, PA: Idea Group.

Chapter IX

Where Knowledge Management Resides within Project Management

Jill Owen, Monash University, Australia

Frada Burstein, Monash University, Australia

EXECUTIVE SUMMARY

This chapter explores how an engineering consulting company creates, manages, and reuses knowledge within its projects. It argues that the informal transfer and reuse of knowledge plays a more crucial role than formal knowledge in providing the greatest benefit to the organization. The culture of the organization encourages a reliance on networks (both formal and informal) for the exchange of tacit knowledge, rather than utilizing explicit knowledge. This case study highlights the importance of understanding the drivers of knowledge transfer and reuse in projects. This will provide researchers with an insight into how knowledge management integrates with project management.

INTRODUCTION

To sustain their competitive edge, businesses are continually searching for ways to differentiate themselves from their competitors. One method of achieving this is for an organization to develop a knowledge management strategy. A knowledge management strategy articulates how the organization creates, values, preserves, and transfers knowledge critical to its operations. The development of an effective knowledge management strategy is important for project management organizations. Crucial factors in achieving these objectives are to manage and more effectively apply and reuse knowledge gained throughout the project life cycle. If useful information is identified, assimilated, and retained within the organization, it represents intellectual capital that can be reused on other projects, reducing the time staff spend recreating what has already been learned. The reuse of knowledge can assist an organization in not reinventing the wheel and ensuring that past mistakes are not repeated. Effective project management is a key enabler for business success. However, where corporate knowledge is ineffectively managed during the project life cycle, valuable intellectual capital is lost, causing rework and lost opportunities.

As a global engineering project management consulting firm Engineering Consulting XYZ consults on projects to organizations worldwide, these projects can potentially reuse knowledge from earlier projects.

The purpose of this case study is to explore how project team members at Engineering Consulting XYZ acquire and reuse knowledge. The chapter analyzes and describes how project staff capture, transfer, and reuse knowledge. The findings are positioned within the Project Management Body of Knowledge's (PMBOK) methodology, the de facto global standard for project management methodology (Project Management Institute, 2000). The case study determines the relative importance and use of tacit, implicit, and explicit knowledge in managing projects.

At the beginning of the research, there was an expectation that the majority of knowledge was obtained via formal means and would provide the most benefit to the organization. However the empirical data suggests that the informal transfer and reuse of knowledge played a more crucial role and provided greater benefit to Engineering Consulting XYZ. The culture of Engineering Consulting XYZ encourages collective learning and sharing.

The chapter initially provides a background to how knowledge management integrates with project management, grounded in relevant literature. The next section looks at how Engineering Consulting XYZ acquires and reuses knowledge on projects, followed by current challenges facing the organization.

BACKGROUND

Project management companies continually compete for business against competitors. The challenge for these companies is to ensure that they deliver their projects faster and more effectively than their competitors. To achieve this, organizations can utilize knowledge gained from earlier projects, or project phases — that is, not reinvent the wheel. Knowledge gained from earlier projects or project phases can be obtained via explicit or tacit means.

Importance of Learning

To succeed competitively and to achieve their business strategies and goals, organizations need to gain knowledge of both the internal and external worlds. An effective knowledge management strategy will help an organization achieve these ends. Stata (1989) suggested that to maintain a competitive advantage, organizations need to learn and obtain knowledge faster than their competitors. Learning allows an organization to respond to changes in the business environment (Baldwin, Danielson, &

Wiggenhorn, 1997). A knowledge management strategy is developed by the organization for improving the way it develops, stores, and uses its corporate knowledge. Both tacit and explicit knowledge are important in the creation and reuse of knowledge. Organizational memory forms the basis of intellectual capital that is held in an organization. Intellectual capital is the knowledge and capability to develop that knowledge in an organization (Nahapiet & Ghoshal, 1998).

If an organization is to continually change, it needs to evolve and learn continuously. Kim (1993) defines learning as the acquiring of skills (know how) and "the ability to articulate a conceptual understanding of an experience" (p. 38). Learning is a process of continual improvement and innovation (Baldwin, Danielson, & Wiggenhorn, 1997). Senge (2002) describes a "learning organization" as one "where people continually expand their capacity to create the results they truly desire, where new and expansive patterns of thinking are nurtured, where collective aspiration is set free, and where people are continually learning to see the whole together" (p. 3).

For a learning organization to continually learn and develop, organizational learning needs to occur. Organizational learning is the capacity or process within an organization to maintain or improve performance based on experience (Nevis, DiBella, & Gould, 1995).

For an organization to learn, knowledge must be created, shared, and reused (Arygris & Schon, 1978). The learning process has identifiable stages: knowledge acquisition, knowledge sharing, and knowledge utilization (Nevis, DiBella, & Gould, 1995).

Arygris and Schon (1978) define organizational knowledge as knowledge about the organization that can be held in individual's heads, files, physical objects, and embedded in cultures and procedures. McElroy (2003) extends this with his concept of organizational knowledge production — at an organizational level, knowledge is created by individuals and groups building on existing knowledge and creating new knowledge.

Schneider (2002) argues that the new or emerging model of an organization is where organizations are characterized by fuzzy organizational boundaries, flattened hierarchies, and work relationships sometimes brought about by contracts (alliances and contingent workers). Knowledge is predominantly created and used across social networks. It could be argued that knowledge creation and sharing at the organizational level relies on a combination of explicit knowledge and social networks.

Project management organizations are a natural arena for knowledge management as project management staff continually interact with and build on both explicit and tacit knowledge as they move between different projects and phases of a project.

In a project management organization, learning is important as it helps project managers deliver not just one but a succession of successful projects, and to develop the right sorts of capabilities, that is, the project management process, the product development process, and the knowledge management process (Kotnour, 1999). Learning within and between projects is required for this. Organizational learning in the project management environment involves both intra- and interproject learning. Intraproject learning occurs within a project at all phases of the project. Interproject learning is applying knowledge gained from previous projects so that it is reused and new knowledge is created (Kotnour & Hjelm, 2002). Knowledge needs to be developed within a project, where it is used and tested, before it can be transferred to other projects.

Projects can have a variety of intra- and interorganizational relationships, especially long-term projects. The challenge within these types of projects is to look at the process for the capture and reuse of knowledge in future projects (or phases of the same project) and to ascertain how intra- and interproject learning occur (McLoughlin, Alderman, Ivory, Thwaites, & Vaughan, 2000).

Learning within a project provides an ongoing store of data, information, and knowledge (Kotnour, 2000). Knowledge can also be transferred between projects (Kotnour, 2000). At a project level, knowledge is created by individuals and groups building on existing knowledge and creating new knowledge (adapting McElroy's [2003] definition of knowledge production at an organizational level).

Definition of a Project

Project Management Institute (2000) in PMBOK defines a project as "a temporary endeavour undertaken to create a unique product or service. Temporary means that every project has a definite beginning and a definite end. Unique means that the product or services is different in some distinguishing way from all other products or services" (p. 4).

For a project management organization to be competitive, project managers need to retain and build knowledge and improve project performance (Cooper, Lyneis, & Bryant, 2000).

Explicit, Implicit, and Tacit Knowledge

Explicit, implicit, and tacit knowledge help to ensure project success. Tacit knowledge is stored in a person's head and cannot be readily expressed in words, while explicit knowledge is knowledge that is expressed tangibly and can potentially be stored in databases or documents (Bollinger & Smith, 2001). Implicit knowledge is knowledge in a person's head that could be coded and stored in databases or documents (Nickols 2000). Tacit and implicit knowledge held within the corporate structure and contexts (e.g., as described by Nelson & Winter, 1982) and from individuals and explicit knowledge together provide a complete picture of the project. Tacit knowledge exists in the corporate structure (in the form of contexts and routines [Nelson & Winter, 1982; Von Krogh & Roos, 1995]) and implicitly and tacitly in members of the organization. Individuals also produce and consume explicit knowledge existing within the organization or from its environment. Sharing of knowledge among multiple individuals with different backgrounds is a critical step in project knowledge creation and reuse. Tacit knowledge based on previous experiences in a similar context is important to project success, as is the transfer of explicit knowledge (Koskinen, 2000). Knowledge can be captured and transferred tacitly within the organization via social networks, while implicit knowledge can potentially be captured and coded.

Knowledge Transfer and Reuse

Knowledge that is gained in a project needs to be transferred to an organization's memory for reuse on other projects; the challenge is to capture and index this knowledge for retrieval while it is available, as project teams are temporary (Damm & Schindler, 2002).

Dixon (2000) identifies five different types of knowledge transfer or reuse: serial transfer, near transfer, far transfer, strategic transfer, and expert transfer.

Project completion is an important phase of the project life cycle in capturing knowledge and preparing it for transfer to other projects. Postimplementation reviews/ lessons learned can either occur via the project team members or an independent reviewer. Lessons learned provide a full description of the project with examples that can be used on other projects. In some instances, lessons learned only focus on the success of the project (Disterer, 2002). There is a need to focus on both the positive and negative lessons to ensure that successes are identified and publicized and mistakes not repeated. At NASA, to ensure that lessons learned get to the right people, they are "pushed" out to people who have similar profiles and can benefit from the lessons (Liebowitz, 2002). The challenge is to ensure that knowledge is captured without taking project team members away from their day-to-day tasks. For lessons learned to be effective (both positive and negative), they need to be indexed or searchable for easy retrieval of knowledge for future projects or project phases.

The reason for knowledge reuse failures can be that knowledge capturing processes are too informal, are not incorporated into the organization's processes, or are not supported by the structure of the organization (Komi-Sirvio, Mantyniemi, & Sepannen, 2002).

The Organization Used in the Case Study

Engineering Consulting is a multidisciplinary global engineering consulting company operating across five different business units: buildings and property, heavy industry, resources environmental, and infrastructure. They are a global, internationally recognized leader in the marketplace. Engineering Consulting XYZ is employee owned and has grown organically and via strategic mergers with organizations with similar cultures and values. Its **mission** is "to focus on valued client relationships to achieve remarkable success for them. The firm has a commitment to **service**, **quality**, and high standards of safety and business **ethics**."

Management of Engineering Consulting XYZ follows a global management structure. The management structure reflects the regional, business, and functional unit structure. Engineering Consulting XYZ employs a wide range of professionals, including architects, engineers, project managers, scientists, economists, and planners servicing a wide range of clients and market sectors.

A key strategy for Engineering Consulting XYZ for the next three to four years is to invest time in the future of the business. This strategy looks at a number of measures where time invested today will secure the long-term future for the company. Knowledge management is highlighted as a key area in which time should be invested on an ongoing basis. To assist in achieving these strategies, there is most likely a reliance on knowledge —explicit, tacit, and implicit.

Engineering Consulting XYZ has recognized the importance of knowledge management within its organization by appointing a knowledge manager and creating an environment that fosters knowledge sharing. The knowledge management strategy is people-centric or personalized rather than systems driven.

In support of its strategy, Engineering Consulting XYZ is pursuing the following:

- **Communities of Practice:** to try and recreate the informal networks in a slightly more formal way across regions.
- **A Human Yellow Pages:** to help identify and contact the right person when faced with a problem.

- **Lessons Learned:** to capture lessons learned through the Communities of Practice (focused by discipline) and through interviews for larger more generic project management-type projects.
- **A Knowledge Management System:** with access to all documents/drawings at a global level.

SETTING THE STAGE

As a global company, Engineering Consulting XYZ utilizes resources globally for certain projects. There are approximately 15,000 projects on Engineering Consulting XYZ's books at any one time ranging in size from $2,000 to $50 million per annum. Engineering Consulting XYZ has achieved yearly revenue in excess of $380 million.

The culture at Engineering Consulting XYZ is open and encourages everyone to achieve their full potential. The culture was developed by the founders of the company and has evolved with extensive staff consultation. Staff members are encouraged to network and share information within this culture.

- "Our culture is based around personal values of competitiveness and challenge, drive and motivation, high professional standards, controlled risk taking, steady wealth creation, and being good citizens through a demonstration of social and environmental responsibility in what we do.
- Our management style is one of openness, support for colleagues, focussing on success through sharing of strategic business information and no game playing.
- Our management approach is adaptive to change and built on exceptional service delivery and adding value.
- Our people philosophy is based on participative employee development to achieve each individual's potential.
- Our ownership structure is one of broad based sharing of equity, targeting continuity of the practice and equitable ownership transfer.
- Our commitment is to innovation in product quality that adds value to our Clients' businesses." (Engineering Consulting XYZ's Web site)

Engineering Consulting XYZ's key goal is to "achieve remarkable success" for its clients. It works with the client to understand the business and then utilizes the best people for the job in terms of skills and knowledge (both technical and local).

While Engineering Consulting XYZ is a global company, a high proportion of the client base is regional and requires project team members with local skills and a knowledge of regional issues; however, there has been a recognition that some of the most appropriate skills (people and technology) need to be obtained globally. The Human Yellow Pages reflects the need to be able to easily identify the appropriate people.

Engineering Consulting XYZ has recognized that people are the key resource of the consulting company and are critical for it to achieve a sustainable future. A part of this focus is to attract and retain talented staff. There are programs in place to ensure that managers are provided with the right people-management skills and staff are able to develop to reach their full potential.

The project management methodology followed by Engineering Consulting XYZ is based on the Project Management Institute's (2000) Project Management Body of

Knowledge (PMBOK) covering the following:

- Initiation
- Planning
- Execution
- Controlling
- Closing

The project management methodology at Engineering Consulting XYZ is an evolutionary process broken into three stages: proposal stage (initiation), project stage (planning and execution), and finalization stage (closing). The controlling phase underpins the process with regular key review points. In addition, progress is monitored on a monthly basis. As part of the development and retention, staff project managers and team members are put through a project management course as well as other appropriate development courses.

As a consulting and project management company, Engineering Consulting XYZ has realized the importance of knowledge management; it tries not to reinvent the wheel on new projects. As part of its knowledge management strategy, a knowledge management system was purchased and implemented, and communities of practice were set up. Both of these were in the very early stages during the reviewed projects.

CASE DESCRIPTION

Engineering Consulting XYZ participated in an alliance project, with a major public client, where all alliance partners were encouraged to focus on agreed-upon project objectives. The role of Engineering Consulting XYZ was to provide the detailed design component of the project, with the deliverables being the design, documentation, and specifications. This case study looks only at Engineering Consulting XYZ's component, and does not take into account other alliance activities. The two phases of the project were treated as two separate projects by Engineering Consulting XYZ with separate deliverables, and as such, have been analyzed as separate projects. At its peak, the project consisted of 30 project team members, with a core of between 15 and 20 members (including the project director and project manager). Of the core project team, eight (including the project manager) worked on both projects.

For the first project, Engineering Consulting XYZ, along with other alliance partners, won an excellence award in their category of industry as

- new knowledge that furthered the knowledge base of the profession was developed;
- new process knowledge was developed; and
- existing knowledge was enhanced and transferred via documented reports.

This case study analyzes and describes how knowledge was captured, managed, and reused in these two projects. In addition, the role that social networks play in the project(s) will be analyzed.

Execution of Company Strategy

Projects are used to execute Engineering Consulting XYZ's strategies. Engineering Consulting XYZ's present vision is to continue to be a sustained consulting group and to be the premier consultant for valued clients. The strategies to achieve the vision focus on identifying and looking after key clients.

Processes

Engineering Consulting XYZ has a robust project management methodology with strong links to the methodology employed by the Project Management Institute's (2000) PMBOK. Each project in Engineering Consulting XYZ undergoes initiation, planning, execution, and closing phases. Business processes and project management systems also support the project.

One of Engineering Consulting XYZ's five business units assigns a project manager to the project. The project is structured according to the work breakdown structure. The project has a project director who provides a mentoring role and is responsible for client relationships, progress monitoring, and performance (quality time costs resources), and overall quality assurance, including risk. In addition, there are review points linked to the project management methodology and quality assurance procedures; these reviews assist in managing the project risks.

Knowledge Management Processes in Engineering Consulting XYZ

Engineering Consulting XYZ supports knowledge management processes throughout the organization. In recognition of this, it has appointed a knowledge manager to develop its knowledge management activities, including the introduction of communities of practice, capturing of lessons learned, and implementation of a knowledge management system.

Knowledge Reuse

Knowledge reuse occurred between projects. New technical knowledge that was created in the first project was reused in the second project. Specific knowledge from the first project facilitated improved designs in the second project.

In Engineering Consulting XYZ, knowledge is reused at all stages of the project life cycle. Project team members continually reuse knowledge and expect to reuse it; one project team member stated that:

In most instances, I expect a level of success. I expect to be able to reuse the information. In fact, if we can't, it will more than likely result in an unpleasant commercial outcome. It's really usually necessary to reuse that information. Every now and then, though, you'll stumble across a piece of information which is so beautifully presented, so valuable that it will deliver a result very quickly, indeed.

At the plan stage, both explicit and tacit knowledge are used. Explicit knowledge is in the form of tenders, proposals, project plans, general project documentation, project methodology, and technical documentation from earlier projects. Documents are stored by project number in hard copy and on the network server. At the tacit level, project team members reused knowledge from earlier projects, either their own knowledge base or via informal networks. Explicit knowledge is usually originated from earlier projects that the project team member has worked on, implying that they do not search electronically or physically for a document but rather use their tacit knowledge to obtain the documentation. Documentation is used as a starting point or for convenience while there is a reliance on networks to obtain more detailed and complex knowledge. As one project team member said:

We use the proposal for convenience because all the words and text are there, so it's readily used and saves you having to reinvent the wheel. But the hard questions like financials and methodology you will usually talk through with the person from the project.

Lessons learned from earlier projects are used at the plan stage to try and ensure that mistakes are not repeated or successes are applied. Most of the lessons learned that are applied are informal lessons. As one person interviewed stated:

Particularly when you are setting it up, you try and incorporate the lessons learned. So if something didn't work last time, you might set the team up a little differently and have different steps in your methodology to try and capture lessons learned previously. There's a lot more in your head than you are able to document.

During project implementation, there is a reliance on both explicit and tacit knowledge; however, there is a greater reliance on personal knowledge. If explicit knowledge is reused, it is obtained by asking an expert for the documentation rather than an electronic search being carried out. A key reason that knowledge is reused is to deliver a solution where any potential pitfalls are known in advance allowing them to be overcome. As one project team member interviewed stated:

You start by discussing how to go about solving a technical problem and how they go about it to ensure that mistakes are not repeated.

Knowledge Creation and Transfer

Knowledge is continually created and transferred within and between projects. In one area of Engineering Consulting XYZ, to overcome the issue of knowledge transfer a mentoring scheme has been implemented to allow the knowledge to be transferred to a number of people within and to become part of organizational memory.

A project director is appointed to each project to mentor the project manager, and review the project. The project director mentors the project manager by meeting with the project manager and discussing the project. Roadblocks, issues, potential risks, and risk mitigation strategies are discussed in these meetings. Knowledge is transferred from the project director to the project manager as he generally has more experience, but knowledge is also transferred to the project director in terms of understanding the status of the project and what impact it may have on the other projects and programs of work.

As the project director meets with the alliance partners and the client at a strategic level, the impact that this project may have on the entire body of work is also understood.

Lessons learned, both formal and informal, are an important method of knowledge creation. Formal lessons learned occur at the end of a project or a phase of a project where formal workshops are used to identify issues/lessons and identify how they can be resolved (tacit to explicit knowledge creation and transfer). The lessons are documented and made available on the network server for future use. In addition there is a review process (between the project director and project manager or a reviewer and project manager/project team member), linked to the project methodology, where knowledge gained from one phase is incorporated into the next phase of the process. At the informal level, lessons learned occur throughout the project where project team members meet to resolve issues (tacit to tacit knowledge creation and transfer). At this level, in some circumstances the lessons may be documented in the form of meeting minutes (tacit to explicit knowledge creation and transfer).

Knowledge transfer occurs from the project to the strategic and business unit level allowing it to become part of organizational memory.

Knowledge is transferred from the project director to the project manager. The project director is a member of a formal network — a global group of regional business leaders. This group meets face-to-face three times a year and participate in telephone conferences every two weeks. Knowledge is rolled up from project level and is discussed at a strategic level. As part of this transfer, knowledge is becoming part of organizational memory.

External knowledge is transferred at a strategic level via external meeting that the project director has with alliance partners and customer reviews (monthly).

The project manager participates in a formal section meeting on a regular basis. Participants discuss proposals, projects, and potential business opportunities. This is a forum for knowledge creation, reuse, and transfer where issues can be discussed and resolved. Within this type of culture, knowledge becomes part of organizational memory as it is transferred to other employees.

Networks

The culture at Engineering Consulting XYZ encourages the use of networks. There is a reliance on obtaining tacit knowledge via personal knowledge or networks (both formal and informal). Informal networks are tapped into within and outside working hours. One project team member stated the following:

[You] build up relationships with people over a period of time. You work with them and find out who the specialists are in areas of the company. You talk to a specialist, call that person, and ask questions on how they have approached something and a relationship is established. As you build personal relationships you know who to call.

The project manager and senior project team members initially relied on personal knowledge and then their informal networks. Formal networks (e.g., as established in the corporate e-mail system) were only tapped into if the relevant knowledge could not be obtained from the other sources. In most cases, as well as utilizing tacit knowledge, people sought out explicit knowledge, that is, people interviewed said it was quicker to ask the person who knew where the relevant documentation was rather than searching for it on the server or in folders.

It's a lot more efficient if you know who produced the file last time and you can just go and ask them where it is. It saves having to search.

Informal Use of Knowledge

Knowledge is informally reused or re-created from one project to another (particularly at the plan, implementation, and closure phases) as the culture and system are not in place to formalize it (while a knowledge management system has been implemented, it was not implemented when these project phases were being conducted). Several project team members have worked with Engineering Consulting XYZ for a number of years, and given the length of time that they have been with Engineering Consulting XYZ, they have created informal networks (often with people whom they have worked with on previous projects). Interviewees commented that they just know who to go to. At the more senior levels of the organization formal networks (across the distributed enterprise) also played a crucial role. In addition there was one exception where one team member relied predominantly on informal knowledge transfer but also documented everything so that if he was not in the organization any longer, another person could access the information. The only issue is that as everything (including all e-mails) is stored in hard copy, it may be difficult to find the most appropriate knowledge.

Knowledge Management System

Engineering Consulting XYZ implemented a knowledge management system during the first project; however, it was at an immature stage and the project team relied on a network server to store project documentation in an electronic format. The documents (both project-related and technical documentation) are sorted by project number. In addition to being stored on a network server, they are also stored within files throughout the office making it difficult for people to find explicit knowledge unless they knew what they were looking for. Two areas had their own systems in which to store relevant project documentation; however these systems did not interact with other systems making it difficult for people in other areas to know how to access the knowledge without first asking someone.

The challenge for the sponsors and champions of the knowledge management system was to encourage people to see the benefits of using the systems.

I think the underlying theory and philosophy is pretty sound. The challenge is in the implementation and the culture to get the thing working so the people can see the full benefits of it.

In addition, the culture of the organization needed to change to encourage people to use the system.

It needs to be promoted in the right way from a cultural change perspective. I think it's about getting people to get used to the idea of collective learning and sharing it. It's going to take more time but we need to show people that the benefits outweigh the cost.

Table 1. Knowledge creation and reuse in projects

Area of Analysis	Method(s)	Artifacts	Phase of PMBOK
Knowledge Creation	Tacit Knowledge/ Explicit Knowledge	Personal Knowledge/Networks Tender/Technical/Project Documentation	Plan Implementation
Knowledge Capture	Formal Workshops Informal Meetings Web Portal/E-mail	Lessons Learned – (Tacit/Explicit) Meeting Minutes Files	Closing
Knowledge Transfer	Tacit Knowledge via Mentoring/ Networks Explicit Knowledge	Networks (Formal/Informal) Documentation	Plan Implementation Closing
Knowledge Reuse	Project Review	Review Process Minutes/Notes	Plan Implementation
How Do People Share/Reuse Knowledge	Informal and Formal Networks Mentoring	Informal and Formal Networks Mentoring	Plan Implementation Closing
Knowledge Management Systems	Web Portal/E-mail Server	Server Database	Plan Implementation Closing

Table 1 summarizes the major knowledge processes within Engineering Consulting XYZ, and the methods and artifacts associated with it. The knowledge processes are also related to major stages from the PMBOK project management methodology (Project Management Institute, 2000).

As highlighted in Table 1, within these projects tacit knowledge and social networks play the most crucial role both in terms of knowledge creation and reuse. However, explicit knowledge may have been used more widely if a system allowing contextual searches was used (a knowledge management system is in the process of being implemented within the company). The culture of Engineering Consulting XYZ encourages the use of knowledge transfer and reuse tacitly at an informal level. For a knowledge management system to be used extensively, a culture (and processes) that fosters the use of formal knowledge would need to be implemented. One of the people interviewed stated that

There is a need to change culture to rely on systems and get people used to the idea of collective learning and sharing it.

CURRENT CHALLENGES FACING THE ORGANIZATION

Knowledge management is a key enabler for Engineering Consulting XYZ to maintain and improve its competitive advantage, reduce project costs, and remove the cost of duplicated learning. However, at the end of this project, the organization faced a number of challenges to ensure that knowledge management enabled it to achieve rather than impede its objectives.

The consulting market has become more competitive, and over the last five years, Engineering Consulting XYZ has adopted a strategy of growth to meet the challenge.

This industry sector has also faced the emergence of the generation X with associated higher staff turnover indicative of less long-term organizational loyalty. This means that the informal networks have potentially become diluted and not as efficient.

One of the key challenges that Engineering Consulting XYZ faces is the reliance on informal networks and informal knowledge. As part of its knowledge management strategy, Engineering Company XYZ had purchased and tried to implement a knowledge management system and introduce the concept of communities of practice. Given that there is a reliance on informal networks and informal knowledge and the culture of the organization supports this environment, a key challenge is to encourage employees to belong to communities of practice that are formal and not necessarily linked to their networks or personal relationships. Processes and technology need to be put in place to support these communities of practice. In addition, given that documentation was either kept in hard copy or on a network server, project team members need to be encouraged to use the knowledge management system. In order to be accessible to others, the documents need to be stored in the knowledge management system as well as on a local area network. In addition, the information stored in the system needs to be maintained so that it is relevant and up to date. A culture that encourages the use of the knowledge management system to complement the reliance on tacit knowledge needs to be developed.

Project knowledge needs to be captured, stored, and indexed to allow for easy retrieval and contextual searches. Capturing the context of project knowledge is crucial for Engineering Consulting XYZ; without it, past knowledge may not be relevant and hard to reuse on future projects. Training in utilizing the system needs to occur.

The knowledge management system has been implemented across geographic regions, business units, and functional units. Training has occurred to ensure that staff know how to use the system. The key is to ensure that the culture of the organization accepts the use of a knowledge management system (both utilization and maintenance) and that the explicit knowledge complements the use of tacit knowledge and networks.

EPILOGUE AND LESSONS LEARNED

Epilogue

This chapter looks at how knowledge is created, transferred, and reused in project management. The culture of the organization plays a crucial role within knowledge management. Where there is a reliance on informal networks and informal knowledge and the culture of the organization supports this environment, a key challenge may be to encourage employees to belong to communities of practice that are formal and not necessarily linked to their networks or personal relationships. Processes and technology would need to be put in place to support these communities of practice. Given that culture plays such a key role in knowledge management, if a mature knowledge management system was implemented and the culture changed to reflect this change, tracking will need to occur to ascertain the long-term effects on the organization.

Lessons Learned

1. In this case study, there was an expectation that the majority of knowledge was obtained via formal means and would provide fruitful ground for a knowledge management system implementation. However, the informal transfer and reuse of knowledge played a more crucial role and provided proven benefit to Engineering Consulting XYZ. Thus the implementation of a knowledge management system resulted in a need for major cultural change.
2. The culture of an organization plays a major part in knowledge reuse. If the attributes of a learning organization are part of the culture, then knowledge reuse can occur. An organization can have all the processes, formality, and structure it wants, but without the right attitude or culture knowledge, reuse may not occur.
3. A total reliance on knowledge management systems does not necessarily suit the needs of Engineering Consulting XYZ; the better use of the system would be desirable. However, as this organization has a culture that encourages collective learning and sharing, a knowledge management system needs to complement the reliance on tacit knowledge and networks.

ACKNOWLEDGMENTS

This research is partially funded by the School of Information Management and Systems, Faculty of Information Technology, at Monash University. We are grateful for the support and input from the case study site.

REFERENCES

Argyris, C., & Schon, D.A. (1978). *Organizational learning: A theory of action perspective.* Addison Wesley.

Baldwin, T., Danielson, C., & Wiggenhorn, W. (1997). The evolution of learning strategies in organizations: From employee development to business redefinition. *The Academy of Management Executive, 11*(4).

Bollinger, A.S., & Smith, R.D. (2001). Managing organizational knowledge as a strategic asset. *Journal of Knowledge Management, 5*(1), 8-18.

Cooper, K.G., & Lyneis, J.N. (2002). Learning to learn from past to future. *International Journal of Project Management, 20*(3), 213-219.

Damm, D., & Schindler, M. (2002). Security issues of a knowledge medium for distributed project work. *International Journal of Project Management, 20*(1), 37-47.

Disterer, G. (2002). Management of project knowledge and experiences. *Journal of Knowledge Management, 6*(5), 512-520.

Dixon, N.M. (2000). *Common knowledge: How companies thrive by sharing what they know.* Harvard Business School Press.

Kim, D.H. (1993). The link between individual and organizational learning. *MIT Sloan Management Review, 35*(1).

Komi-Sirvio, S., Mantyniemi, A., & Sepannen, V. (2002). Towards a practical solution for capturing knowledge for software projects. *IEEE Software, 19*(3), 60-62.

Koskinen, K.U. (2000). Tacit knowledge as a promoter of project success. *European Journal of Purchasing and Supply Management, 6*(1), 41-47.

Kotnour, T. (1999). A learning framework for project management. *Project Management Journal, 30*(2), 32-38.

Kotnour, T. (2000). Organizational learning practices in the project management environment. *International Journal of Quality and Reliability Management, 17*(4/5), 393-406.

Kotnour, T., & Hjelm, M. (2002). Leadership mechanisms for enabling learning within project teams. *Proceedings of the 3rd European Conference on Organizational Knowledge, Learning and Capabilities.*

Liebowitz, J. (2002). A look at NASA Goddard space flight center's knowledge management initiatives. *IEEE Software, 19*(3), 40-42.

McElroy, M. (2003). *The new knowledge management.* Butterworth-Heinemann.

McLoughlin, I.P., Alderman, N., Ivory, C.J., Thwaites, A., & Vaughan, R. (2000). Knowledge management in long term engineering projects. *Proceedings of the Knowledge Management: Controversies and Causes Conference.* Retrieved May 19, 2003, from *http://bprc.warwick.ac.uk/km065.pdf*

Nahapiet, J., & Ghosal, S. (1998). Social capital, intellectual capital, and the organizational advantage. *The Academy of Management Review, 23*(2), 242-266.

Nelson, R.R., & Winter, S.G. (1982). *An evolutionary theory of economic change.* Cambridge, MA: Belknap Press of Harvard University Press.

Nevis, E.C., DiBella, A.J., & Gould, J.M. (1995). Understanding organizations as learning systems. *MIT Sloan Management Review, 36*(2).

Nickols, F. (2000). The knowledge in knowledge management. In J.W. Cortada & J.A. Woods (Eds.), *The knowledge management yearbook 2001-2002.* Butterworth-Heinemann.

Project Management Institute. (2000). *A guide to the project management body of knowledge.* Project Management Institute.

Schneider, M.A. (2002). A stakeholder model of organizational leadership. *Organization Science, 12*(2), 209-220.

Senge, P.M. (2002). *The fifth discipline the art and practice of the learning organization.* Random House.

Stata, R. (1989). Organizational learning—the key to management innovation. *MIT Sloan Management Review, 30*(3).

Von Krogh, G., & Roos, J. (1995). *Organizational epistemology.* Macmillan.

FURTHER READING

Cross, R., Nohria, N., & Parker, A. (2002). Six myths about informal networks and how to overcome them. *Sloan Management Review, 43*(3), 67-75.

Fiol, C.M., & Lyles, M.A. (1985). Organizational learning. *Academy of Management Review, 10*(4), 803-813.

Koskinen, K.U. (2004). Knowledge management to improve project communication and implementation. *Project Management Journal, 35*(2), 13.

Owen, J., Burstein, F., & Mitchell, S. (2005). Knowledge reuse and transfer in a project management environment. Special issue of *Journal of Information Technology Cases and Applications, 6*(4).

Schindler, M., & Eppler, M.J. (2003). Harvesting project knowledge: A review of project learning methods and success factors. *International Journal of Project Management, 21*(3), 219-228.

Schon, D. (1995). *Reflective practitioner: How professionals think in action.* Aldershot, UK: Arena.

Turner, J.R. (1999). *Handbook of project-based management: Improving the processes for achieving strategic objectives.* London: McGraw-Hill.

Walsh, J.P., & Ungson, J.R. (1991). Organizational memory. *Academy of Management Review, 16*(1), 57-91.

Section V

Knowledge Management in Support of Knowledge Transfer

Chapter X

Organizational Knowledge Sharing Based on the ERP Implementation of Yongxin Paper Co., Ltd.

Zhang Li, Harbin Institute of Technology, China

Tian Yezhuang, Harbin Institute of Technology, China

Li Ping, Harbin Institute of Technology, China

EXECUTIVE SUMMARY

This case focuses on the effect of knowledge sharing in the process of enterprise resources planning (ERP) system implementation. Knowledge sharing mainly means the sharing and combination of tacit knowledge in the application of new techniques. Up to now, less than 20% of ERP implementations have varying degrees of success in Chinese companies. Yongxin is one such company that used knowledge sharing to successfully introduce an ERP management system. The authors hope that this case will not only inform researchers of a better design for knowledge sharing, but also assist companies implementing knowledge management in effective knowledge sharing.

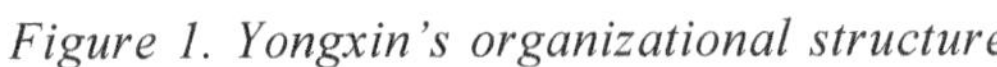

Figure 1. Yongxin's organizational structure

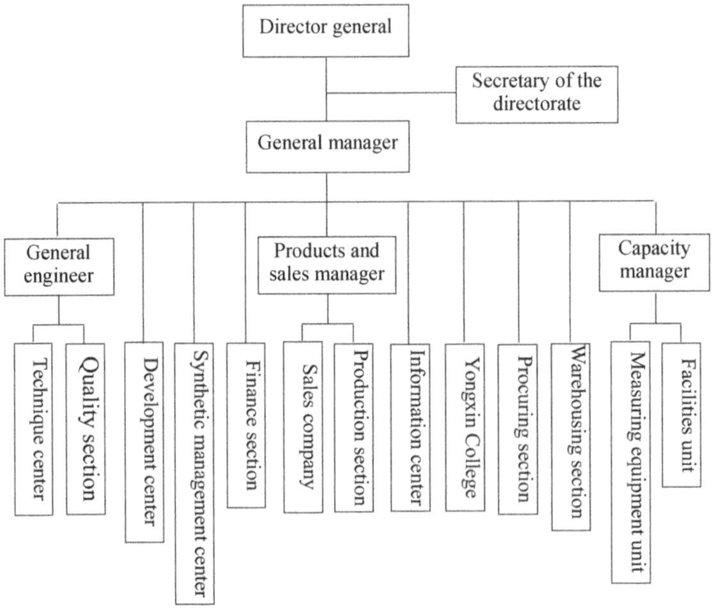

BACKGROUND

Mudanjiang Yongxin Paper Co., Ltd. (Yongxin, for short) is the production base of cigarette auxiliary material appointed by the state, which is located in Mudanjiang city, Heilongjiang province, in northeastern China. Yongxin, previously Mudanjiang paper mill, was founded in 1951. It was transformed from a state-owned enterprise into a joint-stock company in 1997 and became a China listed company in 2000. The total assets of Yongxin are 10.2 billion RMB and the number of employees totals 3,018. Figure 1 presents the organizational structure of Yongxin.

Annual paper production is 33,000 tons and the annual production of self-made pulp is about 15,000 tons. Main products of Yongxin include different kinds of cigarette paper, pulp paper, yellow and white tipping base paper of good printing characteristics, NCR paper, ZnO base paper, and so forth. Currently, Yongxin is one of the most advanced paper-making enterprises in China. Yongxin has accomplished a sales income of 426,230,000 RMB and total profits of 535,500,000 RMB through 2002.

Over the last 50 years, Yongxin has developed its own organizational culture: "booming forever," "creditable forever," which embraces the soul of "human-based" and "honesty and credit" management spirits. The special culture has already won markets, customers, and profits for the company. Now, Yongxin has drawn up its development objectives for the next 10 years. These include raising sales income to 4 billion RMB and production to 0.4 million tons. Planned development strategies are focused on making Yongxin first in the paper manufacturing industry and accomplishing the globalization of the company.

SETTING THE STAGE

ERP Implementation in China

As IT and world economy globalization continues to grow, China has gradually become the world manufacturing center. Currently, one can find products made in China all over the world. However, market competition is also becoming more and more fierce: customer demands are constantly changing; the life span of products is becoming shorter and shorter; technology innovation is accruing exceedingly; and the pressure of globalization is increasing quickly (Chen & Zhou, 2002).

To compete, Chinese manufacturers need to find and implement modern management skills to improve their level of management performance. Fortunately, the Chinese government is aware of and has considerable concerns with the need to improve enterprise information management. However, while ERP systems are a popular solution to managing enterprise information, ERPs may not be the best choice for the Chinese manufacturers to win the global markets. China has 20 years of experience with MRP¢ò/ERP since Shenyang Machine Tool Co., Ltd bought the first MRP¢ò software from the German Engineering Association (Xu, 2003). Unfortunately, ERP implementation results have not met expectations. Many companies do not know the principles of ERP, which leads to the huge waste of human resources, materials, and money. According to the statistics from Andersen, about 1,000 projects have brought in the MRP¢ò/ERP system since 1991 (Fritch & Cromwell, 2001). However, half of them have failed completely; about 30% to 40% have not attained systems integration; and only 10% to 20% have accomplished the expected objectives. Most of these projects were accomplished with investment from foreign funds.

ERP Implementation in Yongxin

As more and more Chinese manufacturers bring in foreign management skills, Yongxin gradually recognized the importance of enterprise information management to the future of the company. The general director, Zhang Wei, considered an innovative and perspicacious person, was appointed to lead the management team to investigate, select, and implement an ERP into the ensemble strategy accounts. Yongxin formed a multisystem integrated management system, which is based on the computer webs and ERP principles. The implementation of the system accelerated the coordination of the business flow, cash flow, and information flow, and has enhanced Yongxin's ensemble management performance.

The general manager, Yin Jicai, is one of the main directors of ERP projects and has participated in the whole process of ERP implementation. He graduated from the School of Management in Jilin University of Technology in 1990, and then served in a variety of positions: clerk in the Enterprise Management office, deputy director, and then director in the branch factory of Yongxin. In 1997, he was appointed as the leader of the Asset Management department. Then he was promoted to vice-general manager of Yongxin Group in 2000. Finally, he became the general manager of Yongxin in 2003. As one of the ERP system initiators, Mr. Yin has led top management in studying ERP principles and knowledge since 1998. Additionally, he guided them in obtaining experiences and lessons learned from companies that have implemented ERP successfully, such as Meiling Co., Ltd and Star Co., Ltd.

The Importance of Knowledge Sharing in ERP Implementation

Consequently, the information center in charge of the implementation and control of ERP was established focusing on knowledge sharing. Yongxin has accomplished the sharing of inside information and technology ever since. Meanwhile, it gradually set up a market-oriented computer-aided management system, which covers all the operational processes of the company. Unfortunately, as a state-owned enterprise, Yongxin confronts many challenges in the implementation of ERP. In one aspect, only a few employees understand the function and effectiveness of an ERP system. In another aspect, the top managers do not realize the objectives of ERP system in each step of the whole circle, which eventually affects the efficiency of the system.

Knowledge sharing mainly means the sharing and combination of tacit knowledge (Tang, 2001). During ERP implementation, Yongxin would have more efficiently achieved management objectives had it understood the concepts of ERP system sooner and had it utilized lessons learned and previous specific practice (Ghosn & Bengio, 2003).

This case analyzes the challenges and countermeasures during the enterprise inner knowledge sharing from this experience.

CASE DESCRIPTION

The Foundation of Information Center

Knowledge management improves the flexibility and innovation capacity of a company by enabling knowledge sharing and leveraging what people know. It provides the right path and management methods for sharing of explicit knowledge and tacit knowledge. Yongxin uses knowledge management in the implementation of ERPs. Operating personnel primarily use explicit knowledge in the design, system operation, and test maintenance of ERPs. ERP management ideas and related techniques utilized by section and middle-level managers are "tacit knowledge." Finally the implementation of Yongxin's ERP consists of the outcome of knowledge innovation, that is, the combination of tacit knowledge and explicit knowledge mentioned above.

Yongxin organized its top managers to learn ERP knowledge early in 1998. At the same time, Yin Jicai, as vice-general manager, led the management team to Meilin Company to learn their successful experience of information management. In 1999, he and the secretaries of all departments went to Star Co., Ltd. — a template enterprise of Chinese information management — where they accumulated a great deal of data about MRP, ERP, CIMS, and the trend of domestic information management development. The effort made a good foundation for the company's structuring of its highly effective knowledge sharing network. At the beginning of 2000, Yongxin started the construction of the infrastructure for the knowledge sharing and shared network project by rebuilding the main production facility and installing the necessary controlling and monitoring system.

In March 2001, Yongxin proposed the company's development plan to each department and district. At the end of 2001, Yongxin founded the information center to make sure that the network's construction ran smoothly with Yin Jicai as the responsible manager for network construction. He quickly realized that the ERP was more than a software system. The ERP implementation required optimum operation flow and integration in the network platform. Also, the design of business processes was unlikely to be carried out thoroughly if the business departments were negative to the project (Desouza, 2003). As a result, he considered it necessary for information center employees to be familiar with basic computer knowledge and the company's everyday operations. Thus, he appointed computer professionals as well as business elites from finance, storage and distribution departments, and other critical departments that played important roles in the process of knowledge and management ideas transference.

The Company Organizational Structure

The ERP management system, which was characterized as "the first in command" project, and affected the whole company, greatly changed the old balance system. This change process could only be coordinated by top management (Mandal & Gunasekaran, 2003). Thus, Yongxin created a three-level project organizational structure within the company to advance the ERP project consisting of a leaders group, project group, and function group (Figure 2).

Zhang Wei, aged 41, general director, a graduate of Northeast Forestry University and an EMBA student at Beijing University, is the head of the leader group. He is considered a strong innovator. Yin Jicai, general manager, acts as associate leader. Other associate general managers, chief engineers, and secretaries of all departments act as members. Most of the members are energetic, well-educated, and young (aged 35-45), who have served more than 10 years in their administrative positions. They are mainly responsible for the whole information administrative system and operation-reconstruction project.

The project group, which consists of top managers and software manufacturer consultants, is the coordinator between leading groups and departments.

The function group is the core group for implementing the ERP network system, and consists of the top operations and software manufacturer operators. Such a rigorous organizational structure becomes the powerful safeguard to the future knowledge transference of ERP.

The First Stage of ERP Implementation

From November 2001 to the end of 2002, the company invested 6,000,000 RMB for network construction and first-stage software development. Several information management systems were modified based on the needs of the computer information network and ERP system.

The first-stage project started in February 2002 with the system going operational in July. It included four phases: total demand analysis, business process project, antitype testing, and data initialization and circulation tests. Yongxin improved the systems for distribution, stock, storage, and finance departments as management considered these the highest priority and difficult to implement. The application of modern, automated

Figure 2. Three-level organizational structure

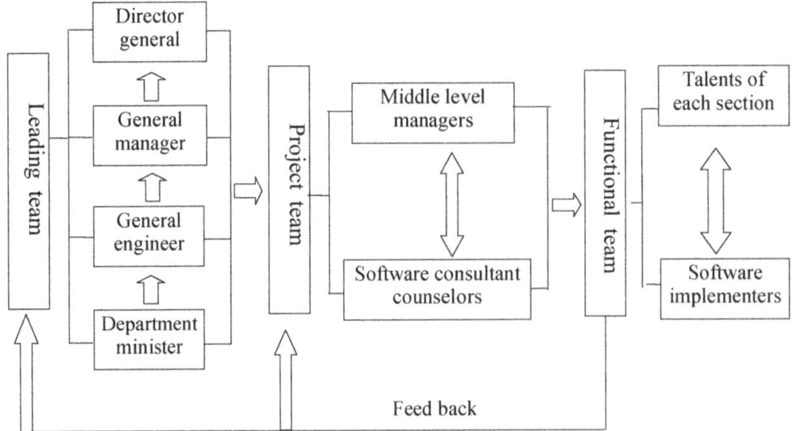

information management approaches, rather than manual management approaches, made the company run more effectively and fit management's need for swift and accurate information for supporting decision making.

During the introduction and implementation of the ERP system, several problems and challenges were identified. When the ERP system was first introduced into the company, managers did not know the function of ERP. Yin Jicai negotiated with dozens of ERP suppliers who were potential partners for Yongxin, and asked them to help the staff understand the advantages of ERP. This process not only deepened managers' knowledge about ERP, but also helped evaluate the potential ERP suppliers. As a result, it also reduced internal resistance to ERP implementation.

Yongxin's finance and supply systems are adapted from two different companies' ERP software systems in order to improve performance. At first, some employees were suspicious about the accuracy of the computer. Therefore, the manual account and system account systems were run in parallel. Yin Jicai convened meetings every morning and compared both ways of account. A month later, the employees understood the convenience of the system account. Half a year later, by forcing electronic office work, the company realized its expected goal of all company information being easily accessible through the intranet, which brought great benefits to the managers and the employees.

To reduce the resistance of other departments, Yin Jicai went to each department to check mistakes. The moment they found mistakes, they held meetings to analyze the reasons and identify the resolution. When the first-stage project was finished, the cost of stock was reduced to 3,000,000 RMB; the inventory subsystem was changed from manual account to computer account; and the distribution subsystem set up customer credit assessment files accurately and fully, so as to respond quickly to customer orders, which helps maintain high-quality service and better customer relationship.

Staff Training

Yongxin realized that the understanding and popularization of ERP needed different arrangement and should be separated into several phases in order to transfer the correlative knowledge to the employees smoothly. To senior administrators, it was of utmost importance to understand the management skills of ERP and any possible risks; to middle-level managers, it was helping to meet the changes of operation flow; to operation personnel, test and operation knowledge is a must. For more effective knowledge sharing, they first send their top personnel to ERP consultants to learn correlative techniques and then transferred the techniques to other personnel through training. In this way, ERP knowledge can be understood and absorbed more readily. Meanwhile, it made knowledge sharing an integral part of the company's practices. A three-level training system was created to assist this transfer:

1. ERP management theories training for top managers
2. ERP system application and maintenance training for operators
3. Daily application training for top department personnel elites

Conclusion

Automating a company's information management is a very complicated learning process. No other approach can take the place of knowledge sharing, and we make it into a reality by learning and practicing ceaselessly (Roda, Angehrn, Nabeth, & Razmerita, 2003). The implementation of an ERP system in Yongxin tells us that it is a system that can assist a company's internal knowledge sharing. Only through integration into a company's strategic plan and infrastructure can it bring a far-reaching influence on the company's development.

CURRENT CHALLENGES/PROBLEMS FACING THE ORGANIZATION

For the Employees

Because of the variance of the employees' levels and resistance to change, training is difficult for Yongxin, a 50-year-old state-owned enterprise. Although the compulsory computer training enhanced employees' familiarity with the technology, it did not give them a deep understanding of ERP; therefore, it is incapable of melding the ERP system into the enterprise's business process making them incapable of capitalizing on ERP's advantages (Ghosn & Bengio, 2003).

For the Managers

Because of the limitation of internal processes in Chinese state-owned enterprises, at the beginning of the ERP implementation, Vice-General Manager Yin Jicai could not coordinate and motivate corresponding departments. In order to promote the ERP, he set aside other vice-general managers, which led to their embarrassment as they were not aware of the value of the ERP system. Even when the ERP system performed well in some departments, the managers did not realize the merit of ERP. Hence, they did not use the ERP system to plan their work, resulting in their work plans not integrating with those from the rest of the enterprise. Training these managers will not work either, as they did not participate in the implementation of ERP. They do not have a thorough grasp of the function that ERP performs in every part of the enterprise. These managers need stronger knowledge transfer. These problems grievously decrease their decision quality.

For the System Itself

Because of the rapid development of the computer technology, Yongxin's original software system cannot satisfy the requirements for the enterprise's automated information management. Meanwhile, the financial and other sections of the ERP system were bought from two different software suppliers. They often conflict with each other during management and control. These problems also obstruct the development of the company's knowledge network.

EPILOGUE AND LESSONS LEARNED

Epilogue

Knowledge sharing is key to the success of the project during the implementation of automated enterprise information management. The implementation of knowledge sharing runs well with a training center. It was important to transfer management skills and manipulate methods to line operatives by effective training. In addition, choosing an information director who is a business expert, skilled technician, and good communicator before the training will enhance knowledge sharing.

Factors that affect knowledge sharing include the information infrastructure of enterprises, internal organizational structure, organizational culture, and staff motivation systems.

First, implement the ERP system and establish an intranet to centralize and administer resources. This is the platform for organizational knowledge sharing, which is a link and a carrier for mass information.

Second, pyramid-like branches of organizational structure prevent knowledge from regeneration and application, hinder the contact and communication among different employees from different knowledge backgrounds, and resulted in distortion in information transfer. It is very necessary to change the company's organizational structure and to make knowledge sharing effective. A good choice is to form a flat organizational structure. This is still a goal for Yongxin.

Third, an incentive and motivation system encourages knowledge sharing more quickly. Enterprises of different cultures should adopt different motivation system accordingly.

It is not difficult for the decision-making level, management level, and the operational level to attain the skills of the ERP system in a high-tech corporation. However, one still needs to show one's respect to the traditional state-owned enterprises for its execution extent and the attitude of the employees toward learning if one acknowledges the ERP implementation of Yongxin, which signifies the knowledge sharing and competence principles in the ERP systems.

At present, ERP systems have been implemented in almost all the departments of Yongxin. Also, the effectiveness of ERP in the circle of each business is gradually being shown, encouraging further implementation of ERP among the company.

All the same, the most rigorous challenge facing Yongxin is the maintenance of the ERP systems. As the computer software fields update quickly, the original ERP systems cannot satisfy their requirements, requiring the company to improve the ERP systems. However, the original financial section of the ERP system was not bought from the same software suppliers as other sections, which brings the challenge of coordinating maintenance of all the sections after the update of the whole system. Actually, the whole ERP system of Yongxin will be ruined if the coordination fails.

Thus, the case study shows that knowledge management is a systemic process which requires all-round strategic planning. Only in this way can it bring its far-reaching influence to the development of enterprises.

Lessons

1. **The applications of theory should adapt to the objective environment.** Different culture environments and organizational structure of companies have differences, so the practices and application of knowledge sharing should complement real environmental situations.
2. **Be careful about methods and modes in knowledge sharing.** Adapting different methods to transfer the same kind of knowledge may affect effectiveness. Therefore, we should pay more attention to choose modes of organizational study and training in knowledge sharing.
3. **Pay more attention to cooperation in a team.** The application of new techniques is a systematic process and it cannot be done by one person. Each member of the organization should cooperate and support each other to achieve the biggest advantage of team work.

FURTHER READING

Barrett, M., Cappleman, S., Shoib, G., & Walsham, G. (n.d.). Learning in knowledge communities: Managing technology and context. *European Management Journal, 22*(1), 1-11.

Koskinen, K.U. (2001). Tacit knowledge as a promoter of success in technology firms. *Proceedings of the 34th Hawaii International Conference on System Sciences.*

Lemken, B., Kahler, H., & Rittenbruch, M. (2000). Sustained knowledge management by organizational culture. *Proceedings of the 33rd Hawaii International Conference on System Sciences.*

Levina, N. (2000). Sharing knowledge in heterogeneous environments. *Reflections, 2*(2), 32-42.

Mangisengi, O., & Essmayar, W. (2003). P2P knowledge management: An investigation of the technical architecture and main process. *Proceedings of the 14th International Workshop on Database and Expert Systems Applications.*

McDaniel, R., & Pollard, L. (2003). Tacit knowledge in information systems. *The Sharp of Knowledge*, 401-404.

Ruppel, C.P., & Harrington, S.J. (2001). Sharing knowledge through intranets: A study of organizational culture and intranet implementation. *IEEE Transactions on Professional Communication, 44*(1).

REFERENCES

Chen, R.Q., & Zhou, S.Y. (2002). *The theory and practice of operation management.* Beijing: Renmin University of China Press.

Desouza, K.C. (2003). Knowledge management barriers: Why the technology imperative seldom works. *Business Horizon, January-February*, 25-29.

Fritch, J.F., & Cromwell, R.L. (2001). Evaluating Internet resources identity, affiliation, and cognitive authority in a networked world. *Journal of the American Society for Information Science, 52*(6), 499-507.

Ghosn, J., & Bengio, Y. (2003). Bias learning, knowledge sharing. *IEEE Transactions on Neural Network, 14*(4), 748-766.

Mandal, P., & Gunasekaran, A. (2003). Issues in implementing ERP: A case study£®*European Journal of Operational Research, 146*, 279-280.

Roda, C., Angehrn, A., Nabeth, T., & Razmerita, L. (2003). Using conversational agents to support the adoption of knowledge sharing practices. *Interacting with Computers, 15*, 57-59.

Tang, X.H. (2001). The approach of tacit knowledge sharing inside enterprise. *Enterprise Study, 5*, 29-30.

Xu, X.F. (2003). The current circumstance, tendency and consideration of the development of ERP technology. *Journal of China Manufacturer Information, 3*, 19-29.

List of Additional Sources

Aspremont, C.D., & Bhattacharya, S. (1998). Knowledge as a public good: Efficient sharing and incentives for development effect. *Journal of Mathematical Economics*, 389-404.

Darroch, J., Shaw, V., & Mcnaughton, R. (2000). Knowledge management practices and innovation. *IEEE*, 684-689.

Dixon, N.M. (2000). Common knowledge: How companies thrive on sharing what they know. *Book Review and Review Briefs, 188*, 270-273.

Edberg, D., & Olfman, L. (2001). *Organizational learning through the process of enhancing information systems*. IEEE.

http://erp.ittoolbox.com

http://knowledgemanagement.ittoolbox.com/

Rowley, H. (2002). Knowledge management needs organizational learning for human context. *Knowledge Management.*

Wahl, S. (2003), Learning at work: The role of technical communication in organizational learning. *Technical Communication, 50*(2), 247-258.

www.cio.com/research/erp/

www.kmbook.com/

www.kmmagazine.com/

www.kmworld.com

www.km-review.com/

Chapter XI

Supporting Research and Development Processes Using Knowledge Management Methods

Thomas Hahn, Profactor Produktionsforschungs GmbH, Austria

Bernhard Schmiedinger, Profactor Produktionsforschungs GmbH, Austria

Elisabeth Stephan, Profactor Produktionsforschungs GmbH, Austria

EXECUTIVE SUMMARY

This chapter shows the integration of formal and informal knowledge and information exchange methodologies for an integrative product development process. It describes in detail how to transfer knowledge between organizational-related units to allow a smooth transition of development projects. Based on communities and information technology support, the concept offers a substantial way to bridge communication gaps to increase efficiency. Furthermore the authors hope that this chapter increases understanding of existing problems in manufacturing companies and enables practitioners to find a basic idea of how to solve their own challenges.

BACKGROUND

Trumpf Maschinen Austria (TAT) was founded 1990 near the city of Linz, Austria, as an independent subsidiary of the Trumpf group. TAT is a competence center for press brake and bending technology and produces TrumaBend® press brakes, the TRUMPF BendMaster®, and laser-hardened bending tools.

TAT had a turnover of 94.5 million euros and employs 168 people, and has a very low fluctuation rate. Two thirds of produced CNC machines are exported worldwide. The main focus of research and development (R&D) is on the process chain of "Blech" (sheet plates).

Currently three TrumaBend® press brakes are delivered every day and production capacities are in the process of being expanded to prepare to meet the constantly increasing demand for TRUMPF press brakes in future. Tool machines and production technology by TAT are in a leading position on the world market.

SETTING THE STAGE

The following case study is based on an information and communication problem between the R&D department and the construction department of a large machine manufacturing company with subsidiaries all over the world.

Problem Details

In the past the development of new machines was done in one big department (construction department) which also had to handle customer orders. Knowledge and experience transfer from R&D activities to order processing was an integrative part of daily business.

Later on, the fast growth of the company led to less R&D activities and required the split into an R&D department and a construction department. The R&D department was then responsible for the development of new machines, and the construction department was responsible for processing customer orders. In this department special needs of the customer concerning a machine had to be implemented within the general technical specifications. The specialization allows a more focused work and clear responsibilities for customer adoptions versus new product development.

Dividing the department caused cultural side effects. The staff of the construction team lost the status of being members of the "creative" R&D department and were very disappointed about this fact. This cultural problem resulted in a structural and emotional gap between these newly formed departments, which was reflected by less communication. Additionally, the formal information exchange has not been defined anew, so the handover happened only after the finalization of the R&D activities.

Now the big challenge is to handle the formal and informal transfer of knowledge and experience produced in the development projects within the R&D department to the construction department, which has to use the project results when processing customer orders. So the overall target of a new concept for exchanging and sharing knowledge and experience is to include know-how and experiences of all departments of the company within development projects and to bridge the emotional gap and friction between these two departments.

General Conditions

Development projects in this company are of highest complexity and last up to three years, and a normal lifetime of such a machine (including modifications) is about 10 years. A development project in this context is defined as a project that develops a machine type in several similar specifications. Additionally the machine manufacturing company required that a new concept for optimizing knowledge and information transfer among the different departments, should support

- integration of know-how of all company departments (e.g., sales, assembly, production);
- reduction of the cycle time for machine development projects;
- serial production has to start right after finishing the R&D project;
- providing up-to-date information about R&D projects for all employees;
- and should also be complementary to an overall "integrated product development process," which was worked out and applied in this company.

CASE DESCRIPTION

To solve the problems, a new concept concerning exchange and transfer of information, knowledge, experience, and know-how had to be developed. Current literature and cases only provide theoretical background and some examples for large firms, which made it necessary to adapt existing approaches and mix them with a new solution.

Current State Analysis

During the current state analysis the existing "integrated product development process" as well as the split of functions among the departments were analyzed. Additionally the employees' concerns have been integrated during an online survey about special topics, which was completed by 35 employees from several departments. This was a very good response rate (47 employees had received an invitation). Some completed questionnaires made no sense, so they had to be omitted.

Results of the current state analysis were (including questionnaires and interviews) as follows:

- No clear work order between development and construction
- Demand for an increase of informal communication to foster the exchange (large projects involve up to 40 employees)
- Employees think that the workload of their own and their branch is very high
- A structured project result handover is needed (Figure 1)
- Reuse of essential documents is often not possible

The organizational analysis (structure, products) detected further problems caused by the strong increase of staff, no existing team or project coordination structures, and extreme pressure from market. New product development is often the starting point for a complete replacement of a whole product series. Based on the high complexity of the development process, changes during the prototype design and later on during the series production cause high efforts.

As a major point of the survey, the project handover between development and construction department had been analyzed in more details:

- Delivery of project results can be done by exchange of documents, but parts must be supported by communication or discussion processes.

Figure 1. Current state of project handover

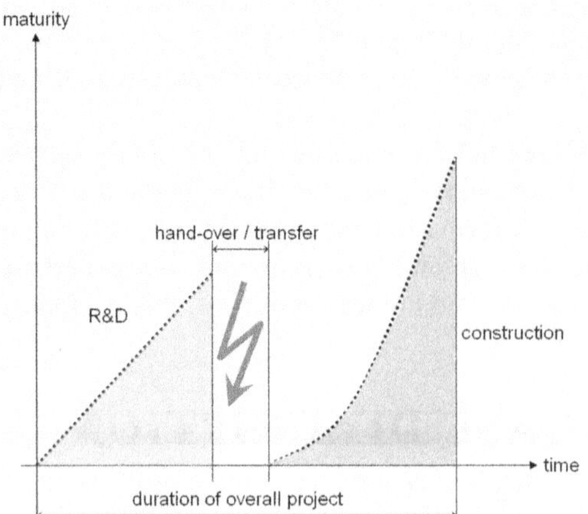

- In principle, all results and interfaces of components or assembly groups are described as complex and time critical (for the delivery process).
- Results about new technologies are also time consuming at the delivery.
- The employees are positively motivated to use a project management tool as support for delivery.
- The construction department should be informed about the current status and content during the project to be able to bring in its know-how for optimal results.
- After delivery, there should be responsible persons at the development department for each technical aspect for assistance with various problems.

One important activity within this phase was to review existing knowledge management methods regarding their applicability within the context of this machine manufacturing company.

Theoretical Backgrounds

Before the concept is described in detail, it is important to emphasize that this solution is not an existing knowledge management approach but a combination of existing tools and instruments. In this section we explain the theory the authors used for designing the concept. Main sources are the approaches of community of practice, moderation and coaching aspects, project and team meetings, lessons learned, and aspects of organizational learning.

First of all, it is important to say that with the concept we intend to approach the existing structure of the organization to the structure of hypertext organization. This kind of organization is characterized on the one hand by a hierarchical structure, and on the other hand by the cooperation of the employees in projects in their department but also to projects with members of different departments. The advantage of this kind of organization is the contact between experts in different areas and, as a result, the exchange of their knowledge (Nonaka & Takeuchi, 1995).

We distinguish the concept of formal and informal dissemination of knowledge. For the formal spread of information, there is a start-up meeting to inform all employees about the new project. Moreover, the project manager immediately sends out important news so that all employees are "on the same page." Standardized templates support the optimal documentation during the whole development process. The existing project management tool stores these documents. One example of a template is the Project Transfer Matrix, a generated knowledge management tool for efficient planning, controlling, and managing the transfer of the project results. The matrix is described more in detail later on. Last but not least, the accomplishment of "lessons learned" in each project group is very important at the end of the project. The team members together document the positive and negative aspects of the whole project and describe how problems could have been avoided. As result, future project teams can learn from their experience (Probst, Raub, & Romhardt, 1999).

The theoretical background of the informal exchange of knowledge provides as basic principle Etienne Wenger's communities of practice concept. A community of practice is a group of people with the same interest in a certain topic, informally bound together with the aim of building and exchanging knowledge. Everyone with interest in the certain topic can participate in sharing knowledge on a Web site. The community runs as long as the members are interested (Wenger, McDermott, & Snyder, 2002). Furthermore, we distinguish between work groups and project teams. A work group has the aim of delivering a product or a service. The members are employees reporting to the same manager and work together until the next reorganization or reassignment. A project team has to accomplish a certain task, is assigned by management, and has a specific deadline. In our concept, thematic groups are built (see section on applied knowledge management methods), which are a combination of the three types.

Furthermore, regular meetings, discussions between the employees, and workshops are possibilities to generate and exchange knowledge. It is also possible to invite an external moderator to accomplish workshops with the advantage that he/she is not involved in the processes of the organization.

To encourage employees to discuss and talk about the new project, it is useful to place charts or whiteboards at meeting points in the company. Meeting points, such as a cafeteria, where members of different areas of the organization meet, facilitate contact between employees. One possibility is the creation of a "topic of the week" to enhance discussions. Possible results and new ideas can be noted on the charts.

There is one more approach of knowledge management in the concept: organizational learning. It describes how groups and so also organizations can learn from the knowledge of the individual and how the knowledge can be spread (Van Heijst et al., 1998). Learning through communication and feedback should be an additional point of this concept, which involves a combination and distribution of existing knowledge.

Having discussed the theoretical background in knowledge management, the concept and its development are described in detail below.

Action Plan

In a workshop with the management team and the project managers, the results of the analysis have been discussed and an optimized situation was drafted. This draft did not contain any idea about the new concept but it described the "to-be" situation within

Figure 2. Planned smooth project handover

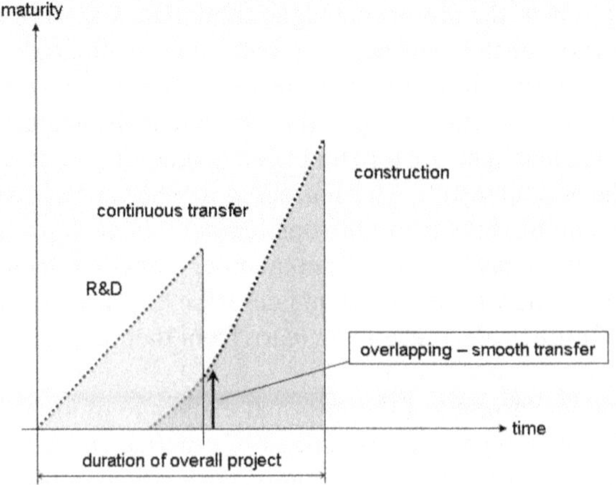

the company very clearly. Derived from this "to-be" description, a list of main goals was prepared, which is divided into three major parts: organization/structure, information/ communication, and project management/documentation.

The optimization of the existing interface between development and construction cannot be taken under consideration separately from other departments of TAT. This means that there is a higher demand for structural and organizational handling of development projects (Figure 2). The following steps have been planned:

- Definition of work distribution among involved departments in development projects
- Definition of specialized technical topic groups (a mixture of teams and communities of practice) for supporting information and communication in projects
- Standardization of documentation and storage of project documents
- Usage of a project management software

For better information and communication during the project delivery, the concept defined the following:

- Support of informal communication of employees of both departments (development and construction)
- Formal communication to grant feedback and commitment of employees to official project documentation
- Information of employees about ongoing development activities and current status of development projects

The last points of the concept handle project management and documentation. The main goal is the structured documentation of project results. To reach this, we planned the following:

- Common vision and mission in the project management
- Structured way of delivering project results

Concept Overview

To solve the existing problems, the concept is oriented along the integrated production development process of TAT (Figure 3). Project management is done very well and clearly defined by internal processes, but information and knowledge interchange must be increased and structured. As a conclusion from the analysis phase, the concept concentrates on communication via different stages, structured and informal information, know-how transfer, and documentation of relevant or critical information handover.

TAT's integrated development process follows the defined process for development of new products which is based on the strategic development program. The first two stages, "Development Program" and "Product Definition," are mainly influenced by the Trumpf Group, which defines every three years development visions for the subsidiary companies. The vague specifications of the development program define the direction of future R&D efforts. Derived from this input, the local subsidiary defines new products or product families in a more detailed way such as a functional specification and technological details, which are worked out in more details in the development department. This functional specification is a starting point for the integrated product development and provides the first input for the knowledge management concept phase — the Initialization Phase.

As shown in Figure 3, the concept consists of five main phases, of which some are partly overlapping. These overlapping parts are necessary to handle preparation activities (e.g., planning workshops), although the actual phase is not completed. Phases I (Initializing), II (Development), and III (Transfer) focus on the product development process and the ongoing interaction of all included departments (development, construction, production). Phase IV (production support) accompanies the whole development project and contains activities and measures to support tasks that are performed in phases I, II, and III. Caused by the identification of optimization potentials beside the interface of development and construction department, we developed Phase V (project-independent activities) which contains activities and measures to increase transparency and information transfer in the whole organization.

The following sections will describe the five phases of our approach and the included measures in more detail.

Procedure Model in Detail

Figure 4 shows a closer look on Phases I and II. The special task here is the *target definition workshop*, which is responsible for the definition of knowledge goals, responsibilities, exchange and feedback, information, and communication tasks, which are necessary for project execution (for details take a look at regarding chapter).

Initializing Phase (I)

Phase I (Initializing) handles all preparation activities for the execution of the development phase, which starts overlapping with it. Preparation means securing ongoing information exchange, communication, and exchange of experiences between all participating departments.

Figure 3. Concept overview

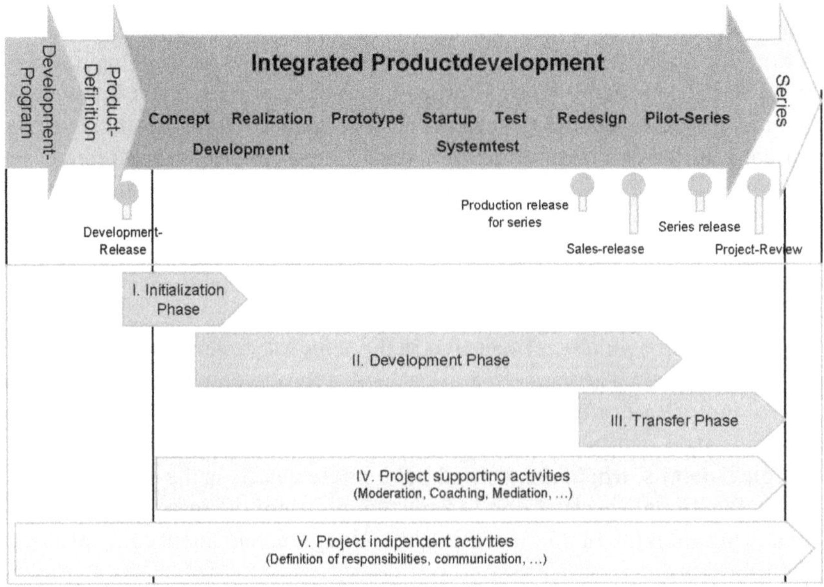

Subphase I.1 – Preparation

In this subphase, the project manager of the development project prepares a presentation of the idea behind a new product (e.g., machine or new series), which contains the news and makes the differences to actual products more transparent.

After this, the project manager holds a presentation in front of leaders and experienced employees of all departments of TAT to obtain initial feedback. This also fosters initial discussion processes among employees and guarantees the same amount of information to all personnel, which is highly important for motivating employees (Davenport, 1998).

Presentation of ideas:

- **Participants:** leaders and experienced employees of departments (selected by heads of departments)
- **Responsibility:** project manager and management
- **Content:** presentation of idea of new machine (or series), special differences to existing machines. Technological details are not presented in detail
- **Goal:** collecting initial feedback and initiating first discussion processes in the company

The second important activity of this subphase is the creation of a concept presentation, which can be done after finishing the concept subphase in the integrated development process (Figure 3). The presentation contains the most important facts such as technological requirements, innovations, or complex elements.

Figure 4. Concept detail – part 1

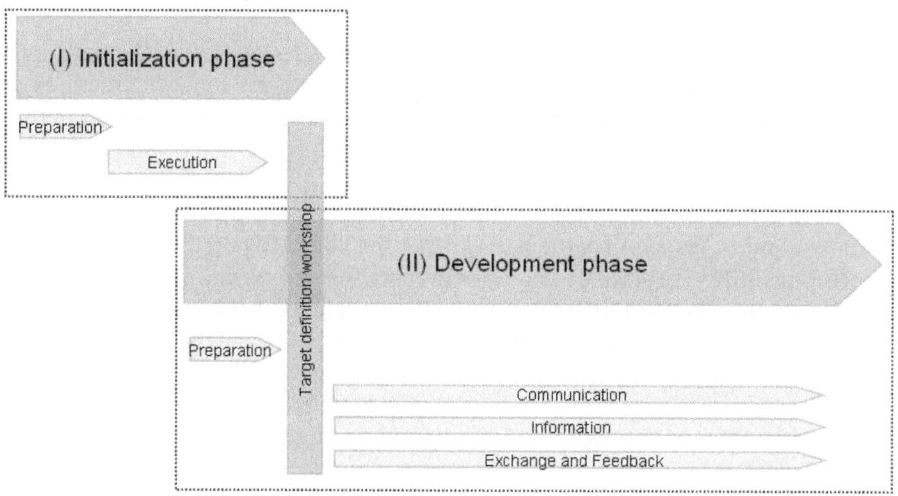

Concept presentation:

- **Participants:** if possible, all employees of TAT
- **Responsibility:** project manager
- **Content:** presentation of machine concept, including all defined technological details, requirements, and performance facts
- **Goal:** identification of all employees with new machine and motivation of employees by early involvation, intensivation of discussion processes eased by equal information level

Subphase I.2 – Execution

This subphase handles the execution of all presentations that are not part of the target definition workshop. The main idea besides the equal information level and discussion processes is the identification of employees with "their" machine.

Target Definition Workshop

The preparation of the target definition workshop is done in subphase 1 of Phase II—preparation (see section on subphase II.1). Content of this workshop is the definition of so-called "knowledge goals." These knowledge goals are relevant for cooperation of the different departments within the development project. The result of the workshop should be a way to secure the communication, information, and experience exchange and feedback between employees of these departments. It is NOT the goal of this workshop to work out technological requirements, because these are defaults already defined by product idea and concept of the new machine (series).

Participants are all heads of units and selected employees (if possible opinion leaders) of participating departments. The participants document their commitment by signing the protocol of the workshop.

As another result of this workshop, technical topic groups (see section on applied knowledge management methods) are defined to build project support structures and activities. Special technical topic groups could be electronics, mechanics, and so forth, which handle a smaller field in the development process.

Target definition workshop:

- **Participants:** leaders of participating departments and (if possible) opinion leaders
- **Responsibility:** project manager (for preparation and execution of workshop)
- **Preparation:** meeting schedule, invitations, preparation of agenda, preparation of short presentation about critical elements of the new machine. Critical means elements with "high effort for TAT," "completely new for TAT," or "success factor for TAT"
- **Content:** discussion of critical elements and the ongoing information and experience exchange in the development process across department borders. Definition of technical topic groups and their leaders/participants
- **Goal:** definition of cooperation in development process across departments. No technological goals for machine (which are already stored in the concept)

Possible goals out of such a workshop are as follows:

- **Goal 1:** securing feedback from all TAT departments
- **Goal 2:** monthly exchange of project status, experiences, and problems between development and construction staff
- **Goal 3:** quarterly information of all departments about project status and experiences

All defined goals are tracked with adequate measures in the development phase (see following section).

Development Phase (II)

The development phase is of great importance for the successful implementation of the procedure model, because in this phase the interaction of all participating departments occurs. Substantial for this phase is the definition of knowledge and communication goals in the target definition workshop.

The three subphases (1-3) execute and track the defined and committed goals out of the target definition workshop. This fosters efficient cooperation, successive construction of know-how in all departments, following the development department, usage of know-how of the following departments, and last but not least, securing the ongoing information about the project realization of all TAT employees.

Subphase II.1 – Preparation

As preparation work is already done before the target definition workshop, there is an overlapping part with subphase 2 of the initialization phase. A suggestion for the workshop is to take an external moderator for efficiency and meeting targets. During this preparation phase, the heads of units also select members of their departments for participation.

Subphase II.2 – Communication

Communication, meaning active and directed information transfer, is established in group meetings (see section on applied knowledge management methods) and an electronic project management tool. Van Heijst et al. (1998) described the act of organizational learning through communication. As one can see in Figure 5, the communication of experience brings an increase in organizational knowledge.

This constellation works both ways for learning out of communication (Van Heist et al., 1998): supply-driven and demand-driven learning. In supply-driven learning, the individual employee gains experience and deeper know-how and communicates this to his/her colleagues. Demand-driven learning describes the situation of an employee, who is searching for an answer for a specific problem or topic.

In TAT, the members of the service department obtained input from customers and thus learned about problems and failures. Structured meetings where this customer knowledge is spread among concerned employees led to constructive innovations and improvements during the series production.

Fostered by the heterogeneous participants of such group meetings, new and important information is spread very efficiently to all departments of TAT. The more formal communication is handled by a project management tool which is described in more detail later. This tool secures the documented information broadcast and supports feedback rules, which force people to react and provide input. As a result from former studies and projects, it is necessary to force people at a certain point to commit or to provide feedback.

Subphase II.3 – Information

Based on committed information goals, the project manager informs all participating employees by e-mail about the actual situation of the project or further news. In parallel, the same information will be published on posters or blackboards in all central areas (e.g., kitchen, coffee machine, smoking area, etc.) to keep all employees informed.

Different to the communication phase is the fact that in this phase (information), the communication runs one way. This is a push methodology, the goal of which is to spread information.

Figure 5. Organizational learning through communication (Van Heijst et al., 1998)

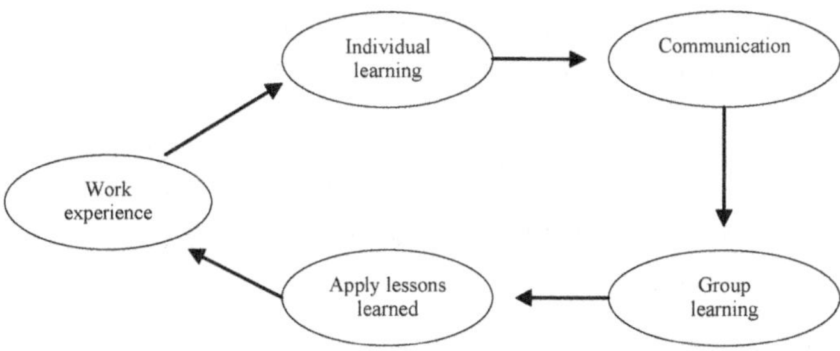

All group meetings are documented in a protocol which is published via the electronic project management tool to all relevant employees (mostly all participating employees), which grants that all involved people have the actual information about decisions, problems, or facts. The IT solution also enables employees who are not directly involved to keep in touch and stay informed, for example, marketing or purchasing department as members of the information group.

Information means, therefore, creating the possibility for facing future situations. In a special case, the purchasing department was so able to check possible suppliers in advance to obtain better conditions.

Subphase II.4 – Exchange and Feedback

The exchange process defines the interaction between all technical topic groups to prevent information gaps. In their group meetings, the technical topic groups work out important elements of their special areas of interest. Important elements include those that are of highly complex or are very time critical during the transfer between development and construction department. These elements are gathered in a structured collection which is periodically reviewed.

A possible way to increase the quality of work is to establish an internal (or if possible, external) feedback group, consisting of experts or experienced people. The optional involvement of external specialists could be done by cooperations with universities or research institutes, which is an upcoming topic in Germany (Edler, 2003).

The results (relevant elements, part concepts, solution concepts, or important experiences) of a technical topic group are sent to a defined feedback group. This group reviews the results and brings in their own opinion and also experience. The main goal is here to use synergies between the knowledge of different groups and also to avoid technological or organizational blindness.

Communication, information, exchange, and feedback:

- **Participants:** all employees (partly), technical topic groups for communication, exchange and feedback are managed by members of the development or construction department
- **Responsibility:** project manager (for informing all employees) group responsible for the work in the group
- **Preparation:** information for all employees; in special cases (confidential information), it is useful to involve the top management, organization of technical topic groups and search for group manager (this task is performed during the target definition workshop)
- **Content:** information about project realization status; communication, exchange, and feedback about important (development or transfer) topics
- **Goal:** ongoing information of all employees during the project run time in all departments following the development department. Usage of existing know-how in following departments. Creating an increased "our product" feeling in all participating employees for securing efficient and target-oriented cooperation

Figure 6. Concept detail – part 2

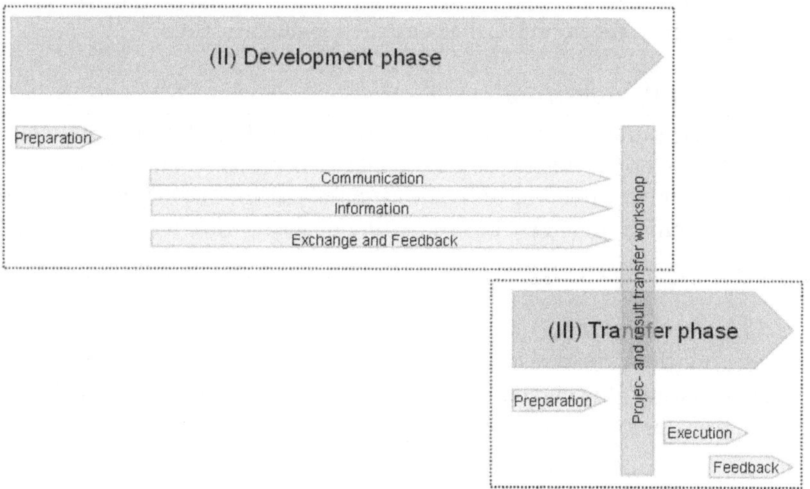

Project and Result Transfer Workshop

As described in Figure 6, the concept includes also a workshop for defining how to transfer the project itself and special results between development department and construction department. This workshop initializes the transfer phase and must already be planned for in the overall project plan. The main subject of the transfer workshop is the formulation of a detailed transfer plan. Participants are largely the same as in the target definition workshop.

A moderator (external) prepares afterward a protocol and a transfer plan in digital media. The protocol and transfer plan must be committed by each participant of the workshop, which is done by using the project management software and its feedback functionality. The project transfer plan provides a summary of what, who, with whom, when, and in which way it has to be delivered. As an instrument for planning, execution, and control, a transfer matrix has been developed, which is described in more detail in another section.

A precondition of a successful application is the ongoing documentation of activities and results done by technical topic groups during the development process.

Project and result transfer workshop:

- **Participants:** leaders of participating departments and (if possible) opinion leaders
- **Responsibility:** project manager (for preparation and execution of workshop)
- **Preconditions:** activities and outputs are already in required form included in the project transfer matrix
- **Content:** specification of single elements of project transfer matrix, such as priority, start-end dates, responsible persons, and participants of transfer
- **Goal:** detailed planning of transfer, which is done during the execution of the transfer phase (III)

Transfer Phase (III)

The execution of this phase grants the efficient transfer of project results to following departments, for example, the construction department.

Subphase III.1 – Preparation

Like the preparation of the target definition workshop, the preparation of the transfer workshop overlaps the preliminary phase. The project manager plans with the (external) moderator the workshop to fix the essential points. The target is to grant after the workshop a detailed transfer plan (consisting of what, who, with whom, when, in which kind) is available.

Subphase III.2 – Execution

The execution this subphase handles mainly the implementation of the transfer plan and the documentation of occurring problems and responding solutions. To document these steps, a transfer protocol is used.

Subphase III.3 – Feedback

The subphase feedback is the final step of the cooperating project handling. Of importance for future projects is the documentation of gained experiences from the current development project. To grant the best possible reuse of experience, it is necessary to collect "lessons learned" of the technical topic groups, from the project manager and subproject managers. This can be done by collecting special topics, such as problem-solution combinations, or by using a storytelling, "light" approach (or something like action reviews). Resulting documents will be collected and provided in the project management software.

It is crucial to encourage or to "force" project managers to take a look at the "experience database" before they start a new project. This is a point to change organizational culture. Accepting know-how out of the experiences of others. "Moreover, they must clearly explain the rationale for their final decision, including why they chose to accept some input and advice while rejecting other suggestions. By doing so, leaders can encourage divergent thinking while building decision acceptance" (Roberto, 2002, p. X).

Project Supporting Activities (IV)

Project supporting activities are not directed to a certain stage of the project but chronological delimited by the project duration. So measures lasting the whole period such as established technical topic groups are started at the project start and finished by a structured closing. Structured closing means the collection of gained know-how, findings of lessons learned, and review of managed processes (including communication processes) as described in subphase III.3 – Feedback.

The following measures could be defined as project supporting activities:

- Establishing of technical topic groups
- Organization of group meetings
- Providing IT support
- Creation of a standardized documentation and folder structure

- Moderation, coaching, mediation (providing staff or competence)
- Information activities (e.g., topic of the week)

Information Activities

As part of the information strategy, the publication of special topics for a short period (a week) is done by publishing posters on blackboards or similar information points in central communication areas such as coffee corners, buffet area, or smoking areas. A future idea could also be the establishing of "infopoints" with specially configured PCs accessing the intranet. Such information and knowledge markets (Davenport, 1998) foster communication, information transfer, and knowledge exchange concerning this special topic. The topic responsible person is the project manager.

Project-Independent Activities (V)

Project-independent activities are institutionalized in the organization. These activities affect the organizational structure more than the virtual organization of a project management structure.

The following activities are defined as independent from a running project and can be initiated every time:

- Definition of a responsible contact person for each department
- Supply of communication means
- Clearly defined work distribution

The first two activities increase internal (and external) communication by providing methods and structures and another topic, clearly pointed out in the online survey, is the clearness of work distribution. A solution for the last point is a team around the head of unit, which describes the work of the department.

Definition of Contact Person for Each Department

To increase the efficiency of communication, especially after delivery of machines that reached the maturity phase, it is necessary to define a responsible contact person per department. Additionally, the technical topic group agents could be defined as contact persons for the individual development topics.

Communication Means

To support informal discussions (which lead to the most creative solutions), it is possible to provide whiteboards or flip charts in communication areas. Ideas could so be described more easily and worked out in more detail than only telling it. Additionally more people could take part in the discussion because it is documented.

Applied Knowledge Management Methods

To achieve the final result of a knowledge-oriented R&D process, the following knowledge management methods have been used and implemented: teams and communities of practice (CoPs) (Wenger, McDermott, & Snyder, 2002); interface handling methods such as workshops; early information system to create awareness; IT system support for decisions; information transfer; and process documentation (Maier, 2004).

As a final step, a reflection step has also been integrated to obtain lessons learned and further improvements along the process.

Technical Topic Groups

These groups are a mixture of CoPs and teams, a semi-open community with a more-or-less defined goal — development of special topics of a new machine (e.g., electronics, mechanics). Like other constructs (CoPs) (Lave & Wenger, 1991), Ba (Nonaka & Konno, 1998), communities of creation (Sawhney & Prandelli, 2000), or networks of collaborating organizations (Powell, Koput, & Smith-Doerr, 1992), such technical topic groups are an extremely important issue for knowledge creation within a company.

Technical topic groups are not organizational units. They consist of participants from *different* departments (not only development or construction department) who are also involved in the topic of the group (e.g., technical topic group for hydraulic systems). Technical topic groups should not exceed seven members for efficiency (Fay, Garrod, & Carletta, 2000).

Each technical topic group nominates an agent who acts as feedback responder. This means the agent answers and comments all feedback inquiries from other groups. All other participants of the technical topic group will only be informed and deliver their comments to their agent.

Results and developments (including relevance) of technical topic groups are documented later on in the transfer matrix.

Organization of Group Meetings

To optimize the cross-department information and communication, it is necessary to institutionalize group meetings of technical topic groups. Each meeting should have a certain topic: development problem, development status, new technology, and so forth. These topics should be primarily suggested by development staff, and the other participants provide input and participate in discussions (bringing in their experience). Group meetings should be arranged periodically (e.g., starting with one meeting per month at the beginning up to weekly). To keep the organizational effort per meeting as small as possible, the meeting organization could be done in a rotating system. The organization could be kept simple: agenda, reservation of meeting room, sending out invitations, and documentation of meeting in meeting protocol.

Like CoPs, technical topic groups share knowledge among different departments and increase the amount of knowledge carriers (not only one person, who could get lost) and also organizational knowledge (institutionalization of know-how and best practices) (Van Heijst et al., 1998).

Project Management Tool/Software

IT support of development is split into two major parts: first is the project documentation (structured documents and folders) and second is the project management software itself. All documents and templates for protocols are provided by the project management software; that is the reason for combining these points into one topic.

Creation of Standardized Documents

The creation of a standardized documentation and folder structure should increase the efficiency in project management. The structure provides information about the point of time when documents have to be created and how they must be structured. To ease the access to these documents, it is useful to create a project-independent folder structure or to implement a document management system.

Implemented standard documents are as follows:

- Feedback document: for feedback groups to obtain feedback in structured and similar form
- Status document: designed for ongoing overview about project status and relevant results. This document is also used for the project information group. The project plan must contain points of time when such documents have to be created
- Agenda and protocol templates for technical topic groups: for a consistent documentation
- Transfer protocol template: for consistent documentation of project-result transfer among involved employees

Project Management Software

During the conceptual planning, it was necessary to plan the application of the existing project management software. As described above, the project management tool supports, additional to the provision of documents, information and feedback processes. To reach this, it was necessary to implement the following roles and dedicated functionalities:

- Project manager: person responsible for project, who accepts document release
- Project member: according to the field of activity in the development project, these persons are responsible for providing and creating documents
- Technical topic group leaders: can create documents to inform their group and project members
- Project feedback group: consists of one agent per technical topic group. The members of this group must give their feedback to documents from project management, project members, and other technical topic groups.
- Project information group: this group contains all other technical topic group members and employees who must be kept informed about the ongoing development activities. This is necessary to prepare early upcoming activities. This information process enables employees to keep a complete overview and it also initiates an informal communication about new developments.

Project Transfer Matrix

During the transfer workshop, the team fills the project transfer matrix, which is used for planning and controlling the transfer of the development project results. The matrix contains all necessary information for the transfer of elements, responsibilities, and status (Table 1).

In detail, the complete TAT matrix consists of the following columns:

- **Project steps:** contains all process steps that have been executed during the product development. This column is filled out by the project members in the technical topic group meetings.

Table 1. Project transfer matrix (excerpt)

Project steps	Executing division	Output	Status (in per cent)	Transfer relevance	Transfer complexy	Transfer responsibility
List of Requirements; Functional Specification and Specification Sheet for the whole project and for the teams	D		100	C	C	
List of suppliers and possible suppliers	D		95	A	B	
List of specific assembly instructions	D		0	A	B	
Project documentation of the R&D	D		running	C	C	
Update list of risks	D		running	B	C	
Test planning and supervision	D		running	C	C	
Training Service	D/C		0	A	A	
Creation of acceptance report	C/D		10	A	A	
Creation of maintenance timetable	C/D		0	A	A	
Training Production	C/D		20	A	A	
Training Assembling	C/D		20	A	A	
Training Sales and Marketing	C/D		10	A	B	

- **Executing department:** the current step is managed and executed by department (XY), or in combination with department (AB).
- **Output:** describes the output of the current project step.
- **Status:** current status of execution in percent.
- **Transfer relevance:** (priority) the definition of A (high), B (medium), or C (low) describes the importance of the transfer of these elements (and defines the order of the transferred elements).
- **Transfer complexity:** the definition of A (high), B (medium), or C (low) describes how difficult it is to transfer this element.
- **Transfer responsibility:** name of employee who is responsible for transfer of this element.
- **Transfer start:** date of when transfer should start.
- **Transfer end:** date of when transfer should be finished.
- **Status of transfer (%):** the transfer responsible person documents in this weekly updated column the transfer status. If a delay arises, the project manager can intervene.
- **Transfer protocol (yes/no):** during the transfer workshop, it is defined if it is necessary to create a protocol for this transfer element, because if the element is not important and there is only low complexity, it is not always necessary to prepare a protocol. To prepare useless protocols would lead to less motivation.
- **Target department:** department that gets output of current project step.
- **Target responsible:** employee of target department who is responsible for transfer.
- **Notes:** additional information for documentation, for example, reasons for delay.

The project transfer matrix is a vital document that describes not only the transfer process but also documents it.

CURRENT CHALLENGES FACING THE ORGANIZATION

Challenges During the Project and Current Status

Based on the fact that the project has been initiated under the pressure of an existing development project, at the beginning the concept could only support this project in the last phases — transfer of experiences and information. The departments used the transfer matrix and managed a structured handover. In parallel, the organization established two technical topic groups (hydraulic systems and electronic systems) and built up the reporting, information, and feedback groups within the project management software.

Current status is now a broad acceptance of the concept. The employees of the R&D and construction departments are now aware that they need each other and work more cooperatively. Company representatives lead this back to team meetings and technical topic groups, where they sit together and discuss constructively — "work is easier if we approach a challenge together." As a tool for measuring this fact, one employee told us that employees now go for coffee break together. Another result is the involvement of the service and after-sales department in the development process. Due to the good experiences with the supporting project management tool, there will be further activities to improve its functionalities. Information providers, for example, like the possibility of the tool to check who read the information and who gave feedback. Project-independent activities (e.g., posters, etc.) have also been implemented and the top-down information flows.

General Challenges

Companies have to concentrate on their own core competencies to compensate the pressure arising from the market and the increasing complexity of processes, products, or surrounding environment. Modern companies are specialized on similar fields and form work groups, work lines, or even companies for this ones. Specialization in this context means, on the one hand, highly qualified employees and very special know-how, but on the other hand, a large amount of communication work. A holistic view and a long-term plan are necessary to achieve such ambitious goals as knowledge management in a diversified or spread company.

Today, employees need not only physical material for their daily work, but also an increasing amount of information and knowledge. Codification of knowledge and dedicated sharing of this information is used for keeping knowledge within the company and to support all working steps where this information is needed. This requires also knowing more than one simple task for a further understanding of the whole process. Employees must be able to get more than a local view to notice barriers or critical interfaces to neighbor tasks. This consciousness enables innovation and further improvements on the process. The same is valid for departments and their organizational borders.

The more specialized a department, the higher the need for a common understanding of company goals and project goals. Employees from different departments work together on different projects and interact in teams. These teams form a special kind of dynamic information network cross to typical information channels of a company. Nonaka called this a "hypertext organization" (Nonaka & Takeuchi, 1995) and later an organization as organic configuration of ba (Nonaka & Konno, 2003), because the structure is dynamically formed on demand and changes over time.

REFERENCES

Davenport, T. (1998). *Working knowledge*. Cambridge, MA: Harvard University Press.

Edler, J. (2003). *Knowledge management in German industry. Study in the framework of an OECD initiative of the Centre for Educational Research and Innovation (CERI)*. Karlsruhe: Fraunhofer Institute for Systems and Innovation Research (ISI).

Fay, N., Garrod, S., & Carletta, J. (2000). Group discussion as interactive dialogue or serial monologue: The influence of group size. *Psychological Science, 11*(6), 487-492.

Lave, J., & Wenger, E. (1991). *Situated learning – Legitimate peripheral participation*. Cambridge, UK: Cambridge University Press.

Maier, R. (2004). *Knowledge management systems* (2nd ed.). Berlin: Springer.

Nonaka, I., & Konno, N. (1998). The concept of "Ba": Building a foundation for knowledge creation. *California Management Review, 40*, 40-54.

Nonaka, I., & Takeuchi, H. (1995). *The knowledge-creating company*. Oxford: Oxford University Press.

Nonaka, I., & Toyama, R. (2003). The knowledge-creating theory revisited: Knowledge creation as a synthesizing process. *Knowledge Management Research and Practice, 1*(1), 2-10.

Powell, W., Koput, K., & Smith-Doerr, L. (1996). Inter-organizational collaboration and the focus of innovation: Networks of learning in biotechnology. *Administrative Science Quarterly, 41*, 116-146.

Probst, G., Raub, S., & Romhardt, K. (1999). *Managing knowledge*. : John Wiley and Sons.

Roberto, M. (2002). *Lessons from Everest: The interaction of cognitive bias, psychological safety, and system complexity*. Harvard Business School Press.

Sawhney, M., & Prandelli, E. (2000). Communities of creation: Managing distributed innovation in turbulent markets. *California Management Review, 41*, 63-74.

van Heijst, G. et al. (1998). Organizing corporate memories. In U. Borghoff & R. Pareschi (Eds.), *Information technology for knowledge management*. Berlin: Springer.

Wenger, E., McDermott, R., & Snyder, W. (2002). *Cultivating communities of practice*. Harvard Business School Press.

FURTHER READING

Bohm, D. (1996). *On dialogue*. Routledge.

Brown, J., & Duguid, P. (2000). *The social life of information*. Harvard Business School Press.

Firestone, J. (2003). *Enterprise information portals and knowledge management*. Butterworth-Heinemann.

Holsapple, C. (Ed.). (2003). *Handbook on knowledge management.* Berlin: Springer.

McDermott, R. (1999a). The role of communities of practice in team organizations. *Knowledge Management Review,* May/June.

McDermott R. (1999b). Nuturing three dimensional communities of practice: How to get the most out of human networks. *Knowledge Management Review,* Fall.

Pfeffer, J., & Sutton, R. (1999). *The knowing-doing gap: How smart companies turn knowledge into action.* Harvard Business School Press.

Rogers, E. (1995). *Diffusion of innovations* (4th ed.). New York: The Free Press.

Scharmer, O. (2000, May 25-26). Presencing: Learning from the future as it emerges: On the tacit dimension of leading revolutionary change. *Conference on Knowledge and Innovation*, Helsinki School of Economics, Helsinki, Finland.

Teece, D., Pisano, G., & Shuen, A. (1997). Dynamic capabilities and strategic management. *Strategic Management Journal.*

Chapter XII

Know-CoM: Decentralized Knowledge Management Systems for Cooperating Die- and Mold-Making SMEs

Florian Bayer, Martin-Luther-University Halle-Wittenberg, Germany

Rafael Enparantza, Centro Technológico Tekniker, Spain

Ronald Maier, Martin-Luther-University Halle-Wittenberg, Germany

Franz Obermair, Profactor Produktionsforschungs GmbH, Austria

Bernhard Schmiedinger, Profactor Produktionsforschungs GmbH, Austria

EXECUTIVE SUMMARY

The die- and mold-making industry can be characterized by small and medium enterprises (SMEs), sophisticated technologies, and highly skilled employees who have to cooperate in order to fulfill orders of customers with which they are engaged in an intensive process of knowledge exchange. The knowledge-intensive production process of die and mold makers consequently requires an integrated organizational and technical solution to support the sharing of documented knowledge as well as collaboration. Standard knowledge management systems (KMS) primarily target the organization-internal processes and documented knowledge of large organizations. Know-CoM intends to overcome the limitations of these solutions and explicitly targets

SMEs as well as knowledge processes that cross organizational boundaries. Know-CoM is a European Commission-funded CRAFT project that provides an advanced concept of decentralized management of access privileges to personal, protected, and public knowledge spaces. An easy-to-use solution supports the capturing of experiences. A joint knowledge structure brokers context across organizational boundaries and eases discovery of knowledge and experts. Finally, a knowledge management certification technique allows for a coordinated reuse of knowledge that is integrated with the daily work practices of die and mold makers.

BACKGROUND

Dies and molds are characterized by hard, low-wear materials, complex geometry, and structures. Their production requires sophisticated technologies, for example, five-axis machining, high-speed cutting, and so forth, and highly experienced and qualified staff (Antoñana, 2000). Dies and molds are used in many industries, for example, by suppliers of components in the automotive industry. Their prices vary by an average of 45,000 from 20,000 to 800,000, whereas the margins are about 6%. The lead time for the production of a die or mold ranges from one to 10 months. For toolmakers, the most important competitive factors are time to market, personnel costs, and quality of the resulting tools. The last ISTMA Annual Report (Antoñana, 2000) highlighted some of the handicaps of the European tool and die industry competitiveness:

- Continuous pressure to reduce time to market
- Strong pressure on prices and high personnel costs
- Growing difficulty to attract and acquire skilled workers

In many SMEs, these handicaps lead to bad working conditions, accidents, and even social problems (Antoñana, 2000).

The market size is 25,000 million euros worldwide (Antoñana, 2000). The European die- and mold-making industry is composed mainly of small and medium-sized enterprises (SMEs) with an average of 23 employees. There is a wide variety of dies and molds (e.g., die casting, plastic, or glass molds) for different purposes and industries. Typically, die- and mold-making companies (DMCs) specialize in certain areas of the industry. Many products require the combination of several dies and molds from different fields and thus customers regularly need to obtain them from more than one producer. Thus, cooperation between DMCs holding complementary competencies is necessary in many cases, particularly to acquire large orders. Producers have to coordinate their activities closely and communicate intensively in order to jointly execute orders. However, the specialization of the DMCs is not only complementary, but also overlapping. Therefore, the relationship between the DMCs can be described as coopetition, because they cooperate and collaborate on the one hand during the joint execution of orders and on the other hand, they compete in markets. Regarding the introduction of knowledge management (KM), the state of coopetition on the one hand requires advanced instruments that create an environment for unobstructed knowledge exchange between the cooperating DMCs and on the other hand, competition poses a significant barrier for the exchange of knowledge across organizational boundaries. In addition to the cooperation and exchange of experiences with other die and mold makers, the DMCs often need to exchange and jointly develop knowledge with their suppliers and customers. Suppliers hold expertise concerning characteristics of materials, tools, and about standard parts needed to manufacture dies or molds. Customers possess knowledge about how the parts that are produced using these dies or molds meet the requirements of the customer's customers. For example, when a plastic part for the automotive industry, such as a car dashboard, is produced, the part has to fulfill requirements regarding surface structure or stability. These requirements must be considered by the die and mold maker during the design phase of the tool with which later the car dashboard will be produced. Additionally, customers of DMCs use different injection-molding and die-casting machines to manufacture parts, which vary in the dimensions power, feed, stroke, clamping surface, force, and so forth. Die- and mold-making companies depend much on experiences with customer machines and materials because the produced tool has to fit in the injection-molding or die-casting machine.

In the next section, we discuss the representative knowledge-intensive core business process of DMCs and study the main issues concerning knowledge exchange, application, retention, and securing.

SETTING THE STAGE

For the detailed analysis of the core process and the technical environment of DMCs, we used questionnaires as well as expert interviews with CEOs, designers, and production planners of seven European die- and mold-making companies. Based on the actual state and requirements identified, we derived a number of knowledge-related challenges. The questionnaires were composed of questions concerning the following areas:

- IT infrastructure and use of IT in the companies
- Production process and its information and knowledge flows
- Handling of knowledge in the company
- Cooperation with partners, customers, and suppliers
- Software requirements and expectations from a KMS

The IT part investigated the technical environment of DMCs as well as the employees' technical expertise. Alongside the hardware available and the software used, we studied the media preferred for internal and external communication.

The questionnaire was used to obtain information about typical development processes of DMCs and to distill the core process. For each process step, it was analyzed which data, information, or knowledge is needed; which sources it comes from; which data, information, or knowledge is created; and where knowledge gaps or potential for improvement exist. Furthermore, experts and persons responsible for process steps were determined.

We asked which kinds of knowledge (e.g., knowledge about products, partners, skills) are stored in which way (e.g., electronically, on paper, or in the heads of people), which criteria were used to structure documents, and what were the main topics. Next to the handling of knowledge, the use of KM-related tools was analyzed. Concerning cooperation, it was examined which roles perform cooperative activities as well as which activities the DMCs intend to carry out with Know-CoM in the future. Additionally, we examined confidentiality of the knowledge shared with partners and customers as well as barriers that prevent knowledge sharing across organizational boundaries.

Finally, it was analyzed which KM-specific functions should be integrated in the software (e.g., knowledge maps, automatic classification, personalization).

The Core Process

The typical development process of die- and mold-making companies derived from expert interviews and questionnaires (see section "Setting the Stage") is depicted in Figure 1. The symbols below the process illustrate some examples of data needed or created during the particular process phases.

Offer creation is carried out in parallel to mold *conceptual planning* and is triggered by customer requests. Customers send a drawing of the part and a list with required mold or die materials. The documents have different formats such as sheets of paper (hand-made sketch, printings, etc.) or electronic documents (CAD files, etc.). Having received the request, the company calculates an offer and sends it back to the customer. Calculation depends on different information gathered or delivered by the customer, for example, type and characteristics of the materials and the part's complexity. The more detailed the request is, the better the company is able to plan and provide a solution for the request. Independent of the information delivered by the customer, calculating offers is difficult due to the high variety of dies or molds formerly produced. Particularly, estimating the number of cost-intensive redesign cycles is very hard (see process step, *mold design changes*). The systematic comparison of the die or mold to be produced to already-produced ones with respect to geometry, material, and so forth, can ease the offer creation process, particularly the estimation of the redesign loops significantly and improve the margin. Based on our interviews and questionnaires, we observed that previous offers, CAD drawings, and so forth, are stored unsystematically.

Mold conceptual planning is based on the customer's requirements regarding functionality, behavior, number of parts per mold or die, number of injections per mold or die, and structure of the planned form. *Conceptual planning* requires information about preconditions related to the construction such as data of the injection mold or die machines, and usability of standard parts. Internal information about availability of production lines and production skills are also needed for suggestions and decisions.

Figure 1. Core process of die- and mold-manufacturing SMEs

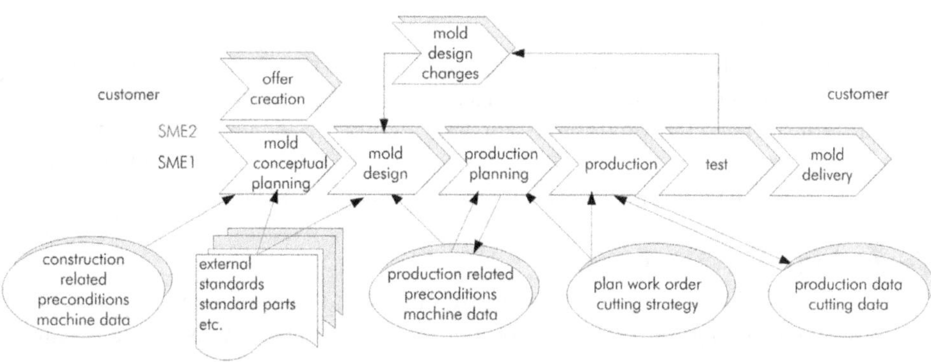

As identified by the questionnaires, the required information is rarely delivered completely by the customer and therefore further time-consuming inquiries are the consequence.

When an order is placed, the *design* starts from an in-depth study of the use of the final product and consists of optional mold-filling simulations, construction and creation of technical documents (e.g., in AutoCAD, CATIA, Solid Edge), specification of CNC (computerized numerical control) programs, as well as the design of inserts, sliders, and cooling system. Examples for the variety of information required during this phase are production-related preconditions, customer machine data, as well as internal machine tool data, and information about standard parts and their specifics.

Based on the product's specifications, the production planner uses information about production-related preconditions such as the company's capacities and capabilities to plan further steps. To implement CNC programs, select cutting strategies or plan work orders, detailed information, and experiences are necessary.

In *production,* dies and molds are produced using CNC machines or other production facilities. Examples of information required in this process step are standard part information, cutting data and cutting strategies, machine data, as well as production plans. Particularly, the choice of an adequate cutting strategy including selection and sequence of cutting tools is strongly based on experience. To define cutting strategies, the mold material, the tool used (diameter, length, notation, supplier, number of cutting edges, coating), and the cutting parameters (revolutions per minute, cutting speed, feed rate, radial cutting depth, axial cutting depth) have to be taken into account. Knowledge about cutting data and cutting strategies is mostly tacit and therefore not documented. Quality criteria for a cutting strategy are, for example, the wasted material or the lifetime of a cutting tool that is additionally influenced by characteristics of the machine tool used.

The following step *test* is dominated by extensive testing of dies and molds in compliance with the customer's requirements. Tested parameters are especially surface structure, dimensions of the mold/die, or stability of critical parts. Possibly, improvements concerning *design* are necessary, if the injection mold or die cast part does not meet the expectations of the customer or the requirements catalog. Insufficient test results can lead to changes of mold *design*. These changes are expensive, because the process has to restart from the mold *design*. Every point mentioned as failure in the test phase has to be corrected in the *production* phase. The number of redesign cycles ranges from 4 to 20 cycles per mold or die and has in Europe an average of seven cycles. Regarding costs, the reduction of the number of redesign cycles promises large improvements in time and costs.

Redesign can be handled by reducing some areas of the die or mold (e.g., milling, grinding, etc.) or adding some material (through welding), if necessary. Adding material to forms reduces the quality extremely and most companies do not give a high lifetime guarantee for such dies or molds. Thus, new *design*, *production,* and *test* cycles can be necessary. When all requirements are fulfilled, then the form is delivered to the customer.

Technical Environment

The degree of process automation and of the use of IT varies much from company to company depending on its size, the region, the type of product, and the customers.

However, an average die- and mold-making company has a number of PCs that are distributed in all departments (production, design, management, commercial, after-sales) and are connected by a LAN.

Computer-aided systems such as CAD (computer-aided design), CAE (computer-aided engineering), and CAM (computer-aided manufacturing) are widely used in the business. Although many companies have licenses for three-dimensional CAD tools, two-dimensional basic tools are still used for designs and drawings of the parts and their assembly. However, a full migration to three-dimensional tools seems inevitable, because of its advantages in terms of design flexibility and visualization. Software for the simulation of injection molding is useful, but requires a high investment in terms of personnel. Therefore, many companies avoid these costs by subcontracting this task to consultants or relying on their experience and test protocols. Additionally, many European DMCs use ERP (enterprise resource planning) systems to store data concerning products, their structure, production routes, orders, suppliers, customers, and so forth.

A substantial part of the data is stored in an unstructured way on individual PCs of the employees. This can range from worksheets or data created and maintained with tailor-made programs that support, for example, the offer creation process, tools for solving technical problems, or project management applications.

Concerning the communication infrastructure, telephone, fax, and face-to-face meetings still dominate information exchange within the company, with partners, as well as with suppliers and customers. E-mail is increasingly gaining acceptance, especially when complex surface parts are the object of orders. However, for simpler 2-D parts, a handmade drawing transmitted via fax is still popular.

In general, die- and mold-making companies are quite familiar with a number of IT tools and systems, but there is a lack of integration of the different systems.

Challenges

The key challenges in the die- and mold-making industry gained from expert interviews and questionnaires during our research (see section, "Setting the Stage") are as follows:

- **Lack of experience management:** Experiences are crucial in many process steps of die or mold manufacturing. Missing documentation of experiences, lessons learned, or good practices can lead to mistakes and design failures. Also, relevant experiences from production and production planning are not available for the conceptual design of molds. Information about testing and redesign is also not provided in the conceptual design step.
- **Insufficient knowledge about customer production facilities:** Missing or insufficient customer machine and environmental data can also cause design changes after delivery of a die or mold which worked fine in the test scenarios at the toolmaker's site, but does not work on the customer's machine. Testing thus requires exchanging experiences about these working conditions as well as (planned) changes between representatives of the customer and designers.
- **Need for collaboration environment:** Subcontracting and splitting of orders require extensive coordination between the DMCs due to minimal tolerances of dies and molds. In some cases, problems arise concerning assembly of the mold or die

parts manufactured by various DMCs. Therefore, it is important that an appropriate basis for context-based sharing of knowledge and context-based collaboration between DMCs is established.

- **Management of intellectual property:** DMCs cooperate on the one hand in certain areas and on the other hand, they compete in markets (coopetition). This fact creates a significant barrier for knowledge sharing across organizational boundaries and requires measures to ensure confidentiality and protect the individual company's intellectual property.
- **Distributed incompatible sources of data:** Publicly available information about standard parts or cutting data has to be collected from several sources for each single process step. These retrieval activities are extremely resource consuming and it is not guaranteed that they deliver up-to-date information.

CASE DESCRIPTION

The Know-CoM solution aims to bridge the gap between a technology-oriented and a human-oriented KM approach (Maier, 2004, p. 355). On the one hand, there is a substantial amount of documented knowledge that is spread across the knowledge bases of cooperating SMEs, customers, and suppliers that have to be semantically integrated. On the other hand, important knowledge resides in the heads of highly skilled die and mold makers that act in a number of roles with respect to the production process. Thus, the Know-CoM solution consists of an organizational design of the knowledge processes that have to be supported by a technical solution and a procedure model that guides the implementation of KM in the toolmaking companies.

Standard KMS have a centralized architecture and normally aim at large organizations, but do not focus on the cooperation between multiple small companies in different locations. However, decentralized KMS seem to fit better for SMEs because they help (see Maier, 2004, p. 284)

- to reduce the substantial costs of the design, implementation, and maintenance of centralized knowledge management suites, in terms of hardware, standard software, as well as the often underestimated costs of designing, structuring, and organizing a centralized knowledge server;
- to reduce the barriers of individual knowledge workers to actively participate in and share the benefits of a KMS, because knowledge-sharing procedures are integrated in their daily work processes;
- to include individual messaging objects (e-mails, instant messaging objects) into the knowledge workspace that are rarely supported by centralized KMS; and
- to overcome the limitations of a KMS that (almost) exclusively focuses on organization-internal knowledge whereas many knowledge processes in die- and mold-making companies cross organizational boundaries.

Concerning DMCs and cooperation between them, particularly the low-cost criterion and the consideration of knowledge processes across organizational boundaries are specifics that have to be considered and seem to be better supported by decentralized KMS.

Regarding the company-specific part, we focus on capturing as well as providing experiences in the relevant process steps whereas concerning the cooperation across organizational boundaries the solution focuses on enabling knowledge exchange in a controlled environment on the basis of a shared context. Therefore, a multidimensional knowledge structure should foster a joint understanding between cooperation partners and to provide documented knowledge in the process steps of the core process.

The following section comprises the definition of a joint knowledge structure as basis for cooperation and the definition of knowledge spaces. Additionally, we describe in this section a method to capture experiences and the technique KM certified which aims at the systematic application of previously documented experiences. Afterward, we discuss to what extent the challenges of the die- and mold-making industry could be solved or reduced by the Know-CoM solution. Finally, we outline the reasons of the platform decision and present a procedure model for the rollout.

Definition of Knowledge Structure

A knowledge structure contains knowledge elements and the relations between them as well as metadata, which give further information about their content, and associations. To facilitate knowledge sharing, a joint knowledge structure has to be established in order to create a joint understanding between cooperating partners. Simple hierarchical knowledge structures are not suitable for cooperation, because different enterprises classify their knowledge elements or documents on the basis of different criteria (e.g., processes, topics, etc.) and end up using individual, incompatible taxonomies. Thus, it is difficult to find a structure that meets the needs of all participating companies. Additionally, nontext files (e.g., CAD drawings), which are important in the die- and mold-making industry, are hard to find by navigating the structure. Therefore, we developed a multidimensional knowledge structure on the basis of expert interviews and questionnaires (see section, "Setting the Stage") that classifies knowledge elements and documents using metadata according to the following dimensions (Maier & Sametinger, 2003, p. 4):

- **Time**: classifies a knowledge element according to time-related characteristics such as time of creation, time of last modification, or time of last access.
- **Process**: represents the step of the core process and comprises, for example, the subdimensions offer creation, design, production planning, production, or test.
- **Topic**: provides keywords intended to be relevant for the user. In the case of Know-CoM, the topics represent the most relevant knowledge areas of the die- and mold-making industry (e.g., molds, machines, parts, etc.).
- **Person**: includes suppliers, manufacturers, customers, and enterprise-internal persons, as well as their different roles within the organization. Regarding messages, the subdimensions, sender or receiver are relevant.
- **Format**: comprises formats specific to production industry (e.g., CAD file, CNC programs, etc.) next to widely used formats (e.g., .xls, .doc, .html, etc.).
- **Type of knowledge**: can be classified in contextualized data, experiences (approved, unapproved, private), lessons learned, good or best practices.
- **Location**: refers to the location described in a knowledge element which a knowledge element or in which a knowledge element was developed, for example, production facilities of customers as well as DMCs.

Figure 2. Joint knowledge structure

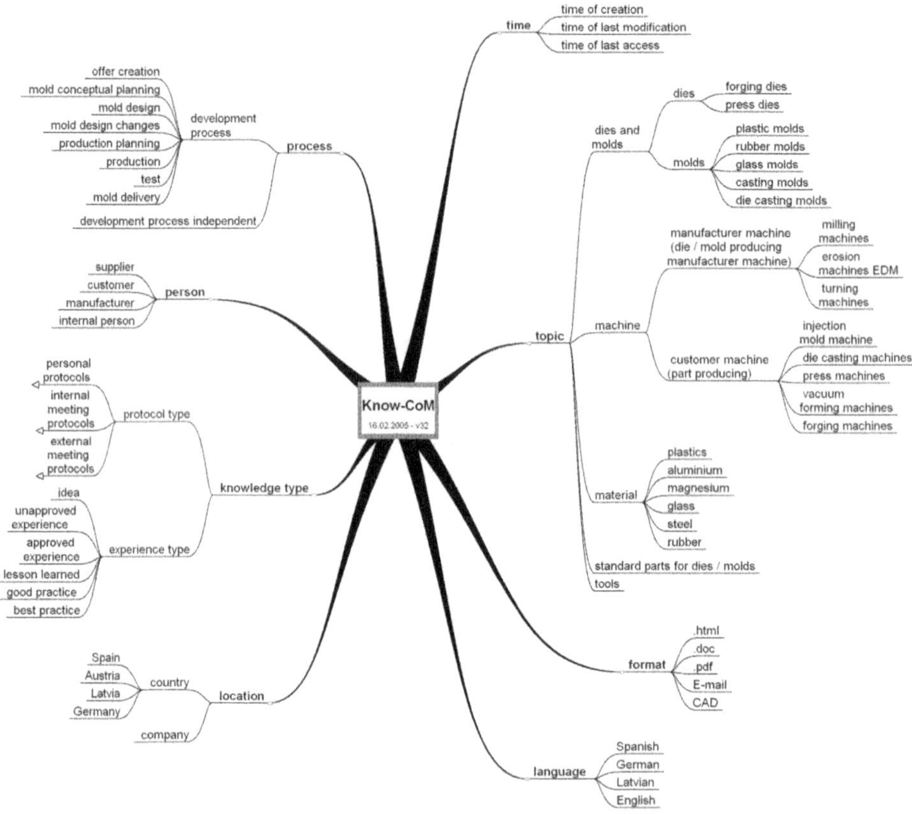

- **Language:** is required because Know-CoM is used by companies in several countries.

Figure 2 depicts the dimensions described above as a MindMap, which represents a minimal joint knowledge structure for the enterprises participating in Know-CoM.

According to these dimensions, nearly every document can be classified (semi)automatically. With the following example, the classification of a document corresponding to the eight dimensions will be illustrated:

If a tester xy (1) from the Spanish (2) company z (3) gains experiences (4) during the mold-testing phase (5) related to the plastic press mold (6) functionality on August 10 (7) and documents these experiences in the format .doc (8), then the following characteristics of the dimensions result from this documentation:

(1) person: → internal person → tester → tester xy
(2) language: → Spanish
(3) location: → company z in Spain
(4) knowledge type: → experience type → unapproved experience
(5) process: → development process → test

(6) topic: → dies and molds → mold → plastic mold → plastic press mold
(7) time: → time of creation → August 10, 2004
(8) format: → .doc

The metadata are collected automatically according to the actual working context of the employee or semiautomatically applying, for example, wizards, to guide users through a subset of metadata that cannot be derived automatically. Based on the knowledge structure, specifications of the dimensions are suggested and the user only has to approve or reject these suggestions. This multidimensional structure builds the basis for joint understanding, which is necessary for cooperation with knowledge spaces that are outlined in the following section.

Definition of Knowledge Spaces

Knowledge elements are stored in so-called knowledge spaces. Referring to the fact that SMEs in the die- and mold-making industry on the one hand cooperate in certain areas and on the other hand, compete in markets, we chose to trisect the knowledge spaces on the particular company server in private, protected, and public ones (Maier & Sametinger, 2003, p. 5) in order to reduce barriers for knowledge sharing and to protect the company's intellectual property:

- **Private knowledge spaces:** Every employee has a private knowledge space, which contains knowledge elements that are only accessible to the employee.
- **Protected knowledge spaces:** We distinguish two kinds of protected knowledge spaces: (1) team or role-oriented protected and (2) private protected. The first kind of knowledge space is used for sharing knowledge with a limited group of people based on predefined roles. The group can be, for example, an organization-internal or external defined role, group, or project team (e.g., designers, sales persons). Additionally, the individual knowledge worker can apply for a protected knowledge space, share knowledge independent of roles or teams, and grant as well as revoke access rights as he/she pleases.
- **Public knowledge spaces:** Every company server has one public knowledge space, which includes contents that are accessible for every employee in the company as well as for all members associated with Know-CoM.

In this environment, significant barriers of knowledge sharing can be reduced, because participants or organizations can decide on their own who is allowed to use their knowledge spaces and have in this way control over their intellectual property. Because of limited user groups, it can be assumed that trust between cooperating employees is higher than without such a limitation and thus sharing of explicit as well as implicit knowledge (e.g., informal exchange of ideas or experiences) is fostered. Access rights which work on the basis of user profiles and the knowledge structure can be adjusted, if a cooperation (e.g., a project spanning enterprises) is dissolved or an employee leaves the cooperation.

Every enterprise participating in Know-CoM has its own company server (Figure 3), which is trisected in different kinds of knowledge spaces. Dashed arrows show connections between the company servers and the cooperative shared-knowledge server, whereas solid arrows illustrate connections between several company servers.

Figure 3. Network of the company servers

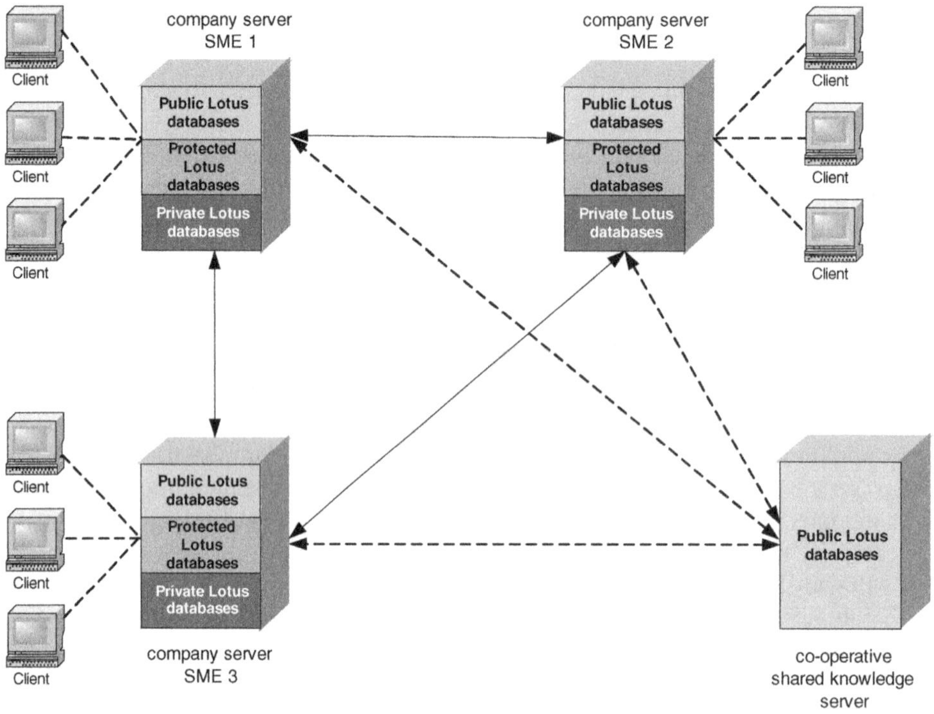

The role of the cooperative shared server is twofold. On the one hand, the server is used to provide publicly available industry-specific information, such as standard part catalogs, cutting data, and so forth, as well as community home spaces for topic-related knowledge exchange of the DMCs. On the other hand, the server should help to localize other companies, find expertise, and bring them together for cooperation. The identification of other companies is supported by company portraits stored on the cooperative server and comprise information about the companies′ areas of competency, machines, capacities, number of employees, location, contact data, and so forth, whereas the cooperation itself occurs in a peer-to-peer mode via protected knowledge spaces of company servers. Concerning roll-out of the Know-CoM solution, this server supports the creation of awareness (see section, "Rollout").

Search inquiries collect relevant documents from the adequate private database of the employee, accessible protected databases and public databases of the company servers, as well as documents from the cooperative shared-knowledge server according to user profiles and access rights. Figure 4 illustrates processing of search inquiries.

If an employee (here: user X) of a company (here: SME 1) formulates a search inquiry concerning any topic, the company server of the SME the employee works for executes the request and scans his/her private knowledge space and protected knowledge spaces, for which the employee has permission to access. As depicted in Figure 4, the employee

Figure 4. Processing of search inquiries

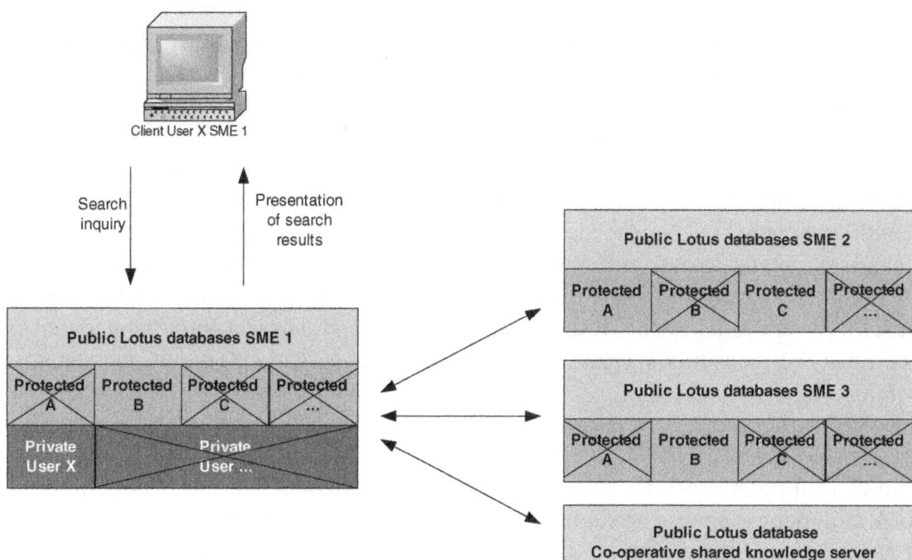

can access only the protected knowledge space B in SME 1. Additionally, the company server forwards the request to other connected servers. Also, only protected knowledge spaces accessible for the employee are scanned as well as public knowledge spaces that are not limited to a certain user group. In the example, user X has access to the public knowledge spaces of SME 2, SME 3, and to the cooperative shared-knowledge server as well as to the protected knowledge spaces A and C of SME 2 and the protected knowledge space B of SME 3. Private knowledge spaces of other SMEs are generally not accessible. After scanning the knowledge spaces, the company server of SME 1 presents the results of the search inquiry to user X. Depending on the privileges, the user can also insert, update, comment, or delete knowledge elements in the workspaces of participating companies.

After describing the knowledge structure and the network of the Know-CoM solution, including the different kinds of workspaces, the next section focuses on capturing experiences from business processes.

Capturing Experiences

The analysis of DMCs (see section, "Setting the Stage") showed that most experiences are collected in an unstructured way via paper-based or individual electronic notes (e.g., commented test results, etc.) or remain in people's heads. Therefore, the systematic and collective reuse of previously gained experiences is at the actual stage of nearly impossible and the same problems or failures occur over and over again. Thus, the KM solution aims at a technically supported and structured gathering of experiences as well as at providing these experiences in an appropriate format in relevant process steps.

The systematic documentation of experiences enables a company to solve recurring problems more effectively and can lead to sustainable competitive advantages. However, there are some barriers, that prevent documentation of experiences or reuse of already-documented experiences. The required time is a critical factor, because employees have to document in addition to other organizational duties. Therefore, the organization has to provide time tolerances to their employees. However, it must be considered that the effort concerning documentation has to be as low as possible, but simultaneously, sufficient context of the experience has to be provided. The detection of context is important, because reusability of documented experiences depends much on the context. Next to these organizational barriers, personal barriers hinder distribution or application of codified experiences. Typical personal barriers are for example insufficient willingness to share knowledge or to apply knowledge that was created by other employees (not-invented-here syndrome). Regarding the cooperation in a competitive environment, particularly the latter seems to be a serious barrier, which has to be considered by accompanying measures, such as change management, trust management, and incentive systems.

Several approaches exist for capturing experiences such as micro-articles, learning histories, RECALL, after action review, and postproject appraisal (for details, see Schindler & Eppler, 2003; Disterer, 2002; Willke, 2001; Sary & Mackey, 1996). In Know-CoM, experiences should be captured as small articles supported by templates that are structured according to *topic*, *story*, *insight,* and *conclusion* of the micro-article (according to Willke, 2001). *Topic* considers the context provided by the knowledge structure. *Story* describes the experience or learning context. *Insight* stands for the learning reason (e.g., the cause of the problem). *Conclusion* comprises the solution (e.g., a procedure) of the problem or a specific situation based on the insight. Experiences that are structured in this way might have a high reusability and traceability due to the provided context. In order to ease codifying experiences, the employees have to answer questions supported by wizards according to the context (*story*) and document their insights and solutions.

During the whole development process of dies and mold, characteristics of the multidimensional structure are collected. For every order, the collected information is forwarded and extended along the steps of the development process. Metadata are added step-by-step either automatically or semi-automatically by the application of predefined checkboxes that comprise the elements of the joint multidimensional knowledge structure. Intelligent metadata management means that based on the knowledge structure, specifications of the dimensions are suggested to the user for approval. Particularly, the automated suggestion and filling of predefined checkboxes with check marks minimizes the employees' documentation effort. This means that, for example, during work on an incoming order, metadata are added according to part, part's material, customer, customer's machine, and so forth. Metadata already collected are extended in the following steps of the core process (e.g., design, production, and test).

Additionally, employees can document experiences in every process step. After completion of the process step or of one task, wizards ask the employee whether there were specifics or problems he/she solved. The following example should explain the procedure of the capturing of experiences in detail:

A toolmaker uses in the process step *production* not the cutting tool suggested by the production planner and changes the tool supplier, because he knows that tool wastage is above average due to the material's hardness and machine characteristics.

Table 1. Example for capturing experiences

Topic:	High tool wastage
Insight:	The material was too hard and therefore the tool not suitable.
Conclusion:	Use cutting tool xx when you mill material z on machine y.

This experience has to be documented during or after the execution of the production step in order to avoid this problem, especially when another less experienced toolmaker uses this cutting tool on a similar mold. Table 1 illustrates a possible documentation, which contains the elements topic, insight, and conclusion.

Cause and solution of the problem or the specific situation are free-text fields. This kind of documentation helps on the one hand to increase traceability for other employees and on the other hand, implicit knowledge could be externalized when employees write down their interpretations. The context variables (*story*) can be detected according to the order document forwarded and extended because metadata regarding material, material's hardness, machine, cutting tools, and so forth, are in this example already collected in former process steps such as design and production planning.

Search inquiries are formulated automatically according to the context variables of the actual process step. The results are presented and ranked in dependency on the matching of the documented experiences' context variables with the variables of the actual working context.

Next to capturing experiences, their systematic application is crucial for the success of the KM initiative. This is supported by the technique KM certified.

KM Certified (KMC)

It cannot be taken for granted that employees apply previously documented knowledge. Additionally, success of the application of knowledge in business processes is hard to identify. Know-CoM contains a dynamic checklist (a kind of work flow) according to the core process which shows what KM-related activities they have to do or should perform. The following example illustrates this technique:

When the price for an offer is estimated, the sales person has to search for documented knowledge (e.g., approved documented experiences, documented lessons learned, or good practices) concerning previous similar offers. After viewing the knowledge elements, the sales person encloses or references them. The designer has the task to evaluate CAD drawings by using previous drawings and has to attach the viewed drawing and his/her annotations and eventually the e-mail traffic with cooperating designers. Additionally, he/she should comment on his/her experience-based assumptions related to possible design changes or other problems he/she identified. The die and mold maker has several tasks concerning the offer pricing. He/she also has to attach the knowledge elements viewed and his/her experience-based annotations. In analogy to the work flow activities described above, the tester as well as other employees involved can review all annotations and enclose the documented knowledge viewed according to their tasks. After completing the tasks in the checklist and after reviewing the attached knowledge elements, the audited object, for example, an offer, becomes KM certified.

If a participant identifies a good practice that seems useful or necessary for integration in the work flow, he/she proposes an item to be supplemented to the checklist.

An approval process is important in this context to coordinate and check the addition of KM tasks. The possibility of suggesting new tasks renders the KM certification checklist dynamic. Moreover, the checklists are predefined for each process step and designed so that the systematic reuse of experiences and particularly good or best practices are considered. Good practices are proven as valuable for an organization, whereas best practices are worthwhile for the whole community of Know-CoM users. Subsequently, some core tasks of the development process are outlined:

During offer creation, especially experiences and information concerning the number of redesign cycles of similar molds are needed. Therefore, the checklist for offer creation comprises tasks regarding the estimation of the number of redesign cycles of similar molds as well as the application of good or best practices in this area, next to the use of templates for the collection of customer information. During conceptual planning, valuable experiences about standard parts in particular have to be reused. Additionally, employees from the areas of production, design, and test might have to be contacted when this contact turned out as worthwhile in the past. The design is a process step, which has a high potential for improvement for the lowering of costs when proven test experiences are reused systematically. Therefore, typical tasks included in this checklist are, for example, the application of test protocols and documented test experiences to similar molds as well as discussion with the die and mold maker and/or the tester. Such discussions can be supported by the use of application sharing and aim at exchanging knowledge as well as at avoiding mistakes. Particularly, when designers of cooperating enterprises communicate, tools for application sharing (e.g., for CAD) are useful and provide additional context.

The main focuses of the checklists for the production planning and production steps lie in the reuse of good or best practices regarding cutting tools, their sequence, and the sequence of the machines as well as the cutting strategies. Additional tasks aim at fostering communication and knowledge exchange with the toolmaker. The checklist of the tester comprises tasks such as the consequent application of former test protocols or the discussion of test results with the die and mold maker and the designer.

KM certified should help to ensure or foster the application of existing knowledge in the process phases described, to reduce previously made mistakes, and to increase the quality of the dies and molds produced.

Discussion

In the following section, we discuss how the elements of the Know-CoM solution could meet the challenges described.

- **Lack of experience management**: Know-CoM aims at capturing experiences during the execution of process steps supported by templates. In particular, templates and wizards ease the codification and lower documentation effort. The main target is ensuring high reusability by other employees, which is supported by semiautomatically detected context. By the technique KM certified, feedback loops between the steps of the core process are established and previously documented experiences and good/best practices are provided systematically after verifying their value. Thus, quality and efficiency can be enhanced, because especially the missing feedback loops from later to early stages in the development process as well as between cooperating SMEs impact these two factors.

- **Insufficient knowledge about customer production facilities**: Gathering of customer information is supported by prestructured protocols for customer correspondences with mandatory fields. The information collected in customer communication is documented and forwarded by work flows along the core process. Thus, the information is available in all steps. In order to avoid misunderstandings and to identify problems concerning the mold or die, application sharing and instant collaboration (e.g., Lotus Sametime. See section, "Know-CoM Software Prototype") between the customer and manufacturer can take place.
- **Need of collaboration environment:** The joint multidimensional knowledge structure provides a shared context and builds the basis for a collaborative environment. Concerning the technical infrastructure, tools for application sharing and instant collaboration provide additional context and support cooperation between DMCs. Moreover, the use of protected workspaces improves flexibility, because access rights can be assigned and revoked depending on the requirements of the companies.
- **Management of intellectual property**: The management of intellectual property and particularly its security is the basic requirement for the cooperation in a competitive environment. The trisection of the individual company servers in public, protected, and private knowledge spaces provides such a secure environment and flexibly adaptable access rights foster the controlled knowledge exchange.
- **Distributed incompatible sources of data**: The distributed sources of data such as standard parts, cutting data, machine characteristics, and so forth, are stored on the cooperative shared-knowledge server or on the public knowledge spaces of the DMCs. Thus, search time can be shortened. The shared knowledge structure also provides context for linking previously incompatible sources of data.

Figure 5 visualizes the elements of the Know-CoM solution. Every company participating in Know-CoM has its own company server, which is trisected into public, protected, and private knowledge spaces. Next to the trisected company servers, a cooperative shared-knowledge server supports cooperation between DMCs by providing community home spaces and tools for expertise retrieval. Both the company and the cooperative server work on the basis of the joint multidimensional knowledge structure, which provides a shared context to the participating enterprises and eases knowledge exchange between the companies. The internal core processes of the SMEs are supported in two ways. On the one hand, experiences are captured during the execution of the process steps and on the other hand, the management of good or best practices is supported by the technique KM certified that is symbolized in Figure 5 with the KMC icons. The management of experiences aims at a low documentation effort as well as at high reusability and is therefore supported by an intelligent metadata management. The latter helps employees to classify knowledge elements according to the dimensions of the knowledge structure. Next to capturing of experiences, particularly their approval and the systematic anchoring in the core process are important in order to ensure that valuable experiences, good or best practices are applied in processes and thus improvements concerning costs, time, and quality are realized. The management of good or best practices is realized by the technique KM certified.

After summarizing the elements of the Know-CoM solution, the following section describes the software prototype.

Figure 5. Overview of the KM solution for die- and mold-manufacturing SMEs

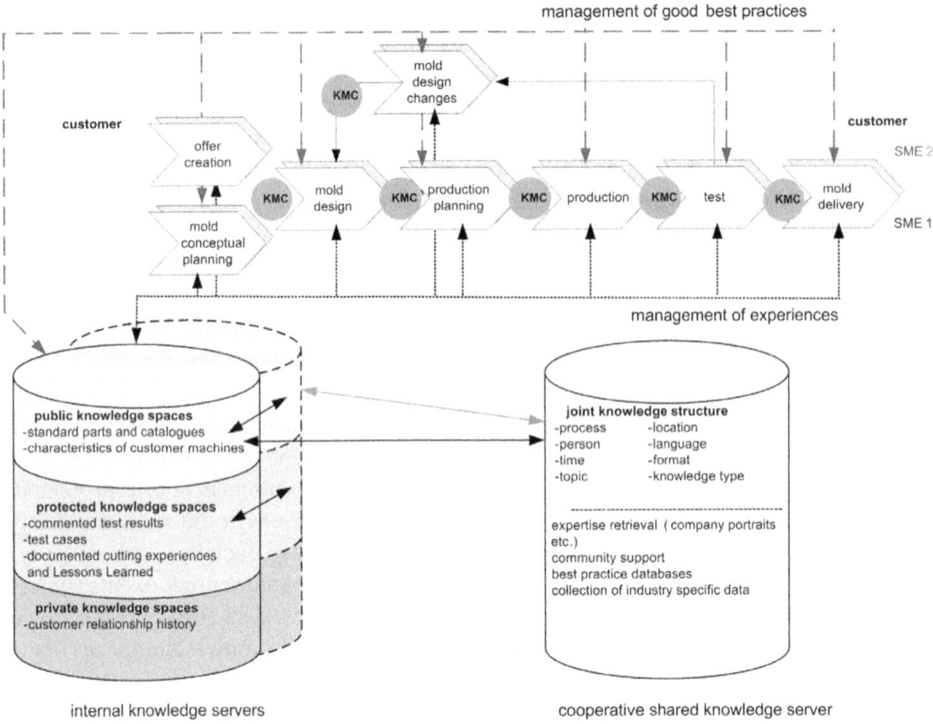

Know-CoM Software Prototype

The Know-CoM software is currently implemented as a Web-based application on a Lotus Notes system (www.lotus.com). Lotus Notes was chosen as the platform for the software prototype, because it provides a set of advanced functions to support database and document management, communication, coordination, collaboration, administration of users, and security mechanisms in a Web-based environment. The CSCW (computer-supported cooperative work) approach provides easy access to communication solutions such as Lotus Sametime (instant messaging and Web conferencing) and Lotus Quickplace (team workplace). Additionally, Lotus Notes comprises integrated discussion boards and supports work flows. Particularly, an integrated and easy-to-use CSCW approach is important in order to foster cooperation between DMCs. Additionally, a VPN (virtual private network) connection is not needed to access a Lotus Notes server, because an encrypted data transfer between clients and servers is supported. This allows secure data or information sharing. Further, advanced applications are full-text retrieval on the local server, mail and calendar integration, the possibility to replicate data of local databases on portable computers, the provided security features, and a policy-based management for different roles. Next to the CSCW integration, particularly the fact that Lotus Notes stores documents on the basis of metadata, influenced the platform decision because this approach fits well with the multidimensional knowledge structure.

As described in the section, "Technical Environment," die- and mold-making companies are quite familiar with a number of IT tools, but their collaboration and communication infrastructure is weak. Actually, much time is lost in communicating details off-line, by sending printed drawings between customer and manufacturer. So the possibility of sharing a CAD application in combination with discussion functionalities and session protocols will bring an enormous time benefit for the participating companies.

Furthermore, a Web-based application needs no local client or sophisticated configuration and can be accessed via Web browsers. As mentioned in the section, "Technical Environment," die- and mold- making companies normally do not have powerful hardware and software systems in production areas, and also lack advanced knowledge for the administration of sophisticated software. Thus, a Web-based application has been chosen because it is easy to use.

As basis for this software system, the decision was taken to create an application out of the box. This means the delivery of the Know-CoM system with a preconfigured server. A company has to configure the network address and local (company-specific) parameters, such as roles and shared-knowledge spaces, and so forth, to start working with the software. The server does not influence other servers and there is no need for advanced integration efforts.

Lotus Notes provides full support for existing layers of the architecture of a KMS (see Maier, 2004, pp. 257–259). The Notes Web client allows full access to all existing databases and solutions, included in the Know-CoM software. Concerning knowledge services, Lotus Notes provides full-text retrieval for information and knowledge discovery, push-and-pull functionalities in work flows, and a wide range of applications for collaboration like Sametime, Quickplace, team calendars, online communication, and so forth. As complete solution provider, Lotus comes with these last two areas: integration services and infrastructure services. These services are part of the Lotus Notes database philosophy, which is the basis for all applications on upper architectural levels.

The Know-CoM software prototype builds upon this Lotus Notes solution and implements the services required in order to support the organizational KM instruments laid out in the previous sections.

Rollout

Concerning the process-oriented introduction of knowledge management, the literature provides several approaches. The phases of the process-oriented approaches GPO-WM[1] (Heisig, 2002) and PROMOTE (Hinkelmann et al., 2002) build a basis for this KM solution. Additionally, a "road map" for the introduction and customizing of standard software (e.g., SAP) is considered for the amalgamation of the procedure model. Based on these literature studies, we developed the procedure model depicted in Figure 6.

- **Creation of awareness and definition of KM goals:** The DMCs analyzed are normally not aware of the potential benefits of knowledge management. Therefore, one of the focuses of the introduction of KM is creation of awareness for the KM initiative. The technical initiatives are rather concentrated in basic ICT infrastructures than in sophisticated KM functions. A preconfigured company server is installed that ensures some basic functionality. Thus, in this stage the employees can explore the cooperative shared-knowledge server and the public knowledge

Figure 6. The Know-CoM procedure model

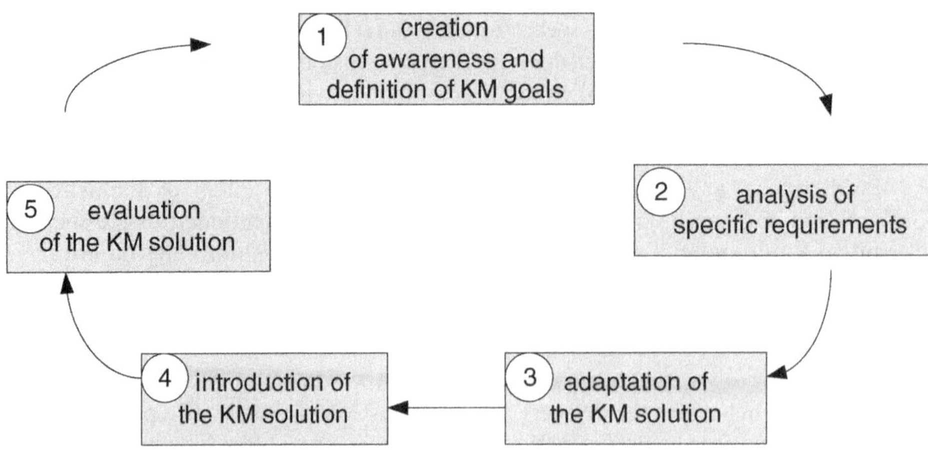

spaces of other DMCs participating in the Know-CoM community. Additional support is delivered by FAQ databases that contain questions and answers concerning KM in general and the Know-CoM solution in particular and by an employee who is responsible for the introduction of the solution.

Finally, the communication of the predefined Know-CoM-specific KM goals, such as the improvement of knowledge exchange or the systematic application of documented knowledge and their extension by enterprise-specific KM goals, is important in order to create transparency in the goals and benefits.

- **Analysis of the specific requirements**: Before the adaptation of the KM solution can occur, an analysis of the company-specific requirements has to take place. The analysis concerns the organizational structure, the development process, the work flows, and the existing knowledge structure. Within the organizational scope, especially the roles and the intra- as well as inter-organizational collaboration structure have to be analyzed in order to consider additional roles or deduce the need for the definition of knowledge spaces. The analysis of the dimension "process" comprises the matching of the core process with the development process of the enterprise concerned in order to consider variations and variants. The analysis of the work flows is necessary for the implementation of KM certified. Additionally, specifics concerning the technical infrastructure of the SME on which Know-CoM should be installed have to be taken into account.
- **Adaptation of the KM solution**: Based on the analysis of the specific requirements, the Know-CoM solution has to be adapted. During this phase, two different areas of customizing are relevant, on the one hand the technical customizing of the solution and on the other hand, the conceptual customizing of the knowledge structure, the core process, the roles, and the knowledge spaces.
- **Introduction of the KM solution**: The introduction step comprises the connection of the clients with the company server, the registration of the users, and the setup

of private and protected knowledge spaces according to the user profiles on the server.

Information about an employee has to be registered and user profiles created when the Know-CoM solution is introduced. Person-related information that has to be collected is, for example, skills, topics of interest, and work experience. Additionally, roles, organizational tasks and process steps have to be assigned to the employee for which he/she is responsible or works on. In analogy to the partition of the knowledge spaces in private, protected, and public, this trisection should also be used for the employees′ profiles. Recommendations of interest- or task-related knowledge groups can occur automatically according to the user profile of the employee. Based on the analysis of the organizational design, protected knowledge spaces are introduced for teams, projects, and so forth.

- **Evaluation of the KM solution**: After the introduction of the solution, there may be needs for improvement that lead to the adaptation of the solution. There are a number of indicators that allow for a systematic evaluation of the use of the solution. In particular, the experiences captured and the dynamics observed in the KM-certified processes as well as the establishment and regular use of knowledge workspaces give hints for subsequent improvements of the KM-supported core processes of the die and mold makers.

Next to the evaluation of the solution aiming at the identification of the needs for improvement, the measurement of the solution's success is also a central issue. Based on the interviews and questionnaires (see section, "Setting the Stage") the most important factors for success measurement in the die- and mold-making industry are lead time from (mold) order to delivery as well as the production time required. A shortened delivery in general or production time in particular also affects production costs of a mold or die. Quality is another key factor in this industry. Referring to the development process, there are a number of indicators that can be used to assess the effects of the Know-CoM solution on time, cost, and quality. These indicators have been documented at the beginning of the project and will be measured again one year after the introduction of the solution. Subsequently, some of these indicators are outlined in Table 2.

The average number of design-test-redesign cycles is one of the most important indicators because it affects time, cost, and quality. This means that the more cycles needed, the longer the lead time, the higher the costs, and eventually, the lower the quality. The quality is not necessarily affected negatively by a high number of redesign cycles, but in some cases, a high number of redesign cycles can reduce the stability of the mold and so its lifetime. Also the number of external rejects from the customer is an indicator that affects the quality of the mold and, in particular, thc reputation of the toolmaker.

The integration of distributed sources of data can reduce the time required for searching data. Particularly, the systematic reuse of previously documented experiences can shorten lead and production time and can also reduce personnel, production cost, and wastage as well as the number of rejects.

Table 2. Indicators for success measurement

Criteria	Indicator
Time	• average number of design-test-redesign cycles and time required • average lead time • average time required for the execution of the process steps • average time needed to get complete customer information • search time
Cost	• average production costs/mold • average personnel costs/mold • average material wastage • average cutting tool wastage
Quality	• average number of internal rejects • average number of external rejects • average lifetime of mold

CURRENT CHALLENGES

This case presents an organizational and a technical KM solution that specifically targets die- and mold-making SMEs. Know-CoM particularly considers capturing, sharing, and reuse of experiences both within the knowledge-intensive business process of a die and mold maker and across the organizational boundaries with customers and cooperating DMCs.

In the following section, some preliminary results concerning the application of Know-CoM by the industrial partners are reflected. We concentrate on the management of protocols and experiences, which have been the first focus of the application of Know-CoM. First, those process steps were analyzed where an immediate benefit could be identified as highly feasible. These are the processes not governed by an ERP system, which in this case were the offer creation and the die setting up and testing. The procedure was to detail subprocesses, assign documents to them if necessary (protocols and experiences), and extract the references required to define and manage the mentioned documents. For example, the following subprocesses were identified in offer creation: (1) offer request reception, (2) information request to the customer, (3) obtain main die parameters (pitch and bandwidth), (4) obtain costs, (5) decide on the probable delivery time, and (6) decide on final price.

Protocols used currently include the die characteristics sheet, the offer calculation sheet, and the formal offer document. These protocols are linked mainly to the first four tasks. The need for establishing protocols in the remaining two stages is being discussed at the moment.

Experiences are gathered for any of the mentioned processes. Guidelines or good practices were elaborated for the process of obtaining main die parameters, a key task that was not documented and greatly relied on the experience of certain key personnel in the company. The formalization of this task has allowed a far shorter training period for newcomers and has lowered the dependency that the company as a whole had on certain personnel for running this process with a guarantee for the final result. A number of references were extracted to be used as metadata for the process of searching and filtering the documents mentioned. Examples in the case of the die characteristics sheet are the number of stations, die dimensions, bandwidth, band pitch, number of columns, type of sliding, number of pieces per year, and number of pieces per stroke.

However, there are a number of challenges for the implementation of the solution since there are possibly significant barriers in DMCs that prevent the effective use of the KM solution. In the following, some of these barriers are outlined.

SMEs are characterized by the scarcity of resources. Particularly, limited human resources make it hard for SMEs to assign employees who are dedicated to the KM implementation or perform tasks that are related to the KM initiative (Wong & Aspinwall, 2004, p. 56).

The protection of intellectual capital is an important issue for SMEs since the unintended loss of knowledge to partners can erode competitive advantages of the company. In particular, compared to larger organizations, SMEs that are less diversified and more dependent on the knowledge of key employees fear losing competencies or employees to cooperation partners. These fears create significant barriers concerning interorganizational collaboration and knowledge exchange and it remains unclear if a secure environment for knowledge sharing is sufficient.

Compared to larger organizations the processes and procedures of SMEs are less formalized and standardized, which increase the probability that employees resist the introduction of the KM solution (Wong & Aspinwall, 2004, p. 52) or resist to perform tasks associated with it.

Capturing and applying experiences can also be prevented by individual barriers such as lack of skills to explicate knowledge or low reliability of the knowledge providers as well as by limited absorptive, processing, or learning capacities of the knowledge seekers. Furthermore, on the organizational level, factors like lack of management support or lack of time can prevent the success of the solution as well as interorganizational factors such as groupthink or an exaggerated unified organization culture that particularly affect the external relationships. Individual, organizational, as well as interorganizational barriers can affect the implementation and the use of the solution as well as knowledge sharing across organizational boundaries negatively (Maier, 2004, p. 130).

Finally, building and management of trust will be a crucial factor that influences the use of the protected knowledge spaces significantly. Due to the shared context supported by the knowledge structure, the cooperative shared-knowledge server and the joint KM principles underlying the solution, a community of Know-CoM users might be fostered that ensures trust.

Epilogue

It seems that centralized KMS offered on the market increasingly live up to the expectations of large organizations ready to apply ICT to support a KM initiative. These solutions are too complex, time-, and resource-consuming for SMEs. Peer-to-peer KMS promise to resolve some of the shortcomings of centralized KMS, especially concerning the time-consuming effort to build and maintain a central knowledge repository. However, major challenges still lie ahead until decentralized systems can truly be called KMS and used to support the still-growing share of users involved in knowledge work. Examples for technical challenges that have to be overcome in decentralized KM concern connectivity, security, privacy, fault tolerance, availability, scalability, and interoperability. Moreover, applying the peer-to-peer metaphor to KMS requires a substantial shift in the perspective on organizational knowledge. Executives might fear losing control over the organization's knowledge assets if all documented knowledge is handled by autonomous knowledge workspaces. Consequently, future KMS solutions might attempt to include the "best of both worlds."

Lessons Learned

- In SMEs, particularly the creation of awareness is an important issue concerning the implementation of a KM solution since SMEs are normally not aware of KM and its benefits. Thus, the availability of some basic functionalities and a person responsible for the implementation is favorable.
- Referring to the fact that processes and procedures in SMEs are compared to larger organizations less formalized and standardized a KM solution that is more rigid or directive seems to be appropriate for SMEs.
- SMEs in general and die and mold makers in particular are less diversified and strongly specialized as well as depend often on key employees. These facts combined with the state of coopetition require the providing of a secure environment for cooperation.
- Die- and mold-making SMEs are familiar with certain IT, but concerning the design of KMS, it has to be considered that the solution is easy to use.

REFERENCES

Antoñana, J. (2000). European tool and die making. *Proceedings of ISTMA Europe Colloquium "Tool and Die Making of the Future,"* Aachen, Germany.

Disterer, G. (2002). Management of project knowledge and experiences. *Journal of Knowledge Management, 6*(5), 512-520.

Heisig, P. (2002). GPO-WM: Methode und Werkzeuge zum geschäftsprozessorientierten Wissensmanagement. In A. Abecker et al. (Eds.), *Geschäftsprozessorientiertes Wissensmanagement* (pp. 47-64). Berlin.

Hinkelmann, K. et al. (2002). PROMOTE, Methodologie und Werkzeug für das geschäftsprozessorientierte Wissensmanagement. In A. Abecker et al. (Eds.), *Geschäftsprozessorientiertes Wissensmanagement* (pp. 65-90). Berlin.

Maier, R. (2004). *Knowledge management systems. Information and communication technologies for knowledge management* (2nd ed.). Berlin.

Maier, R., & Sametinger, J. (2003, July 1-3). Infotop – A shared-context information workspace. *Proceedings of the SEKE 03 – 15th International Conference on Software Engineering and Knowledge Engineering,* San Francisco.

Sary, C., & Mackey, W. (1996). Implementing RECALL: A case-based reasoning system for the access and reuse of lessons learned. *Proceedings of the Sixth Annual International Symposium of the National Council on Systems Engineering,* St. Louis, MO.

Schindler, M., & Eppler, M. (2003). Harvesting project knowledge: A review of project learning methods and success factors. *International Journal of Project Management, 21,* 219-228.

Willke, H. (2001). *Systemisches Wissensmanagement* (2nd ed.). Stuttgart.
Wong, K.E., & Aspinwall, E. (2004). Characterizing knowledge management in the small business environment. *Journal of Knowledge Management, 8*(3), 44-61.

Online References

Lotus Notes, Lotus (IBM). *www.lotus.com/*

FURTHER READING

Beijerse, R.P. (2000). Knowledge management in small and medium-sized companies: Knowledge management for entrepreneurs. *Journal of Knowledge Management, 4*(2), 162-179.
Borghoff, U.M., & Schlichter, J.H. (2000). *Computer supported cooperative work: Introduction to distributed applications*. Berlin.
Huotari, M.-L., & Iivonen, M. (2004). *Trust in knowledge management and systems in organizations*. Hershey, PA: Idea Group.
Maier, R. (2004). *Knowledge management systems. Information and communication technologies for knowledge management* (2nd ed.). Berlin.
Maier, R., & Hädrich, T. (2004, April 2-3). Centralized versus peer-to-peer knowledge management systems. *Proceedings of the 5th European Conference on Organizational Knowledge, Learning and Capabilities (OKLC),* Innsbruck, Austria.
Staab, S., Studer, R., & Sure, Y. (2003). Knowledge processes and meta processes in ontology-based knowledge management. In C.W. Holsapple (Ed.), *Handbook of knowledge management, vol. 2: Knowledge directions* (pp. 47-69). Berlin.
Susarla, A., Liu, D., & Whinston, A.B. (2003). Peer-to-peer enterprise knowledge management. In C.W. Holsapple (Ed.), *Handbook on knowledge management – vol. 2: Knowledge directions* (pp. 129-139). Berlin.
Szulanski, G. (1996). Exploring internal stickiness: Impediments to the transfer of best practice within the firm. *Strategic Management Journal, 17*, 27-43.
Wong, K.E., & Aspinwall, E. (2004). Characterizing knowledge management in the small business environment. *Journal of Knowledge Management, 8*(3), 44-61.

ENDNOTE

1 The German abbreviation GPO-WM stands for process-oriented KM.

Section VI

Issues in Knowledge Management

Chapter XIII

Reserve Bank of New Zealand: Journey Toward Knowledge Management

Yogesh Anand, Reserve Bank of New Zealand, New Zealand

David J. Pauleen, Victoria University of Wellington, New Zealand

Sally Dexter, Victoria University of Wellington, New Zealand

EXECUTIVE SUMMARY

This chapter outlines the adoption and implementation of knowledge management within the New Zealand Reserve Bank. In 1999, the Bank recognised that it had a very high exposure to loss of knowledge on departure of key staff. This was mainly due to two factors: recruitment of staff from a limited global pool of specifically skilled labour, and an average length of service of more than nine years during which time staff members accumulated an extensive knowledge of the Bank and its operations. In response to this and other challenges, the Bank embarked on an ongoing knowledge management program. The Bank invested significant resources into the program and from an initial corporate vision developed a knowledge management framework that led to the identification of potential areas of improvement within the organisation. The resulting knowledge strategy encompassed several key initiatives, the most significant of which was the goal of changing the organisational culture. Other initiatives included the consolidation of the Bank's contact management into a single system, a review of the existing document management system, and information mapping. To date, while some initiatives have been achieved, others remain to be done. The challenge for the Bank now is to move from structured to unstructured processes for knowledge management and maintain the knowledge management focus while balancing available resources. The Bank must also consider how best to progress initiatives without necessarily attaching a specific knowledge management label, and identify ways to move ongoing development of knowledge management strategies to the next level.

BACKGROUND

The Reserve Bank is the central bank of New Zealand and a unique entity. Due to its exclusive status, it is not therefore afforded the recruitment opportunities available to organisations in more prolific industries. In addition, the average lifetime of staff members is more than nine years, resulting in a significant potential loss of knowledge on departure. Consequently, the Bank has identified knowledge loss as a high risk within the organisation. In response to this risk, an extensive knowledge management program has been initiated that now spans a five-year period.

This paper presents a background to the case study organisation, and details the steps taken to implement knowledge management through the organisation.

Organization Background

The Reserve Bank of New Zealand (RBNZ) is wholly owned by the New Zealand Government and serves as the nation's central bank. The Bank has the mission of building national and international confidence in the stability and integrity of New Zealand's currency and the country's monetary system. The Bank has three main functions:

- Operating monetary policy to maintain price stability;
- Promoting the maintenance of a sound and efficient financial system; and
- Meeting the currency needs of the public.

More specifically, the Bank is charged with:

- the registration and prudential supervision of banks, and the promotion of a sound and efficient financial system;
- the provision of interbank settlement facilities and related payment services to New Zealand banks;
- advising the New Zealand Government on the operation of the financial system;
- the provision of cash and debt management services to the Government as well as secretariat services to the Overseas Investment Commission; and
- the issue of New Zealand currency and management of foreign exchange reserves.

The Bank's core functions also include the management of NZ $4+ billion of foreign reserves and the management of relationships with international bodies such as the World Bank and the International Monetary Fund (IMF) in order to ensure that the interests of New Zealand are promoted.

Management Structure

The governor leads the Reserve Bank. The minister of finance, on the recommendation of the board, appoints the governor for a five-year term. In accordance with the RBNZ legislative framework (RBNZ Act of 1989), the governor is the single decision maker for the organization and accountable for all activities of the bank.

The minister of finance is responsible for appointing the board of directors. It is the task of the board to regularly review both the performance of the governor and the bank, and provide feedback to the minister of finance. The board must comprise not less than seven, but not more than 10 non-executive members, and does not have any decision-making authority, although they do make recommendations to the minister regarding the appointment of the Reserve Bank governor.

The governor is provided advice from a number of internal committees, including the following:

- the Governor's Committee;
- the Monetary Policy Committee;
- the Official Cash Rate Advisory Group;
- the Financial System Oversight Committee;
- the Risk Management Committee;
- the Reserves Oversight Committee; and
- the Communications Committee.

The Bank is structured into nine departments including the Knowledge Services Group. The senior management team consists of the governor, a deputy governor, and the heads of the various departments as detailed in Figure 1.

Financial Status

The Reserve Bank income is mainly derived from investing the proceeds that the Reserve Bank receives from issuing currency. The Bank spends some of the money to pay its operating costs, the extent of which are fixed in a five-year funding agreement with the Government. The remaining earnings are passed directly to the Government. The balance sheet of the Reserve Bank is shown in Table 1. Further financial information is included in Appendix 1.

Organizational Climate

The Reserve Bank employs approximately 220 staff, a figure which has been much reduced from the mid 1980s, mainly as a result of a "rightsizing" program.

The Bank works to ensure that it has the right people, systems, and structures in place. In keeping with this policy, in 2002, the Bank carried out a review of its human resource and corporate policies with the aim of ensuring flexibility in responding to changing priorities. The Bank has a commitment to a process of staff consultation and involvement when making changes and believes that the presence of a very flat organizational structure provides greater integration, flexibility, and cooperation across departments.

More recently, the results of a staff survey focused the Bank on the need to develop leadership and communication programs for its staff. The purpose of the survey was to identify areas that would improve the overall organisational environment to make the

Figure 1. Reserve Bank management structure (adapted from Reserve Bank, 2002)

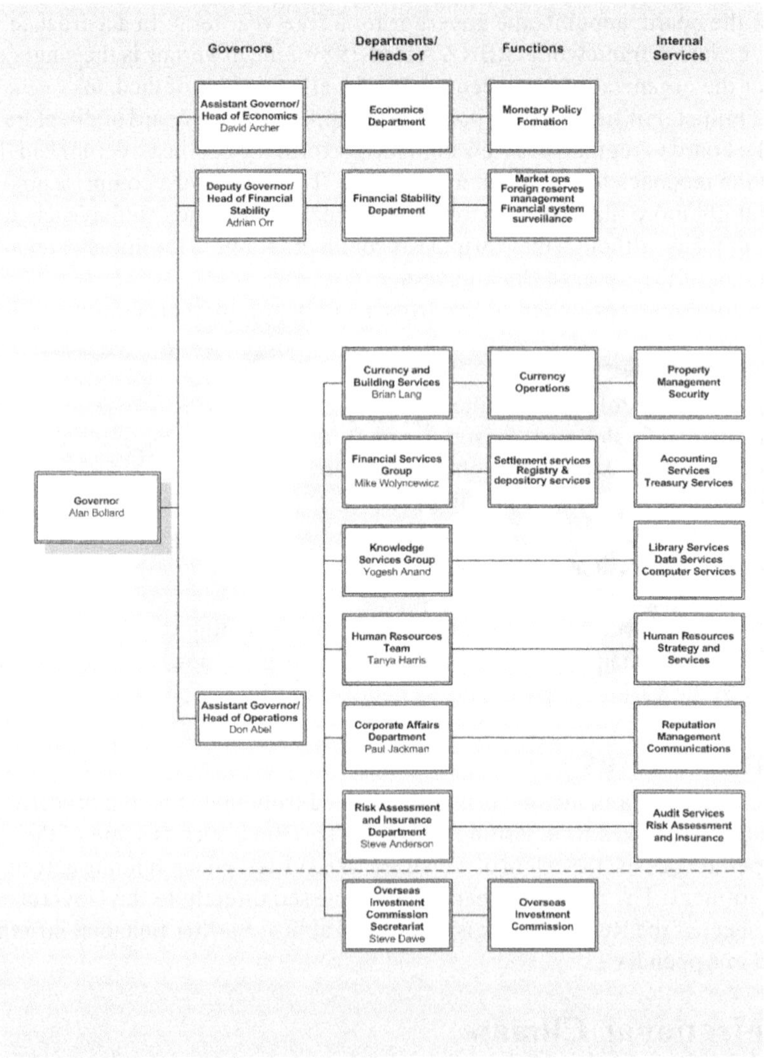

Governors
Departments/ Heads of
Functions
Internal Services
Governor Alan Bollard
Assistant Governor/ Head of Economics David Archer
Economics Department
Monetary Policy Formation
Deputy Governor/ Head of Financial Stability Adrian Orr
Financial Stability Department
Market ops Foreign reserves management Financial system surveillance
Assistant Governor/ Head of Operations Don Abel
Currency and Building Services Brian Lang
Currency Operations
Property Management Security
Financial Services Group Mike Wolyncewicz
Settlement services Registry & depository services
Accounting Services Treasury Services
Knowledge Services Group Yogesh Anand
Library Services Data Services Computer Services
Human Resources Team Tanya Harris
Human Resources Strategy and Services
Corporate Affairs Department Paul Jackman
Reputation Management Communications
Risk Assessment and Insurance Department Steve Anderson
Audit Services Risk Assessment and Insurance
Overseas Investment Commission Secretariat Steve Dawe
Overseas Investment Commission

Bank a more effective and better place of work. The results identified several opportunities for the Bank including the following:

- Changes to the management practices;
- Improvement in communication within the Bank;
- Better tools and information; and
- Recognition for work done.

The Bank is an advanced and proactive user of technology, comprising predominantly technology-literate, highly skilled specialist staff. Due to the nature of policy development, there is a requirement for collaboration across business units and this has

Table 1. The Reserve Bank's balance sheet (adapted from Reserve Bank, 2002)

Assets	**2002/2003**	**Liabilities**
Foreign Reserves	$5.1 billion	Debt to fund the purchase of foreign reserves
Assets arising from managing the Crown's cash operations	$3.4 billion	Obligation to repay the Crown's and others' deposits with the Reserve Bank
Government bonds purchased with monies received from issuing currency	$2.8 billion	Obligation to replace bank notes and coins already in circulation
		Equity
Assets, including the Reserve Bank building in Wellington, and so forth, and government stock, bought with equity	$0.4 billion	The Government's net investment in the Reserve Bank
	Total $11.7 billion	

been primarily facilitated through either face-to-face meetings or through the use of e-mail. The Bank was an early adopter of a document management solution as a way of encouraging collaboration and the sharing of unstructured information across business units.

At an early stage, management identified issues related to collaboration and investment in both human and technology capital. However, business case justification of any major investments in technology has been challenging, given the size of the organization, particularly in the last five years. This has been countered by a management philosophy that accepts that some initiatives are strategic and, as such, may not always stand to business case justification in the traditional sense. The management also had the foresight to recognise the risks related to management of intellectual capital and embarked on initiatives to mitigate these risks.

SETTING THE STAGE

In the early 1990s, the Bank employed approximately 800 staff, many of whom had been with the organization for a considerable period of time. In one instance, a staff member had been with the Bank for over 40 years. In another, a governor of the Bank recently left after 33 years of service. The length of service, combined with the specialist skill set required by Bank staff, resulted in a high percentage of knowledge workers. Consequently, there was a significant risk of potential loss of knowledge as a result of a staff member leaving.

Towards the end of the 1990s, with the rapid advances in technology and the accompanying shift to a global community, the Bank began to experience a slight rise in the level of staff departures. Initially, staff were leaving from predominantly operational areas where the loss of knowledge was not as critical. In these areas, much knowledge had been captured through documented processes and procedures. However, when staff concerned with policy started leaving, it became critical to consider how to deal with this potential loss of knowledge.

As a policy-making organization, the Bank had always been reasonably good at sharing information. When any development was taking place, it was normal practice for information to be readily exchanged with problems arising only where previous actions had been forgotten about, or staff members had left the organisation and, as a result, the information was not readily accessible. However, despite this seemingly strong knowledge-sharing practice, there was still a culture of structural silos within the organisation, with little boundary crossing between departments. This was emphasized in the policy areas where staff members were closeted in offices and were rarely seen to leave other than at lunchtime or at the end of the day.

Concurrent to the increasing level of staff turnover and problems arising from structural silos, the Bank was going through an organisational "rightsizing" program. There was also growing interest in knowledge management within the wider environment at a national level from the government and public sector as well as within commercial and academic circles.

Knowledge management, as it is currently understood, has been around for more than a decade. The term has, however, spawned a proliferation of definitions. Snowden defines it succinctly (1999) as:

The identification, optimisation, and active management of intellectual assets, either in the form of explicit knowledge held in artefacts or as tacit knowledge possessed by individuals or communities (p. 63).

The predominant focus of organisations embracing knowledge management has been the potential for higher levels of profitability, greater market share, and increased innovation. However, there are wider potential benefits for organisations that successfully manage their knowledge, including a flexible approach to change and better workplace morale (Scherer, 2001). In the public sector, Wiig (2002) contends that knowledge management can enhance decision making, assist public participation in decision making, build competitive societal intellectual capital capabilities, and assist in the development of a knowledge-intensive workforce. It can also bring much needed assistance in the area of knowledge sharing, which has historically been an area of difficulty for the public sector (OECD, 2003).

Much academic research pertaining to knowledge management has been predominantly published in the information science/information technology (IS/IT) literature (Newell et al., 2002) and has led to information systems and technology becoming synonymous with knowledge management. More recently, the field has undergone a change in focus from a predominantly technological approach to a more integrated approach (Gold, Malhotra, & Segars, 2001), which has encouraged organisations to bring a more holistic approach to their knowledge management efforts.

Implementation of knowledge management has proved a problem for many organisations. Despite recognition of the potential benefits that knowledge management may offer, many organisations simply did not know where to start (Earl, 2001). Knowledge management best practice has been well documented (Davenport, De Long, & Beers, 1998; Chourides, Longbottom, & Murphy, 2003; Mertins, Heisig, & Vorbeck, 2001) and is often an approach advocated by knowledge management consultants. The downside of best practice is that while it provides examples of implementation approaches that organisations may adopt, it does not take into account the individual factors of the organisation, including the external environment, the internal environment, technology, culture, and infrastructure. Knowledge management is not a "one size fits all" solution,

Table 2. Human resource statistics (adapted from Reserve Bank, 2002)

	1994/ 1995	1995/ 1996	1996/ 1997	1997/ 1998	1998/ 1999	1999/ 2000	2000/ 2001	2001/ 2002	2002/ 2003
Total staff at June 30 (FTE)	293	290	289	281	283	237	199	182	193
Average years of service at June 30	8.6	8.6	8.7	8.3	8.8	9.4	9.4	9.2	9.2
Annual staff turnover	9.6%	15.0%	10.6%	8.8%	10.0%	10.4%	14.9%	13.5%	11.3%

but must be carefully tailored to meet the unique organisational characteristics. By contrast, Snowden's principles of "organic knowledge management" and interest in complex adaptive theory support the view that knowledge management solutions are unique to the organisational context in which they are created (Lelic, 2002).

As a quasi-government department, the Reserve Bank was able to leverage public sector interest in knowledge management in support of its knowledge management journey.

CASE DESCRIPTION

The nature of the work of the Reserve Bank was such that it required a range of specialist skill sets that were not readily available within New Zealand. This was mainly due to the fact that each country has only one central bank, and therefore does not have a large pool of individuals with the specialist skill sets, such as macro-economics and banking supervision, that are required. Consequently, recruitment of staff was effectively limited to a global pool of specifically skilled labour drawn from central banks around the world.

In addition to the scarcity of skill sets, the average length of service at the Reserve Bank was more than nine years, as shown in Table 2.

During this time, staff members accumulated an extensive knowledge of the Bank and its operations, resulting in a very high exposure to loss of knowledge on the departure of key staff. As a consequence of this exposure and of the "rightsizing" program that the Bank was then undergoing, the Bank recognised that it needed to take action to minimise the risk of knowledge loss. Although the NZRB was one of the first to recognise the significance of these issues, other central banks such as the Bank of Canada have also expanded their research programs to include the issues of talent and knowledge sharing (Bank of Canada, 2002).

In 1999, the Bank was not alone in recognising the growing importance of knowledge management. At the same time, the Information Technology Advisory Group (ITAG), comprising academics and representatives from the business community and public sector, presented a report to the New Zealand Government, titled "The Knowledge Economy." The report focussed on the need for New Zealand to change its economic mix and warned that if the nation failed to make the transition from a pastoral to a knowledge economy, then it was destined to become nothing more than a holiday destination for visitors from countries where the knowledge economy had been embraced (ITAG, 1999).

As a result of this report, the New Zealand Government developed a vision of New Zealand as a world leader in e-government, with the Internet being the dominant means of access to government information, services, and processes. In addition, it was their intention that public sector innovation should support a wider knowledge based society. Hearn and Rooney (2002) posit that it is the role of governments to facilitate the technical, cultural, and social aspects of waves of innovation. This role is widely supported throughout the Organisation for Economic Co-operation and Development (OECD), where the majority of central government organisations regard knowledge management as a priority and have knowledge management strategies in place (OECD, 2003).

It was at this point, and with the combination of national and local drivers, that the Bank developed a corporate vision that focussed on knowledge management as a key component. The vision was led by the then deputy governor, whose involvement signified the high level of importance that the Bank attributed to knowledge management. This was an important first step and allowed the Bank's vision to permeate the organisation, providing staff with a needed sense of purpose that transcended everyday activities (Gold, Malhotra, & Segars, 2001). The Bank's new corporate vision prompted the required changes within the organisation (Kanter, Stein, & Jick, 1992). In this case, the vision encapsulated the contribution that knowledge-based value creation can make (Earl, 2001).

The first step after development of the corporate vision was for the Bank to develop a business case to move forward in developing a knowledge management program. Development of a business case for knowledge management is difficult given the seemingly intangible benefits and difficulty in quantifying or measuring the potential outcomes of initiatives. Although the Government vision and the national drivers arising from this were a key source of support for the Reserve Bank vision, they did not assist in the development of a direct business case for the undertaking of a knowledge management program. However, the Bank's status as a quasi-government department enabled it to leverage government interest in building the knowledge economy and positioning the public sector as the driver of the knowledge economy was of particular importance to the Bank. The Bank also emphasised its view that government departments should be showing leadership. By emphasising the importance of leadership from the public sector, the Bank was able to add significant weight to its own business case.

One of the most significant steps in the Bank's journey to knowledge management was the establishment of the Knowledge Services Group. This group, comprising staff from across the organisation, was charged with identifying the importance of knowledge management for the Bank and, subsequent to this, implementation and maintenance of organisational knowledge management practices. The Bank appointed Yogesh Anand to the role of chief information officer (CIO). His role was to head the Knowledge Services Group and take overall responsibility for the Group's combined areas of knowledge management, information management, and technology. A critical part of Anand's role was to take the knowledge management vision and understand what it meant for the Bank, to refine it, to elaborate it, and finally to replace theory with action.

From the outset, involvement in the knowledge management initiative came from all levels. The Bank's governor directly sponsored the initiative, and this top-level support was particularly helpful in communicating the importance of the initiative to all staff. A clear corporate vision (Kanter, Stein, & Jick, 1992; Nonaka & Takeuchi, 1995) and top-level support (Blackler, 1995; Nonaka & Konno, 1998) are widely acknowledged as fundamental to the development of a strong knowledge culture. At the same time, staff from the library and records management area as well as other parts of the Bank came together to form an informal, grassroots network. This network followed the growth of thinking on knowledge management theory and could be categorised as an early community of practice, defined as one of three key critical components of knowledge management (Cohen & Prusak, 2001). Other critical components were identified as the trust of the organisation's staff and the presence of appropriate social norms and organizational culture, both of which were confirmed by the experience of the Bank. Communities of practice have an important role to play in sharing learning and knowledge across an organisation (DiBella & Nevis, 1998), as evidenced within the Bank, where this informal network initiated brown-bag lunchtime sessions, where those interested in finding out more about knowledge management and how it would work in the Bank could meet and discuss the various issues. This group also helped to identify the barriers that existed in terms of knowledge sharing.

Building a KM Framework/Strategy

Thus far, the Bank had developed a vision and seen the formation of both the Knowledge Services Group and more informal knowledge management-friendly networks. However, although knowledge management was much discussed, very few organisations were actually implementing knowledge management programs. Despite recognition that knowledge management could be beneficial to an organisation, many organisations simply did not know where to start (Earl, 2001). The Bank found itself in a similar position and determined that the most logical starting point was to gain an understanding of knowledge management, to investigate global best-practice thinking, and to identify a preferred development process or framework that would be most appropriate to the Bank. Development of knowledge management frameworks can assist organisations to understand the sorts of knowledge management initiatives that are possible and to identify those that are most suitable to the context of the organisation (Earl, 2001).

To enable this development, the Bank sought to develop its own local framework with the help of an outside individual who could bring in best practice and knowledge in terms of what was happening in other parts of the world. However, a critical concern for the Bank was loss of control of ownership of the process. In order to maximise potential of the appointment, the Bank secured the services of an individual through whom it could gain access to established networks and the individual's organisation. By doing this, the Bank was able to harness significant information on what other organisations were doing in relation to knowledge management, and assessment of this information would assist the Bank to develop its own knowledge management strategy. The aim of a strategic approach to knowledge management is "to build, nurture, and fully exploit knowledge assets through systems, processes, and people and convert them into value as knowledge-based products and services" (Earl, 2001, p. 228). This was the Bank's objective.

The Bank then undertook a 12-week program that effectively developed the framework into a workable strategy.

Strategy Development

Developing the Bank's knowledge management strategy involved all areas of the organisation, and contained four main phases as shown in Figure 2. As part of this work, examination was made of the organisational culture, structure, and infrastructure to determine what changes would be needed.

In the initial three-week phase, the Knowledge Services Group worked with the external consultant to gather and review the knowledge management data and best practice from around the world.

The second phase focussed on internal data gathering during which a number of structured interviews and workshops were carried out throughout the organisation to investigate the knowledge required by each function and to understand what individuals saw as being the opportunities (see Appendix 3). Additional input was sought from the members of the informal brown-bag network who had been meeting prior to the onset of the strategy development. This group had valuable information regarding knowledge management thinking at the grassroots level and had helped to identify some of the existing barriers to knowledge sharing within the Bank.

One area of the strategy development that posed particular difficulty was the identification of specific knowledge that would have to be managed in each function. In order to overcome this difficulty, three separate categories were identified for classification purposes:

1. Structured data (S)
2. Unstructured and semistructured information (U)
3. Experience/knowledge (E)

The information gathered through the interviews and workshops was then structured into these three categories as denoted in Figure 3. For example, one workshop focussed on experience and information into the development of monetary policy. Feeding into the process was structured (data) and unstructured information (reports,

Figure 2. Knowledge management strategy development process (adapted from Anand, 2003)

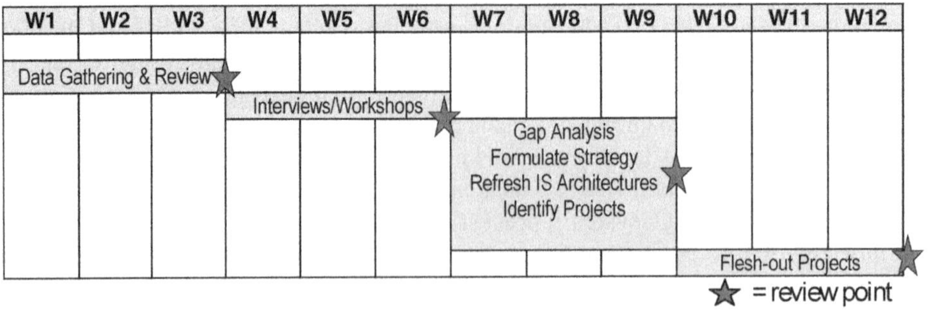

Figure 3. Categorisation of information (adapted from Anand, 2003)

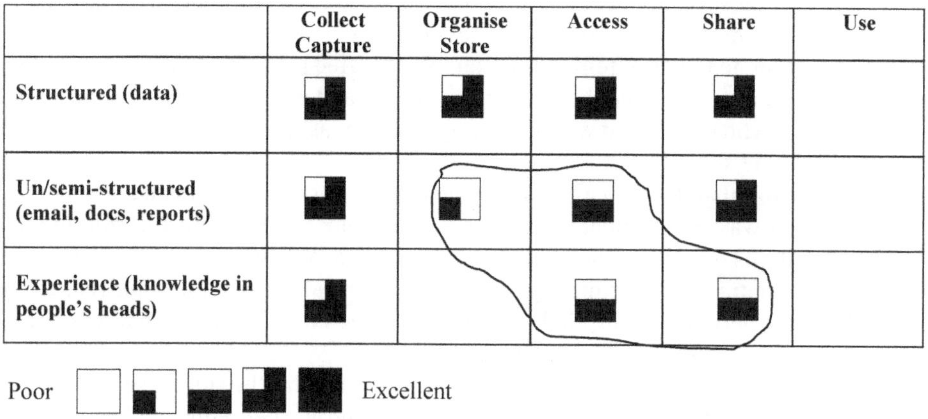

	Collect Capture	Organise Store	Access	Share	Use
Structured (data)					
Un/semi-structured (email, docs, reports)					
Experience (knowledge in people's heads)					

Poor Excellent

Note: Sharing within departments is much stronger than sharing between

etc.) along with experience from external and internal organizations. This was then used to identify where the exposures may be in terms of risks or barriers.

The three categories were also analysed in terms of their collection, storage, access, sharing, and use as shown in Figure 3.

This outcome of this process indicated that, as expected, the Bank was reasonably good at managing the structured information (data) in terms of sharing it and providing access to it. With unstructured or semistructured information, the Bank considered it was good at its collection, but not so good at organising and storing it. For example, although a document management system was in place, it did not integrate well with the e-mail system and so e-mails tended to be held personally. The same thing was found with experience — while the Bank considered it was good at recruiting both graduates and globally experienced staff, its view of their experience then tended to become limited to their specific role rather than their entire experience, which was often far wider. The Bank also found that sharing of information within departments was far better than the sharing between departments.

Armed with this knowledge, the Bank then carried out phase three of the program, which included a gap analysis that would be used to formulate the strategy. The gap analysis identified four threads:

- **People to Information.** This category consisted of infrastructure-type activities aimed at improving knowledge repositories as well as making them easier to access. This ensured that individuals had timely, secure, and accurate data and information to be able to carry out their work. These infrastructure-type activities operated at two levels: management of information coming into the organization, and handling the dissemination of captured information. To carry out the activities required an understanding of what information was needed, or at least, anticipation of the broader requirements. To achieve this, staff in the Bank's information centre worked closely with the different departments to ensure that they knew all that was available within the organisation.

- **People to People.** This category was identified primarily as a culture issue and focussed on sharing the experience and knowledge of staff and making it easily accessible through maintaining and developing contact networks. In this instance, an environment was required, for example, "coffee machine discussions," which enabled and encouraged the exchange of ideas, and which ensured that staff were aware of who knew what within the organisation, as well as allowing new experiences to be shared.
- **Institutionalise Knowledge.** While the Bank was good at capturing decisions, it was not always as efficient in its responses to them. For example, the thinking that went into its decisions, the alternatives discussed, and market reactions were not always captured. Consequently, there was little learning captured for reuse. The challenge here was to turn individual knowledge into an institutional repository, so that it became part of the corporate memory.
- **Collaborative Culture.** The intent of this was to change the culture so that sharing became second nature within the organisation, and as a consequence, moved away from the view that "knowledge is power" to one of "knowledge sharing is power." From an organisational perspective, this meant ensuring that the organisation allowed sharing to happen, with executives leading by example to develop and actively reinforce the organizational culture (Schein, 1992).

An example of facilitating opportunities to share is the recognition of the importance of staff mixing in the cafeteria. When the existence of the cafeteria came under review, the Bank decided to keep it as its benefits in this regard had been recognised. Activities in this area were focussed on creating a collaborative culture in order to make the most of the resources that the Bank had, and a collaborative working environment in which sharing is active and deliberate.

The completion of the gap analysis allowed the Knowledge Services Group to identify a number of specific initiatives that would enhance knowledge management within the Bank. These initiatives were developed and categorised in terms of cost and importance as shown in Figure 4.

In general, the initiatives were aimed at improving the accessibility to structured and unstructured data and to the knowledge held by people, improving the corporate memory, and developing the right culture. In particular, they focussed on infrastructure issues such as the tools required. These issues could be regarded as the low-hanging fruit since they were more easily understood by people and provided a catalyst for a change in culture. However, they also included more difficult cultural and leadership issues. In keeping with the complex nature of knowledge management, these initiatives presented a multifaceted approach that included cultural, technological, and organisational infrastructures as identified by Gold, Malhotra, and Segars (2001).

During the strategy development process the general feeling amongst many within the organisation, apart from the knowledge management enthusiasts, seemed to be one of nonchalance. In many respects, it was recognised that the concept of knowledge management was not new, and there was an underlying feeling of a new label being placed on an old problem. The Knowledge Services Group countered this by talking not about knowledge management, but about the specific issues that were being identified and how these might be resolved. While the term "knowledge strategy" or "knowledge frame-

Figure 4. Reserve Bank knowledge management strategies (adapted from Anand, 2003)

	Low cost	High cost
A (highly recommended)	❑ Develop policies/standards & training programs for document management and email usage ❑ Work with departments to review file classification and handling of records/physical files ❑ Scan selected incoming correspondence ➢ Document lessons learned in formal manner ➢ Make corporate history more visible using timelines o Implement the Learning and Development Project and evaluate outcomes o Assess job rotation, multi-department projects and committees as part of development plans for all staff o Develop communications strategy to support culture change o Continue with Leadership Project & evaluate outcomes o Job evaluation, rewards and motivation initiatives • Grow info publishing and data analysis with DU	❑ Work toward integrated KM system. Start by reviewing document management system and using this as an opportunity to review KM solutions available in marketplace. ❑ Web enable applications ❖ Develop a bank wide contact management system • Data warehouse pilot
B (should do)	• Review data acquisition • XML enable external data feeds ➢ Build knowledge into standard operating procedures and systems	• Standardise data storage • Develop data warehouse
C (could do)	• Develop high level data map ❖ Implement e-collaboration tools (project & chat rooms) ❖ Develop a who's who directory within the Bank ❑ Review Bank's document scanning/OCR requirement	

LEGEND

- • Make structured data more accessible
- ❑ Make unstructured information more accessible
- ❖ Make knowledge held by people more accessible
- ➢ Develop corporate memory
- o Develop the right culture

work" was found to be useful in terms of discussions with the senior management team and in the development of individual business cases, at the grassroots level, people wanted issues to be resolved. In removing the "knowledge management" label, more credibility was able to be added to the initiative.

Specific Initiatives

The most significant knowledge management initiative to be undertaken at the Bank was aimed at changing the organisational culture. The Bank recognised that although this change had the mandate of the senior management group, it would require much more than this. To facilitate the change, three key areas were identified. First, it was understood that it required leadership by example. Shaping culture is critical to an organisation's ability to manage its knowledge more effectively (Gold, Malhotra, & Segars, 2001), and an important aspect of culture is the vision that is presented from top-level management

(Davenport, DeLong, & Beers, 1998). The initial vision had been shaped by the then deputy governor, and mandated by the governor, it was important that this high-level support was seen to be continued. Unlike many organisations embarking on knowledge management initiatives, the relatively small size of the Bank was to prove advantageous, as it was possible to sustain strong lines of communication. As the CIO points out:

There are about 215 people located in this building. If I can't walk to everyone of them and tell them something, there is a problem. In this way, it could be seen that the initiative was being supported at the highest levels in the organization (Anand, 2004).

To further enhance the leadership role and embed knowledge management into the organisational psyche, the Bank identified knowledge management as being a core competency for all managers, and a key element of the appraisal process. Within the performance appraisal, knowledge sharing was broken into multiple statements and the employees measure themselves as to where they think they are at on a scale of one to five, with one being "needs lots of development" and five being "walking on water." The manager then carries out the same assessment. The idea being that once both parties have completed the assessment, they then sit down and look at any gaps or discrepancies in the assessment. This method of assessment has been received well and has prompted staff to look at how they are sharing knowledge in terms of documentation and both internal and external networking. The appraisal is not linked to pay, therefore there is no disincentive attached.

Knowledge management also became an integral part of the Bank's recruitment program, and was used during the recruitment process to capture candidates' thinking on knowledge management and determine their likely approach.

The second key area of priority in terms of changing the organisational culture was to increase opportunities for collaboration. Prior to the onset of the initiative, the Bank had begun to move to open-plan offices for the whole organisation. Only the chief executive and the deputy chief executive retained their own offices. The driver for the change had not been an overt attempt at increasing knowledge sharing. Rather, it was the initiative of a new head of department in the policy area. One of his first observations was that the current environment, comprising individual offices, was not conducive to facilitating policy making, and did little to promote communication between staff. This initiative initially met with strong resistance principally because staff equated offices to status. By removing the offices, individuals felt that they no longer had particular status within the organisation. Having observed the resentment toward the plan, the head of department first took the time to explain the reasons behind the change. However, there continued to be resistance within the workforce, with some staff feeling so strongly that they threatened to leave. This did not eventuate and the change was made. Ironically, three years later, with the Bank still located across a number of floors, the staff requested that the Bank relocates to a single floor location to remove barriers to communication. Another of the key concerns put forward by the staff prior to the change, was that an open-plan layout would be noisy and interfere with their ability to concentrate. In the initial stages, the open-plan approach was found to be noisier; however, complaints about this soon died away and people were now talking far more than when there had been the physical barrier of the offices.

The third area identified as a potential contributor to facilitating a change in organisational culture was the provision of incentives for knowledge sharing. This area has generated much thought within the knowledge management literature and the Bank was not convinced that the introduction of incentives, particularly in terms of financial rewards, was necessarily a positive step. Through careful research, the Bank found that although this approach had appeared to work in other organisations, some problems had occurred. These problems included determining the value of the knowledge and the need for increased payments for greater amounts of knowledge to avoid some being held back. The literature in this area is also divided. While some posit that that productivity and quality occur within corporate cultures that systematically recognise and reward individuals, both symbolically and materially (Willmott, 1993), others argue that extrinsic rewards, such as monetary awards, will have a negative impact on intrinsic motivation (Deci & Ryan, 1985). The Bank decided that while it would continue to monitor developments in this area, the incentive approach was counter to what it was trying to achieve in terms of its culture.

The gaps analysis also made apparent difficulties in the availability of information in terms of access and integrity. A good example of this was the proliferation of contact databases operating within the Bank. It was common for each database to contain the same or similar information as that contained elsewhere and there was no common system for updating or deleting material. As a consequence, there were significant overlaps, data redundancy, and integrity-type issues. In addition, access was not available to everyone and some staff were still operating using business cards. The approach to this problem was to consolidate the databases in order to bring the contact information into one location.

On the surface, consolidation of the various contact databases appeared to be a very low-level issue. In reality, it was one of the most difficult and time-consuming projects that was undertaken. The main difficulties arose from the reluctance of individuals to move from their own contact database, which in some cases had been used for over 15 years, to a database that would be maintained centrally and where access would be available to all.

A large project team was formed to work through the issues that the changeover presented. The project team consisted of three working groups each consisting of 12 people. With the participation of the working groups, a new intranet solution was identified, and the changeover commenced. In order to ensure that the changeover ran as smoothly as possible, the Bank ran multiple training seminars and carried out a great deal of one-on-one hand-holding. Today, the intranet is the primary contact source within the Bank and has been extended to include a contracts link so that all the contracts held within the bank are also held centrally. However, as the CIO states:

I know that probably some people have still got business cards. You can't force people to give them, but now if you spot an anomaly you can fix it, and that updated information is available to everyone (Anand, 2004).

In total, this process took 18 months, which was longer than expected, and was mainly due to the reaction to the change and the feelings of loss of direct control.

The Bank also undertook a review of all of its electronic records and document management activities. The Bank had been an early adopter of document management and had a system in place since 1993. The gaps analysis had shown there were several areas in which the Bank could improve its document management activities, including better management of all external and internal information resources such as the integration of e-mail. Although the current system captured a significant amount of external documentation, the aim was to now electronically capture internal documentation as well. Successful capture of both internal and external documentation would result in staff having a wide and ready access to a range of information.

In contrast to many organisations, the Bank operated as a totally open organisation, which meant that there was no security on any documents, including the discussions of the senior management group. The culture within the senior management group was to discuss why such documents would not be shared in the organisation, as opposed to shared. The only exceptions to this policy were around market-sensitive information on monetary policy where information remained private to protect staff from the results of any leakage, and the staff understood and accepted this. Mintzberg (1979) sees this form of semiadhocracy as one that facilitates knowledge sharing and an intensity of knowledge work, and is particularly appropriate in a knowledge-based organisation comprised of professional knowledge workers.

The review of the document management system was initially considered in terms of a data warehousing issue; however, as the review progressed, it became clear that the issues were more about providing a single point of access to information. As a result, data warehousing was removed from the agenda.

The review is ongoing, with the project team about to introduce the potential new solution to the wider organisation. With the experience gained from the integration of the contact databases, it is at this point that the CIO believes the document review program may encounter possible resistance as the current solution has been in place for 10 years. To counter this, the Bank has in place an extensive change management strategy, which includes "fun parts," strong messages, as well as heads of departments taking an active role in promoting and selling the messages to their respective departments.

There were also a number of smaller initiatives, including increased use of information mapping techniques, as well as use of scanning with a pilot on how best to enable access to documents that were not currently available online.

As well as improving the Bank's infrastructure tools, some of these initiatives are also intended to reinforce the values of the organisation, for example, in support of providing a family-friendly environment.

CURRENT CHALLENGES/PROBLEMS FACING THE ORGANIZATION

The Bank has committed sizeable resources to the initial development and subsequent implementation of knowledge management strategies. These have resulted in significant benefits to the organisation, the most important of which was to mitigate the risk of loss of knowledge through staff departure. There are several other subjective benefits that the Bank attributes to knowledge management, including the culture of the organisation, the extent of current knowledge-sharing practice, and the accessibility of a wider range of documentation of all staff. Despite the difficulty in quantifying the potential benefits of knowledge management, the Bank was, from the outset, comfortable with the idea that the potential benefits were not easily measurable.

The Bank's journey to knowledge management has been a holistic one, and has focussed on culture, structure, and infrastructure. In some ways, the CIO regards technology as the easy part and believes that the greater challenge is in bringing about the change, especially when benefits are more intangible. Change is easier to enact when it can be hooked to something rather than change for the sake of change; therefore, technology is often used as the hook. However, he stresses, that from the Bank's viewpoint, knowledge management is not all about technology. It is not the technologists but the information manager who has responsibility for the Bank's knowledge management strategy. He said:

They're the ones who are used to thinking about unstructured information, whereas if I was to give it to a technology person, they'd be trying to put a structure round it. When you do that, you're going to lose a lot of value from it (Anand, 2004).

There are still several strategies that have not yet been put into place. Although the review of the document management system is partially completed, the introduction of a potential solution is seen to be one that will potentially meet some resistance. The Bank will approach this with the insight gained from previous initiatives and with the experience of knowing that while the road may at times be difficult, the view from the other side is generally better.

There has certainly been progress made in terms of recording past decisions. This has mainly been achieved by targeting individuals developing an e-mail-centric organisation whereby the majority of discussions and debate are captured in threads within e-mails. This has proved successful to date, but moving forward, there may be less use of e-mail and so the Bank will need to initiate alternative approaches to formalise some of the processes.

There are also a number of legacy systems operating within parts of the organisation, such as Human Resources. The integration of these is being addressed in the single point of access activity. At this point, the project is still largely in the stages of trying to understand exactly what is the boundary and scope of the project.

The Bank is also investigating the idea of "yellow pages," a system of identifying those within the organisation with specific expertise. The context of the system will be somewhat wider than other systems in operation in that the extent of the experience will relate not just to that of the person's job but in terms of their wider experience. A good example of this is a staff member who survived the Kobe earthquake in 1995. He has talked to many groups within the Bank about preparedness and issues such as business continuity. Although that experience may not relate directly to his position at the Bank, it is invaluable in the wider context and makes him an excellent knowledge source for a yellow pages system.

An ongoing challenge for the Bank, like several other organisations, is that of continuing to meet the ongoing business demands with the level of available resources. In that environment, keeping knowledge management in the forefront is a challenge and needs to be achieved through practical initiatives that can demonstrably provide tangible and/or strategic benefits. This requires commitment from within the organisation as well as ongoing communication. In the Bank's case, it looked on knowledge management as a sunk investment and focussed on getting acceptance to the framework. Once this was completed, it provided a reference point for the specific initiatives that could be looked at in terms of how well they delivered against the framework.

Culturally, the Bank is at an interesting crossroads. The organisation is becoming wary of what might be termed as "consulting labels." As the organisation's awareness of knowledge management concepts has increased, the term "knowledge management" has become a less favoured label. As a result, one of the challenges for the Bank is to progress the knowledge management initiatives but package them differently.

There is also a need to move the Bank's ongoing development of knowledge management strategies to the next level. To date, a best-practice-based approach has provided a good framework for the Bank. However, one school of thought for ongoing evolution is to explore the more unstructured process for developing knowledge management strategies. Embracing complex adaptive systems theory, this approach can be used to create a sense-making model that utilises self-organising capabilities to identify a natural flow model of knowledge creation, disruption, and utilisation (Snowden, 2002). Snowden concludes that the enabling of such descriptive self-awareness within an organisation will provide a new simplicity that can facilitate new meaning through the interaction of the formal and informal in a complex ecology of knowledge (Snowden, 2002).

EPILOGUE AND LESSONS LEARNED

Epilogue

This case illustrates the challenges inherent in implementing knowledge management initiatives into knowledge-intensive organisations. With no tried-and-true frameworks or models to follow, organisations, such as the Reserve Bank, must grapple with devising and implementing strategies appropriate to their own needs and circumstances. Although it is unlikely that prescribed knowledge management implementation strategies will ever be off the shelf in the sense of providing an easy and effective solution for any given organisation, it is possible to foresee a time when a great enough body of research and practice has been accumulated to offer an organisation such as the Bank enough successful models of knowledge management implementation to pick and choose strategies that might be appropriate to at least begin working with. This case helps point the way forward for others by detailing the journey of one organisation that is seriously pursuing a comprehensive programme.

Lessons Learned

Knowledge management is not a project; it is a continuum

At the outset, the Bank viewed knowledge management in terms of a project, with a distinct time frame and process. In broad terms, knowledge management was viewed as a problem that required fixing. In retrospect, the Bank considers that knowledge management is not a distinct task, but rather as the way you work, encompassing all aspects of the organisation. Essentially, it is an intrinsic part of an individual's approach to work, as well as intrinsic to the Bank's culture.

Committing to a framework that will evolve in a more organic way

In keeping with the view of knowledge management as a continuum, commitment to an organically evolving framework retains a close alignment to the individual nature and requirements of the particular business environment. This avoids the need to put a tight structure around things, which is likely to constrain thinking and result in a less-than-optimum result. While best practice can work well, essentially it is transferring someone else's idea to your individual business circumstance, and can stifle innovation because you are constraining yourself to what others have done. Rather than applying scope and boundaries from others, the challenge is to say, "let us just throw everything up in the air and see where it lands."

It is not exclusively about technology or business process or culture; it is a combination of culture-change initiatives with technology as an enabler.

The combination of technology and business process were important components of the Bank's knowledge management initiative, but neither was considered in isolation. The Bank's knowledge management program necessitated changes to the way things had previously been done. Change is often easier to enact when it has a hook. Often, technology is used as the hook for facilitating change.

High level of commitment from within the organisation

The Bank's knowledge management program was sponsored from the highest level, the governor. If this top-level support had not been apparent, it is believed that the Bank would not have made as much progress as it did. Although it could have been pushed, to a certain extent, by the CIO, there were a number of business cases where the projected benefits were intangible and not able to quantified. Without high-level support, it would have been difficult to secure funding for these business cases in the absence of a tangible return on investment.

The intangible nature of benefits

The benefits derived from knowledge management initiatives are often intangible and hard to quantify. Most organisations require a strong business case to be in place before committing funds to an initiative or project. The Bank found it difficult to identify and measure benefits in terms of financial return and was therefore unable to present these as part of its business cases. The Bank took the approach that by addressing the problems that existed, this would result in intangible benefits, such as a happier workforce, thus leading to increased productivity. The investment was, therefore, more a strategic investment in the business in the long term. Success of earlier business cases has also added support for future business cases.

REFERENCES

Anand, Y. (2003). Reserve Bank of New Zealand: Knowledge management. Presentation. Wellington, New Zealand.

Anand, Y. (2004). Personal interview with Reserve Bank CIO, Yogesh Anand.

Bank of Canada. (2002). *Annual report*. Retrieved July 2004, from *www.bankofcanada.ca/en/annual/2002/bank.pdf*

Bartol, K., & Srivastava, A. (2002). Encouraging knowledge sharing. *Journal of Leadership & Organizational Studies, 9*(1), 64-76.

Blackler, F. (1995). Knowledge, knowledge work and organizations: An overview and interpretation. *Organization Studies, 16*(6), 1021-1046.

Chourides, P., Longbottom, D., & Murphy, W. (2003). Excellence in knowledge management: An empirical study to identify critical factors and performance measures. *Journal of Business Performance Management, 7*(2), 29-45.

Cohen, D., & Prusak, L. (2001). *In good company*. Boston: Harvard Business School Press.

Davenport, T., DeLong, D., & Beers, M. (1998). Successful knowledge management projects. *Sloan Management Review, 39*, 43-57.

Davenport, T.H. (2002). Some principles of knowledge management. Retrieved July 2004, from *www.bus.utexas.edu/kman/kmprin.htm*

Davenport, T.H., & Prusak, L. (1998). *Working knowledge: How organizations manage what they know*. Boston: Harvard Business School Press.

Deci, E.L., & Ryan, R.M. (1985). *Intrinsic motivation and self-determination in human behaviour*. New York: Plenum.

DiBella, A., & Nevis, E. (1998). *How organizations learn: An integrated strategy for building learning capability*. San Francisco: Jossey-Bass.

Drucker, R.E. (1993). *The post capitalist society*. Oxford: Butterworth-Heinemann.

Earl, M. (2001). Knowledge management strategies: Toward a taxonomy. *Journal of Management Information Systems, 18*(1), 215-233.

Gold, A., Malhotra, A., & Segars, A. (2001). Knowledge management: An organizational capabilities perspective. *Journal of Management Information Systems, 18*(1), 185-214.

Hearn, G., & Rooney, D. (2002). The future role of government in knowledge-based economies. *Foresight, 4*(6), 23-33.

Information Technology Advisory Group (ITAG). (1999). *The knowledge economy*. Retrieved December 14, 2004, from *www.med.govt.nz*

Kanter, R., Stein, B., & Jick, T. (1992). *The challenge of organizational change: How companies experience it and leaders guide it*. New York: The Free Press.

Mertins, K., Heisig, P., & Vorbeck, J. (Eds.). (2001). *Knowledge management. Best practice in Europe*. Berlin: Springer-Verlag.

Mintzberg, H. (1979). *The structuring of organizations: A synthesis of the research*. Englewood Cliffs, NJ: Prentice-Hall.

Nahapiet, J., & Ghoshal, S. (n.d.). Social capital, intellectual capital, and the organizational advantage. *Academy of Management Review, 23*(2), 242-258.

Newell, S., Robertson, M., Scarbrough, H., & Swan J. (2002). *Managing knowledge work*. New York: Palgrave.

Nonaka, I. (1994). A dynamic theory of organizational knowledge creation. *Organization Science, 5*(10), 14-37.

Nonaka, I., & Konno, N. (1998). The concept of "ba": Building a foundation of knowledge creation. *California Management Review, 40*(3), 40-54.

Nonaka, I., & Takeuchi, H. (1995). *The knowledge creating company: How Japanese companies create the dynamics of innovation*. New York: Oxford University Press.

Organisation for Economic Co-operation and Development (OECD). (2003). Conclusions from the results of the survey of knowledge management practices for Ministries/Departments/Agencies of Central Government in OECD member countries. Retrieved February 12, 2004, from *www.oecd.org/document/20/0,2340,en_2649_201185_1946900_119826_1_1_1,00.html*

Reserve Bank of New Zealand. (2002). *Annual report 2002/2003*. Wellington.

Schein, E. (1992). *Organizational culture and leadership* (2nd ed.). San Francisco: Jossey-Bass.

Scherer, K. (2001, July 27). Knowledge as a power tool. *New Zealand Herald,* p. C7.

Snowden, D. (1999). A framework for creating a sustainable knowledge management program. In J.W. Cortada & J.A. Woods (Eds.), *The knowledge management yearbook, 1999-2000* (pp. 52-64). Boston: Butterworth-Heinemann.

Snowden, D. (2002). Complex acts of knowing: Paradox and descriptive self awareness. *Journal of Knowledge Management, 18*(1), 1-28.

Teece, D. (n.d.). Capturing value from knowledge assets: The new economy, markets for knowhow and intangible assets. *California Management Review, 40*(3), 55-79.

von Krogh, G. (1998). Care in knowledge creation. *California Management Review, 40*(3), 133-153.

Wiig, K.M. (2002). Knowledge management in public administration. *Journal of Knowledge Management, 6*(3), 224-239.

Willmott, H. (1993). Strength is ignorance; slavery is freedom: Managing culture in modern organizations. *Journal of Management Studies, 30*, 515-552.

FURTHER READING

Alavi, M., & Leidner, D. (2001). Knowledge management and knowledge management systems: Conceptual foundations and research issues. *MIS Quarterly, 25*(1), 107-136.

Cohen, D., & Prusak, L. (2001). *In good company*. Boston: Harvard Business School Press.

Davenport, T.H., & Prusak, L. (1998). *Working knowledge: How organizations manage what they know*. Boston: Harvard Business School Press.

Earl, M. (2001). Knowledge management strategies: Toward a taxonomy. *Journal of Management Information Systems, 18*(1), 215-233.

Gold, A., Malhotra, A., & Segars, A. (2001). Knowledge management: An organizational capabilities perspective. *Journal of Management Information Systems, 18*(1), 185-214.

Nahapiet, J., & Ghoshal, S. (1988). Social capital, intellectual capital, and the organizational advantage. *Academy of Management Review, 23*(2), 242-258.

Nonaka, I. (1994). A dynamic theory of organizational knowledge creation. *Organization Science, 5*(10), 14-37.

Snowden, D. (1999). A framework for creating a sustainable knowledge management program. In J.W. Cortada & J.A. Woods (Eds.), *The knowledge management yearbook, 1999-2000* (pp. 52-64). Boston: Butterworth-Heinemann.

ENDNOTE

1 "Foreign Currency Financial" and "Local Currency Financial" mean assets and liabilities denominated in either foreign currency (e.g., US dollar bonds) or local currency (e.g., New Zealand government bonds).

APPENDIX 1: RESERVE BANK FINANCIAL POSITION 2002 / 2003

	2002 June ($m)	**2003 June ($m)**
Assets:		
Foreign Currency Financial[1]	5,606	**6,216**
Local Currency Financial	5,821	**5,430**
Other Assets	38	**38**
Total Assets	11,465	**11,684**
Liabilities and Equity:		
Foreign Currency Financial	5,253	**5,102**
Local Currency Financial	2,962	**3,165**
Currency in Circulation	2,659	**2,806**
Other Liabilities	180	**195**
Equity	411	**416**
Total Liabilities and Equity	11,465	**11,684**

Graph 1

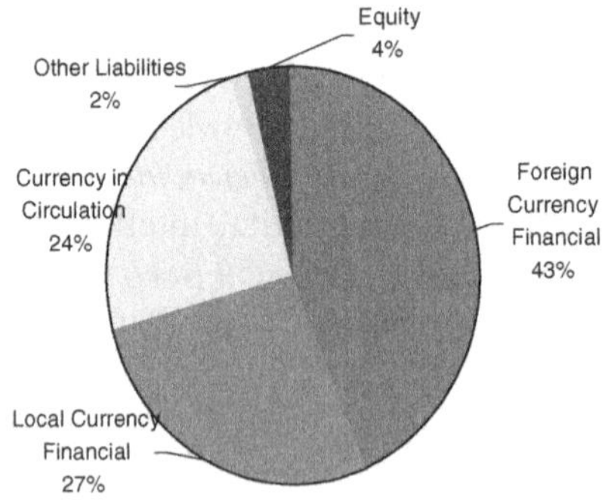

APPENDIX 2: THE RESERVE BANK FINANCIAL PERFORMANCE 2002 / 2003

	2002 June ($m)	2003 June Budget ($m)	2003 June **Actual ($m)**
Operating Income:			
Net Investment Income	200.7	221.0	**215.6**
Other Income	10.3	9.0	**9.3**
Total Operating Income	211.0	230.0	**224.9**
Operating Expenses:			
Personnel	15.6	16.0	**15.6**
Asset Management	5.0	4.0	**4.0**
New Currency Issued	4.7	4.5	**6.1**
Administration	1.1	1.4	**1.0**
Other	9.3	10.5	**9.1**
Loss on Disposal of Property	0.3	0	**0**
Total Operating Expenses	36.0	36.4	**35.8**
Operating Surplus	175.0	193.6	**189.1**
Net Expenditure under Funding Agreement	24.9	26.9	**26.3**
Surplus for Appropriation	175.0	193.6	**189.1**
Transfers to Equity	6.1	4.1	**4.7**
Payment to Government	168.9	189.5	**184.4**

Graph 2 *Graph 3*

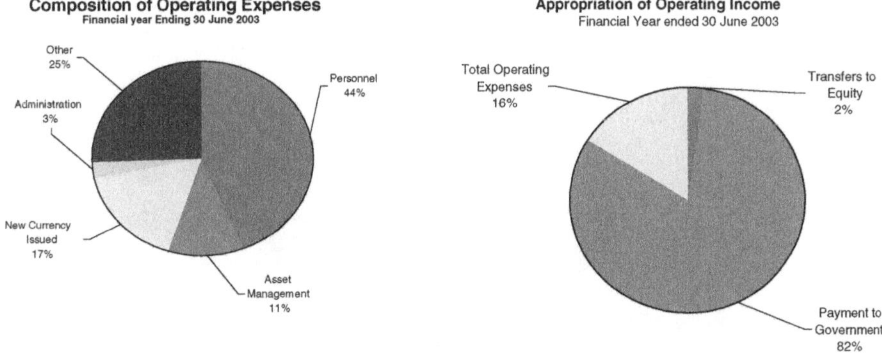

APPENDIX 3: WORKSHOPS USED TO IDENTIFY AREAS OF FOCUS

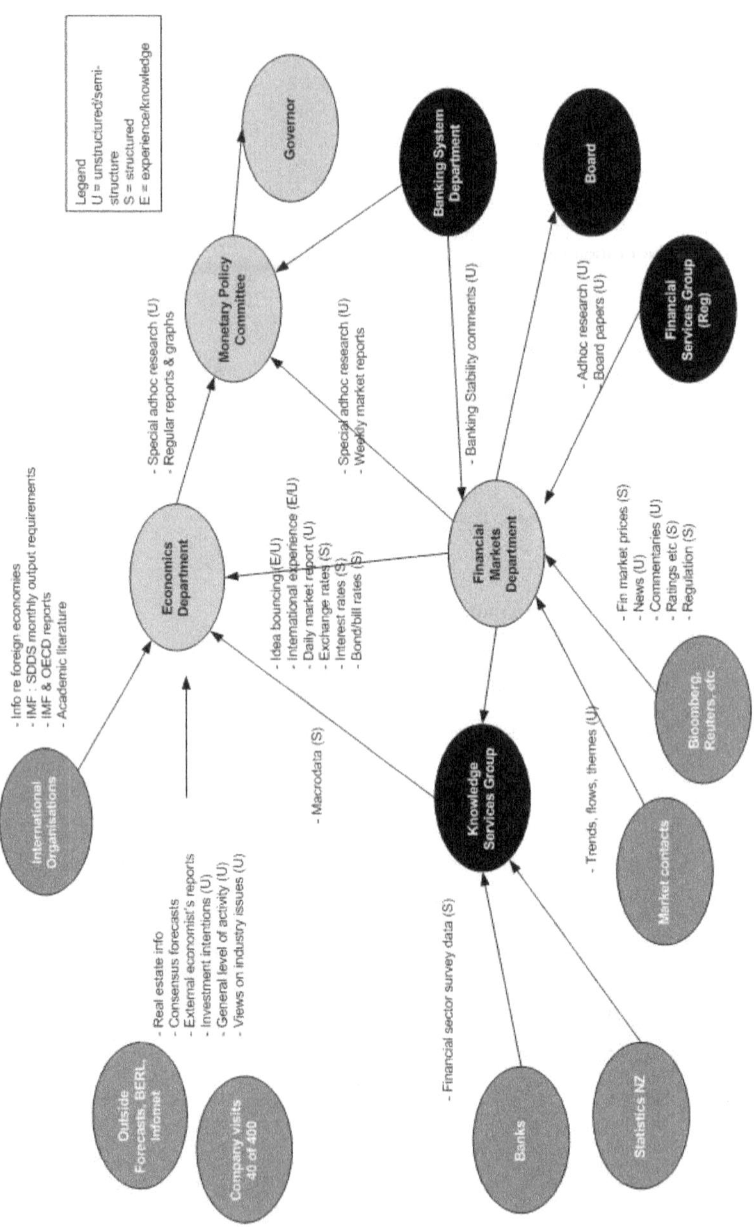

Chapter XIV

A Comparative Case Study of Knowledge Resource Utilization to Model Organizational Learning

Colin White, Deloitte Consulting, USA

David Croasdell, University of Nevada, Reno, USA

EXECUTIVE SUMMARY

The ability to store and manage data has not kept pace with the rapid evolution and growth of information resources. According to TechWeb.com, companies are doubling their storage capacities every year. This action is driven primarily by data warehousing and the necessity to provide instant access to data and supply-chain management. The trend does not look to be slowing. Isolated and undermanaged data resources have become a common practice in the industry despite the fact that the capacities of these systems keep improving while their prices continue to fall. This chapter draws four related cases to assess methods for organizing data and data resources in organizations. Further, the chapter provides examples for organizations to become learning organizations based on their ability to actively collect and distribute knowledge and their ability to become highly coupled socially and technically.

INTRODUCTION

Between 1937 and 1942, John Atanasoff and Clifford Berry designed and built the world's first electronic digital computer. This simple "ABC" computer introduced the ideas of binary arithmetic, regenerative memory, and logic circuits. In the years that have followed the construction of that first computer, business organizations have come to rely on computing technologies along with the data and information generated by those technologies. From early transaction processing to more contemporary "intelligent" systems, organizations have come to depend upon the technologies, systems, and tools that facilitate managing information within organizations. Tools such as the Internet, World Wide Web, and Web-enabled applications have enhanced the ability to collect and disseminate information. However, these tools can also create an overload of information. The ability to filter relevant information and apply that information to decision processes can be a significant challenge for organizations and organizational decision makers.

The ability to store and manage data has not kept pace with the rapid evolution and growth of information resources. According to TechWeb.com, companies are doubling their storage capacities every year. This action is driven primarily by data warehousing and the necessity to provide instant access to data and supply-chain management. The trend does not look to be slowing. Isolated and undermanaged data resources have become a common practice in the industry despite the fact that the capacities of these systems keep improving while their prices continue to fall. *CIO* magazine reports that the percentage of information technology (IT) costs devoted to data storage have risen as much as 50% in recent years. Storage area networks, network-attached storage devices, data redundancy practices, and the labor required to manage increasingly vast amounts of data have all contributed to the rise in costs. The cost of managing storage is now as much as eight times greater than the purchase price of storage hardware. Escalating costs of equipment and labor have placed data storage in the majority of IT budgets. Unfortunately, many of these expenditures are incurred by enterprises that continue to grow disorganized data storage facilities.

This chapter draws on four related cases to assess methods for organizing data and data resources in organizations. In particular, the chapter explores the practice of consolidating data and information to establish knowledge repositories necessary for organizational learning. The cases are used to build a case for prescribing steps organizations can take to develop capabilities consistent with learning organizations. A brief introduction to organizational learning includes a discussion on knowledge capture and knowledge representation. In addition, the discussion argues the importance of existing knowledge resources in relation to the organization's ability to be competitive. The practice of enterprise resource planning (ERP) is presented as a tool for consolidating knowledge resources within organizations. Four organizations are examined to highlight organizational opportunities that were addressed by knowledge solutions. Common practices for collecting and sharing knowledge are described. Each case highlights problems incurred by specific business units, the actions taken to address the problems, and outcomes of the actions. Measurements, such as return on investment (ROI), are included for each firm to aid in the illustration of results. Old processes are compared to recently modified processes. The changes to organizational processes and practices are presented as lessons learned. Finally, a review of all four cases is used to offer insight into the value of consolidating and centralizing knowledge resources. A comparison of the organizations provides evidence to suggest that knowledge consolidation and centralization are important for enabling effective knowledge capabilities.

BACKGROUND

Four organizations were examined in this comparative case study. Three cases come from a review of relevant literature. The fourth case is based on actual work experience the organization described in the case. Lessons from the literature-based cases are drawn upon to consider the last case.

SETTING THE STAGE

Fortune magazine predicts that the most successful corporations will establish themselves as learning organizations (i.e., enterprises that are completely adaptive) (Domain, 1989). In support of this claim, a study by Shell Oil found that companies that last over 75 years have had the ability to explore new business and organizational opportunities to create potential new sources of growth (de Geus, 1988). In an increasingly dynamic, interdependent, and unpredictable world, it is no longer possible to "figure it all out at the top." The key to organizational longevity is the ability to continually explore new business and organizational opportunities that create potential new sources of growth (Senge, 1990). The top-down model whereby "the top thinks and the local acts" gives way to integrating thinking and acting at all levels. Flatter organizational structures and employee empowerment are marking the way in contemporary organizations. The following passages present an overview of organizational learning and ERP in order to provide insight into knowledge practices in organizations.

The Learning Organization Perspective

A learning organization looks for differences between its actual and expected results and tries to correct the errors that have caused the difference. This type of company seeks to improve its actions through acquiring knowledge and understanding. It not only captures knowledge but utilizes its ability to respond and adapt to changing organizational environments (Hashim & Othman, 2003). A key to becoming a learning organization is to achieve a state of generative learning (Senge, 1995). Organizations practicing generative learning are able to observe the big picture — the whole of systems that control events. When a company fails to identify the entire source of problems, the prescribed solution addresses only the symptoms of the problem rather than eliminating the underlying causes.

In addition to generative learning, learning organizations must be capable of creating extrinsic and intrinsic visions of their company. Extrinsic visions focus on achieving something relative to an outsider, such as a competitor. Intrinsic visions focus on creating a new type of product or taking an established product to a new, higher level (i.e., a new level of creativity and innovation). Both visions need to coexist for a learning organization to emerge. To illustrate, consider a company that focuses solely on extrinsic competition. The purpose of such a vision is to defeat an adversary. However, the vision will eventually weaken the organization and lead to negative consequences (Senge, 1990). Focusing on purely intrinsic visions can also create harmful circumstances. For example, managers at the Facit Company, a mechanical calculator manufacturer, did not recognize the development of the electronic calculator industry as a new technological advancement. As such, the managers lacked the intrinsic vision to improve upon and redesign their mechanical calculator. The intrinsic vision carried only memories of their success in the mechanical market. Unfortunately, this vision blinded them to changes in technologies, namely electronic calculators. The lack of intrinsic vision took the company to the brink of bankruptcy and a resulting takeover (Walsh & Ungson, 1991).

Learning organizations have successful leaders who often are "systems thinkers," who focus less on day-to-day events and more on underlying trends and forces of change. They learn not to view an event in isolation but to find its interrelation with other events and to take action at the highest point needed; thus when a leader understands the interrelation of events and problem points in the larger design, implemented solutions will be longer lasting (Senge, 1990).

Harnessing the collective intellect of the people in a company is another challenge for learning organizations (Senge, 1990). In part, the challenge is addressed through a practice called knowledge management (KM). KM is concerned with the way businesses collect and utilize the knowledge that exists within their organizations. The practice of managing knowledge involves allowing new ideas to emerge and the processes that are involved in implementing those ideas (Brown & Duguid, 2000).

Organizations can establish legitimacy by grounding themselves in nature and reason. A firm does this by controlling the memory of its employees, causing them to forget experiences incompatible with its practices (Walsh & Ungson, 1991). In doing this, prior inefficient practices used by employees are discouraged from being continued. These conducts are recorded by the company as a lesson to learn from but are forgotten by the employees. In this way, more effective processes and procedures are incorporated. A strategy that achieves this level of control is the data-oriented approach.

The data-oriented approach focuses on the organization of data, rather than where and how data are used. This idea encourages the independence of data from the system that uses it, thus creating a more enduring organizational design, as the data needs of a business do not change rapidly. The data-oriented approach decreases the risk of generalization errors. These include the errors of commission and errors of omission. The errors of commission involve the entering of irrelevant information into a system. The errors of omission occurs when transferred information is selective, resulting in important parts of what it pertains being omitted (Walsh & Ungson, 1991). Tools that facilitate ERP help enforce a data-oriented approach and limit the type of input a user inserts into the system.

Consolidate Knowledge Resources Using ERP

Many data-oriented organizations use ERP software as a means to disseminate data to all areas of the company. ERP is used to integrate departments and functions across a company onto a single computer system that can serve departments' needs (Koch, 2002). Normally, a department utilized its own stand-alone computer system that was optimized for the particular ways the department did its work. However, ERP combines them into a single, integrated software program that is divided into modules that appear roughly like the old systems. Each department still gets its own software, except now the software is linked together so that someone in finance can look into the warehouse's software to see if an order has been shipped. This enables the various departments to share information and communicate with each other more easily.

A reason an application like ERP is utilized by resource-consolidating companies is to aid in improving business processes. For example, a typical customer order makes a paper-based journey from in-basket to in-basket around the company, being keyed and rekeyed into different departments' computer systems along the way. The time spent in these in-baskets causes delays and lost orders, and the rekeying into different computer systems invites errors. Meanwhile, no one in the company truly knows the status of the order. At any given point, there is no way for the finance department to get into the warehouse's computer system to see whether the item has been shipped.

By having this information in one software system rather than scattered among many different systems that do not communicate with one another, companies can keep track of orders more easily, and coordinate manufacturing, inventory, and shipping among many different locations at the same time. When one department finishes with the order, it is automatically routed via the ERP system to the next department. To find out where the order is at any point, an employee would need only to log in to the ERP system and track it down. People in different departments view and update system information easily. This method allows customers to get their orders faster and with fewer errors.

The Knowledge Life Cycle

The ability to share knowledge across an organization can be a critical organizational asset. Information technologies are used in modern organizations to facilitate corporate communications, store corporate information, and support corporate transactions. These capabilities, among others, allow corporate information technologies to assist in storing, organizing, and accessing the corporation's collective knowledge. Recollection of past events using an automated information system can help users understand the context of activities and learn how the organization has operated under past circumstances. Thus, they are better able to conduct themselves and make decisions in the context of the provided knowledge.

Managing knowledge in organizations includes capturing, encoding, storing, filtering, and disseminating information that can be actualized into valuable organizational know-how. One basic assumption of KM contends resource constraints such as time, capital, and understanding limit the ability to reasonably expect that all necessary and relevant knowledge can be captured and disseminated throughout an organization. Nonetheless, mechanisms to capture, encode, and store process knowledge in organizations provides (1) a starting point for future projects and (2) a basis for avoiding similar mistakes in future projects. Knowing the how and why (i.e., process knowledge) behind what (i.e., factual knowledge) leads to greater abilities to generate insight and better understanding.

Experience and expertise in the workplace provide valuable real-world artifacts for study. However, personal knowledge associated with a specific project can deteriorate overtime. If knowledge can be captured and encoded in a relatively quick and painless way, knowledge assets could be incorporated and shared through the collective organizational knowledge base. Hoffman et al. (1995) describe several methodologies for eliciting knowledge from experts. Methods for capturing process knowledge have had mixed results. The need for corporate amnesia along with resource constraints and the monumental effort that is often required to capture knowledge have conspired against the regular and consistent gathering of useful knowledge.

COMPARATIVE CASE STUDIES

The following sections present the approach four organizations have taken to consolidate and utilize knowledge resources. There are identifiable similarities in knowledge practices along with differences in each organization's approach to organizational learning. The first case demonstrates the effect of standardizing information between business units. The second case discusses integration as a means of migrating from dozens of dissimilar legacy systems and applications to a single data model. The third case provides a KM solution that helps employees share local knowledge around the world. The final case describes the integration of technology and learning processes necessitated by a corporate merger. Consideration of all the cases in total could lead to prescriptive models for implementing organizational learning policies and practices.

Nestlé USA

Nestlé USA is the United States subsidiary of Swiss-based Nestlé SA. The $8.1-billion-a-year company is located in Glendale, California. The company is comprised of seven business divisions including beverage, confections and snacks, food services, foreign trade, nutrition, prepared foods, and sales. Popular product brands include Carnation Instant Breakfast, Stouffer's Lean Cuisine, PowerBar, Baby Ruth, Taster's Choice, and Alpo.

Prior to 1991, Nestlé was a collection of independently operating brands owned by Nestlé SA (Worthen, 2002). In 1991, the brands were unified and reorganized into Nestlé USA. However, the new company continued to function as a group of independent organizations, each making its own business decisions. The only real change was in the way each unit reported to corporate Nestlé USA executives in Glendale, California, rather than to executives in Vevey, Switzerland. The new company was trying to introduce economies of scale and common practices, but years of independent operation made the transaction difficult.

In 1997, a team examining the various systems across the company found that Nestlé USA brands were paying 29 different prices for vanilla to the same vendor. This problem stemmed from each individual plant contracting for vanilla from a single vendor. The vendor was able to charge whatever it thought it could get from each plant. Nestlé USA did not detect the dysfunctional practice because every division and factory had the liberty of naming vanilla according to plant-specific coding guidelines. For example, one plant coded vanilla "1234" while another used "7778." Such practices made comparison difficult. Along with multiple purchasing systems, the company had no idea how much volume it was doing with a particular vendor because every factory set up its own vendor masters and purchased on its own. In addition to the vanilla trouble, many other redundancies were uncovered. The team also found nine different general ledgers and 28 points of customer entry.

Managers at Nestlé USA initiated an ERP project using SAP to address redundancies and inconsistencies within the organization. The project, code named Business Excellence thorough Systems Technology (BEST), was implemented to transform the firm's separate brands into a more tightly integrated company. The vice president and CIO of Nestlé USA joined with executives in charge of finance, supply chain, distribution, and purchasing to form a key stakeholders team. The team conducted an audit of processes and practices to determine what was working well in addition to what areas could be improved within the company. The team recommended changes that could be made within three to five years and presented its report to the Nestlé management. An ERP solution formed the cornerstone of the recommendation.

A team of 50 top business executives and 10 senior IT professionals were assembled to implement the project using SAP's ERP solution. The team was to identify a set of best practices that would become common work procedures for every Nestlé division. A smaller team worked concurrently with the executive team. Members of this team examined data in each division in order to implement a standardized structure across the company (e.g., vanilla would be coded consistently across divisions). After months of development, the key stakeholders planned an implementation incorporating purchasing, financials, sales and distribution, accounts payable, and accounts receivable using SAP and a supply-chain module from Manugistics Corporation, a supply-chain management advising company. Each of the modules was deployed across every Nestlé USA division.

Four of the modules were scheduled to be completed by 2000. The new systems doubled as code fixes for changes due to the millennium date problem. Nestlé USA made the deadline but created other problems in its haste to implement the solution. The BEST project team had overlooked integration points between the modules. The departments now used standardized names, systems, and a common process, but the systems were not well integrated. For instance, a salesperson could give a customer a discount rate and enter the rate into the new system. Unfortunately, the lack of integration prevented accounts receivable from knowing about the discount. Consequently, when the customer paid the discounted rate, it would appear to the accounts receivable operative as though the invoice were only partially paid.

Projects also met employee resistance before three of the SAP and Manugistics' modules were implemented. The groups being directly affected by the new processes and systems had not been represented on the key stakeholders team. As a result, the stakeholder team was always surprising the heads of these divisions. The workers did not understand how to use the new system or the new processes. Moreover, the divisional executives, who were just as confused as their employees and even more upset, did not help. No one wanted to learn the new way of doing things, including the firm's planners who were unwilling or unable to abandon their familiar spreadsheets for the more complex Manugistics' models.

To address these problems, 19 key stakeholders and business executives from Nestlé USA gathered for a three-day meeting. The group members decided that to finish the project they would need to start with the business requirements and reach an end date, rather than trying to fit the project into a mold shaped by a predetermined end date. They also concluded that they had to do a better job of obtaining support from divisional heads and that all the employees knew exactly what changes were taking place. Therefore, a liaison between the divisions and the project team was added to fix the poor relationship between the divisions and the project team. The new liaison and the CIO began meeting more with the division heads and conducting regular surveys on how the employees affected by the new systems were dealing with the changes.

In the end, the BEST project took six years and cost more than $200 million to complete. However, with all of Nestlé USA using the same data, the company was able to better forecast its demand. That allowed the firm to reduce inventory and redistribution expenses that occur when too much of a product is sent to one place and not enough to another. Those supply-chain improvements accounted for a major part of the $325 million Nestlé USA says it saved from its ERP implementation as of May 2002.

Colgate-Palmolive

Another company to consolidate its data is Colgate-Palmolive. With its headquarters in New York, New York, the Colgate-Palmolive Corporation is the owner of some of the most recognizable and widely used personal, household, and oral care products in the world. This includes Colgate toothpaste, Mennen Speed Stick, Softsoap, Palmolive dishwashing liquid, and Ajax detergent.

In 1994, the corporation used a series of IBM AS/400 minicomputers, several mainframes, and a disparate set of business applications. The varied applications along with the existence of 75 independent data centers contributed to an environment that made it very difficult to track organizational resources. To address the problem, Colgate-Palmolive embarked on a project to address inefficient processes arising from poor data management practices (Barlas, 2002).

Colgate-Palmolive's strategy was to integrate the dozens of dissimilar legacy systems and applications into a single data system using a single data model. In addition, the company wanted to decrease the amount of time products spent in the supply chain by getting closer to a single information flow. Like Nestlé USA, Colgate-Palmolive chose an ERP solution. The solution composed of SAP's R/3, which is a comprehensive set of integrated business applications. The system uses client-server architecture to provide storage, retrieval, analysis, and processing of corporate data. The system supports financial analysis, production operation, human resource management, and most other business processes. This entire process began in 1994 (Konicki, 2000).

The corporation looked at its entire supply chain, from the purchase order to cash in the bank, as an integrated process. Colgate-Palmolive analyzed all of its processes and made appropriate changes (Barlas, 2002). The firm then implemented R/3 in its North America division creating an operational template from business, IT, and data management perspectives. Having established the template, Colgate-Palmolive extended R/3 to its other geographies around the world (Barlas, 2002).

Colgate-Palmolive also used its new integrated approach for its e-business strategy (Barlas, 2002). This business-to-business strategy included a mySAP.com-based private exchange to connect the company with its suppliers through Transora, a consumer-packaged-goods (CPG) manufacturer-supplier exchange company. Colgate-Palmolive's SAP applications were also integrated with its suppliers via XML (eXtensible Markup Language) messaging so that the suppliers could retrieve Colgate-Palmolive's SAP information (Konicki, 2000). The company also engaged in vendor managed inventory (VMI) with its various retailers' distribution centers. The change made it possible to do collaborative planning, forecasting, and replenishment (CPFR), and promotional planning with a number of its partners (Barlas, 2002). This enabled the suppliers to look at Colgate-Palmolive's product plans and inventory levels and automatically replenish materials (Konicki, 2000).

At the finish of the project, Colgate-Palmolive managed most of its global operations on SAP's ERP platform while integrating some of its older legacy systems. The corporation has seven different instances of the ERP software applications to manage operations in 47 countries (Konicki, 2000). Ultimately, the company is able to operate using a single data center and one backup. Legacy assets and redundant IT positions were combined. Standardization was implemented across every computer desktop. The change created a capability to move rapidly in response to changing conditions. For example, when it came time to move to the euro, the corporation did it once on the ERP system for 15 countries (Barlas, 2002).

As of August 9, 2002, the company had saved $225 million, including the $75 million saved at Colgate-Palmolive's pet food division, Hill's Science Diet (Barlas, 2002). Much of the saving was earned through the reduction of working capital and inventory (Konicki, 2000). The firm's gross profit margins also increased consistently, going from 39.2% in 1984 to 54.4% in 2000 and expected to hit 60% margin by 2008 (Barlas, 2002).

Xerox

The Xerox Corporation is a $17 billion corporation headquartered in Stamford, Connecticut. The company employs 79,000 workers to offer document solutions, services, and systems (including color and black-and-white printers, digital presses, multifunction devices, and digital copiers) designed for offices and production-printing environments. The firm also sells associated supplies, software, and support for all its products.

The company is examined in light of problems that had arisen from an inability to share experience across the organization. The Xerox Corporation had troubles fostering best practice among its group of printer maintenance employees. The problem centered on an inability to circulate employee expertise using existing organizational infrastructure. The community of Xerox employees who repair the company's machines found that machines were not as predictable as documentation suggested. The organization needed a way to help its technicians share their local knowledge around the world.

To help the maintenance technicians share their experience and expertise, Xerox wanted to create a database to hold top repair ideas in order to share those ideas with other technicians in all areas. This plan also called for only the most favored ideas to be kept in the database as it often occurred that what one person thought useful others found the same the idea absurd or redundant (Brown & Duguid, 2000).

In order to create a useful database for all of its repair technicians, Xerox created a database of the technicians' top reserve ideas. This database also doubled as a resource for repair technicians who had developed the habit of calling engineers in Rochester, New York, to answer customer problems (Issac, 2003).

Before the creation of the database, the firm realized that many databases were created by managers who filled the databases with information they thought would be useful for their employees. However, most of those databases were rarely used by the employees. When Xerox created its Eureka database, it also formed a process for entering and updating the ideas within the database. The process is based on a peer-review system. Within this practice, the representatives, not the organization, supply and evaluate tips. In this way a local expert would work with the representative to refine the tip. Representatives and engineers evaluate the tips, calling in experts where appropriate.

After the Eureka database was implemented and ideas were being added, Xerox offered to pay for tips being inserted. However, the pilot group of representatives who designed the system thought that would be a mistake, leading people to focus on quantity rather than quality in making submissions. Instead, the representatives chose to have their names attached to tips and those who submitted good tips would earn positive recognition in their work community and build social capital as well as career advancement through the quality of their input. This way, the representatives got much-welcome recognition for their creativity, and local best practices would be deployed company-wide (Brown & Duguid, 2000).

As of July 2000, after continually encouraging employees to use the system, the Eureka database held nearly 30,000 ideas and was being utilized by 15,000 Xerox technicians who answered a quarter-million repair calls per year. The shared knowledge in Eureka has saved Xerox about $11 million in 2000 (Stewart, 2000). Customers of Xerox also have saved money in terms of the reduction in downtime (Issac, 2003).

Eureka later extended the role of the Eureka database to collect, share, and reuse solutions to software and network problems as well as those involving hardware (Stewart, 2000). Additionally, Xerox Web-enabled, or made available over the Web, the Eureka database system. This allowed technicians to gain access to the system from anywhere in the world though the Internet. The system added features including a search function, called "Search Light," and a wizard that aids in searching for tips including those waiting to be validated. Eureka even added a feature that shows the most current updates to technicians when they logged into the system (Issac, 2003).

The technicians trust the Eureka system and constantly use the system because it helps them get any problem fixed quickly. In the old process, many technicians would have to call a specialist to find solutions to problems they could not solve themselves. This new process has increased productivity and efficiency (Issac, 2003).

One of the database's core values is illustrated by a case in Brazil where an engineer was about to replace a problematic $40,000 machine for a customer. However, when the engineer looked in the database he found a tip from a Montreal technician that led him to replace a defective 50-cent fuse instead (Brown & Duguid, 2000). Another example includes a control counsel in a Kinko's printer that kept blowing out. After looking at the tips contained in the database, it was realized that the real problem was the voltage switch. The switch was a manufacturing error that was allowing too much electricity to go through the printer's mainframe and causing the control counsel to fry out (Issac, 2003).

The Eureka database has even been praised as a prime example of vernacular knowledge sharing, which is the harvesting, organizing, and passing around of ideas that come from lower-level employees of an organization. This collective knowledge is extremely valuable to the employees as well as the corporation (Stewart, 2000).

Chevron-Texaco

On October 9, 2001, Chevron Corporation, Texaco Incorporated, and Caltex (a global gasoline distributor) underwent a corporate merger to form ChevronTexaco (CT). The merged corporation has a presence in more than 180 countries and ranks as one of the world's largest and most competitive global energy companies. Worldwide, CT is the third largest publicly traded company in terms of oil and gas reserves, with some 11.8 billion barrels of oil and gas equivalents. It is the fourth largest producer of oil and gas with a daily production of 2.7 million barrels. Twenty-two refineries create a global refining capacity of more than 2.3 million barrels a day feeding more than 21,000 branded service stations worldwide.

Headquartered in San Ramon, California, CT is engaged in every aspect of the oil and gas industry, including exploration and production, refining, marketing and transportation, chemicals manufacturing and sales, and power generation. The corporation is also engaged in a chemicals venture (called the Chevron Phillips Chemical Company), an interest in Dynegy Incorporated, and equity interests in 47 power projects worldwide. Moreover, the company is in the process of developing and commercializing several advanced energy technologies such as fuel cells, hydrogen storage, and gas-to-liquids. CT is also a leader in gasification technology. This technology converts low-value materials, such as refinery residue, into clean synthesis gas. In addition, the company develops and commercializes advanced energy technologies, including fuel cells, photovoltaics, advanced batteries, and hydrogen storage. At the same time, the company's workforce of over 50,000 participates in community partnerships, social responsibility, and environmental awareness worldwide.

During the 1980s and early 1990s, the refineries at CT used a mainframe system called the Plant Equipment Information System (PEIS). The system was scrapped because CT saw it as an old technology that was becoming too expensive to maintain. PEIS cost the company nearly $2.5 million annually. After PEIS was cancelled, refineries were allowed to store their information however they saw fit. This action resulted in inefficiencies due to issues with dissimilar practices at the refineries. These dissimilar practices included applications being used by the refineries to store inspection data as well as placing these applications in disparate server locations. This caused great difficulty for all refineries and CT headquarters to find the data for inspection and updating reasons.

In order to address its inefficiencies, maintain its focus on reliability, and continue to identify its lost profit opportunities (LPOs), the company felt it needed to come up with a better way of consolidating business practice and standardizing data formats. An application package called the Enterprise Reliability Management System (ERMS) is the solution eventually selected to address the problems brought about by the merger. The system, developed by Meridium, utilizes distributed client-server technology to track, evaluate, and improve plant reliability. Companies that have adopted the Meridium solution include Exxon Mobile, BP, Chevron Phillips Chemical Company, Marathon Ashland Petroleum, and Coca-Cola. The ERMS application has many of the same features as the old PEIS. However, the new system is advantageous because it can be implemented using personal computers rather than a mainframe and ERMS utilizes an Oracle 8i database backend.

Meridium's ERMS carried an initial investment of $1.2 million. Subsequent upgrades and additional modules have raised the ante even more, but initial returns tend to validate the investment. The ERMS assists CT in recognizing and incorporating the best practices of the firm. These practices include efficient process control, work flow, condition monitoring of piping, technical information, repair tracking, and equipment forecasting. During the 2001 merger, ChevronTexaco's ERMS implementation processes were affected by best practices and data being introduced and incorporated from Texaco and Caltex. New data and information created an environment in which CT would need to upgrade its networks and infrastructure to enable the company to provide newly incurred services it did not have before, such as streaming video.

ERMS has also helped to decrease inspector turnaround in detecting and dealing with reoccurring equipment failures. This enables CT to identify problems in their early stages so that these problems do not become bigger. For example, some equipment failures occurred due to faulty or substandard components provided by a vendor partner. The ability to identify bad equipment and patterns of poor performance has allowed CT to manage its vendor partnerships. Vendors are given the opportunity to repair or replace defective components. Consistently underperforming vendors are replaced.

ERMS has also decreased the probability of piping and electrical equipment failure and increased the reliability on electrical systems by finding "weak links" within the system. For example, if an electrical part fails multiple times within a year, CT can look at the electrical system as a whole and see if redesigning the system is required. The application has decreased unnecessary condition inspections of piping and electrical equipment.

As part of the implementation, ChevronTexaco has developed a plan for supporting the system and its service level. CT had to be certain to incorporate competent IT professionals and to have all employees continually communicate with one another. For example, there was an instance when CT had a problem with entering data via the front end of the ERMS module. The module would not accept the data. The problem was later solved. It was discovered that one of the database administrators (DBA) was changing the relationships between the tables and updating column names within the same tables without informing coworkers of his actions.

Even though CT managers feel ERMS may be underutilized, the system has shown itself to be exceptional in its ability to help maintain equipment reliability in the refineries. The company judges the value of the system by its ability to provide a platform that extracts data more quickly than the corporation's old process (and from any place), controls different sections of the company simultaneously, predicts equipment failures, allows for a more efficient maintenance schedule, and produces more accurate reports (which allows for faster responses). CT has numerous lessons learned from the ERMS implementation. Changing the work process has been discovered to be difficult. Training employees to use ERMS without disrupting daily work flow has been very challenging. CT managers now realize how important it is to understand and utilize the entire work process. Ignorance of this holistic "system" view eventually leads to more errors and redesign of existing business practices. To this end, CT has worked hard to ensure that all employees are on board with its new business practices.

DISCUSSION

All four companies presented have learned the importance of consolidating knowledge resources. Such resources are needed for best practices to be incorporated and kept within a company by minimizing corporate inefficiencies and redundancies. Nestlé USA was able to address data redundancies across operating brands by implementing an ERP solution to share knowledge and create consistency across functional units. The solution also allowed Nestlé USA to manage vendor relationships and enjoy economies of scale across product offerings.

In the case of Colgate-Palmolive, the corporation was spending excess funds trying to manage dispersed data and applications. The problem was made worse because the corporation spans multiple countries and continents around the globe. The case illustrates the value of consolidating data resources. The practice allowed the firm to eliminate unneeded jobs and equipment, thus saving the company time and money.

In Xerox, the organization experienced difficulties in gathering and disseminating ideas and tips to other field technicians. This case illustrates problems generated due to "space-based amnesia." This form of forgetfulness occurs when an organization fails to move or disseminate lessons learned at one point in the company to other points in the same firm. Xerox displayed this behavior with regard to its technicians having to find answers to problems that technicians in other areas had already solved. There was no medium for the technicians to communicate and share their experiences with one another. The net effect was technicians continuously "reinventing the wheel." Xerox addressed its knowledge needs by implementing the Eureka database to share process knowledge and tips among its employees across time and space.

ChevronTexaco presented a different perspective for measuring success knowledge. The corporation's ERMS has been in for less than a year. It is too early for the company to gather enough information to give a monetary figure (i.e., ROI) on the new system's success or failure. However, the view that a project has to be justified with a solid business case that includes an estimated ROI may not be the right way to think about measuring the project's payoffs (Sawhney, 2002).

In this instance, CT uses metrics such as time saved by inspectors in checking measurements for accuracy and ensuring that correct information is continually being entered and recorded. The company sees value in being able to create better forecasts for declining refining piping. Such forecasts allow the corporation to avoid unnecessary replacement of piping that had no need to be replaced.

Success is ultimately measured by what the project accomplishes (Worthen, 2002). In the four cases presented in this chapter, the ends met the expectations each firm desired. This could include a high ROI or it could just be the benefit of creating a system that helps a corporation's employees do their job better. However, for those companies that do look at monetary benefits, a Meta Group study of 63 companies found that the average annual savings from a new consolidated system, in this case an ERP system, was $1.6 million (Koch, 2002).

CONCLUSIONS

This chapter investigates the practice of consolidating data and information to establish knowledge repositories necessary for organizational learning. The discussion argues the importance of existing knowledge resources in relation to the organization's ability to be competitive. The practices for three learning organizations are reviewed and compared. Additionally, knowledge sharing and common practices at CT refineries are described.

A review of all four cases is used to offer insight into the value of consolidating and centralizing knowledge resources. A comparison of the organizations provides evidence to show that corporations of different sizes and across different industries can become a learning organization by maximizing opportunities to utilize knowledge resources, thereby creating more efficiency within their companies. While each company followed different paths to get to their end, each share the strategy of consolidation of company data and resources.

In this chapter, the resource consolidation information from articles and review papers further supports the idea that centralization aids corporations in their operational efficiencies. Efficiencies gained from these practices provide ways for companies to maximize organizational functionality, thus allowing greater returns for firms.

REFERENCES

Barlas, D. (n.d.). Colgate-Palmolive. Retrieved August 9, 2002, from *www.line56.com/articles/default.asp?ArticleID=3896*

Brown, J.S., & Duguid, P. (2000). Balancing act: How to capture knowledge without killing it. *Harvard Business Review*, May-June, 3-7.

Cruz, F. Personal interview. February 7, 2003.

de Geus, A.P. (1988). Planning as learning. *Harvard Business Review*, March -April, 70-74.

Dumaine, B. (1989, July 3). What the leaders of tomorrow see. *Fortune*, 48-62.

Hashim, N.A., & Othman, R. (2002). Organizational amnesia: The barrier to organizational learning. *Proceedings of the 3rd Annual Conference on Organizational Knowledge, Learning and Capabilities,* Athens, Greece.

Hoffman, R.R., Shadbolt, N., Burton, A.M., & Klein, G.A. (1995). Eliciting knowledge from experts: A methodological analysis. *Organizational Behavior and Human Decision Processes*, 62, 129-158.

Issac, M. Personal interview. February 6, 2003.

Koch, C. (2002, February 7). The ABC's of ERP. *CIO.com*. Retrieved from *www.cio.com/research/erp/edit/erpbasics.html*

Konicki, S. (2000, December 18-25). Break out. *Informationweek.com*. Retrieved from *www.informationweek.com/817/lockin.htm*

Moozakis, C. (1998, June 14). Storage demands soar. *TechWeb.com*. Retrieved from *www.techweb.com/wire/story/TWB19980614S0003*

Rethinking enterprise storage strategies. (2002, October 15). *CIO Magazine's Strategic Directions*, 3-4.

Sawhney, M. (2002, July 15). Damn the ROI, full speed ahead. *CIO Magazine*, 36-38.

Senge, P.M. (1990). The leader's new work: Building learning organizations. *Sloan Management Review*, August-December, 7-23.

Stewart, T.A. (2000, July). Water the grass, don't mow, and wait for lightning to strike. *Business 2.0 Magazine Online*. Retrieved from *www.business2.com/articles/mag/0,1640,8104,00.html*

Walsh, J.P., & Ungson, G.R. (1991). Organizational memory. *Academy of Management Review*, *16*(1), 57-91.

Worthen, B. (2002, May 15). Nestlé's ERP odyssey. *CIO Magazine*, 62-70.

Chapter XV

Implementing Knowledge-Enabled CRM Strategy in a Large Company: A Case Study from a Developing Country

Minwir Al-Shammari, University of Bahrain, Bahrain

EXECUTIVE SUMMARY

This case study is aimed at developing an understanding of the various aspects and issues concerning the implementation of a knowledge-enabled customer relationship management (KCRM) strategy at a telecommunications company in a developing country. The KCRM program was composed of three major parts: enterprise data warehouse (EDW), operational customer relationship management (CRM), and analytical CRM. The KCRM initiative was designed to automate and streamline business processes across sales, service, and fulfillment channels. The KCRM program is targeted at achieving an integrated view of customers, maintaining long-term customer relationship, and enabling a more customer-centric and efficient go-to-market strategy. The company faced deregulation after many years of monopoly. The company initiated a customer-centric knowledge management program, and pursued understanding customers' needs and forming relationships with customers, instead of only pushing products and services to the market. The major result of the case study was that the KCRM program ended as an Information and Communications Technology (ICT) project. The company did not succeed in implementing KCRM as a business strategy, but did succeed in implementing it as a transactional processing system. Several challenges and problems were faced during and after the implementation phase. Notable among these was that the CRM project complexity and responsibilities were underestimated, and as a result, the operational CRM solution was not mature enough to effectively and efficiently automate CRM processes. Changing organizational culture also required a tremendous effort and pain in terms of moving toward customer-centric strategy, policy and procedures, as well as sharing of knowledge in a big organization with many business silos. Employees' resistance to change posed a great challenge to the project. As a conclusion, the KCRM case study qualified as a good case of bad implementation.

INTRODUCTION

Business organizations are experiencing significant changes caused by the growing dynamics of business environments. Organizations are faced with fierce competitive pressures that come from the globalization of economies, rapid technological advancements, rapid political and governmental changes, and increases in consumer's power, sophistication, and expectations as customers become more knowledgeable about the availability and quality of products and services. Such environmental challenges place a huge demand on firms to remain flexible, responsive, and innovative in delivery of products and services to their customers (Drucker, 1995; Teece, Pisano, & Shuen, 1997).

The resource-based view of the firm recognizes the importance of organizational resources and capabilities as a principal source of creating and sustaining competitive advantage in market competition. According to this approach, resources are the main source of an organization's capabilities, whereas capabilities are the key source of its competitive advantage (Grant, 1991; Davenport, 1995). Establishing an effective knowledge management capability is a challenge in 21st-century organizations.

The importance of customers to business firms has created tough "rivalries" among competitors over acquiring new customers or retaining/expanding relationship with current ones. In order to build good customer relations, it is necessary for companies to serve each customer in his/her preferred way, therefore requiring the management of "customer knowledge" (Davenport, Harris, & Kohli, 2001). Customer Knowledge (CK) is increasingly becoming a principal resource for customer-centric business organizations. As a consequence, acquisition and effective usage of such knowledge is increasingly becoming a prerequisite for gaining competitive advantage in today's turbulent business environments.

Establishing an effective KM initiative is a challenge for most organizations. Particularly difficult is the capture of tacit knowledge that resides primarily in the heads of experienced employees. Knowledge involves three overlapping factors, namely, people, organizational processes (content), and technology (ICT) and can be approached in two ways:

- **Personalization:** human-based information processing activities such as brainstorming sessions to periodically identify and share knowledge

- **Codification:** systematic processes for regularly capturing and distributing knowledge

The personalization strategy is more focused on connecting knowledge workers through networks, and is better suited to companies that face *one-off* and unique problems that depend more on tacit knowledge and expertise than on codified knowledge. The codification strategy is more focused on technology that enables storage, indexing, retrieval, and reuse of knowledge after it has been extracted from a person, made independent of person, and reused.

Objective and Structure of the Case Study

This case study aims at developing an understanding of various aspects and issues related to the implementation of knowledge-enabled customer relationship management (KCRM) by a telecommunications firm in a developing country. The telecommunications company, referred to as Global Telecom (GTCOM) from now on, seeks to move from an engineering-led organization toward a customer-centric strategy as the backdrop for implementing the KCRM. The KCRM initiative was designed to allow GTCOM to automate and streamline its business processes across sales and service channels. The KCRM strategy was targeted at achieving an integrated view of customers, maintaining long-term customer relationship, and enabling organizational transformation from product-centric to customer-centric.

The case study starts by providing a background to the motivation for moving toward a customer-centric organization, followed by setting the stage to the case, and exploring the details of the case. Then, the chapter describes the current challenges facing the organization, and ends with a discussion and conclusions.

Methodology

In order to gain an understanding of the organization as a whole and the KCRM initiative in particular, 11 in-depth face-to-face interviews, and one in-depth telephone interview were carried out to solicit the viewpoints of the concerned managers from different managerial levels and business functions. In addition, appropriate organizational documents and reports were consulted.

The interviews were systemically analyzed, and the result of the interviews was tape-recorded voice descriptions of the main aspects and issues when implementing the KCRM initiative.

BACKGROUND

Drivers for Becoming Customer-Centric

The telecommunications sector in this developing country was in a monopolistic position with respect to virtually all telecommunications, data transmission, and Internet services for many years. As part of the government policy to liberalize different business sectors, an autonomous body was established to regulate the telecommunications sector. The Telecommunications Regulatory Commission (TRC) by the end of 2002 issued expressions of interest for a second GSM license, and awarded a second license in 2004. The market was due to be fully open to competition in all telecommunications areas by July 2004.

Never had the external environment of GTCOM been so competitive, turbulent, and challenging with respect to attracting and keeping customers and controlling costs. The delicate market position of GTCOM, due to the liberalization of the telecommunications market, was aggravated by organizational dysfunction manifested by a strong hierarchical structure, indigenous culture, and a product-centered business. The fear was that unless GTCOM undertakes substantial change, its competitors would move ahead and it would be left behind.

In an attempt to face the challenge, the main thrust of activities in the past months was to make GTCOM more customer friendly and efficient so that consumers will be less inclined to "jump out of the ship" and defect to new players in the market. As a result, GTCOM decided to adopt a knowledge-based customer-centric response strategy, that is, KCRM, in order to diffuse existing business problems and exploit future business opportunities.

The KCRM initiative targets the achievement of a more integrated approach toward serving customers through a multitude of channels. By implementing the KCRM program, GTCOM sought to transform its customer-centric data into complete knowledge, and to apply that knowledge to the development of a longer-term relationship with customers. The complete understanding of existing customers enables GTCOM to meet current market challenges and represents a new potential market and source of gaining competitive advantage, retaining existing customers, repeating profitable sales, increasing revenue, and improving customer satisfaction.

Corporate History

GTCOM came into being in 1981 as a national telecommunications shareholding company. GTCOM is now working toward meeting the demands of the new info-communications age — the convergence of communications, computing, entertainment, mobility, and information.

As one of the country's largest organizations, GTCOM makes a difference in people's lives. To improve this, besides creating business and employing citizens, it is committed to addressing the impoverished and underdeveloped sections of the community, and allocates 2% of its profits every year to educational, cultural, environmental, charitable, and social causes.

Type of Business and Products/Services

GTCOM is an integrated communications solutions provider that offers a wide range of products and services in the data, Internet, mobile telephony, and fixed telephony market segments.

In the Internet service provision market, GTCOM has services that include one-stop shopping, integrated services digital network (ISDN), messaging switching system (MSS), budget Internet-access service, and asymmetrical digital subscriber line (ADSL). In telephony, though the broadest market is fixed lines, mobile services grow ten times faster.

GTCOM also provides a portal to mobile users, accessible by SMS text messages, WAP, or Internet, delivering Internet content, information services, e-mail, and business applications. In addition, it offers a wide range of e-commerce services to its customers.

Financial Status

The financial highlights of GTCOM showed a 4% growth rate in gross revenue in the first half of 2003 compared to the second half of 2002, and 5% growth rate in net revenue in the first half of 2003 compared to the second half of 2002. However, expenses grew up by 23% in the first half of 2003 compared to the second half of 2002, and net profit dropped by 20% in the first half of 2003 compared to the first half of 2002.

Strategic Planning

GTCOM's vision is to be the first-choice communications partner for customers in the local market and in chosen markets across the region and to serve as a role model for other communications companies. Its mission is to deliver a simple and complete customer experience — offering a full range of reliable, competitively priced communications services and solutions.

Among its core values is commitment to performance improvement and efficiency in conduct, customer and employee satisfaction, and socioeconomic well-being of its communities. Customers have available a 24-hour call center and customer service through GTCOM's e-shop, an Internet-based self-service facility. GTCOM's corporate objectives are as follows:

- Enhance customer satisfaction.
- Deliver impressive year-on-year profit growth.
- Increase efficiencies across GTCOM and its subsidiaries.
- Ensure that employees are properly train, motivated, rewarded, and retained.
- Protect and build upon its outstanding corporate image.

Organizational Structure

GTCOM is considered one of the largest companies in the region in terms of employees and revenue. GTCOM employs more than 2,000 employees with different skills such as engineering, ICT, business management, and support. The command structure of GTCOM is rather traditional, hierarchical, and "functional" in nature. In functional organizations such as GTCOM, work is conducted in departments rather than customer-centered business processes that cut across business functions. The organizational structure is composed of four hierarchical levels. The top level represents the board of directors and chief executives (CEs), the second level represents the chief executive officer (CEO), the third level represents the chief operating officer (COO) for Customer Services (CS) and the COO for Support Services (SS), as well as the general manager (GM) for Human Resources (HR), whereas at the fourth level — underneath the COO for CS and SS — comes a number of business units, each headed by GMs, senior managers, or managers. The CS units look after all types of front-office customer transactions and include a number of units, namely, major, business, residential, and new business development units. On the other hand, the SS units work toward supporting all customer units in offering back-office services to customer transactions and include units such as IT support, finance support, engineering support, and services support units.

Corporate Culture

The ability, willingness, and readiness of people to create, share, and transfer knowledge heavily depend on the corporate culture and business integration. Although many attempts have been made at GTCOM to encourage knowledge sharing, it seems that there is still a lack of cultural preparedness for intradepartmental knowledge sharing that was aggravated by lack of business integration across different silos, which had its profound adverse effect on interdepartmental knowledge sharing.

The knowledge-sharing culture at GTCOM has been hindered by additional factors; among these are position/power differences, lack of self-confidence, fear of loss of power or position, and/or misuse or "no use" of knowledge-sharing collaborative technologies. An example of the misuse of knowledge-sharing technologies is when an employee finds hundreds of e-mails waiting for him/her in his/her "in-box" simply because other employees kept on forwarding received e-mails to him/her whether these e-mails concern him/her or not. A customary practice of the no use of knowledge-sharing collaborative systems may be evidenced by an employee who asks his/her boss or another colleague on how to invoke a particular computer procedure instead of searching the intranet for retrieving such a command.

SETTING THE STAGE

Description of KM Context

GTCOM has traditionally been product focused and overwhelmed with supply-side issues rather than customer-side needs. Until GTCOM made a serious effort to understand its customers better, its initiatives designed to improve efficiency and effectiveness in the customer interface had little chance of success.

The description of KM context provides an exploration of what customer knowledge is, assesses who hold and should hold that knowledge, outlines KM problems, identifies KM directions needed, sketches the overall KM plan, and assesses the way in which that plan relates to KM problems.

What is CK?

Customer knowledge (CK) refers to understanding customers' needs, wants, and aims when a business is aligning its processes, products, and services to create real customer relationship management (CRM) initiative. Sometimes CK can be confused with CRM. Although there could be some overlap, CK works at both micro and macro levels and includes a wider variety of less structured information that will help build insight into customer relationships. CK should include information about individuals (micro) that helps explain who those individuals are, what they do, and what they are looking for, and should also enable broader analysis of customer base as a whole (macro). Similarly, CK may include both quantitative insights (i.e., numbers of orders placed and value of business), as well as qualitative insights (tacit or unstructured knowledge that resides in people's heads).

The aim of building up a strong body of CK is to enable GTCOM to build and manage customer relationships. CRM is an interactive process that achieves optimal balance between corporate investments and the satisfaction of customer needs to generate the maximum profit. CRM emerged as an amalgamation of different management and information system (IS) approaches, and entails the following processes (Gebert, Geib, Kolbe, & Brenner, 2003):

- Measuring inputs across all functions, including marketing, sales, and service costs as well as outputs in terms of customer revenue, profit, and value;
- Acquiring and constantly updating knowledge on customer needs, motivation, and behavior over the lifetime of the relationship;
- Applying CK to constant improvement of performance through a process of learning from successes and failures;
- Integrating marketing, sales, and service activities to achieve a common goal;
- Continuously contrasting the balance between marketing, sales, and service inputs with changing customer needs in order to maximize profit.

CK that flows in CRM processes can be classified into three types:

1. **Knowledge about customers:** accumulated knowledge to understand customers' motivations and to address them in a personalized way. This includes customer histories, connections, requirements, expectations, and purchasing pattern (Davenport et al., 2001).
2. **Knowledge for customers:** required to satisfy information needs of customers. Examples include knowledge on products, markets, and supplies (Garcia-Murillo & Annabi, 2002).
3. **Knowledge from customers:** customers' knowledge of products and services they use as well as about how they perceive the offerings they purchased. Such knowledge is used in order to sustain continuous improvement, for example, service improvement or new product development (Garcia-Murillo & Annabi, 2001).

Knowledge about customers is gathered through interactions with customers through processing of customer orders as well as through different customer interaction channels such as phone, e-mail, interactive voice recognition (IVR), fax, mail, e-commerce, and front-office stores (Figure 1). Operations knowledge about customers, for example, customers' personal information and purchasing history are held in computerized operational data stores (ODS), that is, billing and provisioning data stores, and accessed by staff of these units. For example, each time a customer makes contact with the company, the customer's needs, as well as the actions taken to satisfy these needs, represent information that may be captured and processed to benefit future customer interactions.

The knowledge about customers should be used to determine what to offer, when to offer, and how much to charge. In the long term, the company has to design new products, offer new services, compete in new markets, but even in the short term, the top salesperson could get sick or be headhunted. What companies currently know about their customers may not be sufficient in order to build and sustain stronger relationship with customers. Companies may need to put in processes and systems to gather more information and data about who their customers are, what they do, and how they think in terms of future purchasing decisions. Therefore, analytical, or deduced, knowledge about customers such as prediction of customers' expectations and future-purchasing patterns, using advanced computer models and business intelligence (BI) systems is becoming a prerequisite to establishment of strong customer relationship.

Knowledge for customer sources relate to personal knowledge possessed by employees themselves or related to employees' work such as corporate manuals, guidelines, memos, and meetings. Knowledge that resides in people's heads can be extracted through person-to-person contacts or through the usage of computer-supported collaborative work (CSCW) technologies, that is, intranets and Lotus Notes, or through e-mails.

Knowledge from customers is another important knowledge for GTCOM that is collected through market surveys.

Therefore, the focus of this case study will be on the most vital form of business knowledge, namely, knowledge about customers and will be referred to as KAC from now on.

Who Hold and Should Hold CK?

Comprehensive CK is created through acquisition and processing of fragmented information found in files and databases specific to the particular application which was designed to process whatever transactions were being handled by the application, for example, billing, sales, accounting, and so forth. Currently, each of GTCOM's customer contact/delivery channels (e.g., phone, e-mail, fax, store) as well as front-office departments (marketing, sales, and customer services) was operating as a silo with its own island of automation; information from each customer contact/delivery channel was owned as a separate entity by that unit. However, with each unit having its own information, leveraging information across the myriad of customer contact channels was not carried out nor was it possible to provide a consistent customer service experience. For example, a customer may telephone a call center to inquire about a transaction conducted through the Web site only to be told to call the Internet department.

GTCOM does have knowledge about its customers, but frequently this knowledge is in a fragmented form, difficult to share or analyze, sometimes incomplete, and often unused for business decisions. Advances in ICT are increasingly providing GTCOM with opportunities to support customer service operations, and integrate KAC through several contact/delivery channels.

Direct users of KAC are power users at customer-facing departments, namely, sales, marketing, and customer services. Managers of these departments currently hold KAC, but that knowledge doesn't provide analytical 360-degree view of customers. In addition to power users, there are other users with authorized access to GTCOM's KAC. These users are as follows:

- **Basic users:** operational staff at the clerical level
- **Administrative users:** IT people
- **Executive Users:** senior managers, GMs, and CEs

The organizational structure of GTCOM does not reflect the needs for effective utilization of knowledge resources. No special unit was found in charge of promoting KM activities and programs where knowledge ideas can be computerized and shared across different departments. In addition, no person was found in charge of the generation, storage, sharing, distribution, and usage of KAC, that is, there is no Chief Knowledge Officer (CKO).

KM Problems

The problem faced by GTCOM in creating a customer-centric business was that its organizational structure was centered on multiple isolated silos or functions, which led to fragmentation of KAC. Multiple silos represent multiple obstacles that undermine full exploitation of enterprise-wide business knowledge. A silo or stovepipe structure is a function-based form of organization, supported with islands of data, which does not promote communication across departments or units. Information on customer demographics and usage behavior, for instance, were scattered among numerous databases, which forced users to query multiple systems when an answer to a simple query was required or when making a simple analysis or decision related to customers.

KAC-related challenges that face GTCOM are as follows:

- Current ICT systems are unable to create complex KAC required by the business decision makers for facing fierce competition;
- Increasing demand for multidimensional customer view;
- Diverse data sources and platforms, that is, Windows, LINUX. UNIX, impeding customer data management.

Directions Needed

There is a need for GTCOM to fill a gap between what it thinks customers want and will put up with, compared to what customers really want and will go to its competitors for. Management of KAC requires effective capture of customer information, conversion of information into useful relationships, and efficient dissemination of knowledge to the places within the organization that need it most for decision making. Management of KAC requires the usage of processes and tools that build and distribute that knowledge.

This requires implementation of an enterprise-wide solution that relies on a single comprehensive data repository, namely, Electronic Data Warehouse (EDW), utilized by multichannel customer service contact/delivery points in order to achieve true enterprise data integration. The EDW is a comprehensive resolution of customer service issues over any and all channels, and a single customer view across the entire enterprise containing all information about the customer, their transactions, and the data they are likely to require during those transactions.

Successful management of a single customer view requires formulation of comprehensive KCRM strategy that translates GTCOM's mission and vision into a long-term customer-centric course of action. The objective of the desired KCRM initiative is to capture and organize comprehensive KAC, allow it to be shared and discussed, and to build customer relationships now and over the longer term. A comprehensive KCRM may entail the following components:

- Identification of business/units requirements
- Readiness assessment (manpower, technology, finance, etc.)
- ICT infrastructure upgrade
- Implementation of knowledge-based technology solution
- Organizational transformation
- Cultural change
- Measurement and evaluation of performance metrics
- Change management

Overall KM Plan

Although GTCOM's overall KM plan is not found at a formal, corporate-wide level, several KM activities were conducted but rarely categorized as KM. However, a customer-centric KM plan has been formulated, clearly articulated, and formally addressed through many formal KM undertakings. One manager clearly explained the fact that the overall KM initiatives at GTCOM were predominantly informal, fragmented, and not part of a corporate knowledge plan or strategy. In his words:

I think we are at the stage where we need to formalize it [KM]. It [KM] is being addressed in general and informally on the basis of ideas we are linking to corporate objectives. So there is nothing specifically to say; like in the past we came with TQM [time quality management], we wanted to introduce this TQM concept into the organization or process reengineering and staff like that, they would be addressed within the departments' sections. We will say these are the targets: better customer satisfaction, revenue growth, efficiency, and corporate image.... So we gave the owners and the concerned people the chance to come up with the ideas; we do not go to them with the exact solution because it is them who know what is happening in their department sections, and our role is basically to explain to them to think out of the box.

GTCOM adopted a mixture of codification and personalization approaches in its KM activities, but the codification strategy prevailed over the personalization strategy. The following is a description of KM activities undertaken by GTCOM, grouped according to the three pillars of knowledge: people, process, and technology.

People

Job rotation is almost the only notable human-based initiative formally undertaken by GTCOM. The company has placed a high value on applying job rotation principles for several years now. Not only did it transfer people within the same department but transferred them into other departments or into joint ventures outside the country. One manager maintained that "Engineers who are working in HR [Human Resources] and HR people who are working at marketing, and we have finance people who are serving in the front office. This is the way that we have been adopting perhaps not to the degree that we would like because not everybody is prepared to the challenge but 2% of our employees, that is our KPI [key performance indicator], will rotate annually. And we have managed to achieve not exactly 2%, but something close to that, and we are happy with it, but we would like that to be expanded."

Processes

Sporadic initiatives regarding the sharing of best practices and lessons learned are conducted at GTCOM. For example, the IT department holds an annual review of projects whereby lessons learned and selected best practices are reviewed and distributed to participants. The concept of best practice is also applied to customer service by scripting and compiling frequently asked questions, which are used at the call center as the best practice or standard proven solution for problems presented by customers.

Voice of the customer (VOC) is a KM initiative that aimed at assessing customer satisfaction using a market survey. There are many variables that go into it; it is huge, and is carried out annually. It explores customers' feelings and level of satisfaction toward a great number of things, including wait time; accuracy of bills; the level of the knowledge and the courtesy and the attitude of the technicians, account managers, help desk, SMS news, call center staff; prices; communication; and branding. Once the VOC knowledge is captured, it will be properly disseminated and reported to top-level executives for management actions. GTCOM has got a project champion who is basically a person who looks after the survey results, ensures there is an action plan, and ensures that the action plan is implemented.

ICT

GTCOM undertook several ICT-based KM activities. It introduced a new module called the Competency Dictionary or Performance Management Review module as part of the human resource management system (HRMS). The module enables employees to use their terminals to assess their competencies from their own point of view; then their line managers assess them again. This knowledge map allows identifying the gap between the required knowledge and the existing knowledge. The gap is used as a knowledge repository to take HRM decisions related to promotion, transfer, rotation, training, and recruitment. Finally an employee self-service allows access to completed training in the last two years, application to loans, and other services.

Another initiative was project portals, where every project at the company opens a session in the intranet and links the financial area, the project manager and all members of the project. It allows sharing documents and exchanging e-mails. This initiative aimed at creating a collaborative environment for sharing knowledge and work in progress. Similarly, every department has a home page in the intranet to join members of the department and to spread information such as procedures, templates, reports, and folders.

Computer Supported Collaborative Work (CSCW) solutions such as intranets, Lotus Notes, and document work flow systems were also utilized by GTCOM. The intranet supported knowledge dissemination in various ways. Employees heavily use e-mail and Lotus Notes for e-mail, calendar, contacts, and memos to organize meetings, events, and deadlines. The Integrated Document Management System (IDMS) covers document management and work flow and allows moving documents from one place to another when there is a need for approval, for instance. It is still used only in purchasing and in human resource management for performance appraisal review, but it is planned for usage in other areas in the company.

The KCRM is a major technology-based KM program formally conducted at GTCOM. It aims at understanding the "customers' lifetime value," and includes three projects: the EDW, operational CRM, and analytical CRM projects. Details of the KCRM strategy will be provided in the Case Description section.

Connection Between Overall KM Plan and CK Problems

Only two of the many KM activities, namely, the VOC and KCRM, formally addressed KM problems. However, knowledge from customers obtained through the VOC is not as valuable, comprehensive, and timely as KAC obtained from the KCRM. Many advanced analytical features such as customer profiling, segmentation, one-to-one selling, cross-selling, up-selling, campaign management, individual pricing, risk analysis, sales prediction, loyalty analysis, and easy customization. In the words of one manager, "It was not possible to bring about an integrated, one single view of the customer by solely focusing on market research activities. The worry was certainly that competitors will come and we certainly have to have competitive edge over competitors, a competitive edge over the customers is our database. Nobody will know our customers' behaviors, who they are, where they live, when they make the call, but us."

Additionally, when market researchers go and interview people to generate knowledge from customers as part of the VOC initiative, the results of interviews cannot just be taken as the right solutions. The KCRM intends to make a contribution to that, but again the challenge is to analyze the CRM reports, and to extract knowledge from customers the way users want when there are so many variables to consider. For example, when studying the potential demand for a new product, the need is to understand and make the best guess for a market demand, and if the tool is not used properly, then wrong results might come about.

CASE DESCRIPTION

The desired goal of the customer-centric KM plan of GTCOM was the acquisition of cross-functional customer-centric knowledge in order to help it sustain competitive advantage in a highly competitive and dynamic business environment. The focus of this part of the case study will be on providing details of the KCRM components as well as evaluation of the progress made leading to an identification of new or remaining challenges.

KCRM Strategy Fit within Customer-Centric KM Plan

In 1998/1999, GTCOM foresaw that knowledge was key to being able to establish long-term relationships with customers and improving profitability in the impending competitive environment. In 2001, it decided to initiate the development of a threefold KCRM strategy composed of the EDW, operational CRM, and analytical CRM projects to be able to manage its customer-centric knowledge resources.

The development process of the customer-centric KM plan involved several decisions and activities, which are as follows:

1. Transformation toward a customer-centric organization
2. Organizational restructuring to align its structure with the new business strategy
3. Streamlining the value chain of most processes
4. Formulating an action program or business case which involved the following activities:
   a. Correction and cleansing of customer data (e.g., customer names, addresses, ID numbers, etc.)
   b. Enhancement of customer contact channels
   c. Establishment of KPIs to include factors such as return on investment (ROI), head count reduction, speed of customer service, and response rate to customer calls

Although GTCOM has no solid overall KM plan, a customer-centric KM plan derived from the vision of improving customer relations has been articulated. Real customer relationships are formed through interaction and by anticipating user needs, not by providing custom products. Therefore, KCRM has been adopted as an enabling strategy for the achievement of that vision. The KCRM strategy will provide GTCOM with a mechanism to further understand customer behavior and anticipate customer demand for its telecom services across all sales and service channels, and respond quickly to changing customer needs.

The vastness and complexity of customer-centric knowledge required in today's service operations demand advanced technology capabilities. There is no doubt that today's ICT power has opened the door to a new breed of codified knowledge that can help in addressing customer-centric knowledge problems, that is, EDW and CRM, and it is obvious that ICT has dominated GTCOM's customer-centric KM plan.

KCRM strategy aims at providing GTCOM with an integrated environment to track its sales opportunities, build accurate sales forecasts, provide an outstanding multichannel customer service, and deliver speedy fulfillment of customer orders. "Service is proving to be a key differentiator in the region's increasingly competitive telecoms sector, and GTCOM's CRM initiative is targeted at achieving one integrated approach toward serving our customers through a multitude of channels," commented one IT manager. The CRM program manager noted, "CRM is expected to give [GTCOM] a single, updated view of our client base, enabling us to create more targeted sales offerings while providing enhanced service capabilities."

However, in light of fierce competition facing GTCOM, there is a need to do much more and much faster to increase its customer-centric knowledge base, invest in training their staff, and take advantage of the new ICT for acquiring and disseminating knowledge throughout the company. GTCOM also needs to carefully analyze the potential costs and benefits of introducing ICT-based customer-centric knowledge programs, and adapt these ICT solutions to its KM and corporate context. Also, one needs to remember that KCRM is not only a technology solution to customer-centric knowledge problems. Rather, it is a long-term integrated strategy that combines processes, people, and structural changes.

KCRM Architecture

The KCRM strategy was enabled by three ICT-based solutions: operational CRM, EDW, and analytical CRM (Figure 1). The operational KCRM is composed of three layers. The first layer is customer contact/interaction channels or "touch points," that is, phone, e-mail, integrated voice recognition (IVR), fax, mail, e-commerce, and person walk-in retail stores. The second layer represents customer-facing departments, that is, marketing, sales, and customer services departments. The third layer is composed of several front-office operational systems:

- **CRM:** Fixed telephone line service provisioning system (replaced the old CSS provisioning side)
- **FODS1:** Fixed telephone line billing (replaced the CSS billing side)
- **FODS2:** Internet protocol billing
- **FODS3:** Prepaid mobile telephone line service provisioning
- **FODS4:** Postpaid mobile telephone line provisioning and billing

The second part of the KCRM is the EDW. Incoming transactional data from all front-office systems as well as many back-office operational systems feed into the EDW. The EDW operates as follows:

1. Extracts data from operational databases, namely, sales, service, and marketing systems.

2. Transforms the data into a form acceptable for the EDW.
3. Cleans the data to remove errors, inconsistencies, and redundancies.
4. Loads the data into the EDW.

In addition, there is an enterprise application integration (EAI) layer that was decided to be there to address the problem of diverse customer data sources and platforms. It integrates the front-office CRM provisioning system with the three back-office *billing* systems, namely, BODS1, BODS2, and BODS3, which then feed into the EDW. While all front-office ODS applications feed data into the EDW, only three out of five major back-office ODS applications feed into the EDW. Main back-office application systems are as follows:

- **BODS1:** Geographic information system (GIS) *billing* system (integrated with the EDW)
- **BODS2:** Mediated *billing* for fixed telephone lines (integrated with the EDW)
- **BODS3:** Back-office *billing* gateway for mobile telephone lines (integrated with the EDW)
- **BODS4:** Enterprise resource planning system (ERP)
- **BODS5:** Human resource management system (HRMS)

The third major part of the KCRM architecture is the analytical KCRM, which is composed of data marts created from the EDW, followed by analytical applications using BI system, and finally development of an integrated customer view. Data mart is customized or summarized data derived from the data warehouse and tailored to support the analytic requirements of a business unit/function.

EDW Project

The EDW is a subject-oriented, time-variant, non-volatile (does not change once loaded into the EDW) collection of data in support of management decision processes (Inmon, 1996). The EDW represents a "snapshot" or a single consistent state that integrates heterogeneous information sources (databases), is physically separated from operational systems, and is usually accessed by a limited number of users as it is not an operational system. EDW holds aggregated, tiny, and historical data for management separate from the databases used for online transaction processing (OLTP). The EDW is a repository of data coming from operational legacy systems, namely, customer care, billing system (including the three customer profiles: IT, GSM, and fixed line billing), finance system, account receivables, and others. The EDW was thought to be a strategic system and major enabler for GTCOM's continued success in the fierce competitive environment.

The EDW has become an important strategy in organizations to enable online analytic processing. Its development is a consequence of the observation that operational-level OLTP and decision support applications (online analytic processing or OLAP) cannot coexist efficiently in the same database environment, mostly due to their very different transaction characteristics.

Data warehousing is a relatively new field (Gray & Watson, 1998) that is informational and decision-support-oriented rather than process oriented (Babcock, 1995). The strategic use of information enabled by the EDW helps to solve or reduce many of the

Figure 1. GTCOM's knowledge-enabled CRM architecture

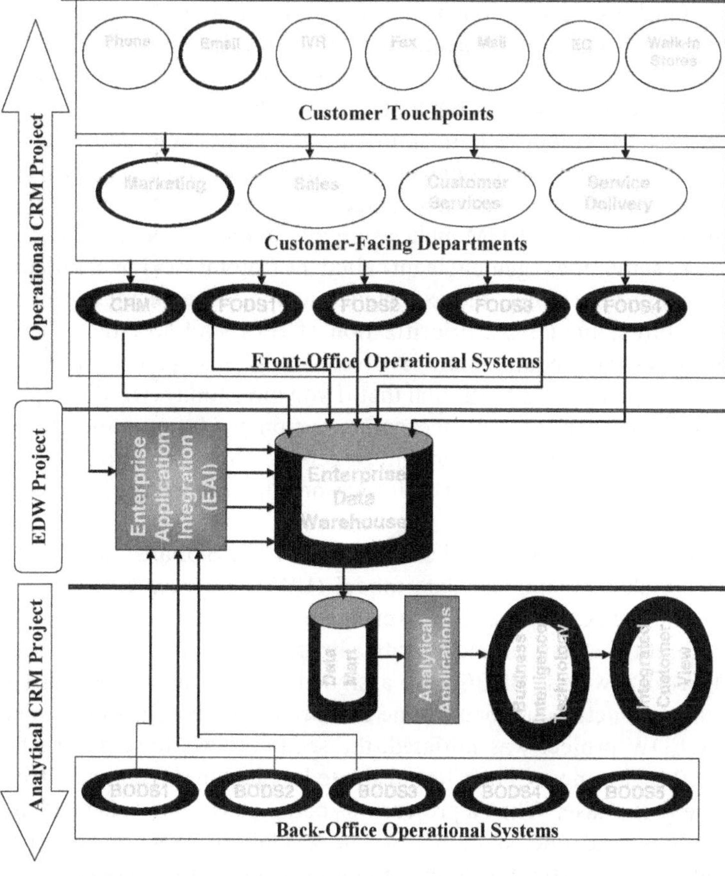

negative effects of the challenges facing organizations, reduce business complexity, discover ways to leverage information for new sources of competitive advantage, realize business opportunities, and enable quick response under conditions of uncertainty (Love, 1996; Park, 1997).

GTCOM realized that it could not continue to run business the same traditional way by using the same old ICT and the same old focus of a product-led business in a highly competitive and turbulent business environment. The competitive nature of today's markets is driving the need for companies to identify and retain their profitable customers as effectively as possible. GTCOM perceived the key to the achievement of this objective was the usage of rich customer data, which could be sitting unused in a variety of databases.

EDW Planning and Initiation Stage

In 1998/1999, GTCOM had some foresight that knowledge was crucial to establish long-term relationships with customers. Although the company's leadership commitment played a key role in the implementation of the initiative, the main driver for EDW initiative was the fierce competition due to deregulation of the local telecommunications market that was announced in 2001 but took effect in 2003.

GTCOM has its own approach for approving new business initiatives and converting ideas into concrete projects. From a business management perspective, new initiatives at GTCOM pass through three major stages. Prior to the commitment of resources and initiation of a project, GTCOM makes sure that it adds value; managers present a business case to a senior management team called the Capital Review Board to agree on the capital expenditures, timing, and expected outcomes. The business case covers all the business requirements (BRs), prioritization of BRs, and how they fit within the corporate objectives. The requirements revolved around this open question: "What are the most important pieces of information that if you have today, would help you make better or more informed decisions?", for example, customers' information which includes type of customers, age, location, nationalities, gender, education and professions, and geographic distribution, and products' information which represent historical data for all services and products.

Business questions (BQs) were then established. The BQs are documents that help in modifying the standard logical data model (LDM) to meet GTCOM's business requirements. One BQ example is, "Which customers generate most of the total traffic?" Then, BQs are carefully examined and prioritized to determine what information is needed for each BQ. Also "owners" of BQs are assigned, so that any further discussion of meaning can be conducted on a one-to-one basis rather than a full-house meeting.

Once the EDW project was initiated, the second phase took place wherein the Project Review/Management Committee evaluated achievements compared to the plans approved in the first phase. When a project was completed, it was checked in terms of its deliverables, cost, and time. Since many of the KM initiatives were supported by ICT, they also followed a specific development and implementation process based on the methodology used by the IT department.

GTCOM then tendered the EDW system and selected a vendor, who formulated strategies and presented experiences and recommendations of processes and structures to best exploit knowledge. In the first quarter of 2001, the initial stages of the project began. To understand business processes and objectives, the vendor of the EDW redefined processes, identified key business deliverables, and prioritized them into about 100 business cases, for example, customers, products, revenue, traffic, and sensitivity analysis. The vendor played a leading role in being the main source of knowledge for GTCOM and in partnering with business units to define their business requirements. The vendor formulated strategies, presented them to management, and came up with experiences and recommendations of how to best exploit knowledge in terms of processes and structure. At the same time, GTCOM formed a committee in order to align the system to business objectives in terms of who should be getting what access, what sort of information should be going on it, and how to structure the project phases.

EDW Design and Customization Stage

The EDW project is a very multifunctional and multitasking endeavor that transcends functional boundaries, for example, technology, product, marketing, market research, and finance. In 2000, GTCOM formed different committees to oversee the first phase of the project. These were the Business Intelligence Steering Committee (BISC) representing GMs (high-level senior managers) and Project Management Committee (PMC) consisting of the IT project manager and key business representatives from marketing, sales, back office, and customer care. There were also subcommittees looking into technical details of the system such as format of reports, quality of data, and others.

Soon, GTCOM finalized the design and started customizing the EDW and transferring information from the source systems into the EDW system. The end of 2002 witnessed the completion of the first stage called Increased Business Value. During 2003, the second phase (Expansion and Growth) began.

The high-level design of the EDW was composed of the following:

- The data warehouse itself, which contains the data and associated software;
- Data acquisition software (back-end), which extracts data from legacy systems and external sources, consolidates and summarizes the data, and loads it into the data warehouse (operational side);
- The client (front-end) software, which allows users of business intelligence, tools such as decision support systems (DSS), executive information systems (EIS), data mining, and customer relationship management (CRM) to access and analyze data in the warehouse (analytical side).

The design and customization process involved the following decisions/activities:

- Customizing the standard;
- LDM of the vendor to meet GTCOM's BRs and rules;
- Designing a high-level data sourcing and architecture design to support the established BRs;
- Designing data access architecture and user access points;
- Designing management and maintenance structure, which includes system, management, user administration, security management, as well as backup, archive, and recovery (BAR).

EDW Testing and Support Stage

The testing process consisted of activities such as defining the test environment, defining test cases and test data, assembling the components to be tested, executing the test, analyzing results, correcting identified problems, and revising/updating the testing process throughout the life of the project.

The support function involves a number of processes and tools that will be used to give the users the access priority adequate for them according to the service level agreement (SLA). This is done via a number of processes and tools.

EDW Implementation and Operation Stage

This harmonizes well with the concept of EDW, which is an interdisciplinary endeavor that needs to transcend functional boundaries, that is, technology, product, marketing, market research, and finance, and it capitalizes on shared knowledge and expertise from different business units.

EDW Implementation Team

The EDW project actively involved senior management, IT managers, business managers, and the vendor during the development process. Although knowledge users are business people from various functions, an IT manager at the beginning championed the project. Soon they understood that it had to be business driven and one of the general managers was appointed as the sponsor. The technical mind-set of IT people may not fit the business nature of the EDW project; EDW was part of a business strategy, not just a suite of software products. The following roles were performed by the EDW implementation team:

- **Business representative:** this role provides the leadership necessary for project success, facilitates the decision-making process for current and emerging business needs and requirements, as well as facilitating users' training and project budgeting decisions. The role provides link between the business side and the IT side. While he/she doesn't need to understand the details of system installation and configuration, business representative must be aware of CRM configuration and maintenance requirements. The GM for the Residential Customer Business unit handled this task.
- **Executive sponsor/owner:** this person is a major business player who plays both the role of sponsor and owner, provides the link between the project manager and upper management, guides funding and financing decisions, as well as decisions about when and where to deploy the CRM system. This person must understand the details of the installation, configuration, and schedule. The EDW sponsor was the manager for the Customer Marketing unit.
- **Project manager:** the project manager directs the work, makes things happen, and works with the vendor. This person must understand the details of the installation and configuration, and the schedule. The EDW project manager played this role.
- **Project team leader:** the role of this person is same as that of the business representative but from the IT point of view. This person is responsible for coordinating the IT side of the project with business needs and requirements. A database administrator handled this task.

EDW Content

The EDW is a data-based rather than a process-based system. Therefore, it does support data capturing and processing but not business processes. The data captured by the EDW relate to the following entities:

- **Customers:** relate to residential or business customers (age groups, living areas, etc.).
- **Products:** represent the number of mobile or fixed telephone lines, Internet lines, and so forth.
- **Traffic:** related to the usage behavior of customers (in terms of volume, duration, and time of calls).
- **Revenue:** referred to the amount of money generated per category of customers, products, age groups, or living areas.

- **Sensitivity analysis:** derived information that results from advanced analysis of the previous components.

Many reports can be generated from the EDW. Products/services reports, for instance, provide the following information:

- Revenue breakdown as one-time/recurring usage for each product family per quarter;
- List of customers based on the number of offers a customer has;
- List of customers who do have a selected product/s but has other selected product/s;
- List of customers and the products (leased equipments) and the age of the equipment;
- Sold products in the last 12 months, in addition to cross-selling reports;
- Top/bottom N products based on the number of customers subscribed to those products;
- Customer-level profiling based on bills issued, payments, overdue amount, and number of bills with amount overdue;
- Segmentation of customers based on the average current charge per invoice ranges;
- Top N rank customers based on revenue, usage/recurring/one-time revenue by party type;
- Revenue growth over a period of 12 months with respect to customer category.

CRM Project

The CRM project was composed of two parts: operational and analytical. The operational CRM project was delivered in May 2004. The goal of the CRM project was to enable GTCOM to focus on its "customers' lifetime value." Typically, operational CRM has the potential to respond to customers' priorities in terms of their value and being able to answer customers promptly and efficiently and would feed at the inbound and outbound directions into the EDW (bidirectional). To do so, the agent dealing with them would have online information about their identity, spending, products and services, and needs. And on the other hand, anything customers ask online would be captured into the marketing side of the CRM straight away by the front-end units such as call center and customer care, and will be used for customer segmentation and profiling by the analytical CRM.

The analytical side of the CRM is scheduled to start the planning phase in September 2004, and is due to be delivered in 2005. CRM feeds the transactional processing data into the EDW and then conducts analytical processing on these data. The analytical CRM typically includes OLAP, data mining (DM), and business intelligence (BI). However, only the BI option has been part of the analytical CRM at GTCOM. Analytical CRM provides power users with sales cubic view of their customers through slicing and dicing, back-end marketing management activities, such as campaign management and sales management; and allows users to feed on certain business rules for customer groups into the operational side, as well as predict future trends and behaviors and discover previously unknown patterns. It also facilitates marketing campaigns and surveys. The rest of discussion will be confined to the operational side of CRM.

CRM Implementation

The operational CRM development process passed through the following major decisions and/or activities:

- Approval of the business case and project budget after analyzing its benefits, costs, and potential risks;
- Selection of a vendor and ICT application. The vendor was itself the consulting company that managed the implementation of the CRM initiative, drawing on the software company's extensive expertise in the business needs of the telecoms sector;
- Integration of the old technology (CSS provisioning and billing system) with the CRM project in the transitional phase;
- Identification of project implementation team members who represented major business units as well as the IT unit;
- Establishment of best work flow practices for provisioning of services;
- Mapping of customer data flow in line with the new process flow;
- Deciding on the right time to discard the old customer service system (CSS), a system for telephone line provisioning and billing, and the right time to go live with the new operational CRM system, as well as deciding on the criteria of acceptance of the system from the vendor.

CRM Implementation Team

The implementation team of the operational CRM project performed the following roles:

- Business representative: this role provides the leadership necessary for project success, facilitates the decision-making process for current and emerging business needs and requirements, as well as facilitating users' training and project budgeting decisions. This role provides link between the business side and the IT side. While he/she does not need to understand the details of system installation and configuration, the business representative must be aware of CRM configuration and maintenance requirements. The GM for Customer Services handled this role.
- Executive sponsor/owner: this person is a major business player who plays both roles of sponsor and owner, provides the link between the project manager and upper management, guides funding and financing decisions, as well as decisions about when and where to deploy the CRM system. This person must understand the details of the CRM's installation, configuration, and the implementation schedule. The business representative was a senior manager for IS Development and Analysis.
- Project manager: the project manager is the person who directs the work and makes things happen. This person must understand the details of the installation and configuration, the implementation schedule, work with other team members and understand their contributions, and work with the outside vendor. The CRM project manager handled this role.
- System owners: set up and configure hardware, and install operating systems and supporting software. Different IS specialists in charge of ODSs handled this role.

CRM Processes

Unlike the EDW, the operational CRM system is a process-based system that automates customer-facing business processes, and is accessed by a large number of users who operate or manage the operational systems as well as their ODSs. It automates the following groups of processes:

- Sales processes
- Service processes (both fault and complaint processes)
- Marketing processes
- Call center/contact channels processes

CRM Content

In addition to automating business processes, the operational CRM system captures the following types of transactional data:

- Customer demographic data
- Service fulfillment information
- Sales and purchase data and their corresponding service order number, status, etc.
- Service and support records
- Profitability of products and customers
- Other types of customer-centric information

Organizational Transformation

Alongside the KCRM program, GTCOM undertook an organizational transformation initiative in its quest for achievement of customer-centric business. In 2000, GTCOM felt that it was time to reengineer business processes by cutting out the non-value-adding ones, and integrating ISs together. There were many fragmented or stand-alone systems that were doing many important things but were not "talking" to each other.

Starting from 2001, GTCOM foresaw the need for a transformation of the organization from engineering-led to customer-led. The end of 2002 witnessed the completion of the first stage called Increased Business Value. In 2003, several work teams looked at the various functions and processes for possible improvement and reengineering. Phase 3 of the organizational transformation program, known as Get Ready, was a continuation of the first and second phases that was almost paralleled with the EDW project. Phase 3 mainly sought to help GTCOM face the business competition by transforming GTCOM from product-led to customer-led business.

An outside consultant was called in to lead the organizational transformation process. However, the consultant faced some resistance from employees, especially when the issue of restructuring was tackled. Restructuring became part of the organizational politics and inertia emerged as a result.

One of the specific restructuring initiatives launched by GTCOM under the newly emerged customer-led form was a "Knowledge Exchange" to increase the cross-functional cooperation and exchange of knowledge between sales (customer-facing or front-end) and product development (marketing-oriented or back-end) divisions. These two divisions were used not to maintain cooperation and exchange of knowledge with each other as they had a culture of "we got our own things to do; you got your own things to do."

As a direct response to the liberalization program of telecommunications services, GTCOM has been going through a transitional rebalancing program that started in 2003 and is planned to continue until the end of 2005. At the beginning of 2003, the sales and product divisions were merged, and as a result of the combined knowledge of these two units, GTCOM has launched its new Mobile Price Plan on June 2003. This whole undertaking would not have been possible in the past with all of the silos or stovepipes in place.

Following the implementation of required organizational adjustments in the transitional period, GTCOM will be operating in a fully competitive environment by the end of 2005. Table 1 summarizes the major prospective changes that are due to take place following the transformation of GTCOM from a monopolistic to a fully-competitive business.

Results

Financial Performance

On the financial performance side, GTCOM has done extremely well so far in its ability to meet the turbulent and competitive environment. The main favorable result witnessed following the implementation of the KCRM strategy was that it offered GTCOM good financial performance results during the first quarter of 2004. Since GTCOM transformed its business and implemented KCRM, its net profits climbed to about 25.2% against the same period of last year. This increase is attributed to a year-on-year rise in gross revenues of 5%, and a reduction in costs largely due to nonrecurring exceptional items related to restructuring, which were successfully implemented by GTCOM in 2003.

Operational Performance

Unlike its good financial results, GTCOM's performance was not encouraging at the level of operational excellence (i.e., service time, lead time, quality of service, productivity) and satisfaction/loyalty of stakeholders (customers, employees, etc.). It faced and/or is still facing the following problems:

- **System's inefficiency and customers' expectations:** the operational CRM could not capture basic customer data; people at network department, for example, could not trace the work flow of sales order processes, which in turn, adversely affected the ability to meet customer expectations. This inefficiency would result in longer order fulfillment or service completion time, low productivity, customer dissatisfaction, and possible defect of customers to competitors.
- **Work flow problems:** the logical work flow of sales order processes across business units is as follows: *Sales, Network, Programming, Private Branch Exchange (PBX) between users and network, Installation*, and *Accounts,* respectively. Service delivery time now is on average one to two weeks, but was less than one week under the old CSS provisioning and billing system.
- **Testing/migration problems:** during the migration/testing period which lasted for couple of days (roughly between seven to ten days), many data did not go through

Table 1. Major prospective changes in GTCOM's move from a monopolistic to a fully competitive organization

Monopoly	Full Competition
Technology-push	Market-pull
Low-customer value	Non-tariff driven customer
High cost structure	Low cost structure (through re-engineering)
Back-end focused	Front-end focused
Bureaucracy	Meritocracy

the operational CRM, as their data fields were not validated by the system. The nonvalidated data had to be rekeyed manually into the system. The computer system was of no use for the whole transitional migration/testing period, so all costumer operations were processed manually.

- **Vendor-related problems:** although it is a world-class vendor with extensive experience in ICT solutions, the vendor underestimated project complexity and responsibilities. This resulted in missing the delivery target three times, and then followed by a decision by many employees to quit their jobs.
- **Ineffective change management:** in addition to the projects implementations team, there was a dedicated change manager; however, this role was ineffective. The concept of change management was new to GTCOM, and it could not afford to continue funding the post, so the post was cancelled.
- **Management problems:** GTCOM changed the CSS system into CRM in a critical period of time when the market was liberalized. It was very dangerous to phase out the CSS system when nothing was clear on the negative consequences on operational excellence and satisfaction of stakeholders. It had also been decided to proceed with implementation although it was known that the system was not effective and incapable of meeting the objectives of the CRM strategy and its KPIs.

CHALLENGES

Although GTCOM had made some positive moves toward changing the organization from being engineering-led to customer-led, especially in light of changes in its business environment, it still faces a number challenges with respect to the effective management of its knowledge for continued business success. The challenges are as follows:

Overall KM Strategy

There was a need to formulate organization-wide formal KM strategy and programs for learning best practices and for the development of new projects. The KCRM initiative at GTCOM seemed to be created and used on the basis of "technology push," introduced through vendors, rather than "market pull," as a mere response to real business need. The KCRM technology components were driving, instead of enabling, the KCRM strategy and its KPIs. One manager admitted that "suppliers try to push their new products and then there is stage of filtering, studying, and analyzing where there are subjectivities and different opinions." The development of an organization-wide strategy for the generation, sharing, distribution, and utilization of knowledge is becoming imperative for GTCOM's continued success in today's competitive market.

Although it can be said that GTCOM did a good job in putting up the required ICT infrastructure in place, however, it did not develop a robust business solution in terms of knowledge processes that allowed exploiting the information provided by the implemented system. One manager explained, "I don't even think we have the process to look at the customer from A to Z. I think the mistake maybe [GTCOM] has made is that we have been very good in putting up the system, but even the underlying process of capturing the needs of customers hasn't been well though of and hasn't been implemented properly."

Another manager argued, "Unfortunately, this is what I have to say that with respect to EDW: we have done the systems and IT side very well, but the other side of it — the knowledge aspect of it — exploiting that knowledge, exploiting that source, and also the skills aspect of the people, there is quite long way to go."

Corporate Culture

Corporate culture is widely held to be the major inhibitor or facilitator for creating and leveraging knowledge assets in organizations. Low-trust cultures constrict knowledge flow, and companies that have conducted organizational transformation or downsizing, such as GTCOM, face a particular problem in this regard. These companies need to rebuild trust levels in their culture before they can expect individuals to share expertise freely without worrying about the impact of this sharing on employees' value to GTCOM. Such changes require paying considerable attention to the supporting norms and behavioral practices that manifest trust as an important organizational value (Long & Fahey, 2000).

Since 2002, there has been more encouragement for internal knowledge sharing through committees as a result of transformation from a product-centered to a customer-centered business, and from bureaucratic to democratic management. This may be due to the fact that GTCOM will no longer be able to enjoy its monopoly in the market, and will have to improve its competitive position through organizational transformation and capitalizing on its core competencies, namely, KAC.

However, monitoring business pressures that were supposed to be drivers for knowledge creation, diffusion, and application did not seem to have helped in total elimination of knowledge hoarding that fears competition and leak of information. One manager argued, "GTCOM has certain visions along that side [KCRM], it is a big project, it takes a long time, needs cultural changes and stuff like that. So that is the challenge we are facing right now."

Business Requirements

The biggest challenge to the KCRM projects was the determination of corporate-wide business requirements and knowledge strategy. As there was lack of consensus on defining business requirements and goals of every business unit, there was also lack of consensus on defining data elements (e.g., good/bad customer) among business units as every unit may have its own definition of data elements.

Stovepipe Structure

KM is a cross-divisional and cross-functional intricate endeavor. Plans to make better use of knowledge, as a resource, must be built into the structure and culture of the organization in the medium term. KCRM technology alone was not enough to create a competitive advantage unless it has been coupled with the necessary organizational transformation from silo-based to process-based structure, especially in the front-end business operations, and capitalizing on the power of the intellectual assets of people to improve the quality of delivered services while achieving better efficiency and efficacy.

The organizational structure should reflect the needs for better management of knowledge. A special business unit, or a cross-unit task force or team, needs also to be established in order to foster the concept of KCRM in a formal and a holistic approach through experimentation, documentation, sharing, and dissemination of knowledge across different departments. This structural change will allow to improve performance of initiative already in place and to promote new initiative that might be needed, such as the establishment of an electronic library, yellow pages, knowledge maps, that can facilitate the buying and selling of specific knowledge created by workers in different departments within GTCOM.

Stovepipe or silo organizational structure hindered organizational learning among business units, as the organization, as a whole, would not know what it does know. The silo or stovepipe structure led to the fragmentation of activities among many departments, and resulted in the creation of physical and psychological walls separating business functions, for example, information on mobile and fixed phones that appear to be done independently on an ad hoc basis. The functional-based structure of GTCOM was being overemphasized at the expense of knowledge sharing across departments especially in customer services, which are cross-functional in nature.

The workflow of many processes of the CRM system was very slow and not smooth, and streamlining work flow of fragmented processes is still unresolved in many areas. Interdepartmental communication problems (cultural and technological) are still prevailing under the multiple-silos structure.

Business Integration

Once they lacked a single information repository, companies have traditionally spent large amounts of time and money writing integration programs to communicate between disparate systems. A variety of technological options exist for the implementation of KCRM projects. The adopted hardware, software applications, and databases for the KCRM initiative need to be compatible and operable with the existing legacy systems. The chosen ICT infrastructure needs also to integrate well with other systems in the organization. Some adjustments may be required to assure a balance between systems requirements and functionality from one side and flow of business processes from the other side.

Evidence of the ineffective ICT infrastructure is the lack of integration with previous technology initiative and legacy systems. There are several problems with integration. First, integration complexity causes delay. Systems will rarely operate in real time resulting in delays in synchronizing information. This can cause embarrassment to companies and aggravation to customers when updates to one channel are not reflected immediately in the others.

The second problem is that integration adds overhead cost. The integration must be implemented, administered, and maintained independently of the actual customer service applications for each delivery channel. The problems of complexity and costs are magnified each time a change is made to a channel application.

Customer's Expectations and Satisfaction

In addition to being inefficient in capturing some customer data, the CRM system still suffers from limited storage capacity/lack of scalability, complexity, limited processing speed, and lack of technology fitness in terms of growth and implemented capacity of the KCRM projects. These shortcomings of the system could adversely affect customers' experiences and satisfaction, as well as employees' morale.

Power Users

Knowledge/power users are people who are responsible for generating knowledge about competitors, external market, products, and so forth, using the EDW initiative. Actual knowledge users of the EDW may include people from units such as sales, marketing, market research, and human resource management, although potential users could include other departments such as product development. As business-wide requirements were not effectively identified, so the knowledge requirements of different business units were not being successfully transferred into data entities, and many units did not seem to be constantly using the system. It seemed that heavy usage of the EDW system was at the marketing and sales function, as the culture in other units may not have favored the usage of the system as a source for generating knowledge. One manager maintained, "I don't know if the finance people use it enough because they do have a SAP system, I don't know if it is integrated with the EDW."

Knowledge users of major KCRM systems, for example, the EDW, at GTCOM need to be expanded to include functions other than sales and marketing, such as finance, operations and logistics, and so forth.

Quality of Data

Following an identification of business needs and agreeing on a definition of data elements of the system, data cleansing should be conducted before putting up the EDW initiative. Otherwise, false indications and misleading information would be the outcome. Data accuracy is very critical as EDW systems retrieve data and put them in the required format, but if the raw data were not completely filtered, then the validity of the project's information would be at risk. Poor data quality at GTCOM resulted from accumulation of much data inaccuracies over the years, and there is a need for conducting an urgent cleansing of these data.

From a technical perspective, there were great expectations as to the capabilities of KCRM systems, but the systems turned out not to be as successful as expected. The system overpromised but underdelivered as it was hard to use for basic queries due to the unavailability of some data elements in the legacy system and quality of data (some data elements were inaccurate and/or incomplete at the data source and data entry level).

Some managers claimed that project management had not considered some problems from the past and, therefore, problems continue to exist with the new systems. According to one manager, "One of the problems that has happened which we have inherited now putting this integrated knowledge-based systems together is that we know all systems had data corruption in the past, and again [GTCOM] hasn't properly done enough work to clean that data first and then put into the system. Today, for example, [we are] suffering because [we are] basically doing analysis and generating reports and some of it is not accurate."

The GM of HR explained the data accuracy problem in the HRMS implementation by saying, "What has happened during our trial period is that at the end of the year, I discovered that some people have got a lot of leave days, this is one of the short comings of self-service because it has not been handled properly at line management level. Then I discovered that a lot of people have days of leave outstanding so I questioned and when we checked with the line managers they say, 'Oh, I forgot to enter it.' So instead of you having 20 days leave, you were having 60 days leave, and I said to the person or department, 'OK, all staff above 20 pay them those days in cash to do the balance and not have more than 20 days.' You know it would have caused me to make the wrong decision because of lack of responsibility of line management."

Resistance to Change

The KCRM is a core business initiative that is sensitive to the political environment within an organization. Without complete user support, KCRM projects are doomed to failure. People's mind-set and resistance to change posed a real challenge to the KCRM program. Some employees did not accept the new system, as it was too advanced for them to cope with. User training was not adequately provided to the right people, at the right time, and for the right duration.

There is a need for new blood as it is too difficult to fine-tune the mind-sets of some employees. More recruitment and training of staff, for example, new graduates, who are capable of absorbing or generating new knowledge, and the incorporation of knowledge creation, sharing, distribution, and usage of knowledge in the performance appraisal of employees could help in the expansion of knowledge usage.

However, GTCOM did not have any formal mechanism for providing financial rewards to members who create, share, or use knowledge. A direct outcome of the lack of financial incentives is the limited willingness of employees to contribute to the knowledge sharing, creation, and leveraging. Changes in GTCOM's reward system could help in motivating knowledge workers to create, share, and apply knowledge.

Job Losses

The challenge of job losses was a major part of the restructuring exercise. However, one key executive maintained, "That's not the object of the exercise, but a drop in headcount is inevitable — and I think our employees accept that. It is a fact of life that monopoly phone operators all over the world has been forced to slim down to become competitive. [GTCOM] has a duty to its customers, shareholders and employees — and refusing to face economic facts will do no favors for anyone in the long run. In the future, job security will be related to our ability to retain customers."

Vendor's Involvement

It seems that the focus of the EDW and CRM vendors was limited to customizing and implementing ICT tools, but not ensuring that the process and organization elements were in place for effective management of the KCRM project. An effective vendor's role and involvement, as well as effective management of relationship with vendors are very essential to the KCRM success.

Organizational Roles

The lack of structural mechanism for knowledge creation, sharing, and leveraging made it very difficult for many employees to access particular knowledge or even to be aware that knowledge is out there and needs to be leveraged. The absence of a formal position in charge of KM in the corporate structure, for example, CKO, made it very difficult for one group to learn from other groups outside their business functions. The existence of a position such as a CKO helps in defining a formal methodology in synthesizing, aggregating, and managing various types of CK throughout GTCOM.

DISCUSSION AND CONCLUSIONS

The challenge of competition, after many years of monopoly, is shaking off GTCOM and is forcing it to abandon the old product-led traditions of the telecommunication monopoly and, instead, focus sharply on customers and what they want — not what it thinks they should have — in order to please them and win their long-term loyalty. Focusing on customer relations is increasingly becoming a weapon used by many service-oriented firms to face business challenges.

GTCOM has worked hard to maintain its strong market position in a highly competitive and turbulent market. It has introduced a KCRM program that meant to optimize GTCOM's customer-centric knowledge resources, productivity, and procedures by maintaining unified and integrated customer views with greater levels of detail and accuracy. However, the KCRM initiative was faced with a number of problems and challenges.

Following the implementation of the KCRM initiative, GTCOM has achieved mixed results, namely, remarkable performance on the financial side but failure at the level of operational excellence and at the level of customer service and satisfaction. Yet the KCRM initiative has to mature into concrete corporate-wide change effort based on a clear plan and strategy, and GTCOM still has a long way to go before being able to fully realize the benefits of the KCRM.

In light of the case study's findings, one concludes that before launching a KCRM program, there should be a clear understanding of why it is being used, and then focusing on the strategy not technology. One needs to make sure the KM strategy is well defined and well understood before looking at software to implement it. This also means changing long-established business processes and culture.

To conclude, the KCRM initiative at GTCOM was overpromised but underdelivered. Several factors contributed to this failure; paramount among these is the adoption of KCRM as an ICT solution, not a business strategy. The KCRM program at GTCOM proved to be a good case of bad implementation.

LESSONS LEARNED

1. KCRM strategy needs to be enabled, rather than driven, by technology. In order to keep KCRM projects business-driven rather than technology-driven, and to reduce employees' resistance to change and secure a successful buy-in of KCRM projects from end-users, it seems that it would be better to have knowledge/power users champion KCRM projects, alongside active involvement, support, and participation from senior management levels, as well as IT managers.
2. Corporate-wide knowledge-sharing culture should prevail to facilitate implementation of KCRM strategies.
3. Long-term financial performance cannot be secured if customers' expectations are not being met with satisfactory experiences.
4. High quality of data guarantees accuracy and efficiency of KCRM reports.
5. Clear and prioritized identification of business requirements need to be prepared before deciding on the KCRM technology.
6. Effective management of end-user training programs (EUT) offered to the right people at the right time for the right duration is essential to the KCRM program.
7. Continued commitment from top management is essential to the success of KCRM programs.
8. Streamlining work flow processes is as important as adoption of advanced KCRM technologies for the success of KCRM programs.
9. A stovepipe structure with multiple silos hinders business integration, interdepartmental communication, and full realization of KCRM benefits.
10. Resistance to change poses a threat to KCRM problems. It seems that having knowledge/power users champion KCRM projects, alongside active involvement, support, and participation from senior management and IT managers, help in reducing employees' resistance to change, securing a successful buy-in from end-users, and keeping the project business-driven rather than technology driven.
11. Documentation of knowledge gained throughout the KCRM development process, for example, selection, planning, budgeting, scheduling, implementation, positioning, monitoring, challenges faced, lessons learned, future prospects, and so forth, and making this knowledge available possibly through Web-based platform/portal, e.g., knowledge repository, and distribution of this knowledge to all concerned parties (sales, marketing, customer services, IT, as well as senior management) help organizations learn and benefit from their past memories in future projects.

ACKNOWLEDGMENTS

The author acknowledges the very constructive and fruitful comments raised by the reviewer of the case study. The comments have greatly helped in improving this final draft of the paper.

REFERENCES

Babcock, C. (1995). Slice, dice, and deliver. *Computerworld, 29*, 46, 129-132.

Davenport, T.H., Harris, J.G., & Kohli, A.K. (2001). How do they know their customers so well? *Sloan Management Review*, *42*(2), 63-73.

Davenport, T.H., & Prusak, L. (1998). *Working knowledge: How organizations manage what they know*. Boston: Harvard Business School Press.

Drucker, P. (1995). *Managing in a time of great change*. Truman Tally.

Garcia-Murillo, & Annabi, H. (2002). Customer knowledge management. *Journal of the Operational Research Society*, *53*, 875-884.

Gebert, H., Geib, M., Kolbe, L., & Brenner, W. (2003). Knowledge-enabled customer relationship management: Integrating customer relationship management and knowledge management concepts [1]. *Journal of Knowledge Management*, 7(5), 107-123.

Grant, R.M. (1991). The resource-based theory of competitive advantage: Implications for strategy formulation. *California Management Review*, *33*, 113-135.

Gray, P., & Watson, H.J. (1998). *Decision support in the data warehouse*. Prentice Hall.

Inmon, W.H. (1996). *Building the data warehouse* (2nd ed.). New York: Wiley.

Long, D.W., & Fahey, L.(2000). Diagnosing cultural barriers to knowledge management. *The Academy of Management Executive*, *14*(4), 113-127.

Love, B. (1996). Strategic DSS/data warehouse: A case study in failure. *Journal of Data Warehousing*, 1(1), 36-40.

Park, Y.T. (1997). Strategic uses of data warehouses: An organization's suitability for data warehousing. *Journal of Data Warehousing, 2*(1), 13-22.

Teece, D., Pisano, G., & Shuen, A. (1997). Dynamic capabilities and strategic management. *Strategic Management Journal*, *18*, 509-533.

Turban, E., McLean, E., & Wetherbe, J. (2002). *Information technology for management: Transforming business in the digital economy* (3rd ed.). New York: John Wiley.

Chapter XVI

Why Knowledge Management Fails: Lessons from a Case Study

Ivy Chan, The Chinese University of Hong Kong, Hong Kong

Patrick Y.K. Chau, The University of Hong Kong, Hong Kong

EXECUTIVE SUMMARY

Knowledge is increasingly recognized as providing a foundation for creating core competencies and competitive advantages for organizations, thus effective knowledge management (KM) has become crucial and significant. Despite evolving perspectives and rigorous endeavors to embrace KM intentions in business agendas, it is found that organizations cannot capitalize on the expected benefits and leverage their performances. This is a case study of an organization in Hong Kong. It is a typical organization with a strong awareness and expectation of KM, yet its program failed within two years. Our findings show that KM activities carried out in the organization were fragmented and not supported by its members. Based on this failure case, four lessons learned are identified for use by management in future KM initiatives.

BACKGROUND

Founded in 1983, HS (the actual name of the company is disguised for confidentiality) is a Hong Kong-based enterprise with a production plant in mainland China. HS is primarily engaged in the production and export of handbags and leather premium products to the United States and European markets. The current CEO is the second generation of the founder. Like many companies in Hong Kong, HS centralizes all its strategic planning and decisions, as well as sales and marketing functions at its head office in Hong Kong while doing the production and assembly work across the border for low production cost. Appendix 1 is the organizational chart of HS. It is found that the head office has 10 staff including a CEO, a general manager, a sales manager, an operation manager, and six other administrative staff. The production plant in China has 450 staff including 40 managerial, supervisory, or administrative staff and 410 skilled workers. Over the years, HS has expanded its range of products and production capacities and resources in order to seize market opportunities and has enjoyed quite healthy growth in terms of sales turnover and profits.

SETTING THE STAGE

Business began declining with double-digit revenue losses in 1998. This was primarily attributed to the fierce competition in the markets and soaring production cost. For example, some competitors were offering drastic price cuts in order to obtain business contracts. Also, new product designs did not last long before being imitated by the competition. The CEO and the senior management team began planning the future of the company and to look for ways to improve the efficiency and productivity of its employees. Business continued to deteriorate, so that by 2001, in order to find out what had gone wrong, the CEO formed a strategic task force consisting of all managers in Hong Kong, several key managers responsible for the production plant in China, and himself to look into the matter. After two weeks of exploration (including observation and communicating with other staff in the company), the strategic task force concluded that knowledge within the organization was ineffectively managed; specifically, there was low knowledge diffusion from experienced staff to new staff, and high knowledge loss due to turnover. Driven by traditional management philosophy, the CEO and the strategic task force believed that they understood the organizational context better, and thus decided to undertake an in-depth investigation through internal effort instead of hiring an external consultant.

CASE DESCRIPTION

In June 2001, the strategic task force carried out investigation, observation, and interviews of employees in various departments. After three months, they identified the knowledge management (KM) issues summarized in Table 1.

From these findings, the strategic task force determined that open communication and discussion was necessary and effective to further examine the KM problems, and therefore called for a couple of meetings with managers and supervisors. In order to encourage open discussion, the meeting was conducted in an informal manner instead of the frequently used formal discussion (such as predefined order for reporting departmental issues). Furthermore, the room setting was changed with seats arranged in a circle to allow everyone to see each other and a flip chart was made available to jot down immediate thoughts. More importantly, everyone was encouraged to express his/her thoughts, opinions, and feedback from a personal perspective or collective stance (e.g., comments from subordinates).

Table 1. Diagnosis of KM problems in HS

Issues	Problems from a KM perspective
❖ Supervisors complained about the heavy workload as they were merely the experts/ advisers for their team members. ❖ Supervisors had little interest in what other supervisors were doing and practicing as they considered their tasks were the most important agenda. ❖ Employees demonstrated passivity and taken-for-granted passion while they were learning new skills, for example, they implemented instructions without asking.	❖ Knowledge was not shared but solely kept by a small group of people. ❖ Learning initiatives among employees were low due to the silo effect of organizational structure.
❖ When skilled workers left HS, specific production techniques were swiftly acquired by other competitors who employed those ex-staff of HS.	❖ Knowledge was lost to competitors.
❖ Supervisors did not have unified standard to extract best practices from experiences. ❖ Employees encountered difficulties in identifying success stories or effective production techniques for respective clients.	❖ Knowledge was not appropriately defined, captured, and retained.
❖ Employees did not have strong willingness to learn new techniques and practices. ❖ Employees took a long time to acquire techniques yet hardly retained the acquired techniques.	❖ Knowledge creation and development was not encouraged, motivated, and nurtured systematically.

The results of the meeting were encouraging as many participants expressed their opinions and comments eagerly. In particular, staff in the meeting agreed that KM was neither an extension of information management nor solely a technology application to capture, organize, and retrieve information or to evoke databases and data mining (Earl & Scott, 1999; Thomas, Kellogg, & Erickson, 2001). Instead, knowledge was embedded in people (e.g., skills and actions), tasks (e.g., production process), and the associated social context (e.g., organizational culture) that involved communication and learning among loosely structured networks and communities of people. Therefore, individuals/ employees were crucial to the implementation of KM initiatives by utilizing their knowledge and skills to learn, share, combine, and internalize with other sources of knowledge to generate new thoughts or new perspectives.

With the above results, HS decided to devise and launch a KM program with an aim to institutionalize knowledge diffusion among employees and leverage knowledge creation for quality products. Instead of a top-down approach of policy making, the management adopted a middle-up-down approach (Nonaka, 1994) with supervisors as the major force to leverage and promote KM throughout the organization. To enhance acceptance and lessen resistance to change, HS chose a new product series to try out the KM initiative with a focus on the following four main aspects: strategic, organizational, instrumental, and output.

In the strategic aspect, it was considered that knowledge available and possessed at HS would fall short of the core competence necessary for business success (e.g., chic product design). Therefore, effort was needed to fill this gap by acquiring knowledge from both external and internal sources. From the organizational side, it was thought that knowledge was more valuable when it was shared and exchanged. Thus, a knowledge-friendly culture needed to be promoted through encouraging employees to socialize and share their ideas and thoughts such that new knowledge could be created to broaden their knowledge repositories. At the base level, it was determined that knowledge had to be acquired, stored, and disseminated in a systematic way to enable employees to access and reuse it easily. In doing so, essential knowledge, such as experienced practices in production skills and innovative ideas in product design, could be captured and recorded. Individual employees or teams who contributed knowledge useful and relevant to HS were to be rewarded. Last but not least, from an output perspective, it was realized that periodic reviews were crucial for evaluating KM effectiveness and for devising subsequent corrective action, if necessary. Performance indicators such as production efficiency, adoption rate of good practices identified, and clients' satisfaction were required.

A detailed implementation plan was devised based on the above analysis, which was then agreed to and approved by the top management of HS. The KM program was officially launched in April 2002.

CURRENT CHALLENGES/PROBLEMS FACED BY HS

After 15 months, HS found that the KM initiative did not generate the positive impact on organizational performance as expected. Organizational performance remained stagnant, revenue continued to decrease, and staff turnover rate stayed high. Our involvement with HS as an external consultant began after the CEO had determined to find out why and/or what happened. Our assistance to HS was clear — to investigate the situation, to uncover the mistakes, and to look for remedies. A series of semistructured interviews with key employees in the managerial, supervisory, and operational levels were therefore conducted. Table 2 summarizes our findings.

As seen, a good start does not guarantee continuity and success (De Vreede, Davison, & Briggs, 2003). First, two crucial reasons were identified as to why HS was unable to bridge the knowledge gap. They were (1) the top management was too ambitious or unrealistic to grasp and incorporate the "best" knowledge in industry into the company and (2) their insufficient role support in encouraging the desired behavior. Similar to many other KM misconceptions, top management wrongly aimed at incorporating other enterprises' best practices (e.g., product design of the fad) or success stories (e.g., cost cutting and streamlining operational processes) into its repositories without considering the relevance, suitability, and congruence to its capabilities. Therefore, this "chasing-for-the-best" strategy soon became problematic and departed from its KM goals. HS did not gain business advantages, such as unique product design and value-added services to customers, and were still unable to respond to the marketplace swiftly.

Table 2. KM results from 2001 to 2003 in HS

KM Focus	Initiatives in 2001	Results in 2003
Strategic		
❖ To determine knowledge gap	❖ Identified core knowledge that led to business success	❖ Unrealistic aims → created fallacies "all the best in HS" to direct KM development ❖ Volatile support → undermined the KM climate
Organizational		
❖ To establish knowledge-friendly culture	❖ Shared knowledge in various socialization and informal gathering	❖ Unframed socialization → created more confusion or negative perceptions ❖ Ineffective human resources policy to retain knowledge workers → swifted loss of knowledge
Instrumental		
❖ To acquire and stimulate knowledge creation	❖ Acquired knowledge in departmental handbook and rewarded knowledge sharing behaviors	❖ Unlimited definitions or views of sources of knowledge → left individual knowledge untapped ❖ Emphasized monetary rewards to stimulate contributions → created self-defeating mechanism and unfriendly team culture ❖ Perceived IT as cutting-edge solution → led to unduly investment on technology
Output		
❖ To evaluate and audit KM development	❖ Conducted periodic review and measured organizational performance	❖ Reviewed infrequently → created pitfalls to learn from mistakes, then moved ahead ❖ Predisposed on efficiency and profitability → overwhelmed short-term benefits to exploit existing knowledge

Second, the mere presence of KM vision is not sufficient to guarantee KM success. Most employees commented that top management involvement in the KM implementation was volatile and appeared to be a one-shot exercise (Gold, Malhotra, & Segars, 2001). For example, the KM program started well with noticeable initiative to identify untapped knowledge from various sources, yet fell behind the expected goals as top management involvement was remote (e.g., leaving the KM effectiveness as departmental responsibility) and support was minimal (e.g., time resources available for knowledge sharing and creation). Thus, the two factors directly hampered the employees' dedication and belief in KM as a significant organizational move.

Third, from the organizational aspect, even though various social activities such as tea parties were used to foster a friendly and open organizational culture, we found that most of these knowledge-sharing activities were futile because no specific and/or appropriate guidelines for such sharing had been devised (Nattermann, 2000). As a result, instead of having discussions that were directly related to tasks, or least contributed to idea generation, frequent chats (e.g., gossiping) among employees and wandering around were found. Many employees were confused with what the sharing was all about. Some employees even perceived KM negatively as interfering with activities important to their daily tasks, creating resistance to participation in what was perceived to be a temporary fad.

Fourth, the instruments used to help acquire and stimulate knowledge creation and sharing encountered problems during implementation. The fallacy of knowledge acquisition with reliance on external sources (such as the existing practices addressed by competitors) undermined employees' intent to explore the available but untapped knowledge resident in their minds (Bhatt, 2001; Nonaka, 1994). The use of information technology to drive knowledge storage and sharing, in principal, was conducive to employees. Yet, the silo organizational structure of HS with disentangled databases for knowledge capture caused more harm than good. Some employees asserted that they did not have the incentive to access or utilize the departmental knowledge handbook and procedural guidance (available from databases) as it is a time-consuming endeavor to dig from the pile of information. Some employees found knowledge incomprehensible as it was presented and stored in various formats, with jargons and symbols that were neither standardized nor systematized across departments.

Fifth, although a reward system was established for knowledge creation and/or sharing, the emphasis on extrinsic terms, such as a monetary bonus, turned out to have an opposite and negative effect on cultivating the knowledge-sharing culture and trust among employees. Some employees commented that knowledge should be kept as personal interest (i.e., not to be shared) until they felt that they could get the monetary reward when shared or recognized by management. Other employees found that harmony and cohesiveness within the team or among colleagues were destabilized as everyone maximized individual benefits at the expense of teamwork and cooperation.

Sixth, there was a misleading notion that IT could be "the" cutting-edge solution to inspire KM in organization. Despite the introduction of IT tools to facilitate knowledge capture, codification, and distribution, it was found that IT adoption and acceptance remained low due to employee preference for face-to-face conversation and knowledge transfer instead of technology-based communication, and the general low computer literacy that intensified the fear of technology. In addition, given the insufficient support from management for IT training and practices, employees, particularly those who had been with HS for a long time, had strong resistance to new working practices for facilitating KM.

Seventh, it was noted that the KM initiatives were left unattended once implemented. It remained unclear as to how to exceed existing accomplishments or overcome pitfalls of the KM initiatives, as there was no precise assessment available. For instance, the last survey evaluating the adoption of best practices from departmental knowledge was conducted a year ago, without a follow-up program or review session. Another example was that the currency and efficacy of the knowledge recorded in the departmental handbook appeared obsolete as no procedures were formulated to revise or update the handbook.

Last but not least, an undue emphasis and concern with the "best-practice" knowledge at HS to improve short-term benefits (e.g., to exploit existing knowledge in order to achieve production efficiency) at the expense of long-term goals (e.g., to revisit and rethink existing knowledge and taken-for-granted practice in order to explore innovation and creativity opportunities). Some employees pointed out that they were inclined to modify existing practices rather than create new approaches for doing the same or similar tasks as recognition and positive impacts can be promptly obtained.

EPILOGUE

To date, KM is considered an integral part of a business agenda. The dynamics of KM as human-oriented (Brazelton & Gorry, 2003; Hansen, Nohria, & Tierney, 1999) and socially constructed processes (Brown & Duguid, 2001) requires an appropriate deployment of people, processes, and organizational infrastructure. This failure case presents the challenges that could be encountered and coped with in order to accomplish effective KM implementation. The people factor is recognized as a key to the successful implementation of KM from initiation, trial, to full implementation. KM is a collective and cooperative effort that requires most, if not all, employees in the organization to participate. KM strategy and planning should be organized, relevant, and feasible within the organizational context. One's best practices and winning thrusts may not be well fitted to others without evaluation for fit and relevance. A balanced hybrid of hard (e.g., information technology) and soft infrastructure (e.g., team harmony and organizational culture) is needed for success.

LESSONS LEARNED

Knowledge management is increasingly recognized but its challenges are not well understood. To institutionalize a KM program, organizations can draw lessons from this failure case so as to construe what imperatives are needed and what mistakes should be avoided. Management issues and concerns are highlighted as follows.

Lesson 1: Start with a KM Plan Based on Realistic Expectations

The mission and behavioral intentions of leaders have a strong impact on employees and where to aim and how to roll out KM processes (KPMG, 2000). In this case, it is appreciated that top management recognized its organizational ineffectiveness and initiated a KM plan as a remedy. We suggest, however, that planning based on unrealistic expectations undermined its ability to successfully direct future actions. Therefore, management has to be reasonable in setting KM goals, perceptions, and beliefs. It is suggested that a feasibility assessment of organizational infrastructures (e.g., financial resources, technology level) and organizational climate (e.g., employees' readiness to KM, resistance to change) be conducted to define the KM principles and goals. Inspirational aims, which can be reasonably and feasibly accomplished, encourage employees to assess their personal knowledge and transfer others' knowledge when it is shown to enhance existing practices and can help meet new challenges.

Lesson 2: Management Support is a Strong, Consistent, and more Importantly, Cohesive Power to Promote KM

It is evident that vision without management support is in vain and temporary. As valued most by the HS employees, continuous corroboration from top management is indispensable to motivate their commitment toward knowledge-centric behaviors for long-term competitiveness (Lee & Choi, 2003). Therefore, beyond visionary leadership, management should be willing to invest time, energy, and resources to promote KM. At its core, management could show their enthusiasm in a boundless and persistent way, including vocal support, speech, inaugural memo, and wandering around different business units to invite impulsive idea generation and knowledge creation from all levels of staff. Also, management could champion the KM process and lead by example with employees who are receptive to KM.

Lesson 3: Integration of Monetary and Nonmonetary Incentives

To stimulate KM behaviors, specifically sharing and creation, it is important to assure a balanced reward system integrating monetary and nonmonetary incentives that fit various forms of motivation (Desouza, 2003). In the beginning of the KM programs, employees needed to be shown that personal benefits could be obtained from KM success with improvement in products, processes, and competitiveness. Therefore, rewards that are direct, monetary-based, and explicit are useful. For this, management can provide salary increase or promotion. With the passage of time, rewards could be extended to something implicit. For instance, management can publicize those employees' names and respective ideas that contributed to organizational processes, or provide skills-enhancement program to enable employees to see their importance with extended job scopes. Moreover, management can consider rewards systems geared toward individual or team achievement so as to encourage more interaction, creativity, teamwork, and harmony among people.

Lesson 4: KM has to be Cultivated and Nurtured, which is not a Push Strategy or Coercive Task

As shown in this case, KM is not a singly motivated exercise. It requires a collective and cooperative effort to put into effect various resources. Other than the vision and top management support, operational staff can greatly affect the success of the KM program. Their influences affect attitudes, behaviors, and participation in KM and could exert positive impacts on KM effectiveness if managed properly. For attitudinal changes, efforts have to remove or at least alleviate employees' negative perception toward KM. For example, the fear and misconception that KM is a means to downsize organizations for efficiency or as heavy workload which requires much IT expertise. For behavioral changes, we highlight a supportive working environment where employees can have ample time to engage in KM endeavors, such as sharing and creation, a fair and positive culture where everyone is valued and encouraged to contribute to KM effectiveness, is needed. To encourage participation, pushing or mandatory activities are least effective. Coupled with the rewards systems, employees should be inspired to take risks as learning steps for KM success. Unexpected failure or unintended results may cause management to call for a break to identify the causes and remedy solutions. Do not quit or blame, otherwise, mutual trust and commitment to work with the KM processes will be lessened.

REFERENCES

Akbar, H. (2003). Knowledge levels and their transformation: Towards the integration of knowledge creation and individual learning. *Journal of Management Studies, 40*(8), 1997-2021.

Alavi, M., & Leidner, D.E. (2001). Review: Knowledge management and knowledge management systems: Conceptual foundations and research issues. *MIS Quarterly, 25*(1), 107-136.

Bhatt, G.D. (2001). Knowledge management in organizations: Examining the interaction between technologies, techniques, and people. *Journal of Knowledge Management, 5*(1), 68-75.

Brazelton, J., & Gorry, G.A. (2003). Creating a knowledge-sharing community: If you build it, will they come? *Communications of the ACM, 46*(2), 23-25.

Brown, J.S., & Duguid, P. (2001). Knowledge and organization: A social-practice perspective. *Organization Science, 12*(2), 198-213.

Desouza, K.C. (2003). Facilitating tacit knowledge exchange. *Communications of the ACM, 46*(6), 85-88.

De Vreede, G.J., Davison, R.M., & Briggs, R.O. (2003). How a silver bullet may lose its shine. *Communications of the ACM, 46*(8), 96-101.

Earl, M.J., & Scott, I.A. (1999). What is a chief knowledge officer? *Sloan Management Review, 40*(2), 29-38.

Gold, A.H., Malhotra, A., & Segars, A.H. (2001). Knowledge management: An organizational capabilities perspective. *Journal of Management Information Systems, 18*(1), 185-214.

Hansen, M.T., Nohria, N., & Tierney, T. (1999). What's your strategy for managing knowledge? *Harvard Business Review, 77*(2), 106-116.

King, W.R., Marks, Jr., P.V., & McCoy, S. (2002). The most important issues in knowledge management. *Communications of the ACM, 45*(9), 93-97.

KPMG Consulting. (2002). *Knowledge management research report 2000.*

Lee, H., & Choi, B. (2003). Knowledge management enablers, process, and organizational performance: An integrative view and empirical examination. *Journal of Management Information Systems, 20*(1), 179-228.

Nattermann, P.M. (2000). Best practice does not equal to best strategy. *The McKinsey Quarterly, 2*, 22-31.

Nonaka, I. (1994). A dynamic theory of organizational knowledge creation. *Organization Science, 5*(1), 14-37.

Thomas, J.C., Kellogg, W.A., & Erickson, T. (2001). The knowledge management puzzle: Human and social factors in knowledge management. *IBM Systems Journal, 40*(4), 863-884.

ADDITIONAL SOURCES

Chen, M. (1995). *Asian management systems*. London: Thomson Business Press.

Fosh, P., Snape, E., Chan, A., Chow, W., & Westwood, R. (1999). *Hong Kong management and labour: Change and continuity*. London: Routledge.

Kaul, V.K. (2002). Knowledge management and innovation in technology-based small and medium sized enterprises. *Management Research News, 25*(8-10), 102-103.

McAdam, R., & Reid, R. (2001). SME and large organization perceptions of knowledge management: Comparisons and contrasts. *Journal of Knowledge Management, 5*(3), 231-241.

Sarmento, A., & Correia, A.M. (2003). Knowledge management: A rewarding challenge for SME's? *Proceedings of the Fourteenth Annual Information Resources Management Association International Conference*, Philadelphia.

Small and Medium Enterprise Center. *www.tdctrade.com/sme/*

Virtual Small and Medium Enterprises Center. *www.sme.gcn.gov.hk/smeop/english/index.cfm*

Zetie, S. (2002). The quality circle approach to knowledge management. *Managerial Auditing Journal, 17*(6), 317-321.

APPENDIX 1: ORGANIZATIONAL CHART OF HS

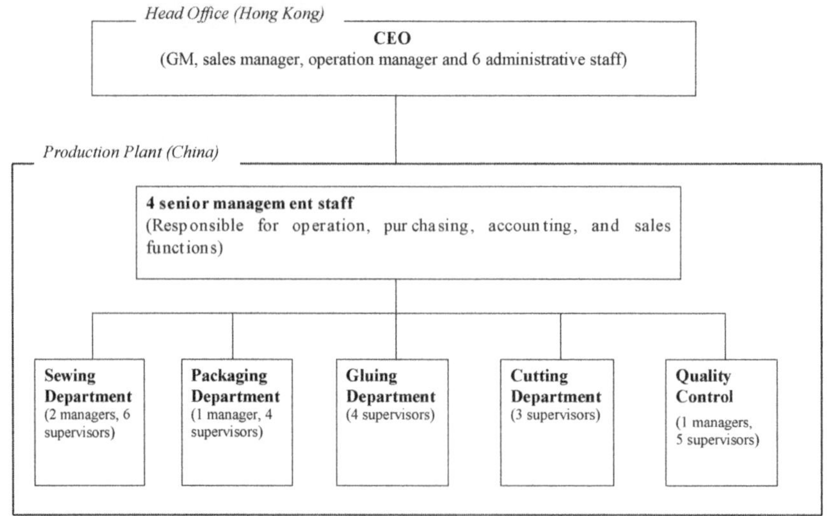

Chapter XVII

Infosys Technologies, Limited

Nikhil Mehta, Auburn University, USA

Anju Mehta, Auburn University, USA

Knowledge has no equal.

– Ancient Indian Scriptures

EXECUTIVE SUMMARY

Despite the emergence of knowledge management (KM) as a critical success factor, few organizations have successfully orchestrated the implementation of a KM initiative. This chapter highlights the implementation efforts of one such firm — Infosys Technologies, Limited. In this case, we discuss how KM emerged as a strategic requirement of the firm, and various capabilities the firm had to develop to fulfill this requirement. In other words, we discuss KM implementation as a confluence of multiple initiatives. We hope that by presenting this idea through the use of a case study we will assist readers to understand the intricate relationships between different facets of KM implementation.

BACKGROUND

Haris, account manager with Infosys's North American operations, pulled out of the multilevel parking lot in downtown Detroit. His meeting with the director of sales management systems of a large automotive manufacturer went fine. The company's sales and order management across the country operated in silos and the director wanted to integrate them. "This will improve our customer service and, at the same time, reduce cost. Can you help?" the director had asked. Haris was slightly anxious as he negotiated the evening traffic of downtown Detroit. He had to get back with the proposed solution by the next day, but the technical team was busy on a client site in Canada.

Late that night, he contacted Infosys's Domain Competency Group (DCG), the company's think tank in India that provides round-the-clock domain knowledge support to practice units around the world. It was morning in India and an automotive expert replied, "This sounds similar to a project we completed for a German automotive company a few months back. We can leverage that experience to propose a solution for the U.S. retail channels. I'll send you the material. And, let me ask the folks in Germany to update you on this."

As Haris presented the proposed solution the next day, the client admitted, "You seem to have clearly understood our problem. I like your approach to integrate our applications and create a unified customer interface layer. Let's get a formal proposal on this."

In the India head office of Infosys, Nandan Nilekani, the CEO, was gratified to notice how knowledge flows had improved across the organization as a result of their KM initiative. The initiative had slowly emerged as the organizational backbone, connecting Infosys's 30 offices around the globe into an intellectual monolith.

Based in Bangalore, the IT hub of India, Infosys was founded in 1981 as an offshore software service provider by a group of seven software professionals led by N.R. Narayana Murthy ("Murthy"). The journey over the past 23 years was a mixed bag. Early years were tough but the founders stuck together, at least for some time. "We had strong hopes of creating a bright future for ourselves, for Indian society, and perhaps even for the world," recalled Murthy, "Confidence, commitment, passion, hope, energy, and the capacity to work hard were available in plenty. However, capital was in short supply. We struggled to put together a princely sum of $250 as our initial seed capital." Revenues in the first decade were an unimpressive $3.89 million. In 1989, when one co-founder left, others became cynical of the future. It was Murthy's unflinching belief in success that finally kept them going.

Strong Leadership

A firm believer in being a role model for the rest of the employees, Murthy had a strong influence on virtually every area of Infosys's operations. His daily life was a blend of austerity and hard work. He reached office by the company bus and typically put in a 12-hour workday. For the past 20 years, he had never denied audience to anyone at Infosys at any time of the workday. People respected him for his tranquility, humility, and simplicity. His non-conventional management style was matched by his singular ideas of doing business. A firm believer in an intellectual, philosophical, ethical, and spiritual management, he once mentioned, "It is better to lose $100 million than a good night's sleep. The softest pillow is a clear conscience." He implemented his management philosophy by infusing Infosys with five core corporate values. Symbolized as C-LIFE, they include Customer Delight (surpassing customer expectations), Leadership by Example (commitment to set standards and be an exemplar for the industry), Integrity and Transparency (commitment to be ethical, sincere, and open in dealings), Fairness (commitment to earn trust and respect), and Pursuit of Excellence (commitment to constantly improve oneself). These values were echoed in company's vision statement: "We will be a globally respected corporation that provides best-of-breed business solutions leveraging technology delivered by best-in-class people."

Murthy's value-driven entrepreneurial paradigm, impeccable corporate governance record, and Infosys's outstanding financial performance won him the Ernst & Young World Entrepreneur of the Year Award for 2003. He and the current CEO and managing director, Nandan Nilekani, were also declared by Fortune as Asia's Businessmen of the Year 2002-2003.

Robust Growth

Things changed dramatically for Infosys in the early 1990s. The economic reforms declared by the Indian government brought a new lease of life to the Indian software industry. Infosys was among the first to ride the wave of resulting opportunities. Strong performance buttressed with planned growth brought impressive results. By 1999, the company had floated a successful public issue in India and the United States, thus becoming the first Indian firm to be listed on NASDAQ. Exhibit 1 summarizes the performance of company's stock over the past few years. The company also topped $100 million in annual revenues, 90% of which came from the IT and business consulting services to Fortune 1000 firms. Exhibit 2 charts company's revenue growth over the years.

By 2003, Infosys employed over 21,000 people scattered over 30 offices and development centers (DC) in 17 countries. With a market capitalization of $10 billion, and 2002–2003 profits of $245 million, Infosys emerged as the second largest IT company in India. The company had grown at a compounded annual growth rate of 70%. Exhibit 3 traces Infosys's corporate journey over the past 23 years. During these two decades, Infosys had a number of firsts to its credit. It was the first Indian company to offer stock options to its employees. It became the first Indian company to include the assessment of intangible assets in its financial results, which it declared in accordance with the accounting principles of seven countries. Exhibits 4a, 4b, and 4c show Infosys's selected financial results per the U.S. GAAP and the Intangible Assets Score Sheet, respectively. It was also the first Indian company to win Asia's Most Admired Knowledge Enterprise (MAKE) award in 2002 and 2003 and the Global MAKE award in 2003.

From Software Services to IT Consulting

Infosys gradually evolved from an offshore software service provider to an IT and business consulting firm. Murthy remembered, "We wanted to expand our portfolio of services and were developing the skills to do more of consulting. We built a team of around 300 business consultants and also started a business process outsourcing arm." The expansion was carefully planned and timely executed across five core domains: software development, software maintenance, software reengineering, Y2K technologies, and ERP and e-commerce systems. Exhibit 5 highlights the past two years' revenue contribution in terms of the service offering.

Software Development: Infosys started with providing piecemeal solutions to small IT-related problems of their clients. Over the years, as its processes matured and its project management skills improved, it started offering comprehensive software solutions for all the IT needs of its customers. The fixed-price tag, fixed-time frame, and stringent quality guarantees attached to the large project responsibilities improved clients' satisfaction as well as Infosys's profit margins. In addition, its ability to manage and successfully execute large projects positioned it as a long-term service provider to its clients. The client list swelled to 350, with more than 85% repeat business.

Software Maintenance: Infosys's early offerings in this field included maintaining legacy systems. Later it developed expertise in updating the systems to keep pace with the changes in the marketplace. Especially for its US-based clients, the 11-hour time difference between India and the United States helped it update the systems while they were idle at night.

Y2K Technologies: One of the earliest areas of growth for the Indian IT industry, Y2K technologies helped Infosys as much as it did any other software company. But Infosys was prudent enough to realize the short-term nature of this domain and to consciously reduce its revenue dependence on Y2K-related businesses. Much before the deadline of the year 2000, Infosys gradually detached resources from Y2K-related projects and allocated them to long-term projects.

Software Reengineering: Infosys helped its customers graduate to new technologies without abandoning the existing ones. The company, for example, developed software solutions to help clients shift from a mainframe-based system to client/server-based system or from a simple database to a relational database.

ERP and E-commerce: Infosys's management was visionary enough to have anticipated an increase in global business opportunities on these two fronts. Before stepping into ERP domain, Infosys implemented SAP for its own operations gaining valuable expertise in the process. Beginning with ERP consulting, the company started offering customized ERP solutions to suit clients' needs. A simultaneous initiative gained ground in the field of Internet-related services, especially e-commerce, and Web services. Infosys developed a comprehensive range of services targeted at start-ups as well mature e-commerce operations, and e-commerce slowly emerged as one of the highest revenue generators for the company.

Scalability Strategy

Back in 1990s when the founders formulated their corporate strategy, they realized that to succeed on a global level would require them to create a positive image among global companies. As Murthy mentioned, "When in the early '90s we went to the US to sell our services, most CIOs didn't believe that an Indian company could build the large applications they needed. The CIOs were very nice to us, of course. They offered us tea, listened to what we had to say and then said, 'Look, don't call us, we'll call you.' We realized a huge gap in our perceptions. We wanted a situation where if you ask CEOs in the US, Europe, or Japan, 'Which is the company you want to outsource software to?' We wanted them to say, 'Infosys.'"

To realize this dream, Infosys started crafting a corporate strategy with a focus on building a high-growth, high-margin, and low-risk company. The management had a mix of completely opposite objectives at hand. They had to maximize profits while reducing risk. They had to choose sustainable sources of revenue and yet remain responsive to new market trends. They had to maintain excellent quality while cutting costs and project delivery times. These opposing sets of objectives required the resource clout of a corporation but the nimbleness of a start-up—yet another paradox. As a result, Infosys developed a complex strategy characterized by:

Scalability

Murthy wanted to build a scalable corporation that could simultaneously grow in terms of revenues, profitability, people, cultural value systems, and value chains. Nandan, the then COO, summarized scalability as "the ability to constantly evolve while avoiding a major disconnect in our operations. We constantly dissect the global IT domain — not just our competition, but also our customers, their businesses, their processes, and then try to foresee problems they would face in the future. Then we test our analyses and learn from our mistakes." Infosys's initial trials with scalability were frustrating, but with time, the management realized benefits of developing a scalable organization. As K. Dinesh, one of the directors, said, "IT firms operate in an environment that, at best, can be described as the sum total of all the business environments in which our clients operate. We have to master numerous technologies, which change very frequently, customer needs are in constant flux, and projects have to be executed across multiple cultural systems. We couldn't have survived as a stable organization!"

Developing scalability required meticulous long-term planning. The management would take a cold hard look at the future and try to project revenues by different growth areas. These projections were used to assess the future requirements of capacity, people, training, and investment in technology. As Nandan explained, "You have to do forward planning, take a long view of the business, which in turn translates into the necessary investments in people, technology, and physical infrastructure."

Scalability ensured that despite the operational rigidity that usually accompanies a firms' organic growth, Infosys remained a flexible organization that adapted with time. Murthy summarized: "The crux of scalability is to ensure that we grow simultaneously on all fronts while maintaining the quality, agility, and effectiveness of a small company."

PSPD Model

Another one of Murthy's brainchild, the Predictability Sustainability Profitability and Derisking (PSPD) model was a robust revenue forecasting system. Exhibit 6 illustrates the model. Predictability and profitability referred to the future revenue situation of the company. For example, Murthy mentioned regarding predictability: "I just cannot imagine how any company can fail to estimate its revenues for the next year and still call itself a healthy business. Which Fortune 500 client would like to depend on a vendor whose CEO is not certain about the company's future?"

Sustainability had a broader meaning and was defined in terms of five parameters that ensured longevity of the corporation. They include: a climate of openness, learning attitude among the employees, a value system ensuring fairness, increased speed of execution, enhanced imagination to pioneer great ideas, and excellence in ensuring a seamless execution of these parameters.

Submodels were developed to achieve the three strategic goals of predictability, sustainability, and profitability. Predictability and sustainability were ensured by the Customer Relationship Model (CRM), and profitability was ensured by the Global Delivery Model (GDM), which required shifting costly project components from the client location to relatively cheaper locations around the world.

The Derisking component was added to the model after an unfortunate incident. In 1992, Infosys had General Electric (GE) as their largest customer accounting for about 40% of its revenues. Realizing their clout, GE exerted pressure on Infosys to bring down their rates. After one year of intense bargaining, Infosys severed its contract with GE. Since then, Infosys decided not to be depend on any client for more than 10% of their business.

Derisking aimed at building risk management abilities, both short term as well as long term. Murthy explained, "Our derisking model says that we must have a balanced portfolio of markets, technologies, and practices." To manage long-term risk, Infosys maintained a strategic balance in its portfolio of clients, accepting only ones that met strict guidelines for revenues potential. It reduced the revenue dependence on its largest client from 15.6% to 6.7% and those of its five largest clients from 43.1% to 29.2%. A similar balance was maintained in its industry focus. Besides assuring predictable revenues, this balance ensured a diverse skill set among the company's professionals. Exhibit 7 summarizes its revenue segmentation by client and industry.

To manage risk in the short run, Infosys formed a risk-mitigation group that monitored 120 parameters, and made risk-related recommendations on a fortnightly basis. These parameters included macro as well as micro aspects of various technologies, customers, and markets Infosys was related with. An internal group of executives met every fortnight to discuss and analyze the recommendations of the group.

Flexible Organization Structure

In 1998 Infosys realized that its Strategic Business Unit (SBU)-based structure was incompatible with its scalability strategy. Nandan explained, "Scalability demanded that Infosys be lithe, agile, and flexible in responding to the new market trends because emerging market trends could be in any new dimension." Murthy had a similar opinion: "We understood the demands of operating in a market where technology changes rapidly and business models quickly become obsolete. Success depended on our ability to recognize and assimilate these changes quickly. SBUs didn't facilitate that." As a result, Infosys reorganized its nine SBUs into a highly flexible Practice Unit (PU)-based structure. The PUs were geographically organized, and each had a dedicated sales and software delivery infrastructure (Nanda & DeLong, 2001). Support functions such as finance, quality, and research were centrally located in India.

Global Delivery Model (GDM)

The underlying framework for the new structure was the Global Delivery Model. Infosys developed the model on the principle of distributed project management, that is, executing the project at multiple locations with flawless integration. "We wanted to do the work where it could be done best, where it made the most economic sense, and with the least amount of acceptable risk," explained Murthy.

The GDM required the PUs to be distributed globally, each made responsible for different markets Infosys was operating in. Each PU had a sales arm, a Global Development Center (GDC) and a Delivery Unit (DU) attached to it. In addition, Proximity Development Centers (PDCs) were opened in Boston and Fremont to take care of the implementation issues in the U.S. market that required close proximity to clients. This reorganization enabled Infosys to work across multiple time zones on a 24-hour work cycle.

GDM envisioned Infosys as a virtual corporation. Marketing teams at the PDCs would pitch in for the projects. Once a project was won, a team of experts would travel to the client's site to assess project requirements. On return, they would quickly assemble a virtual team from multiple GDCs that would execute the project, all this while a small team would stay on-site to update the virtual team on matters related to the project. On completion of the project, the virtual team would be disbanded and redeployed on another project, while a team from the PDC would travel to the client's site to take care of the installation, testing, and training issues. Exhibit 9 illustrates the distribution of project management activities between the client site and the GDCs. Capabilities developed to facilitate the GDM included:

- a highly flexible infrastructure to avoid resource redundancy;
- reliable information connectivity to enhance seamless communication between various GDCs and client sites; and
- standardized processes. To ensure process quality, Infosys attained Level 5 of Software Engineering Institute's Capability Maturity Model (SEI CMM).

GDM accrued many advantages to Infosys:

- Scalability was a natural outcome. Software engineers at all locations had access to organizational resources, a fact that helped them respond swiftly to clients' changing requirements.
- Cost of ownership was drastically reduced for the client as well as for Infosys.
- Derisking of the project was assured, as critical services were available 24/7. GDM enabled a highly networked environment where one project location could act as a complete backup for another to ensure recoverability.
- Time to market was radically reduced. GDM offered extended workdays across multiple time zones all over the world. Also, projects were divided into modules that could be completed independently and simultaneously at multiple GDCs.

SETTING THE STAGE

The Need to Improve the Knowledge Flows

In 1992, a number of multinationals, such as IBM Global Services, Accenture, and EDS, entered India to demand their share of the software outsourcing market. Infosys was faced with a challenge to retain its personnel and the market share. Murthy and other cofounders realized that success would rely on two pillars: developing intellectual resources and constantly innovating the core processes. Time proved them right on both accounts.

Developing Intellectual Resources

A crisp human resource strategy was designed, which initiated the following changes:

- **Formalizing recruiting, training, and retaining processes:** Murthy mentioned, "The biggest challenge was to recruit, enable, and retain the brightest talent." Stringent recruiting standards such as 'academic excellence' and 'learnability' were outlined. Although these standards helped Infosys hire star academic performers, they shrunk the available pool of qualified applicants. For example, only 2% of 250,000 applicants in 2003 were recruited. Rather than relaxing the standards, Infosys attached its recruiting process to the "predictability" component of its PSPD model. The revenue predictions about future were based on assessing the likely availability of qualified workforce.

Heavy investments were made in training. An Education and Research (E&R) department and a Management Development Center (MDC) were created. They developed and imparted about 300,000 man-hours of technical and managerial training annually. This included a mandatory 10-day formal training every year for all employees, and a four-month training program in analytical thinking, problem solving, technical fundamentals, and customer negotiating for the new recruits.

Retaining an attractive workforce was the most difficult part. As Murthy mentioned, "Talented employees trained to deliver excellence attracted corporate headhunters. We didn't want to be a supplier of trained workforce to our competitors. But it wasn't easy to convince our knowledge workers (employees) to stay with us. We planned a series of initiatives like employee empowerment, building the right culture, and wealth sharing."

- **Employee empowerment:** Murthy saw empowerment as a way to improve employees' perspective. For a highly talented IT workforce, this was easier said than done. As he explained, "Most engineers had a strong identity, clear life goals, and flexible yet defined ways of doing things. Talking to them about individual empowerment was a redundant exercise." So Infosys designed a unique approach to empowerment — to develop a strong corporate culture by channeling individual aspirations toward a common objective. "Constant Innovation" was chosen as an objective worthy for knowledge workers. Murthy felt that "the future winners will be firms that escape from the gravitational pull of the past on the fuel of innovation."
- **Building leaders:** The objective of "constant innovation" required building a band of leaders who could raise the aspirations of their associates. Murthy mentioned, "Our focus at Infosys was to breed a whole generation of leaders, mentor them, throw them the challenges, and train them in the practice of management." A Leadership Institute was set up in India that started training selected managers from all the global locations. The institute taught courses on business ethics, cultural integration, mentoring people, and relationship building with global customers.
- **An open culture:** The next step was to create a culture that heightened the desire for innovation, a culture that gave respect to ideas regardless of where they emerged. Murthy opined, "It was vital for our people to be able to deliver, execute, and meet challenges of the future. This required an open culture that recognized merit and encouraged ideas from all. A culture that did not get subdued by hierarchy and was free of politics. A culture of excellence, speed, and execution."

  A critical issue while building such a culture was to integrate employees of over 38 nationalities. The challenge was to develop an environment where all these cultures were at ease with each other. The E&R department, the Management Development Center, and the Leadership Institute were asked to handle this issue through their training sessions. Project managers and team leaders were encouraged to assemble diverse teams to execute projects. On large global projects, employees from different cultures in different offices around the world were asked to propose, win, and execute those projects on collaborative basis.

- **Wealth creation and wealth sharing:** Unlike its competitors, Infosys started offering stock options to its employees. It renounced the practice of signing employment bonds with its professionals going abroad, and started offering higher education opportunities to its employees in foreign universities. Murthy summarized these policies: "We realized that we had to make a value proposition to our people, as we did for our customers."

It took Infosys over four years to fully implement these components of the new human resource strategy. By 1996, Infosys had a perceptible edge over its competitors — employee turnover was at an industry low of 10% and people reported a feeling of pride in working with Infosys.

Continuous Innovation

Murthy was of the opinion that a scalable company could not be built with static processes. "Ensuring innovative processes enables an evolutionary architecture," he said. In 1992, Infosys launched the Excellence Initiative to brace the software development and delivery processes. The excellence statement declared: "A commitment to strive relentlessly, to constantly improve ourselves, our services and products so as to become the best." The initiative had a strong focus on quality and innovation. Over the years, supply chain was tightened using Baldrige's seven criteria, international standards such as Six-Sigma and ISO 9001 were achieved. By 1997, CMM Level 4 was attained, and preparations began to attain CMM Level 5.

By 1999, Murthy had started planning a change in leadership, and wanted the then chief operating officer (COO), Nandan Nilekani, to take over as the CEO. As a part of his mentoring plan for Nandan, he assigned him the responsibility to develop the infrastructure for CMM Level 5, which included building a robust system to continuously improve the software development and delivery processes. Nandan, a product of the Indian Institutes of Technology, approached this issue with a purely technical perspective. With an inkling that system requirements for CMM Level 5 will include steady knowledge inputs, he thought of implementing a small knowledge-based system to facilitate knowledge flows to the operations improvement group — the team governing process innovation within Infosys. He held discussions in this regard with employees at various levels, and was surprised at the results — knowledge flow was more than just a requirement for CMM Level 5; it was also the bane of a different problem of mammoth proportions. Virtually everyone, from software developers to sales managers, complained about the acute lack of knowledge inputs even in their day-to-day operations. Highly trained professionals asked Nandan, "Given the knowledge-related constraints, how do you expect us to attain the corporate objective of continuous innovation?"

The Need Intensifies

Nandan continued to probe this issue further. He remembered, "I got a feeling of a huge knowledge void, as if Infosys was fast becoming opaque to any kind of knowledge flow — from within as well as outside. Most of the time the required knowledge existed somewhere, but no one knew where. I noticed that while I was searching for solutions to enhance complex knowledge flows for CMM Level 5, the mechanisms for even the simplest of knowledge flows were nonexistent." Later, he discovered that the problem was also aggravated by the demands of two of the Infosys lifelines — the Global Delivery Model and scalability strategy.

Demands of Global Delivery Model (GDM)

GDM enabled executing software projects in a geographically distributed environment, yet with high degree of predictability and dependability. Typical software development and delivery units were located at multiple locations across the globe. GDM required a third of Infosys's 19,000 employees to be based at the corporate campus in Bangalore, another 8,000 in four other DCs in India, and the rest across three smaller DCs in India and eight global development centers. Additionally, 10% to 15% of employees were always at client locations.

Despite a robust communication infrastructure connecting these locations, knowledge flows among them were conspicuously absent. Each location operated like a knowledge oasis. For example, people would come up with problems in Boston similar to the ones already faced and resolved by people at Bangalore. Ironically, Boston never heard of that and would waste time on solving the problem again. "There was clear-cut redundancy problem, and there were indications that GDM needed to be buttressed with a knowledge-based system," Nandan explained.

Demands of Scalability

Scalability demanded building a flexible and learning organization that constantly utilized its knowledge assets to replenish its repertoire of resources and capabilities. It was becoming increasingly clear to Nandan that true scalability would elude them unless organizational knowledge assets were made accessible to every employee. He admitted, "We realized that scalability demanded learnability — the ability to extract knowledge from specific concepts and situations and apply it to other situations. And learnability required real-time access to firm's knowledge resources."

Scalability also demanded efficient utilization of capacity. Management had to ensure that they did not overrun the capacity, and yet remained responsive to new market needs. Infosys had to be ready for project-related opportunities in totally new markets and technology domains. This required a highly responsive system that would quickly assimilate knowledge regarding these opportunities and then disseminate it among appropriate groups to enable project execution with exceptional speed and high quality.

In addition to individual demands of GDM and scalability, Nandan also identified problem issues in certain areas of overlap between the two. For example, GDM enabled Infosys to grow exceptionally fast. But the absence of truly scalable knowledge resources and the infrastructure to share them constrained the growth potential. Nandan summarized: "All said, we needed a system to build domain-specific knowledge resources and the technological infrastructure to share those resources."

CASE DESCRIPTION: BUILDING A KNOWLEDGE-BASED COMPANY

Initial Knowledge-Sharing Mechanisms

Since its inception, Infosys had always emphasized knowledge sharing. In the earlier years, the hundred or so software developers usually shared project-specific knowledge over informal gatherings. By 1992, the number of employees had risen considerably, so Murthy asked all project managers to hold brainstorming and mentoring sessions at the completion of every project, and to document these sessions. A central library, called the Body of Knowledge (BoK), was created to catalog and archive these documents for future reference. BoK was later converted to its electronic form.

Over the years, as the knowledge-sharing needs of employees intensified, some other stand-alone mechanisms evolved. They included:

- A technical bulletin forum – set up in 1995 by the employees themselves to generate technical discussions
- Corporate Intranet – rolled out in 1996 to integrated all departmental information
- Process Assets Database – created in 1997 to facilitate software developers' store project-related artifacts for future reuse
- Project Leader Toolkit – assembled in 1998 to consolidate helpful tips regarding offshore project management
- Marketing Assets Repository – built in 1997, it had client presentations, key project proposals, and client case studies

In 1999, following Nandan's recommendations, it was decided to initiate formal KM program. Exhibit 10 traces the evolution of Infosys's KM program.

A steering committee, comprising Nandan himself, some other members of the board, and senior-level employees with diverse profiles, was formed to articulate a formal KM implementation strategy. The committee's first task was to define Infosys's KM vision statement. The steering committee envisioned Infosys "to be an organization where every action is fully enabled by the power of knowledge; which truly believes in leveraging knowledge for innovation; where every employee is empowered by the knowledge of every other employee; which is a globally respected knowledge leader" (Kochikar & Suresh, 2004, p. 249).

Building the KM Infrastructure

The steering committee made four critical decisions while establishing the organizational KM infrastructure:

Focus on Explicit Knowledge

An initial study of various user communities within the organization revealed that a significant bit of their knowledge requirements included reusable documents, reports, software code, and architectural diagrams. Keeping this in mind, the committee restricted its infrastructure-related efforts to enhance the sharing of explicit knowledge.

Tacit knowledge sharing was identified as a long-term goal, and efforts for enhancing explicit knowledge flows were seen as contributing to that goal. Moreover, Infosys already had a number of tacit knowledge-sharing mechanisms including knowledge transfer sessions (KT sessions) among the project team members, impromptu project meetings, formal seminars by experts, and best-practice sessions. Still, it was decided that the KM infrastructure would not ignore tacit knowledge sharing altogether.

Facilitated-Distributed Architecture

Another important decision at this stage was selecting the appropriate KM architecture. Architecture was recognized as key to the success of KM initiative as it would influence issues such as defining the responsibilities of top management and the employees; creating specific roles to own those responsibilities; deciding the nature of knowledge sharing, that is, mandatory versus voluntary; choosing appropriate measures to get people involved; and successfully implementing KM processes.

The committee considered the KM architectures of various pioneers in the field. For example, it compared Hewlett and Packard's decentralized bottom-up model to Buckman Lab's more centrally driven top-down one, and found them inappropriate for Infosys's requirements (Kochikar & Suresh, 2003). Infosys realized that its own values, norms, and practices should dictate the choice of the architecture. So structured surveys backed by extensive interviews were conducted across the organization to identify various knowledge-sharing and application issues typical to Infosys.

The results indicated that a top-down KM model will not fit with Infosys' largely decentralized culture, while a bottom-up approach may lead to a selective dissemination and application of knowledge, thus leaving the genuine knowledge needs unmet (Venugopalan & Suresh, 2003). The KM steering committee and the KM group finally decided on a facilitated-distributed architecture that was more akin to the middle-up-down model proposed by Nonaka and Takeuchi (1995).

The architecture was "facilitated" because a centralized KM Group was created to facilitate the KM program. The Group included (Nanda & DeLong, 2001):

- Behavioral experts to help nurture a knowledge-sharing culture
- A content-management team that would handle content-related issues and also develop the knowledge taxonomy
- A process expert team to identify and initiate core KM processes and to synchronize them with the core business processes
- A technology team that would build and maintain the technical infrastructure

In addition to the KM Group, a team of knowledge champions was organized from various business units and functions to evangelize and promote the KM program.

Foreseeing the immense breadth of organizational knowledge, the architecture was also kept "decentralized." Knowledge creation and application was identified as employees' responsibility. This decision was key in increasing employee commitment to the program. It also helped the KM group to garner support from experts spanning different industry sectors, technologies, and project management areas to build a comprehensive and scalable knowledge taxonomy.

Knowledge Taxonomy

The KM Group anticipated the KM system to handle several terabytes of data. The Group also realized that the analytical nature of company's employees required a robust knowledge taxonomy supported by a sophisticated content retrieval mechanism to improve their search capability.

The taxonomy developed by the content management team covered 1,100 knowledge areas (called knowledge nodes), rearranged in a four-level hierarchy to simplify navigational needs. At the first level, the nodes were organized in terms of broad areas of relevance: technology, methodology, domain, project management, and culture. Each of these level 1 nodes branched out into more granular nodes to populate the subsequent levels. For example, the node *Wireless Application Protocol* could be traced under *Technology → Mobile Technologies → Protocols* (Kochikar & Suresh, 2004).

In-House KM Applications

The KM Group next evaluated some standardized KM software packages to decide the KM applications issue. Packages were assessed in term of their scalability, robustness, ease of use, and ability to accommodate the organizational knowledge taxonomy. After some deliberation, the KM Group found most of the packages unfit for Infosys's needs, and decided to develop its own set of KM applications.

Before developing new applications, it was important to consolidate the existing stand-alone applications under a single umbrella. These included the body of knowledge (BoK), technical bulletin forum, the process assets database, the project leader toolkit, and the marketing assets repository. A front-end KM portal was designed and all the stand-alone applications were added on the back end. Some other applications with substantial usage across Infosys were left untouched. As Nandan explained, "We didn't want to disturb the existing knowledge flow infrastructure too much. Secondly, assimilating these applications would have projected an impression that we were forcing people into the KM program, which was not the best policy to convince talented knowledge workers."

On the tacit knowledge front, an application called the People Knowledge Map (PKM) was added to the KM portal to facilitate tacit knowledge sharing. The PKM kept a record of the skill sets and expertise of people across the organization. The expertise component included a voluntary registration by the experts with this application. Apart from the PKM, a Web-based virtual classroom was also attached to the portal. It allowed access to various courses developed by the E&R department, the MDC, and the Leadership Institute, and incorporated a forum to initiate course-related discussions.

The Program Takes Off

The KM program was launched with fanfare. Seminars and presentations were held at all global locations. Technical quizzes with monetary prizes were conducted, and stock market trends and live cricket scores were constantly flashed on the KM portal to attract first-timers.

Knowledge Currency Units (KCU)

To evangelize the program, a novel incentive scheme was introduced. Reviewers as well as users were asked to award quality points, called knowledge currency units

(KCU), to each submission. Various denominations of KCUs were created for different types of contributions. For example, a body of knowledge submission or a technical white paper was assigned higher denomination than a project snapshot. The KCUs awarded to the submissions accrued to the contributors, who could trade them for books, music, and other products from an e-commerce company.

The KCU scheme was a win-win situation for both the KM program and the employees. The program received the extensive attention and participation — the system was populated with first-time knowledge assets, and many employees earned up to $250 in KCUs. The scheme also ensured a market-driven approach toward keeping the system lean and current. Knowledge assets with low composite KCUs were automatically phased out by the system.

Adding Satellite Portals

Much before the launch of the program, various departments, projects, and even interest groups within Infosys maintained their own portals. After formalizing the program, an option was to phase them out in favor of a single KM portal. But the KM Group decided to add them as satellites to the KM portal. Dr. J.K. Suresh, principal knowledge manager, explained the reasons behind this step: "Employees had a considerable amount of self-pride attached to these portals, and it would have been counter-productive to wean them away from these portals and get them to the KM system. Then, in the initial stages of the KM program, some of these portals had better content than the KM portal itself. So the only way out was to let them grow as stand-alone portals and to integrate their content with the KM portal. This enriched the KM portal and ensured greater organizational visibility to their content. Second, those portals gave us clear hints of emerging communities of practice, and removing them would have discouraged those communities."

Growth and Consolidation

By 2001, the program had captured the attention of the employees. But the KM Group now faced the challenge to convert the initial interest into a long-term involvement. As Dr. Suresh explained, "While the material rewards served the purpose well, they were imperfect instruments in sustaining the involvement of employees. It was time to move up Maslow's hierarchy." The group planned a multipronged strategy to address this issue (Nanda & DeLong, 2001).

Ensuring Recognition

In an organization of nearly 10,000 people, need for recognition emerged as a strong motivator for employees. The KM Group gradually started underplaying the importance of the KCU scheme, and added a scoreboard on the KM portal displaying the top-nine submissions in each content type. The scoreboard was updated every month and the names of winning employees were highlighted in all corporate communications.

Highlighting Benefits

Addressing a still-higher level of employees' needs, the KM group started emphasizing organizational and group-level benefits of knowledge sharing and application.

Quality metrics of high knowledge-sharing projects were compared with those of average knowledge-sharing projects. Initial results indicated a 15% less defect rate in the former projects. These projects were also found to be 13% lower on cost of quality metrics. Project leaders were also queried for possible insights. They reported saving over four man-days per person in the first six months as a direct benefit of knowledge reuse. These benefits, when highlighted across the organization, impressed the professional strata that had, until now, stayed away from the KM initiative.

Consolidating Applications

By this time, the majority of the employees were hitched to the KM bandwagon. Riding the popularity wave, the KM Group made the critical move to consolidate the stand-alone applications that were left untouched initially. These applications were originally developed and used by specialized communities of highly educated professionals, and the KM Group was hesitant of integrating them into the mainstream KM system before winning the interest of these communities. The applications included:

- The Integrated Project Management (IPM) tool, which had a twin functionality as a tool for project life-cycle management and as a huge repository for project-related information
- The Employee Skill System (ESS), which, unlike the People Knowledge Map (PKM), was maintained by the human resource department. It kept mandatory records of employee competencies as they changed over time
- Various online forums for technical discussions

Consolidating these applications still involved a host of behavioral and proprietary issues and Nandan would not allow any official persuasion. The problems were most pronounced in the case of the bulletin board. Infosys typically had a single mammoth bulletin board, which most of the employees would keep open all day. But it lacked any archival and search capabilities, and after detailed discussions with various user groups, the bulletin board was finally split into 45 separate domain-specific discussion forums, and integrated with the KM portal. The initial resentment by some employees petered out once benefits of having technology-specific forums became evident.

By the end of the second round of consolidation, employees could visit the KM portal to access BoKs, case studies, technical white papers, project snapshots, virtual classroom, reusable code, project leader toolkit, and previous client presentations and proposals. They could identify and query experts in various fields and visit bulletin boards to view and participate in various discussions. They could also search the archives for previous discussion threads.

Enabling Knowledge Creation

Although knowledge creation was identified as employees' responsibility, Nandan realized that management had a critical role to play in the overall goal of building Infosys as a knowledge-based company. He explained, "Employees in this industry work in domains defined by the periphery of corporate strategy. So, the knowledge created at their end is limited to these areas. Scalability strategy demands constant upgrading in areas of operation, and it is management's obligation to create appropriate knowledge base to support employees in those areas." This led to the creation of two internal consulting groups: the Domain Competency Group (DCG) and the Technology Competency Group (TCG). DCG had a business focus and was assigned the role of creating knowledge in various domains. It had experts on transformation and business dynamics, current trends, and regulatory and accounting practices of manufacturing, services, and retail sectors. TCG was technology focused and had different subgroups. One of them — the Software Engineering and Technology Laboratory (SETLabs), which developed novel methodologies and technology architectures for use by Infosys's project teams around the world. People from these units were required to publish their research regularly in IEEE journals.

Sensing an increase in business opportunities in e-commerce, ERP solutions, and telecommunications, three new business units were added to scout for opportunities in these fields. An engineering services group was also created to develop new knowledge and competencies in these fields. The group transferred its members to the three units to share competencies.

To involve the global locations in knowledge-creation exercise, knowledge-generating units were added to all the locations. "Proximity centers," as these units were called, internalized knowledge from the local environment. Usually, the centers worked closely with technology start-ups in their respective markets to gain access to the latest technologies. Knowledge pertaining to these technologies was supplied to the local office and to the TCG in India.

Compulsory Sharing and Application

Once appropriate levels of growth and consolidation were achieved, management started reinforcing knowledge sharing and application as core business activities. The process team within the KM Group was assigned the responsibility to design appropriate sharing and application processes.

Strong behavioral issues were attached to mandatory sharing and application. The KM Group realized that highly talented professionals could not be forced to share their knowledge. It would malign the whole rubric of Infosys's philosophy toward its intellectual assets. So they initiated mandatory sharing and application in areas where the information being shared had a low knowledge component. Project management was one such area. Project managers had to input mandatory project information at various project stages in the integrated project management (IPM) application. The IPM was slightly modified to require managers to provide experiential knowledge (Nanda & DeLong, 2001). The idea was to encourage them to contribute knowledge artifacts during the project itself, rather than as a time-consuming exercise at the end of the project. Once completed, the document was uploaded as a project snapshot to the KM portal.

A similar process was initiated for mandatory sharing in project management. Project managers were asked at various stages of the project to search for existing knowledge inputs. The KM system was supplemented with the capability to record the managers' names and the knowledge artifacts they consulted. These records were provided to the respective managers as well as their colleagues to help them decide on potential usefulness of the artifacts.

Measurement Issues

By late 2003, Nandan, now the CEO and managing director, was content with the progress of the KM initiative. It had involved a substantial effort, but initial results were impressive:

- The knowledge taxonomy had developed into a robust four-level structure encompassing more than 1,700 nodes displaying over 18,000 knowledge assets covering various industries, technologies, and project management topics.
- On any typical workday, Infosys employees all over the world downloaded over 1,000 artifacts from KM portal totaling over 150,000 documents every quarter.
- One in every four employees had contributed at least one knowledge artifact to the central knowledge repository.
- Thousands of employees regularly participated in knowledge exchanges on the discussion forums.

"What begun as an effort to improve the knowledge flow situation, ended up giving us a whole new perspective of things — the knowledge perspective," Nandan mused.

The Future: Knowledge Management Maturity (KMM) Model

By 2003, the KM steering committee was of the opinion that an implementation framework would be essential to chart the future course of the KM program. During one of the discussions between the committee and the KM Group, an interesting possibility emerged — to develop a framework in line with the capability maturity model (CMM). The resulting framework was named the Knowledge Management Maturity (KMM) model. The KMM model categorized possible levels of developing the knowledge management capability within a firm. The levels ranged from 1 representing the "default" state of a firm bereft of any form of KM activity to level 5 representing a "sharing" state where robust processes leverage organizational knowledge assets for measurable productivity benefits (Kochikar, 2003). Exhibit 11 illustrates the five KMM levels. Infosys was designated as moving toward the "Aware" stage of level 3.

CURRENT CHALLENGES FACING INFOSYS

An important accomplishment for Infosys' KM program was the company's recognition as one of the Asia's Most Admired Knowledge Enterprises (MAKE) for 2002 and 2003. In 2003, Infosys was also recognized as one of the Globally Most Admired Knowledge Enterprises. (Other winners included Accenture, Amazon.com, BP, GE, Toyota, and World Bank.)

With the initial success of the KM initiative, there also emerged new challenges. As with KM initiatives at other companies, questions were being raised about the program's impact on the firm's performance (Chen, Feng, & Liou, 2004). After 4 years into the KM program, Nandan knew that at some point he would have to justify the economic commitment to the program. As an initial assessment, the KM group started conducting annual and semiannual polls. Employees consistently attributed 2% to 4% increase in operational efficiency to KM. About 90% reported saving at least 1 day every quarter, and about 20% to 30% reportedly saved up to 8 days (Ravindra & Suresh, 2003). But Nandan was not satisfied with the anecdotal evidence. "We really needed a robust set of quantitative measures," he confessed.

As Infosys inched toward level 3 of its KMM model, Dr. Suresh briefed Nandan that although they had started working toward building survey-based and metrics-based value assessment measures, it might still be some time before the efforts fructified. Some questions they were struggling with included what could be the specific approaches to gather evidence of KM's contribution to business value creation? What were the issues involved in implementing each of these approaches? Would it be ever possible to measure KM's return on investment (ROI)?

While the KM Group was busy developing assessment metrics for KM-enabled value creation inside the company, Nandan tried to focus on the potential usefulness of the KM initiative even beyond firm's boundaries. He realized that one of the biggest benefits of the initiative was its contribution to make Infosys a truly scalable company. He could notice the fact that in the past four years Infosys was learning more, and more importantly, it was learning better. Existing knowledge facilitated creation of new knowledge, thus enhancing firm's innovative capabilities and enabling it to exploit business opportunities earlier and better than the competition. "Going at this pace," he asserted, "we should become proactive problem definers than reactive problem solvers. We should be able to tell our clients of the problems they will face in future, and advice them of some solutions leveraging IT. But making this giant leap involves a whole set of scalability issues and I don't even know what they are!"

On a separate note, Nandan also wondered if it would ever be possible to facilitate tacit knowledge sharing within an economically and temporally feasible framework. "That is the final frontier, where we can claim true individual empowerment — every employee having access to every iota of organizational knowledge. Also I can imagine a host of trust issues in such a situation. We need to ask ourselves a whole lot of questions. I wish I knew those questions, and the answers to those questions too."

EPILOGUE

In this case study, we highlight a firm's efforts to implement knowledge management to fulfill its strategic requirements. The case study can possibly be used to develop a theoretical approach to build KM as an organizational capability. A useful building block can be the resource-based and the knowledge-based perspectives discussed in the strategy literature. The resource-based view discusses organizational capabilities as a source of competitive advantage, and the knowledge-based-view highlights knowledge management as one such capability. Utilizing these perspectives and the knowledge inherent in this case study, future researchers can develop, and subsequently test, normative prescriptions for building the KM capability. Current work of one of the authors is a step in this direction (Mehta, Hall, & Boulton, 2004). To practitioners, this would provide an approach to understand, measure, and predict a firm's capacity to create value by implementing a successful KM program.

LESSONS LEARNED

- The case study highlights the emergence of KM as a strategic requirement in knowledge-intensive industries. The fact that knowledge requirements underlie most of the improvements adopted by Infosys to manage growth substantiates the argument. How top management of Infosys took cognizance of KM as a strategic requirement would be an interesting discussion topic.
- The case study brings out, although subtly, the inherent dichotomy in KM implementations. Despite being an organization-wide exercise, it still is a confluence of many separate initiatives to be undertaken in an overlapping sequence. The nature and sequence of the separate initiatives undertaken by Infosys, namely, creating KM roles (KM Group), building KM infrastructure, initiating KM processes, is one possible illustration.
- The case also hints at the centrality of HR issues in KM. Whether the initial success of KM program would still be the same had Murthy not implemented the new human resource (HR) strategy way back in 1996 is an interesting issue for discussion.
- Infosys's knowledge management maturity (KMM) model is an interesting extension of Software Engineering Institute's Capability Maturity Model (SEI CMM). Explicitly, it provides a future road map for organizational KM initiatives. Tacitly, it highlights the cyclical nature of KM implementation. Efforts to attain the higher levels of KMM are substantiated by feedback and insights from lower levels.

REFERENCES

Chen, E.T., Feng, K., & Liou, W. (2004). Knowledge management capability and firm performance: An empirical investigation. In N.C. Romano Jr. (Ed.), *Proceedings of the Tenth Americas Conference on Information Systems*, 2255-2262.

Infosys annual report. (2002). Bangalore, India: Infosys.

Kochikar, V.P. (2003). The knowledge management maturity model—A staged framework for leveraging knowledge. Retrieved January 11, 2004, from *www.Infy.com*

Kochikar, V.P., & Suresh, J.K. (2004). Towards a knowledge sharing organization: Some challenges faced on the Infosys journey. In M. Rao (Ed.), *Annals of cases on information technology* (vol. 6[c], pp. 244-258). Hershey, PA: Idea Group.

Nanda, A., & DeLong, T. (2001). *Infosys Technologies, Limited.* Harvard Business School Case Study no. 801-445. Boston: Harvard Business School.

Nonaka, I., & Takeuchi, H. (1995). *The knowledge creating company.* New York: Oxford University Press.

Ravindra, M.P., & Suresh, J.K. (2004). How Infosys embeds knowledge management to drive customer intimacy. *KM Review*, March/April, 5.

Venugopalan, M., & Suresh, J.K. (2003). Knowledge management at Infosys. Retrieved January 11, 2004, from *www.Infy.com*

APPENDIX

Exhibit 1. Infosys U.S. Stock Data, 1997–2002

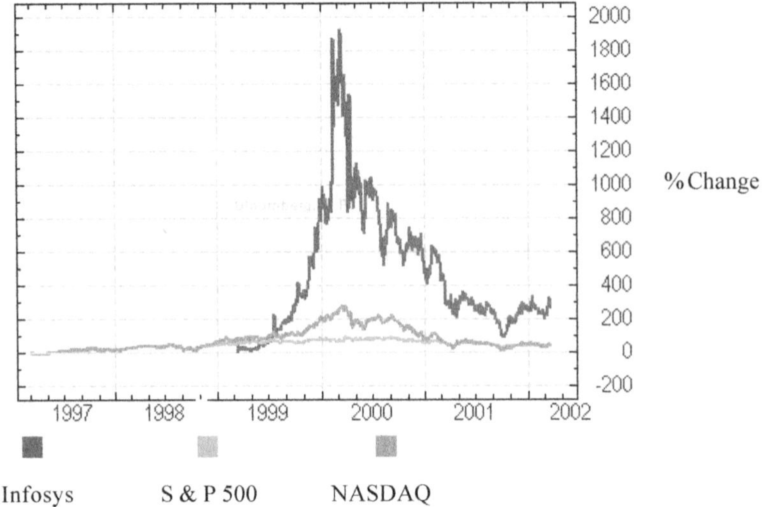

Source: Garud, Kumaraswamy, & Malhotra (2003)

Exhibit 2. Infosys's revenue growth over the years, 1994–2003

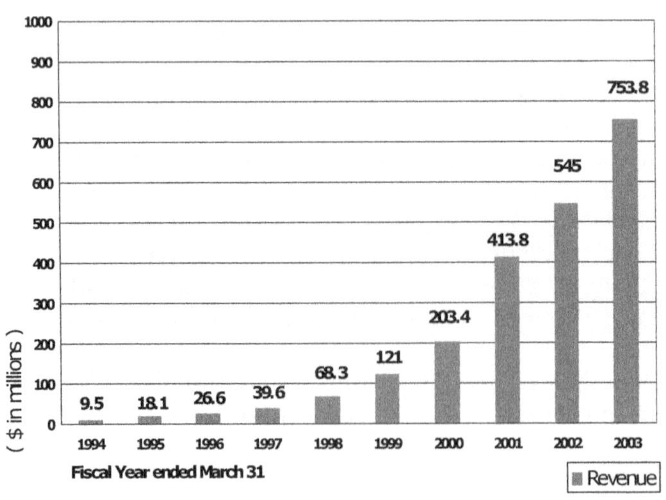

Source: Infosys

Exhibit 3. Infosys timeline (1981–2003)

1981	Year of incorporation in India
1987	Opened first international office in the US
1992	IPO in India
1993	Successfully listed in India Obtained ISO 9001/TickIT Certification
1995	Set up development centers across cities in India
1996	Established e-business practice Set up first European office in UK
1997	Attained SEI-CMM Level 4 Set up office in Toronto, Canada Set up Engineering Services practice
1998	Established Enterprise Solutions practice
1999	Listed on NASDAQ Crossed $100 million in annual revenues Attained SEI-CMM Level 5 Opened offices in Germany, Sweden, Belgium, and Australia and two development centers in the US
2000	Awarded the National Award for Excellence in Corporate Governance by the Government of India Crossed $200 million in annual revenue Set up development centers in Canada and the UK
2001	Crossed $400 million in revenues Rated Best Employer of India in a study by *Business Today*-Hewitt Associates
2002	Touched $0.5 billion in annual revenues Declared Most Admired Knowledge Enterprise (MAKE) for Asia region
2003	Declared Most Admired Knowledge Enterprise (MAKE) globally Banking software chosen by ABN AMRO Bank for China region

Source: Infosys

Exhibit 4a. Infosys financial results, FY03 and FY02

Statement of cash flows - (USD Million)	**FY03**	**FY02**
Cashflows from Operating Activities		
Net Income	194.87	164.47
Gain on sale of property, plant and equipment	(0.00)	(0.02)
Depreciation	37.02	33.61
Amortization of intangible assets	2.36	-
Provision for investments	3.22	-
Deferred tax benefit	(2.42)	(2.00)
Amortization of stock compensation expenses	4.80	5.01
Changes in assets and liabilities		
Trade accounts receivable	(37.66)	(7.20)
Prepaid expenses and other current assets	(5.24)	1.08
Unbilled revenue	(15.44)	(3.13)
Income taxes	(3.92)	0.87
Accounts payable	**0.42**	**(0.03)**
Client deposits	0.92	1.08
Unearned revenue	9.49	(3.75)
Other accrued liabilities	22.76	1.49

Exhibit 4a. Infosys financial results, FY03 and FY02 (cont.)

Net cash provided by operating activities	**211.18**	**191.48**
Cashflows from Investing Activities		
Expenditure on property, plant and equipment	(43.16)	(68.35)
Expenditure on intangible assets	(3.55)	-
Sale of property, plant and equipment	0.07	0.34
Loans to employees	(7.25)	(5.55)
Purchase of investments	(0.05)	(2.20)
Net cash used in investing activities	(53.94)	(75.76)
FINANCING ACTIVITIES:		
Proceeds from issuance of common stock	2.81	0.96
Issuance of preferred stock by subsidiary	**10.00**	-
Payment of dividends	(33.91)	(22.90)
Net cash used in financing activities	**(21.10)**	**(21.94)**
Effect of exchange rate changes on cash	7.73	(7.37)
Net increase in cash and cash equivalents	143.87	86.41
Cash and cash equivalents (beginning)	210.49	124.08
Cash and cash equivalents (end)	354.36	210.49

Source: Infosys Annual Report

Exhibit 4b. Infosys financial results, FY03 and FY02

Balance Sheet as at (US$ million)	**FY03**	**FY02**
Current Assets		
Cash and cash equivalents	354.36	210.49
Trade accounts receivable, net of allowances	109.12	69.02
Deferred tax assets	0.29	0.77
Prepaid expenses and other current assets	24.38	15.24
Unbilled revenue	19.70	3.64
Total current assets	507.85	299.16
Property, plant, and equipment, net	157.19	147.20
Intangible assets, net	6.47	-
Deferred tax assets	7.26	4.56
Investments	4.61	7.78
Prepaid income taxes	4.45	-
Other assets	16.45	12.46
TOTAL ASSETS	**704.28**	**471.16**
Current Liabilities		
Accounts Payable	0.43	-
Client Deposits	3.21	2.22
Other accrued liabilities	46.25	22.42
Income tax payable	-	0.68
Unearned revenue	13.20	3.46
Total current liabilities	63.09	28.78
Noncurrent liabilities	5.19	-
Preferred stock of subsidiary	10.00	
Stockholders' Equity	8.60	8.60
Additional paid-in capital	127.04	123.08
Accumulated other comprehensive income	(31.44)	(45.44)
Deferred stock compensation	(2.82)	(7.62)
Retained earnings	524.62	363.76
Total stockholders' equity	626.00	442.38
TOTAL LIABILITIES AND STOCKHOLDERS' EQUITY	**704.28**	**471.16**

Source: Infosys Annual Report

Exhibit 4c. Intangible assets score sheet

External Structure	2003	2002	Internal Structure	2003	2002	Competence	2003	2002
GROWTH Revenue growth (%)	39	37	IT Value added (%)	4. 31	4. 57	Education Index of all staff	44,972	31,385
% revenue from famous clients	56	56	R&D Value added	0. 47	0. 66			
% revenue from exports	98	98	Total investment / value added (%)	7. 2	14. 4			
No. of new clients added this year	96	116						
			Proportion of support staff (%)	8. 9	9. 8	Value added/ engineer (INR lakhs)	26. 06	23. 95
EFFICIENCY Sales/client (in INR lakhs)	1,050	889						
			Sales/ support staff (INR lakhs)	316	257	Value added/ employee (INR lakhs)	23. 03	21. 61
STABILITY Repeat business revenue/ total revenue (%)	92	88	Average age of support staff (yrs.)	32. 1	30. 9	Average age of all employees (yrs.)	26. 6	26. 6
Sales - top clients/ total revenue (%)	5. 8	6. 1						
Sales - five largest clients/ total revenue (%)	23. 4	24. 1						
Sales - ten largest clients/ total revenue (%)	37. 3	39. 4						
One Million – Five Million $ clients	156	108						
Ten - Forty million $ clients	30	23						

Source: Infosys Annual Report

Exhibit 5. Revenue segmentation by service offering

Revenue Segmentation	**FY03**	**FY02**
SERVICE OFFERING		
Development	32.1%	40.0%
Maintenance including Y2K	28.2%	25.4%
Y2K	0.0%	0.0%
Reengineering	5.5%	9.3%
Other services	29.7%	22.8%
Total services	95.4%	97.6%
Products	4.6%	2.4%
Total	**100.0%**	**100.0%**

Source: Infosys Annual Report

Exhibit 6. Infosys PSPD Model

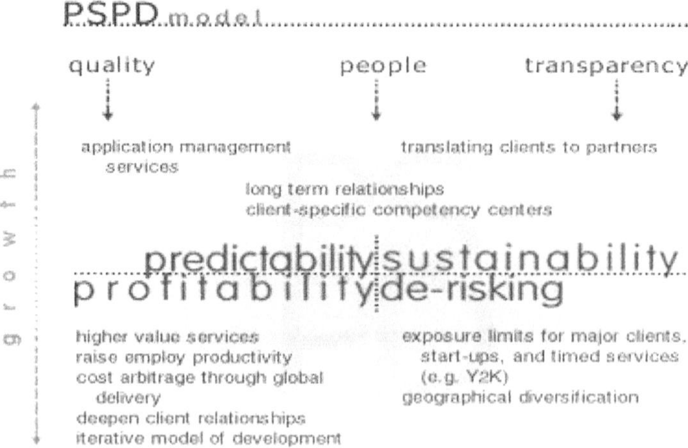

Source: Infosys

Exhibit 7. Infosys client mix

Revenue Segmentation	**FY03**	**FY02**
Client's Industry Class/Vertical Domain		
Manufacturing	16.4%	17.8%
Insurance, Banking, and Financial services	37.6%	33.7%
Telecom	15.2%	18.4%
Retail	11.4%	9.1%
Others	19.5%	21.0%
Total	**100.0%**	**100.0%**
Client concentration		
Top client contribution to revenues	6.1%	7.3%
Top-5 client contribution to revenues	24.1%	26.0%
Top-10 client contribution to revenues	39.4%	39.2%
Number of active clients	345	293
New clients added in the period	116	116
Repeat business %	**92%**	**88%**

Source: Infosys

Exhibit 8. Infosys Global Delivery Model (GDM)

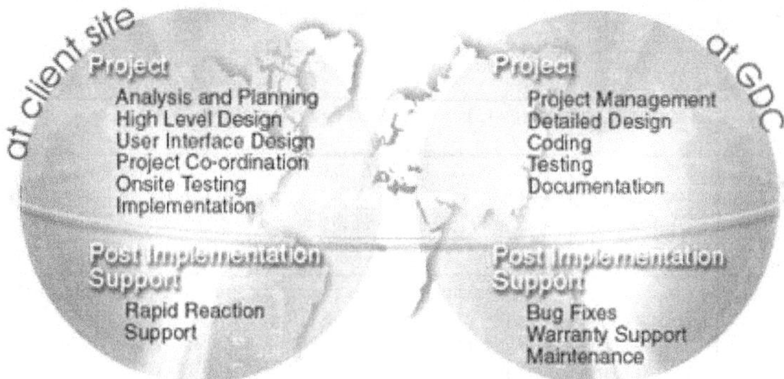

Source: Infosys

Exhibit 9. Infosys KM timeline

1992	Body of Knowledge (BoK)
1995	Online Technical Bulletin Board
1996	Corporate intranet unveiled
1997	Online Sales and Marketing System added
1998	Project Leader Toolkit added
1999	• People Knowledge Map (PKM); • KM initiative formalized
2000	• Integrated KM portal launched • Satellite servers added
2001	Subscription and Customization Services offered
2002	• Skills Database added • Integrated Search Option introduced
2003 +	• KM portal available on the extranet • KM Benefits assessment initiated • Increased focus on tacit knowledge sharing • Various communities of practice formalized across the organization

Source: Infosys

Exhibit 10. Levels of Infosys's Knowledge Management Maturity (KMM) Model

Level	***Label***	***Organizational Capability***
1	Default	Complete dependence on individual skills and abilities
2	Reactive	Ability to perform repeatable tasks
3	Aware	• Restricted ability for data-driven decision making • Restricted ability to leverage internal expertise • Ability to manage virtual teams well
4	Convinced	• Quantitative decision making for strategic and operational applications • High ability to leverage internal and external sources of expertise • Measurable productivity benefits through knowledge sharing • Ability to sense and respond proactively to changes in technology and business environment
5	Sharing	• Ability to manage organizational competence quantitatively • Streamlined process for leveraging new ideas for business advantage • Ability to shape change in technology and business environment

Source: Infosys

Chapter XVIII

Keeping the Flame Alive: Sustaining a Successful Knowledge Management Program

Eliot Rich, University of Albany, USA

Peter Duchessi, University of Albany, USA

EXECUTIVE SUMMARY

This case study looks at how to keep a knowledge management initiative going after it has been successful for a couple of years. This organization found that continuously measuring benefits from the knowledge management system and keeping the knowledge in the system fresh and relevant were key to long-term success. However, achieving this was difficult as improving quality added more work to the already-busy managers and measuring worth was difficult.

INTRODUCTION

Michelle Johnson was in a reflective mood. As director of System Management Solutions International's (SMSI) knowledge management staff, she had led a two-year project to turn the firm's experimental use of groupware into a viable and important corporate asset. Her vision of a technology-driven resource for sharing the corporation's expertise was in operation.

These first two years focused on the start-up issues that had stymied the knowledge management (KM) projects of others. Her team had managed to find a combination of formal and informal incentives that stimulated hundreds of staff members to share their experience with others around the firm. The technology architecture to connect the firm's worldwide offices was in place. Finally, senior management support for the effort was, for the moment, sufficient to fund the current effort.

Now she needed to consider what was next for the program. The satisfaction Ms. Johnson felt over the successful integration of KM techniques into the company was tempered by concerns about the program's future. Surveys showed that staff satisfaction and participation was quite high, and user feedback about the quality and breadth of the KM system was positive, though not as high as earlier in the year. There was particular uncertainty about the attitude of SMSI's partners, who paid for the program but did not receive the direct knowledge benefits seen by the field workers.

The planning for future KM activities at SMSI needs to focus on sustaining the momentum and effectiveness of the program as the firm moved from a booming consulting industry to one where projects were becoming more scarce. Thus, the critical issue becomes maintaining the current success of its KM initiatives and system, given both external and internal changes.

BACKGROUND

SMSI, founded in the early 1970s, is a publicly held business consulting and IT services firm. During the last three decades, the firm has completed tens of thousands of engagements, ranging in intensity from a few staff weeks to hundreds of staff years. While technology implementations were still the main focus of the firm, its expertise in change management and specialized content areas (e.g., human resource management, government operations, financial reporting) have become an important part of the firm's portfolio. By most measures, the firm has been very successful. Gross revenues of the firm have grown steadily since its founding, reaching $1 billion in the late 1990s. In parallel, staffing has grown from about 4,500 employees in 1994 to almost 9,000 by the end of 1999 (Figure 1).

Figure 1. SMSI revenues and staffing

SMSI

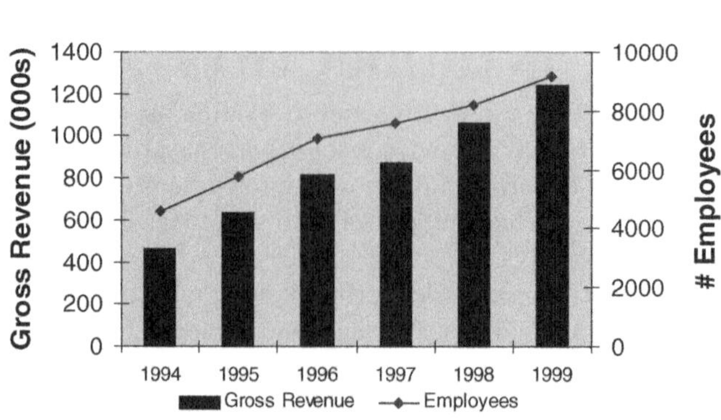

SETTING THE STAGE

The Resource Structure of SMSI

SMSI is organized around lines of business and geographic regions. Within each region, it followed what is more or less a prototypical staffing model, consisting of three professional levels. Consultants are the "worker bees" responsible for the execution of specific tasks. Managers, the next level in the organization, organize, instruct, and review consultant work as well as develop work that requires more experience. Partners, at the high end of the structure, are responsible for leadership of major projects, define strategy for the firm, develop business opportunities, and maintain client relations. These three roles are "the grinders, the minders, and the finders" of the consulting business (Maister, 1997). These professional roles are backstopped by a support organization that sustains the day-to-day operations of the firm.

The Role of KM

Consulting is fundamentally a knowledge-based business. Clients use consultants to provide hard-to-develop skills, retaining them for short periods, the duration of a project, or sometimes longer. Over the last decade a transition has occurred in the consulting business, away from treating every problem as a unique opportunity, and toward rapid leverage of experience. This creates a new perspective on the role of the consultancy, where consultants act as information brokers, using connections across industries and projects to identify classes of problems, and applying their collective skills to solve them (Sarvary, 1999). Consulting firms act as a resource hub, with networks of staff that can reuse their knowledge for multiple clients. Finding the right skills within the consultancy and bringing them to bear quickly is a key selling point. Therefore, consulting firms need to find techniques for sharing their experience quickly, and creating the linkages and team structures that attract clients.

Staffing and Knowledge Retention

Every year consulting firms organize hiring plans based on their projected project demand. Many recruit from undergraduate and graduate programs, preferring to train staff in their unique approach to business and clients. New consultants face a great deal of work pressure and competition for managerial positions, and a large proportion of them leave before moving to the managerial ranks. The combined effects of long work hours, uncertain career paths, and competitive pressure for recognition all exert adverse pressure on junior staff. Similarly, there is churn in the managerial ranks as experienced professionals try to develop the client relationships required to support promotion to partner. A small proportion of managers achieve partner status; the remainder may change firms or launch other opportunities. There is something of an "up-or-out" structure, similar to that seen in law firms.

Concern about turnover is of greater concern during upswings in the market, as there is more competition for talented staff. In these times, firms must replace staff recruited away by competitors as well as recruit new consultants to meet swelling demand for services. These two forces have generated hiring rates as high as 40% per year for some large companies, which in turn create a great strain on the firms to train and integrate these new employees into the firm.

Turnover also affects the knowledge available to the firm. When experienced staff leave the firm, they take their knowledge with them. Rather than risk the loss of this knowledge, consulting firms actively collect and codify project-based materials, write practice guides and methodologies, and synthesize their experience in written, oral, and multimedia forms. When new inexperienced staff arrive, these codified assets provide significant leverage. The "push" model of individual training and mentoring of juniors by seniors has given way to a "pull" model, where experience is made available on demand through databases and communications networks.

KM in Consulting Companies

The staggering rate of change in the volume of information has accelerated the need for information and knowledge management. Individuals and companies that have their fingers on the pulse of the newest and most useful information can command a high price for their knowledge, if they can bring it to their clients quickly. This, in turn, means that the experts must access and leverage their own knowledge acquisition and retention, so that they always have the best information for their clients.

The consulting environment has always required mobility and flexibility, and the knowledge resources of the firm must be at the fingertips of consultants in the field. As one manager put it, "We're all road warriors now." It's not clear if staff spend more time on the road than in the past, or if they are just expected to be available and productive whether in or out of the office. Consultants are expected to use technology, primarily e-mail, and to remain connected to the corpus of the firm. In these firms, successful knowledge management implementations mean that the road warriors can bring the intellectual resources of the firm with them to client sites. It is not surprising that large consulting firms were also early adopters of knowledge management technologies (e.g., Alavi, 1997; Bartlett, 1996; Chard, 1997; Reimus, 1997). Knowledge management is a competency of interest to consulting clients, and the ability to demonstrate internal implementation competence and benefit validates the credentials of the firm to potential clients.

CASE DESCRIPTION

For SMSI, the ability to leverage its existing experience through KM technology came none too soon. The late 1990s were very busy times for technology and management consultants, and SMSI rode the leading edge of the boom. To meet customer demand, SMSI hired staff at an unprecedented rate. At the same time, staff turnover was very high, peaking at about 20% per year, as the combination of work pressure and opportunities in a skill-seller's market makes retaining staff difficult. Much of the turnover was among staff with experience in the most current software platforms. As new skills were learned, many staff left SMSI to chase better offers. This staff churn created a continuing outflow of knowledge from the firm's resources.

Surging growth, technical change, and high turnover created great pressure within the firm to capture and disseminate knowledge and experience. Lessons learned in one project might be immediately useful elsewhere, and certainly would provide value to someone else in the firm. When the firm was smaller, staff with questions could discuss them with others in the same office; now, expertise was more scattered and less available. Individuals did not know each other as well as they did in the past, and there has been a sense of reluctance to contact individuals outside the immediate workgroup.

Long-time employees are concerned about the effects of rapid growth on the organization's culture of information sharing. One termed the effect "intellectual sprawl," where consultants in different business units were re-creating the same work products and techniques independently. In their view, there was not enough sharing of the lessons of technology and engagement management, at a time when the proportion of inexperienced staff grew. While the knowledge management program attempts to facilitate sharing, there was still a sense that the best ideas were not always available, and that human contacts were superior to the use of an information system.

Developing SMSI's KM Program

The development of a formal KM program at SMSI was facilitated by the firm's history in information systems consulting. From a practical standpoint, the firm was well positioned to implement the complex technological infrastructure associated with KM. The firm's leadership committed to solve the technical success and the cultural and social challenges that KM presents. This recognition allowed SMSI to avoid some of the stumbling blocks that less sophisticated firms faced.

Experimentation with KM technologies started in 1992, with the introduction of Lotus Notes as a groupware tool. By 1998, almost 100 Notes servers were in place, and all office-based personnel had desktop access to the tool; most field personnel had shared access through one or more Internet-enabled computers. When the tool was adopted as a firm-wide standard, a number of special interest groups (SIGs) were established, and used Lotus Notes as a tool to facilitate discussions across offices on topics of mutual interest as well as an e-mail backbone. Most were informal discussions on emerging technologies; these discussions rarely lasted more than a few months as individual knowledge needs changed. Often they became places to ask direct questions from individuals across the firm, with additional follow-up through telephone calls. Occasionally some synthesized databases stimulated working papers or, eventually, encapsulations of SMSI's best practices.

To stimulate further development and sharing of information, SMSI established a Knowledge Colleagues program. Staff working in business units proposed short-term technology experiments or projects, resulting in the development of a paper or prototype to share throughout the firm. Individuals were released from their project work for two weeks to work on their tasks, with the expectation that they would also contribute additional time to complete their work. A series of activities dealing with knowledge sharing was established in late 1996, facilitating transfer of information across several core disciplines around the firm. The initial series included systems development, business process reengineering, customer value management, engagement management, change management, advanced technologies, and decision analytics. Knowledge management and electronic commerce were added in 1998, along with the firm-wide rollout of the technology platform.

Figure 2. SMSI Knowledge Colleagues projects

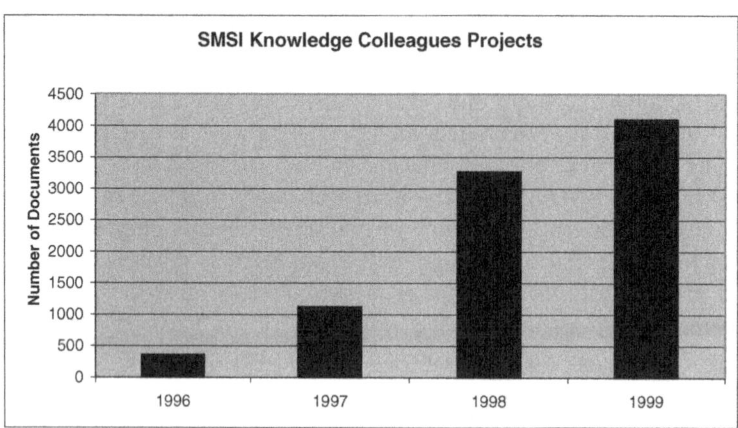

During these first few years, the list of completed contributions grew from 400 to over 4,000 topics (Figure 2). This growth was a mixed blessing. Ms. Johnson noted that the more recent documents were not as useful as earlier ones. The initial topics tended to be of more general interest, and later ones were more specialized to particular problems and industries, and less relevant to the general population. In addition, there was less review of the contents as the number of documents grew.

SMSI's KM program extended beyond the development of the Colleagues program. A small headquarters-based unit acted as a clearinghouse for the firm's current and past activities. Databases of current activities across the firm, model deliverables, and frequently asked questions were made available. They were representative samples of well-received project materials, client proposals, templates, and general advice on the topics at hand. Experts and thought leaders in the topic area were identified, and their particular expertise highlighted. Discussion databases, where questions may be posed to these experts, received several postings a day. These discussion databases could be initiated by anyone in the firm, and there were literally thousands of them. No central repository was maintained, and the contents were often informal and somewhat wild and wooly.

SMSI's Knowledge Colleagues also agreed to participate in the discussion databases and make themselves available for ad hoc questions around the firm. Through their responses, the Colleagues extend the informal information network that corporate growth was dissolving. The time they spend in this role was not billable to any project, and went largely unmonitored. Here, more than anywhere, the altruistic nature of the knowledge-sharing experiment was seen, as individuals who answered questions were often contacted off-line for further explanations.

CURRENT CHALLENGES

The success of the SMSI KM program was quite remarkable. Almost all of SMSI's staff used the KM system in some fashion. The most pleased were the junior and mid-level consultants, who found ready reference for their project needs and routine questions about the firm. Managers and partners used the system to locate experts for use in proposals and to fill staffing gaps for projects. This was particularly valuable when there were few available resources, and there seemed to be a constant scramble to match client needs with experienced consultants.

Of all the various facets, Ms. Johnson was proudest of the Knowledge Colleagues program. Here, more than 800 members of the professional staff, almost 10% of the firm's employees, were volunteering time to share their experience with others around the firm. This was the essence of the cultural change that SMSI needed to leverage its knowledge capital. The program's participants were eager to add new materials to the collections available across the firm, as their contributions were noted in their annual performance reviews as an important contribution to the culture of the firm. While not a large measure, there was clearly some recognition in the review process that was felt to factor into raises and promotions.

Now that the program is in place, Ms. Johnson's challenge is to establish that SMSI's KM can continue to provide value. Will the KM system continue to provide useful information? She considered the primary driver of the KM program's success to date: the perceived positive effect on users and the firm.

User value is subjective, resting in how the user applies the knowledge to the problem at hand. A KM system may provide a specific answer to a direct question, or it may provide some insights into an issue that add value in a new context. In a knowledge-intensive industry, the results of answers may be easy to measure (such as the foregone cost for work that could be borrowed, rather than repeated), or may be very difficult to quantify (as with the value of a confirming perspective prior to taking a decision).

To facilitate the acceptance of the KM program, there was no cost to using the system. It was hoped that a free system to share knowledge would demonstrate its value organically, rather than through a pricing mechanism. It was expected that the free system would demonstrate particular deliverables (i.e., training courses) that might be subject to internal development charges.

With KM systems, as with other types of decision support tools, users who do not like the tool may choose to ignore it or not contribute to it. Thus one measure of user value is the level of participation. In traditional transaction-oriented IT systems, users have little choice about using the technology. They may love it, or they may hate it, but the computer is still integral to performing their jobs, and users are compelled to make do with the system. Thus continued participation and inquiry of a KM system may be used as a surrogate for satisfaction.

In turn, satisfaction with a KM system often generates additional demands for knowledge. The more value users found with the information contained in the system, the more likely staff were to come back with additional requests and inquiries (and the higher the costs of the system to develop new materials). The evidence that requests were growing was the major justification for continued funding of KM efforts at SMSI.

A more formal measure of effect was still elusive. In manufacturing environments, it is possible to identify the value of knowledge through reductions in defects, worker productivity, or other production-based metrics. In consulting, the results of learning and transferred experience through the use of KM tools tended to be a better quality of ideas, rather than simply finishing work more quickly. One consultant noted, tongue-in-cheek, that finishing work more quickly might even be against the firm's principles, particularly if the client was paying by the hour. The senior managers reviewing the effects of KM on the organization were asked to think about softer and more anecdotal measures than they were used to, with user satisfaction being a primary indicator of continued success.

Of course, reasoned Ms. Johnson, this would likely work in reverse as well: A KM system that did not address the needs of the users would get less use. Requests would taper off, starting a possible downward spiral toward obsolescence. Such a spiral would be hard to identify beforehand, and would be difficult to reverse. Thus sustaining a KM program requires several critical adjustments to the KM program to maintain the positive momentum and continually demonstrate the KM system's value to users and the firm. Yet, Ms. Johnson thought, how does SMSI (or any firm for that matter) meet these challenges?

Encouraging the collection of knowledge from a large number of contributors had several unanticipated consequences. The most concrete was a large accumulation of materials, not all of which were adding to the available knowledge for several reasons. First, redundant materials have little incremental impact. At the outset of the Knowledge Colleagues program all contributions were welcome. In response, staff posted their planning tools, interim deliverables, and project documents for use by others. Over time, though, the incremental value of these postings to others decreased. When searching for a topic, many users looked only at the first few hits. Having seven or eight or 15 examples of a project schedule made little difference in outcome, but they do consume resources.

Second, collected materials become obsolete, and their effects on the organization decrease. The collection of project materials and examples permitted the dissemination of new information quickly. Over time, though, the older materials became less useful as techniques change and market requirements shift. In the fast-changing world of information technology consulting, some materials were really only useful for a few weeks or months. After that, they might be misleading or just plain wrong. If users of the KM system find that materials are not current, their satisfaction will drop, and they are less likely to ask for information in the future.

Third, the "core knowledge" needed by the firm was about to change because the marketplace was about to change as well. When SMSI's KM program was launched, the firm was struggling with integrating thousands of newly hired employees into the fabric of the firm. When a new hire arrives, the KM system gives him or her a ready source for contacts around the firm and exposure to SMSI's project portfolio. This eased the transition into the firm, and made these new hires much more productive.

With the slowing of the consulting marketplace, however, the firm may not be hiring staff as quickly, and the value of indoctrination-focused knowledge falls. In a declining market, emergent needs revolve around developing and maintaining customers and looking for new opportunities, rather than sharing knowledge about techniques to complete projects. The SMSI partners, who made up the firm's marketing and management teams, needed support in their quest to obtain work. Internal data sources, while providing information on the firm's existing project and resource portfolios, provided limited value in their search.

SMSI was willing to pay for the KM infrastructure and support participation in knowledge activities. This senior management support came from the desire to retain and reward key employees, and less from any formal calculation of the knowledge benefits to the firm. In a time of high turnover, any reasonable technique to retain staff through formal and informal recognition was deemed useful. Even in the absence of financial value, the firm's partners and senior executives believed that the program was helping the firm manage its growth in a time of technical change and rapid expansion of staff.

The belief in the potential of KM to sustain the company through this period of growth was most manifest in the recognition of Knowledge Colleagues. Participation in the program was specifically considered during staff personnel reviews, and Colleagues were given special business cards that identified them as participants. This provided both financial and psychological incentives to participate.

As she considered these observations, Ms. Johnson saw that they interacted in a complex way. Firm growth stimulated demand for knowledge, and the programs she developed helped to meet that need. The internal programs and incentives created an active knowledge-sharing environment. Was there more "knowledge sharing" than could be maintained while preserving quality? Should there be additional screening or reviews put in place? What effects would such changes have on the culture of the firm and incentives to provide knowledge?

Forces external to the firm would also affect what direction KM should take. SMSI had benefited from the explosive growth in e-commerce paired with the millennial-driven Y2K systems revisions. The suddenness of these industry changes created an extreme demand for information and solution reuse, which provided great leverage from the collected knowledge assets of the firm. There was little expectation that this type of work would continue at the same pace, and much of this previously valuable information would no longer be needed. The cost of keeping existing materials is small, as long as they are correct.

What new knowledge needs would emerge when markets start to decline? Integrating new staff was going to be less important. What knowledge will be needed to maintain SMSI's revenue and opportunities for growth? Are there unmet internal markets for knowledge that might still be exploited? This is another area Ms. Johnson wanted to explore.

The internal KM program at SMSI needed to shift its focus from creating a knowledge-sharing organization to one that manages its knowledge as an asset that depreciates over time. The success of the program would be based on maintaining the value and quality of its contributions to its users. In addition, a somewhat shaky forecast for SMSI's services would affect the willingness to support programs that do not demonstrate bottom-line contributions. Was there a way to directly demonstrate the value of knowledge sharing to the partners of the firm?

She believed that ongoing investment is needed, but was not sure how should it be applied. Is the development of new knowledge more important than cleaning up and review of older information? Are the incentives in place adequate to keep the internal knowledge channels open? What about developing new markets for KM? What should be the focus of her team's activities?

EPILOGUE

The Manager's Actions

In late 1999, Ms. Johnson unveiled her plans for creating a sustainable KM program for SMSI. There were two major threads to her plan. First, she believed that it was necessary to maintain the KM resource as a source of reliable, solid information. While the Knowledge Colleagues program had engaged thousands of people in the firm, some of the materials were not well regarded. Second, she needed to establish the worth of the program in a formal manner.

To meet the first objective, she revised the Colleagues program's structure. Starting in 2000, all new contributions were reviewed by senior managers of the firm to ensure their applicability and accuracy before they were accepted for distribution. In addition, all the existing materials were reread for continuing value, with revisions or deletions as required. A cap of 500 new topics per year was put in place, roughly the same number of contributions as in the first year of the program. Ms. Johnson felt that this was about the maximum number of documents that could be adequately reviewed each year.

At first, limiting the number of contributions did increase the quality of the contributions, as there was now a need to weed out weaker materials. This had a secondary effect, however, as rejected materials discouraged participation in other aspects of knowledge sharing among previously enthusiastic junior staff.

The increased emphasis on quality necessarily also increased the workload on the managers and partners who participated in the Colleagues program. These staff had the experience and breadth of knowledge to evaluate the usefulness of contributions to the firm, and their applicability beyond a particular project. The change of their role from creator to reviewer was unwelcome, and their enthusiasm for the voluntary nature of the program was shaken. To counter this anticipated shift in collegial spirit, SMSI agreed to maintain the formal (i.e., financial) recognition for those staff still participating in the program.

The second goal, establishing the worth of the KM program, remained elusive. Throughout the program's introduction, the KM staff was careful to collect any anecdote about the financial worth of materials obtained through its offices. War stories of projects working on opposite sides of the globe shared information and materials were disseminated. A set of user surveys were conducted to ask for estimates of value from users; these yielded highly suspect results, particularly one that estimated that the KM program yielded half the net revenue of the firm for 1998. The continuing internal support of the program was still largely based on the belief that it was working, and that competitors were doing it as well, rather than concrete value.

Longer-Term Results

The emergent recognition of the need to balance volume of collected knowledge and maintaining quality and was disrupted by forces outside the control of Ms. Johnson and the KM staff. The postmillennial slowdown in IT consulting drastically changed the SMSI workplace, and in turn, the KM program. The initial changes came from a drastic drop in new project work. As projects completed, there were fewer new assignments, and more staff went unassigned. By late 2000, hiring was frozen, and the turnover rate dropped to about 2% as competitors no longer hired skilled staff away.

In an attempt to shore up their finances, SMSI stopped funding all activities that did not directly contribute to revenue. Development of knowledge materials for training and indoctrination work was curtailed, particularly as virtually no new staff was joining the company. KM programs, while believed important, were carried as an overhead expense to the firm, and the financial support was withdrawn.

The nonfinancial incentives for participating dried up as well, as staff became more concerned about maintaining their own positions than assisting others for the good of the firm. There was great pressure to "tend to one's own garden," and use whatever time was available to develop leads for potential projects, rather than participating in the Colleagues program. Indeed, this was a rational perspective, as a series of layoffs dropped the payroll to 7,200 by 2001.

By mid-2001, much of the KM program, including the Knowledge Colleagues program, had been dismantled. Ms. Johnson left SMSI to join a new consultancy firm that specialized in knowledge management, along with many of her staff. The KM program continued at a much smaller scale, focusing on market intelligence and skill building for the SMSI staff.

Lessons Learned

The final straw for the KM system was the weakness in SMSI's markets, and the reaction of its management to reduce funding. This was not in the scope of control of the KM managers. Nevertheless, there are several elements that may be taken away from the case.

- **More is not always better.** Developing a community of knowledge-sharing staff was a particular concern to SMSI's KM managers. To this end, their program emphasized a broad-based, inclusive approach that encouraged participation and knowledge sharing. After some time, however, the quality of the knowledge shared was not equal to the quantity that was available. This perception of dropping quality may have contributed to the program's later weakness. This problem would become more visible as the collection of accepted knowledge grew. A more selective process for accepting contributions, along with a process of vetting and reviewing the content of the system, might have mitigated.
- **Monitoring usage.** Integrating a usage or rating scale into the knowledge system would have assisted in identifying materials that were outdated or not widely applicable. More modern KM systems than that available at SMSI recognize this need, and assign weights to materials that have been evaluated by the users as useful or not. Examples where this is present include the customer service sites at Symantec and Microsoft, which ask users to rate the usefulness of retrieved items.
- **Recognizing the stakeholders.** While the SMSI program clearly recognized the needs of junior consultants and managers, it was less successful in developing the same kind of respect among partners, who ultimately paid for the system. For this group, the anecdotal evidence that the KM program was useful was not sufficient to continue its funding as the financial position of SMSI worsened. In comparison, a competitor firm spent considerable effort developing marketing and prospect management knowledge bases for the partners. When faced with the same declin-

ing market, this competitor continued to fund its own KM system, in large part because it provided direct benefits to those making financial decisions about its future. The axiom "Follow the money" continues to ring true.

REFERENCES

Alavi, M. (1997). *KPMG Peat Marwick U. S.: One giant brain* (Case Study No. 9-397-108). Boston: Harvard Business School.

Bartlett, C. (1996). *McKinsey & Company: Managing knowledge and learning* (Case Study No. 9-396-357). Boston: Harvard Business School.

Chard, A.M. (1997). *Knowledge management at Ernst and Young* (Case Study No. M-291). Palo Alto, CA: Stanford University.

Maister, D.H. (1997). *Managing the professional services firm*. New York: Free Press.

Reimus, B. (1997). Knowledge sharing within management consulting firms. Retrieved June 14, 1999, from *www.kennedyinfo.com/mc/gware.html*

Sarvary, M. (1999). Knowledge management and competition in the consulting industry. *California Management Review, 41*(2), 95–107.

Additional Sources

General Readings on KM:

www.KMWorld.com - *KM World Magazine*
www.km-forum.org/ - The Knowledge Management Forum
www.cio.com/research/knowledge/ - *CIO* Magazine KM Research Center

Specific readings on KM sustainability:

Rich, E. (1998, July 20–23). Limits to groupware-facilitated organizational learning in a consulting firm. Paper presented at the *Proceedings of the Sixteenth International Conference of the System Dynamics Society*, Quebec City, Canada.

Rich, E., & Duchessi, P. (2004, January 5–8). Modeling the sustainability of knowledge management programs. Paper presented at the *Proceedings of the Hawai'i International Conference on System Sciences*, Big Island, HI.

Section VII

Knowledge Management Outcomes

Chapter XIX

Knowledge Management for Healthcare: Using Information and Communication Technologies for Decision Making

A.N. Dwivedi, Coventry University, UK

Rajeev K. Bali, Coventry University, UK

R.N.G. Naguib, Coventry University, UK

EXECUTIVE SUMMARY

This case study is based on data collected from a prominent UK-based healthcare software house (Company X Ltd). The organization specializes in information and communication technologies (ICT) solution development, implementations, support services (including system and application support and telephone hotline support), and training and consultancy services. The organization prides itself on the fact that, by providing unique customized ICT solutions based on the Internet and database technologies, it is able to ensure that its healthcare-based clients (hospitals and allied organizations) have strategic advantages. The case study describes the outcome of a three-year research project, the chief outcomes of which were the development of a knowledge management (KM) conceptual model for use in the healthcare solutions sector as well as detailed advice and recommendations for the organization.

BACKGROUND OF THE CASE STUDY

This case study presents an extensive discussion on the cultural, organizational, and technical implications of introducing the knowledge management (KM) paradigm in the healthcare sector. Company X Ltd ("Company X") is a UK-based healthcare information and communication technologies (ICT) solutions provider. The organization was concerned about the possibility of a sharp decline in its share of the UK healthcare-ICT solution provider market. Company X was interested in identifying the emerging trends in the highly competitive UK-healthcare ICT solution provider market. The market is composed of such organizations as the National Health Service (NHS) Trusts (government-funded hospitals and healthcare centers) which were becoming more skeptical and demanding, both in terms of service and price for new and innovative ICT products.

To accomplish the goal of identifying the emerging trends in this highly competitive market, Company X initiated a research collaboration with the Biomedical Computing Research group (BIOCORE) based at Coventry University, UK. One of the primary objectives of the research was to investigate the efficacy of the KM paradigm for Company X in order to redesign itself to meet the changing healthcare ICT needs.

ORGANIZATIONAL BACKGROUND

Company X is a software house based approximately 40 miles west of central London. Employing 45 persons as well as a number of external associates, the company specializes in ICT solution development, ICT implementations, support services (including system and application support, telephone hotline support), training, and ICT consultancy services, all primarily for the healthcare sector.

Most of the business solutions provided by Company X are based on the Microsoft Windows platform and on Web browser technologies. The company has extensive experience in integrating Web browser technologies with information databases. The company prides itself on the fact that by providing unique customized Web-based ICT solutions and database technologies, it is able to ensure that its clients have strategic and operational advantages.

Provision of such high-quality customized ICT solutions necessitates Company X to work in close collaboration with its clients. As a result, the company has considerable contacts with a wide cross section of the community (such as social services, NHS Trusts, GP practices, councils, care agencies, and charities).

Company X was started approximately 12 years ago by a managerial team that had close ties with the SQLBase development team at ORACLE. The Company X managerial team was responsible for introducing SQLBase into the UK. The company is almost entirely owned by its employees, and all research and development at Company X is remunerated from income generated from its consultancy services.

The original Company X business plan was to focus on the development of client-server solutions using Microsoft Windows, SQL, and information databases. Company X is also a synergy partner of Centura Software (formerly Gupta), an ORACLE reseller, an Informix business partner, and offers the services of Microsoft-certified trainers. Company X is also a Microsoft healthcare solutions partner. Company X also has an excellent relationship with a local telemarketing company that uses Company X to host its strategic telemarketing database for Europe, the Middle East, and Africa. Company X has proprietary rights over several solutions, the most prominent of which are a set of toolkits used for the rapid implementation and maintenance of customized solutions running on Internet-based technologies. The organization provides professional services in the following areas:

1. **ICT Consultancy and Application Development:** The company has specialist skills in creating solutions relating to executive information solutions, management information systems, and office automation systems.
2. **Business Expertise:** Company X has considerable expertise in the use of ICT for creating solutions to assist its clients in achieving their business objectives. The company has created ICT solutions for a wide range of industry sectors including healthcare, banking, distribution, finance, insurance, manufacturing, oil, and gas.
3. **Application Consultants:** Company X has acted as application consultants on a wide range of business issues across diverse industry sectors and has extensive experience in building client-server ICT solutions using component and object-oriented techniques. The unique synergistic use of these two technologies has allowed the firm to develop a reputation for building fast and efficient ICT solutions that are also cost effective. Its solutions allow it to save both time and money for its clients as the software code can be effectively reused. This also allows its clients to reduce their maintenance costs.
4. **MIS and EIS Consultants:** The company also offers services in building management information systems and executive information solutions. The unique selling proposition (USP) of Company X's MIS and EIS solutions is that they include a graphical user interface which provides clients with significant information, allowing them to have more control over strategic business activities.
5. **Technical and end-user training:** The company offers bespoke end-user training for all of its solutions. It offers specialized training courses that cover the key aspects of various application development languages and client-server solutions.
6. **Project Management:** Company X also acts as a project management consultant; in this capacity, its main role involves the coordination of all procedures and operations within the software application development life cycle of each project so as to ensure that other software projects are completed on time and within budget.

The organization has a diverse client base (over 300 clients) that consists of a cross section of industry and public sectors. The company also acts as an adviser and trainer to some of the largest software houses in the UK.

SETTING THE STAGE

The Company X Toolkit

As mentioned previously, Company X offers a set of integrated toolkits which have been customized for healthcare institutions (HIs). Currently, the toolkit has been implemented at over 24 National Health Service (NHS) Trusts throughout the UK. The toolkit consists of four main modules:

1. **Admin:** offers users the ability to control access to databases. It allows authorized administrators to ensure the integrity of the databases. It supports simultaneous management and control of information over several different vendor databases such as Microsoft SQL Server and Oracle SQL Base.
2. **Upload:** supports the rapid development of applications that allow users to automate electronic feeds between different databases. It automatically generates integrity rules whilst establishing connections between different databases.
3. **QuickBuild:** allows users to maintain information (records) that is being held in databases.
4. **Report Organizer:** is a tool that supports information search and retrieval and supports presentation of the same on word processing applications.

As the toolkit has been built using component technology, it is possible to rapidly build customized applications from these modules. This leads to low maintenance costs and saves additional costs for making add-on applications. The use of eXtensible Markup Language and eXtensible Stylesheet Language as primary standards in the development of the toolkit ensures that other software applications have the ability to interact with existing data in the toolkit, thereby ensuring true heterogeneity. As the HTTP interface is an integral part of the toolkit, all applications built with it are accessible via Web browsers.

In recent years, the healthcare ICT solution providers' market in the UK has undergone a rapid transformation, allowing the company to exploit new opportunities in the market. The company has noted that, in recent years, the existing exclusive suppliers to NHS Trusts had become outdated with regard to the quality of services offered to them as compared with the quality of services offered to clients in the commercial sector by other solution providers. This gave the company an opportunity to demonstrate its RAD (rapid application development) techniques to Trusts, allowing it to efficiently develop solutions for the NHS based on components developed for the commercial sector.

Company X has noted that the existing exclusive suppliers to NHS Trusts had also become outdated with regard to after-sales service, which it was offering. The company overcame this by ensuring that it always worked in partnership with Trusts, allowing it to demonstrate its widespread after-sales experience, lessons learned from ICT projects in other industry sectors (i.e., banking, distribution, etc.).

Examples of Relevant Healthcare IT Experience in NHS Trusts

Examples of relevant ICT experience in healthcare organizations include the XYZ Oncology Information System Project, a consortium of 24 NHS Trusts and a regional cancer registry. At the end of a lengthy vendor evaluation process, Company X was selected to be the sole supplier for the entire oncology project. The evaluation board felt that Company X's key attributes were the fact that its solution eliminated programming code, was accessible via a Web browser, and ran on a Windows platform.

Another project involved the ABC Group of Hospitals. The Group was part of the XYZ Oncology Information System Project consortium. After reviewing the results of the oncology solution, the ABC Group decided that they wanted to use Company X's EPR toolkit to implement a Clinical Knowledge Solution (CKS). The CKS was a suite of operational solutions, which shared a common set of information such as patient demographics, but which maintained its own patient-related information. The first applications supplied by Company X were in general surgery, theater management, and endoscopy. Company X and the ABC Group are currently examining ways of implementing a Trust-wide CKS.

Typical of many solution providers, Company X had undergone several organizational changes. In the past year or so, the organization had acquired another healthcare ICT solution provider (which created clinical systems for NHS Trusts). This had led to a rebranding of its healthcare business. The company has entered the financial services sector by creating an alliance with another solution provider in order to cater to business opportunities in the banking sector, particularly in asset management systems and securities trading systems.

At the time of writing, Company X was in discussions with a US-based solution provider that was investigating organizations in the UK healthcare-ICT market in order to form a joint venture, the precise details of which were still at a preliminary stage. Company X was hoping to learn from the proposed American partner's expertise as it employed over 2,000 people, supplies clinical, practice management, and home health solutions to over 100 US-based hospitals and practices, and processes transactions for over 500 physicians.

PREVAILING ROLE OF ICT IN DECISION MAKING

Within Company X, an evaluation of how knowledge was being created, stored, and retrieved was carried out. It was felt that the intranet was being used only as a storage area for company documents and more importantly, it was not serving as an enabler in context of knowledge creation and transfer.

Case Description

The participants in the research program who were specialists in healthcare management were given a brief which required them to formulate a strategy, the adoption of which would enable Company X to be a leading player in the UK healthcare-ICT solution provider market. These participants formulated a strategy for Company X. This strategy was presented in the form of two reports. The first report was a preliminary report, which presented an analysis of the challenges facing UK healthcare-ICT solution providers. In the second report, high-level details for an alternate product (i.e., creation of a software which would allow HIs to create customized KM solutions) which would complement Company X's existing main product offering (i.e., a set of integrated toolkits for healthcare-ICT solution provider market) were presented. The main thrust of the second report was that it was important for Company X's future to start creating clinical knowledge management (CKM) solutions for the healthcare sector.

Report No. 1: An analysis of the challenges facing UK healthcare-ICT solution providers

The research project commenced with an analysis of the global healthcare industry, the findings of which were presented in the form of a preliminary report to Company X's senior management. The salient points of the findings were as follows:

(1) There is information overload for healthcare stakeholders — the average physician spends about 25% of his or her time managing information and has to learn two million clinical specifics (The Knowledge Management Centre, 2000). This is further compounded by the fact that biomedical literature is doubling every 19 years. In the UK, each physician receives about 15 kg of clinical guidelines per annum (Wyatt, 2000). The above indicators illustrate how difficult it is for HIs and healthcare stakeholders (HSs) to successfully meet the healthcare information needs that are growing at an exponential rate.

The impact of the above, particularly from a societal perspective, is enormous. Up to 98,000 patients die every year as a result of preventable medical errors (Duff, 2002). The financial cost of these preventable medical errors cost from US $37.6 billion to $50 billion and, in numerical terms, account for more deaths than from car accidents, breast cancer, or AIDS (Duff, 2002). A study has pointed out adverse drug reactions result in more than 770,000 injuries and deaths each year (Taylor, Manzo, & Sinnett, 2002).

Another study reported in the *Harvard Business Review* noted that, as early as 1995, there were indications that "more than 5% of patients had adverse reactions to drugs while under medical care; 43% of those inpatient reactions were serious, life threatening, or fatal" (Davenport & Glaser, 2002, p. 107).

Advances in biomedical sciences have unalterably transformed the healthcare sector. Modern-day healthcare stakeholders (physicians, nurses, etc.) require information about "10,000 known diseases, 3,000 drugs, 1,100 lab tests, 300 radiology procedures ... 2,000 individual risk factors ... with 1,000 new drugs and biotechnology medicines in development" (Pavia, 2001, pp.12-13). An indicator of the enormity of the exponential increase in biomedical knowledge is witnessed by the growth in the National Library of Medicine's Medline database (4,500 journals in 30 languages, dating from 1996) of published literature in health-related sciences. In 2002, Medline contained 11.7 million citations and, on average, about 400,000 new entries were being added per year (Masys, 2002).

Observations evidence the impact of these exponential advances on individual stakeholders (Masys, 2002). Even if a typical modern-day healthcare stakeholder were to read two articles a day, it would take him or her 550 years to get updated with the new literature added every year (ignoring the existing literature level of 11.7 million). If we assume that about 1% of the new literature added every year is of relevance to a healthcare stakeholder, it would take a stakeholder five years (reading an average of two articles a day) to be updated with the healthcare advances of one year. It would appear that contemporary healthcare stakeholders are always behind the current state of knowledge (Masys, 2002).

(2) In today's information age, data have become a major asset for healthcare institutions. Recent innovations in information and communication technologies

(ICTs) have transformed the way that healthcare organizations function. Applications of concepts such as data warehousing and data mining have exponentially increased the amount of information that a healthcare organization has access to, thus creating the problem of "information explosion." This problem has been further accentuated by the advent of new disciplines such as bioinformatics and genetic engineering, both of which hold very promising solutions which may significantly change the face of the entire healthcare process from diagnosis to delivery (Dwivedi, Bali, James, Naguib, & Johnston, 2002b).

(3) Healthcare managers are being forced to examine costs associated with healthcare and are under increasing pressure to discover approaches that would help carry out activities better, faster, and cheaper (Davis & Klein, 2000; Latamore, 1999). Work flow and associated Internet technologies are being seen as an instrument to cut administrative expenses. Specifically designed ICT implementations, such as work flow tools, are being used to automate the electronic paper flow in a managed care operation, thereby cutting administrative expenses (Latamore, 1999).

(4) One of the most challenging issues in healthcare relates to the transformation of raw clinical data into contextually relevant information. Kennedy (1995, p. 85) has quoted Keever (a healthcare management executive) who notes that "Healthcare is the most disjointed industry ... in terms of information exchange.... Every hospital, doctor, insurer and independent lab has its own set of information, and ... no one does a very good job of sharing it."

(5) Advances in IT and telecommunications have made it possible for healthcare institutions to face the challenge of transforming large amounts of medical data into relevant clinical information (Dwivedi, Bali, James, & Naguib, 2001b). This can be achieved by integrating information using work flow, context management, and collaboration tools, giving healthcare a mechanism for effectively transferring the acquired knowledge, as and when required (Dwivedi, Bali, James, & Naguib, 2002a).

(6) Until the early 1980s, ICT solutions for healthcare used to focus on such concepts as data warehousing. The emphasis was on storage of data in an electronic medium, the prime objective of which was to allow exploitation of this data at a later point in time. As such, most of the ICT applications in healthcare were built to provide support for retrospective information retrieval needs and, in some cases, to analyze the decisions undertaken. This has changed healthcare institutions' perspectives toward the concept of utility of clinical data. Clinical data that was traditionally used in a supportive capacity for historical purposes has today become an opportunity that allows healthcare stakeholders to tackle problems before they arise.

(7) The contemporary focus is only on how best to disseminate the information, which could be fatal for the future of the healthcare applications (i.e., current use is static). Rather than creating or disseminating contextual knowledge, healthcare applications are being used to disseminate data and information. Future healthcare industry applications would have to support the transfer of information with context (i.e., such schemes would have to become dynamic in nature).

Such a scenario is likely to lead to a situation where healthcare institutions would be flooded with large amounts of clinical data. The introduction of the KM paradigm would enable these institutions to face the challenge of transforming large amounts of medical data into relevant clinical information. Future healthcare systems would have to shift their emphasis to deal with the intangibles of knowledge, institutions, and culture.

Healthcare institutions require a framework that would help to assess how best to identify and create knowledge from internal and external organizational experiences and how best to disseminate it on an organization-wide basis in a manner that ensures that the acquired knowledge is available for preventive and operative medical diagnosis and treatment when required. This would call for the contextual recycling of knowledge which has been acquired from the adoption of healthcare industry trials. KM can assist the healthcare industry to become viable by giving healthcare information *context*, so that other healthcare providers can use the healthcare industry to extract knowledge and not information. The healthcare industry is focused on the technology aspect of healthcare and that the key to success of the healthcare sector in the 21st century is an effective integration of technology with the human-based clinical decision-making process. It is therefore important for Company X to develop a conceptual healthcare management framework that encompasses technological, organizational, and managerial perspectives for the healthcare industry.

(8) The first report ended by stating that, from a management perspective, these new challenges have created the need for a CKM (Clinical Knowledge Management) system that can assist healthcare stakeholders in alleviating the problem of information explosion in the healthcare industry. The primary obstacle to the report's recommended integration of the KM paradigm in healthcare was the lack of any established framework or model which had its roots in either clinical or healthcare environments.

KM does not have any commonly accepted or de facto definition. However, KM has become an important focus area for organizations (Earl & Scott, 1999). It has been argued that KM evolved from the applications of expert systems and artificial intelligence (Liebowitz & Beckman, 1998; Sieloff, 1999). Almost all the definitions of KM state that it is a multidisciplinary paradigm (Gupta, Iyer, & Aronson, 2000) which has further accentuated the controversy regarding the origins of KM. It has been argued that the main aim behind any strategy of KM is to ensure that knowledge workers have access to the right knowledge, to the right place, at the right time (Dove, 1999).

One of the main factors behind widespread interest in KM is its role as a possible source of competitive advantage (Nonaka, 1991; Havens & Knapp, 1999). A number of leading management researchers have affirmed that the Hungarian chemist, economist, and philosopher Michael Polanyi was among the earliest theorists who popularized the concept of characterizing knowledge as "tacit or explicit" which is now recognized as the de facto knowledge categorization approach (Gupta et al., 2000; Hansen, Nohria, & Tierney, 1999; Zack, 1999).

Explicit knowledge typically takes the form of company documents and is easily available, whilst tacit knowledge is subjective and cognitive. One of the characteristics of explicit knowledge is that it can be easily documented and is generally located in the form of written manuals, reports, and/or found in electronic databases (Dwivedi, Bali, James, & Naguib, 2001a). As such, it is easily accessible and in many cases available on

Figure 1. The KM cycle (Dwivedi et al., 2002b) (modified from Skyrme, 1999)

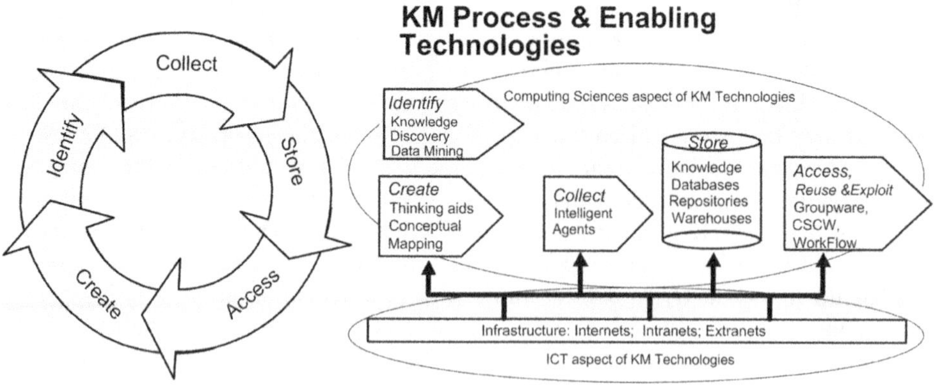

an organization's intranet. The cornerstone of any KM project is to transform tacit knowledge to explicit knowledge so as to allow its effective dissemination (Gupta et al., 2000). This can be best met by developing a KM framework. Authors such as Blackler (1995) have reiterated that the concept of knowledge is complex and, in an organizational context, its relevance to organization theory has not yet been sufficiently understood and documented. This is one of the fundamental reasons why KM does not have a widely accepted framework that can enable HIs in creating KM systems and a culture conducive to KM practices.

Figure 1 illustrates how the KM process revolves around a cycle. As illustrated, KM is underpinned by information technology paradigms such as computer-supported cooperative work (CSCW), work flow, intelligent agents, and data mining. According to Manchester (1999), a common point about software technologies such as (1) information retrieval, (2) document management, and (3) work flow processing is that they blend well with the Internet and related technologies (i.e., technologies that focus on dissemination of information).

Deveau (2000, p. 14) submits that "KM is about mapping processes and exploiting the knowledge database. It's taking people's minds and applying technology." Deveau (2000) also noted that information technology puts the organization in a position to state the currently available information in the organizational knowledge base. At this point, the role of ICT ends and the role of KM commences. As KM deals with the tacit and contextual aspects of information, it allows an organization to know what is important for it in particular circumstances, in the process maximizing the value of that information and creating competitive advantages and wealth.

A KM solution would allow healthcare institutions to give clinical data context, so as to allow knowledge derivation for more effective clinical diagnoses. In the future, healthcare systems would see increased interest in knowledge recycling of the collaborative learning process acquired from previous healthcare industry practices. The report put forward the notion that the healthcare sector has been exclusively focused on ICT

Figure 2. Requirements for a KM framework

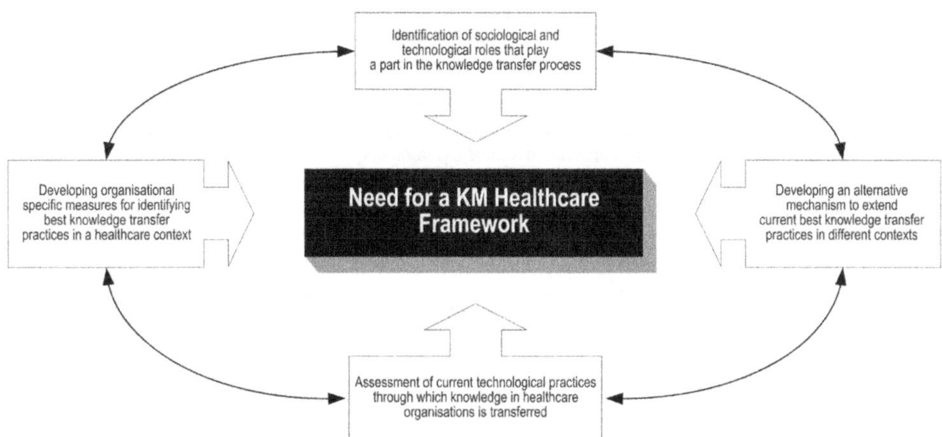

to meet the challenges described above and reiterates that this challenge cannot be met by an ICT-led solution.

KM initiatives should be incorporated within the technological revolution that is speeding across healthcare industry. There has to be balance between organizational and technological aspects of the healthcare process, that is, one cannot exist without the other (Dwivedi et al., 2001a). The report emphasized the importance of clinicians taking a holistic view of their organization. Clinicians therefore need to have an understanding of ICT in a healthcare context and a shared vision of the organization. Clinicians and healthcare administrators thus need to acquire both organizational and technological insights if they are to have a holistic view of their organization.

The KM paradigm can enable the healthcare sector to successfully overcome the information and knowledge explosion, made possible by adopting a KM framework that is specially customized for HIs in light of their ICT implementation level. Adoption of KM is essential for HIs as it would enable them to identify, preserve, and disseminate "best context" healthcare practices to different HSs.

The report additionally identified four elements (Figure 2) that would be integral to any such KM framework for the healthcare industry. It is emphasized that when an attempt is made to formalize knowledge in an institutional framework, the multidisciplinary nature of healthcare knowledge in an organizational context emerges.

Report No. 2: Creation of a template for clinical knowledge management (CKM) solutions for the healthcare sector

Based on empirical data from the healthcare sector, Company X was presented with a four-layer KM framework, the Organization Current Knowledge Design (OCKD) model, which could serve as a generic toolkit for HIs who are interested in developing an understanding on how to develop a KM strategy (see Figures 3 and 4). As one goes on

Figure 3. Four-layer OCKD KM framework

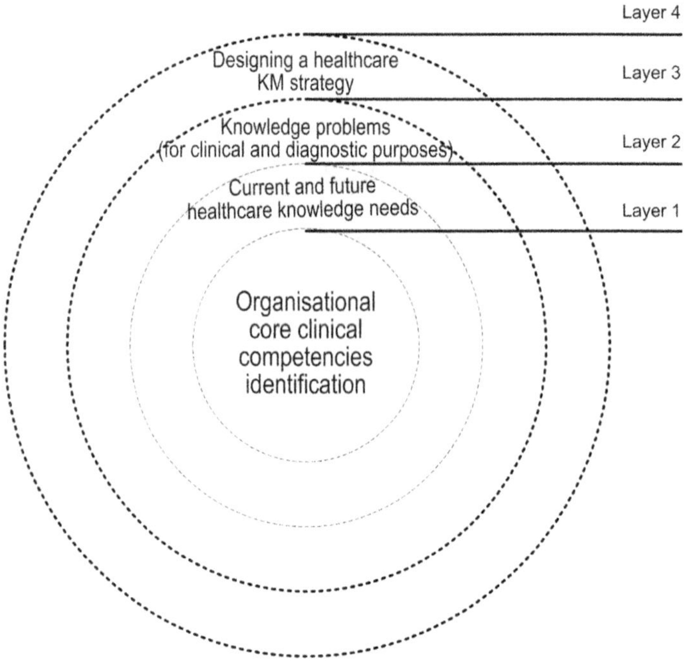

peeling one layer, another layer emerges, cumulating finally on the organizational core competencies.

The first step (layer 1 in Figure 3) in formulating a KM strategy involves the identification of the core competencies of an HI. This can be carried out in a number of ways (i.e., using the traditional five forces model by Porter [1985]). This process will enable an HI to be clear about its MOST (mission, objectives, strategy, and tactics). It would also allow it to notice how its MOST is aligned with its organizational core competencies, the EIC analysis (economic, industry, and company outlook). The next step would be a study to identify the HI's current and future knowledge needs (layer 2 in Figure 3). This would call for an analysis of the current technological infrastructure (i.e., support for m-health applications) that is in place for supporting knowledge transfer. After this process, an HI will need to assess how much knowledge should and can be codified (see layer 3 in Figures 3 and 4). This stage will result in the decision to adopt a KM strategy with emphasis on either personalization or codification. Irrespective of the strategy adopted, HIs would have to be clear on what constitutes best clinical innovative practices. This, to some extent, will help in capturing the tacit knowledge of clinical specialists. At the top layer (layer 4 in Figure 3), an HI has a KM strategy. Each HI can either adopt a KM strategy, which has emphases either on the tacit knowledge that resides in its resources or on a KM strategy that emphasizes the organizational processes: the codification strategy. This leads to the identification of relationships that exist between different types of knowledge (tacit or explicit) being transferred and to dissemination practices. It then results in a spiral transfer between the processes marked with the broken arrow signs (Figure 4).

Figure 4. Elaborated OCKD framework for Company X

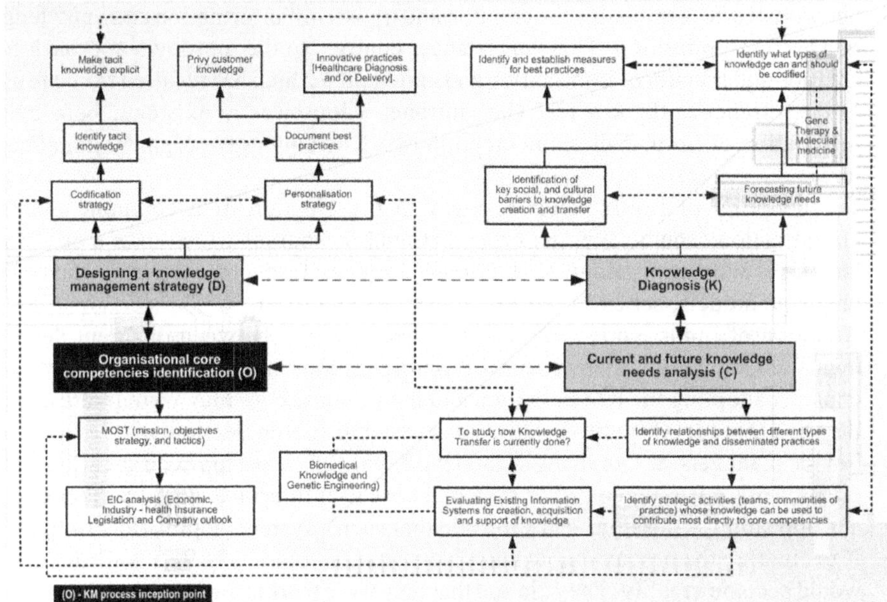

CURRENT CHALLENGES FACING THE ORGANIZATION

Impact of New ICT in Decision Making

Senior management at Company X noted that the existing ICT (i.e., the intranet) was not enabling users to create new knowledge and/or exploit existing knowledge. It was decided to create a new IT infrastructure, one which would be seen as an enabler and which would comprise of various tools. At the same time, it was decided to restructure existing pay and reward schemes (i.e., remuneration), so as to reward information/knowledge sharers (both at an individual and group level). It was also decided to bring about a change in the leadership style and organizational culture, so as to enable members of staff to develop a strong feeling of cultural affinity toward each other.

As a first step, Company X carried out a network-wide installation of Lotus Notes. At the same time, it offered financial and nonfinancial incentives to those teams and individuals who adopted Lotus Notes to capture and share best practices. This scheme was complemented by senior management communication initiatives that emphasized integration of the new IT infrastructure in a new organizational culture—one that emphasized knowledge sharing.

As a result of the above initiatives, the following developments took place:

1. Middle- and lower-level managers have started to enable and promote learning. As a consequence, communities of practice whose focus is on creation and transfer of best practices have evolved.

2. Another interesting observation was in the use of ICT (after the installation of Lotus Notes and creation of a KM-conducive organizational culture) — ICT was perceived to be responsible for creation and transfer of information and knowledge in a bottom-up fashion. This was in sheer contrast to the top-down approach for creation and transfer of information and knowledge which has resulted from the use of the intranet as the key ICT (i.e., intranet, which was in existence before the installation of Lotus Notes and creation of a KM-conducive organizational culture).
3. The adoption of Lotus Notes resulted in the creation of a common process classification scheme (i.e., an organizational thesaurus) which uses a common language and terminology that allows users to find presentations, data and language models, schemas, best practices, and so forth.
4. Adoption of Lotus Notes was seen to create synergy between different departments of Company X. This success promoted senior managers at Company X to consider adopting the KM paradigm and in this context — they were interested in the OCKD model (Figure 4). This is discussed further in Section 5.2.
5. Senior managers at Company X believed that the next step would call for the creation of a customized expert system whose user interface would be as friendly and appealing as possible. They did add that such a system would allow Company X to eliciting the best available knowledge, but it would be quite a while before it would become a reality. They did add that they were working toward their long-term goal of creating a customized expert system, which would complement their initiatives (i.e., Lotus Notes and the communities of practice).

Adoption of the OCKD Framework at Company X

The participants in the research program for Company X presented the OCKD framework to Company X. The accompanying report argued that it was important that Company X starts to create CKM solutions for the healthcare sector. It continued that, as a first step for building an enterprise-wide (i.e., entire hospital) CKM system, Company X should make separate CKM suites for the following key healthcare ICT systems:

1. Radiology Information Systems (RIS)
2. Patient Administration System (PAS)
3. Laboratory Information Systems (LIS)
4. Clinical Patient Record (CPR)
5. Pharmacy Systems (PS)
6. Nursing Systems (NS)

The report stressed that the above-mentioned CKM suites, once implemented individually, should automatically be able to interface with each other, thus making the vision of an enterprise-wide CKM system a reality for the healthcare industry. No UK-based healthcare ICT solution provider has come up with such a product, and in light of its findings in its preliminary report, creation of a product like an enterprise-wide CKM system would ensure that Company X becomes the undisputed market leader in the UK market.

The OCKD framework was very well received within Company X. However, senior management noted that there remained several barriers to the possible acceptance of the OCKD model:

- A key constraint would be getting the top management of NHS Trusts to support any new projects and that Trusts and hospital administrators had first to recommend KM products. This would require NHS Trusts and hospital administrators to be convinced of the utility of the KM paradigm. This would call for substantiation of the results obtained from KM trials, preferably in health-related scenarios.
- NHS Trusts are now particularly more skeptical and demanding, both in terms of service and price, and more so for new innovative ICT products. They felt that the KM concept would take a few years to develop into a mature product.
- The UK solution provider market is driven by the centralized buying procedure of the NHS, that is, the NHS Purchasing and Supply Agency, which is currently very cost sensitive. The need for a new KM system has to be recommended by the Agency.
- There is no measurement tool that could quantify the impact of the OCKD model on the processes of an organization.
- They also noted that there could be legal liabilities for the sellers of the model in case the stated best practices are not properly validated in a healthcare context.
- An additional key constraint was finance. Building an enterprise-wide CKM would require additional funds.
- Detailed supporting technical documentation for each CKM application had to be developed. This would take both time and money.

CONCLUDING COMMENTS

Company X is currently working with several NHS Trusts in an attempt to develop jointly an enterprise-wide CKM product. It remains convinced on the feasibility of the KM paradigm solving the problem of information explosion in healthcare. The company is also in agreement with the fact that the current focus on technological solutions will aggravate the problem of explosion in clinical information systems for healthcare institutions. It remains convinced that any potential solution has to come from a domain that synergistically combines people, organizational processes, and technology, thereby enabling HSs to have a holistic view of the entire healthcare continuum and that an enterprise-wide CKM product, based on the OCKD framework, is the first step in this transformation.

REFERENCES

Blackler, F. (1995). Knowledge, knowledge work and organizations: An overview and interpretation. *Organization Studies, 16*(6), 1021-1046.

Davenport, T.H., & Glaser, J. (2002). Just-in-time-delivery comes to knowledge management. *Harvard Business Review, 80*(7), 107-111.

Davis, M., & Klein, J. (2000, February 7). Net holds breakthrough solutions. *Modern Healthcare*, 14.

Deveau, D. (2000). Minds plus matter: Knowledge is business power. *Computing Canada, 26*(8), 14-15.

Dove, R. (1999). Knowledge management, response ability, and the agile enterprise. *Journal of Knowledge Management*, *3*(1), 18-35.

Duff, S. (2002). It's easier to tell the truth. *Modern Healthcare*, *32*(23), 12-13.

Dwivedi, A., Bali, R.K., James, A.E., & Naguib, R.N.G. (2001a). Telehealth systems: Considering knowledge management and ICT Iissues. *Proceedings of the IEEE-EMBC 23rd Annual International Conference of the IEEE Engineering in Medicine and Biology Society (EMBS),* Istanbul, Turkey.

Dwivedi, A., Bali, R.K., James, A.E., & Naguib, R.N.G. (2001b). Workflow management systems: The healthcare technology of the future? *Proceedings of the IEEE EMBC-2001 23rd Annual International Conference of the IEEE Engineering in Medicine and Biology Society (EMBS),* Istanbul, Turkey.

Dwivedi, A., Bali, R.K., James, A.E., & Naguib, R.N.G. (2002a). The efficacy of using object oriented technologies to build collaborative applications in healthcare and medical information systems. *Proceedings of the IEEE Canadian Conference on Electrical and Computer Engineering (CCECE) 2002*, *2*, 1188-1193.

Dwivedi, A., Bali, R.K., James, A.E., Naguib, R.N.G., & Johnston, D. (2002b). Merger of knowledge management and information technology in healthcare: Opportunities and challenges. *Proceedings of the IEEE Canadian Conference on Electrical and Computer Engineering (CCECE) 2002*, *2*, 1194-1199.

Gupta, B., Iyer, L.S., & Aronson, J.E. (2000). Knowledge management: Practices and challenges. *Industrial Management & Data Systems*, *100*(1), 17-21.

Hansen, M.T., Nohria, N., & Tierney, T. (1999). What's your strategy for managing knowledge? *Harvard Business Review*, *77*(2), 106-116.

Havens, C., & Knapp, E. (1999). Easing into knowledge management. *Strategy & Leadership*, *27*(2), 4-9.

Kennedy, M. (1995). Integration fever. *Computerworld, 29*(14), 81-83.

The Knowledge Management Centre. About the Knowledge Management Centre. Retrieved November 12, 2000, from *www.ucl.ac.uk/kmc/kmc2/AboutKMC/index.html*

Latamore, G.B. (1999). Workflow tools cut costs for high quality care. *Health Management Technology*, *20*(4), 32-33.

Liebowitz, J., & Beckman, T. (1998). *Knowledge organizations: What every manager should know*. St. Lucie Press.

Manchester, P. (1999, November 10). Technologies form vital component: INFRASTRUCTURE: The IT infrastructure will capture, store and distribute the information that might be turned into knowledge. *Financial Times* (London), p. 8.

Nonaka, I. (1991). The knowledge-creating company. *Harvard Business Review*, *69*(6), 96-104.

Pavia, L. (2001). The era of knowledge in health care. *Health Care Strategic Management*, *19*(2), 12-13.

Porter, M.E. (1985). *Competitive advantage: Creating and sustaining superior performance*. New York: The Free Press.

Sieloff, C. (1999). If only HP knew what HP knows: The roots of knowledge management at Hewlett-Packard. *Journal of Knowledge Management*, *3*(1), 47-53.

Taylor, R., Manzo, J., & Sinnett, M. (2002). Quantifying value for physician order-entry systems: A balance of cost and quality. *Healthcare Financial Management*, *56*(7), 44-48.

Wyatt, J.C. (2000). 7. Intranets. *Journal-Royal Society of Medicine*, *93*(10), 530-534.
Zack, M.H. (1999). Managing codified knowledge. *Sloan Management Review*, *40*(4), 45-58.

Chapter XX

Productivity Impacts from Using Knowledge

Murray E. Jennex, San Diego State University, USA

EXECUTIVE SUMMARY

This is a longitudinal case study that explored the relationship between use of organizational memory and knowledge, knowledge management, and knowledge worker productivity within the engineering group at a nuclear power plant. Three data points were taken over five years. The group used a knowledge management system (KMS) and it was found that the system improved effectiveness/productivity of the organization. The organization had not identified measures for determining productivity improvements, so the key results of the case study are models showing the impact of knowledge use on productivity.

INTRODUCTION

Kaplan and Norton's (1992) Balanced Business Scorecard measures the value of IS to the organization with one of the factors considered being the ability of the organization to sustain learning and improvement. Learning and organizational learning are the processes by which experience is used to modify current and future actions. Huysman, Fischer, and Heng (1994) as well as Walsh and Ungson (1991) believe organizational learning has organizational memory (OM) as a component. Stein and Zwass (1995) and Walsh and Ungson (1991) define OM as the means by which knowledge from the past is brought to bear on present activities, thus resulting in higher or lower levels of organizational effectiveness. Improving effectiveness can result in improved organizational performance and adding value to the organization. Organizational learning (OL) uses OM as its knowledge base. Davenport and Prusak (1998) define knowledge as an evolving mix of framed experience, values, contextual information, and expert insight that provides a framework for evaluating and incorporating new experiences and information that in organizations often becomes embedded in documents or repositories and in the organizational routines, processes, practices, and norms. Alavi and Leidner (2001) view organizational knowledge and OM as synonymous labels.

Knowledge management (KM) is defined by Malhotra (1998) as that process established to capture and use knowledge in an organization for the purpose of improving organizational performance. We refine KM to be the process of selectively applying knowledge from previous experiences of decision making to current and future decision-making activities with the express purpose of improving the organization's effectiveness. Jennex and Olfman (2002) view KM and OM as manifestations of the same process only in different organizations. User organizations "do" knowledge management; they identify key knowledge artifacts for retention and establish processes for capturing it. OM is what IT support organizations "do"; they provide the infrastructure and support for storing, searching, and retrieving knowledge artifacts. OL results when users utilize captured knowledge. That OL may not always have a positive effect is examined by the monitoring of organizational effectiveness. Effectiveness can improve, get worse, or remain the same. How effectiveness changes influences the feedback provided to the organization using the knowledge. Figure 1 illustrates these relationships.

Additionally, Strassmann (1990) and Rubin (1994) propose that adding value to the organization or the organization's customers improves the productivity of the organization. Rubin (1994) defines "added value" as being the result of improved organizational performance.

KMS are systems designed to manage organizational knowledge. Alavi and Leidner (2001) clarify KMS as IT-based systems developed to support/enhance the processes of knowledge creation, storage/retrieval, transfer, and application. Additionally, a KMS supports KM through the creation of network based OM, and support for virtual project teams and organizations and communities of practice. A final goal of a KMS is to support knowledge creation.

An organization implements a KMS to improve its ability to capture, store, and reuse knowledge with the expectation that it will improve its learning and overall performance through improved decision making. Ultimately, organizations implement a KMS to help the organization to learn and improve with the expectation that organizational effectiveness/productivity will improve. This case study looks at an organization that manages and uses knowledge to determine if KM truly does improve productivity.

The case study covers 5 years with data collected during three time periods. The first time period was in 1996 with the second time period being in 1998 and the third in 2001. The first data collection period utilized a survey and 40 interviews. The second data collection period occurred after the organization had completed a voluntary retirement program resulting in a 25% turnover in staff and utilized a survey and 10 interviews with new members to the organization. The third data collection period occurred while the organization was undergoing reorganization and reduction in force and utilized 22 interviews, 14 with interviewees from the first period, six with interviewees from the

Figure 1. The KM/OM/OL Model (Jennex & Olfman, 2002)

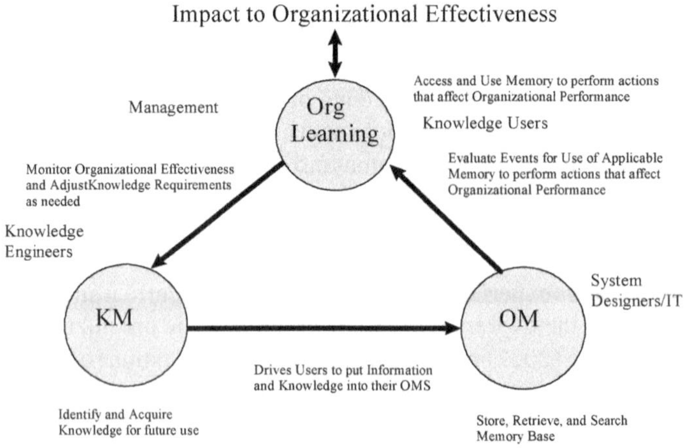

Impact to Organizational Effectiveness
Management
Org Learning
Access and Use Memory to perform actions that affect Organizational Performance
Knowledge Users
Monitor Organizational Effectiveness and AdjustKnowledge Requirements as needed
Evaluate Events for Use of Applicable Memory to perform actions that affect Organizational Performance
Knowledge Engineers
KM
OM
System Designers/IT
Drives Users to put Information and Knowledge into their OMS
Identify and Acquire Knowledge for future use
Store, Retrieve, and Search Memory Base

second period, and two with key managers leading the reorganization. All three data collection periods also included document review and direct observation for a period of several weeks during the data collection period.

BACKGROUND

The subject engineering organization is part of a large, United States-based, investor-owned utility. The utility is over 100 years old, has a service area of over 50,000 square miles, provides electricity to over 11 million people via 4.3 million residential and business accounts, and had operating revenues of approximately $8.7 billion in 2002. Utility net revenue has fluctuated wildly the last few years with a $2.1 billion loss in 2000, $2.4 billion in earnings in 2001 (primarily due to one-time benefits from restructuring and other initiatives), and decreasing to $1.2 billion in earnings in 2002. To service its customers, the utility operates a transmission and distribution system and several large electrical generation plants and is organized into three main line divisions: Transmission and Distribution, Power Generation, and Customer Service. Divisions such as Human Resources, Security, and Information Technology (IT) support the line divisions. The utility has approximately 12,500 employees.

The Power Generation division is organized into operating units dedicated to supporting specific power generation sites. Each operating unit has line organizations such as Operations, Maintenance, Engineering, and Chemistry/Health Physics. Power Generation operating units are supported by dedicated units from the corporate support divisions (Security, Human Resources, IT). The engineering organization used for this case study is part of the nuclear operating unit of the Power Generation division and is located at the largest electrical generation site operated by the utility. IT support is provided to this operating unit by Nuclear Information Systems (NIS), which administratively is part of the corporate IT division and which operationally reports to both corporate IT and the nuclear unit of the Power Generation division. NIS supported engineering through its Engineering Support Systems group. This group consisted of a supervisor, two project manager/analysts, and two developers. This group was tasked with the maintenance of the 11 systems under NIS control. New systems or enhancements to existing systems were done at the instigation of engineering. Engineering through a charge back process paid costs associated with these projects and developers were hired as needed to support the work.

At the time of the study, the engineering organization consisted of approximately 460 engineers disbursed among several different engineering groups reporting to the Station Technical, Nuclear Design Organization, Nuclear Oversight, and Procurement management structures. Industry restructuring was causing large drops in revenues that were driving the nuclear unit to reorganize engineering into a single organization consisting of 330 engineers under the management of the Nuclear Design Organization. An engineering organization was selected for the case study as:

- Engineers are knowledge workers and make decisions as a part of their job function.
- Engineers use knowledge to make decisions.
- Engineer productivity is improved by increasing the speed and/or quality of the decisions they make.

This specific engineering organization was selected because it was accessible. Also, this organization resolves equipment and operational problems within a nuclear facility. They utilize performance and maintenance histories, lessons learned, and previous problem resolutions to arrive at new solutions or courses of action. How well they do this is reflected in how well the facility operates. The organization has approximately 100 engineers organized into groups that support specific facility systems or programs.

SETTING THE STAGE

The organization is driven to capture and use knowledge. Since it is a nuclear plant, it falls under the guidance of the United States Nuclear Regulatory Commission (NRC). The NRC mandates that nuclear plants learn from events so that they are not repeated. Each nuclear site has an independent safety engineering group tasked with reviewing events from other sites for applicability to their site. Additionally, knowledge on event experience is promulgated to each site through official NRC documents. However, the result of this regulatory influence is that an inquiring and knowledge-sharing culture is fostered throughout the nuclear industry. This site had an excellent knowledge-sharing culture and interviews and surveys found that engineers were almost as likely to capture knowledge because they thought it a good idea as they were due to regulatory requirements. Table 1 shows the drivers that influence engineers to capture knowledge. These drivers are shown ranked by their importance. Additionally, their frequency of use is shown as it shows that importance has little to do with how often the driver is used.

The organization did not have a formal KM strategy or KMS when the case began, although by the end of the case, a formal KM organization had been formed. However, the organization did have KMS repositories and components although they were not

Table 1. Knowledge driver ratings

Driver or Reason Something Is Captured in the KMS	*n*	Importance (Std Dev)	*Frequency (Std Dev)*
NRC Requirement	19	1.05 (0.24)	3.26 (1.31)
You believe it is important to capture the knowledge	22	1.18 (0.41)	1.84 (1.30)
Procedure Requirement	19	1.32 (0.47)	2.27 (1.03)
Near-Miss Event	17	1.53 (0.64)	3.39 (0.96)
Management/Supervisor Directive	20	1.55 (0.70)	2.29 (1.36)
Site Event	18	1.56 (0.62)	3.21 (1.22)
AR Assignment	20	1.60 (0.71)	2.19 (1.05)
Data/Trend Analysis	19	1.63 (0.49)	2.67 (0.90)
Lesson Learned	17	1.71 (0.59)	3.08 (0.76)
Other Regulatory Requirement	14	1.71 (0.65)	2.93 (1.54)
Industry Event	20	1.75 (0.55)	3.44 (1.15)
Good Practice	19	1.79 (0.64)	2.67 (1.18)
INPO Recommendation	15	1.80 (0.56)	3.47 (1.25)
Group/Task Force Recommendation	17	1.82 (0.35)	3.86 (1.03)
Coworker Recommendation	18	1.83 (0.66)	2.56 (1.37)

n = # of respondents using the driver; Importance: 1=Very Important, 2=Important, 3=Not Very Important; Frequency: 1=Daily, 2=Weekly, 3=Monthly, 4=more than monthly, less than yearly, 5=Yearly

recognized as such. The organization's knowledge was found to reside in four major locations: documents, databases, employees' memory, and others' memories. Interviews and surveys found several repositories supporting these locations and it was determined that the de facto KMS was these components. Table 2 documents the de facto KMS and shows the type of repository, the system supporting the repository, and the types of knowledge found in the repository.

The above KMS components were found to be overlapping systems with each containing elements from the others. This was especially true for most IT components because process automation and reengineering led to the replacement of many documents and processes with IT substitutes. A few changes in the KMS were noted over the course of the case. The most significant was a decrease in importance of e-mail. This was attributed to changing the e-mail system from CCMail to Lotus Notes. The change was performed without converting e-mail archives with the effect that knowledge was lost. This experience taught the organization not to rely on e-mail as a repository. Another important change was the reduction in the reliance on the "work done" sections of MOSAIC. Cost-cutting process changes resulted in these sections being stored in the Corporate Document Management (CDM) system. This led to the addition of CDM to the KMS, which was the only component added during the course of the 5-year study.

An important observation on KMS use was that amount of use was not a good indicator of the impact of KMS use. Several long-term organizational member during interviews echoed the sentiment that it was not how often engineers used the KMS but rather that it was the one time that they absolutely had to find knowledge or found unexpected knowledge that proved the worth of the KMS. An example of this was the use of the KMS to capture lessons learned and best practices associated with refueling activities. These activities occur on an approximate 18-month cycle that was sufficient

Table 2. KMS components

Repository	System	Contents
Document Based	CDM	Documents: memos, correspondence, drawings, procedures, vendor info, Records: completed procedures, tests, surveillances, Maintenance Orders, Reports
	Engineer Library	Drawings, Licensing Documents, Codes, Standards, NUREGS, Regulatory Guides, Design Basis Documents, System Descriptions, EPRI Documents, Reports, Old Nonconformance Reports, Correspondence, Vendor Info
	Training Master File	Qualification Guides, Answer Keys, Event Evaluations, Lesson Plans, Task Analyses, Various Training Materials
Computer	MOSAIC	Equipment Maintenance History, Problem Reports/Resolutions, Root Cause and Corrective Actions, Lessons Learned
	NCDB	Drawing Revision History, Base Engineering Info, Program History and Info, Document History, Calculations
	TOPIC	Hypertext Files of Licensing Documents, ISEG Evaluations, Reports, Correspondence
	NDMS	Procedures, Procedure History, and Change Basis Documents
	Internet	Vendor/Utility/NRC Info
Self	Your Files	E-mail Archives, Files, Notebooks, In Head Memory, etc.
Other	Coworker	E-mail Archives, Files, Notebooks, In Head Memory, etc.
	External various	Various External Entity Files, includes INPO and NPRDS, EPRI, NRC, Vendors, User's Groups, Trade Groups

time to forget what had been learned during the last cycle or to have new members with no experience taking over these activities.

This made evaluating the impact of the KMS on productivity difficult as a common measure of impact is to multiply impact by the number of times used. This measure would not have reflected the actual impact on productivity had it been the only way of assessing the KMS. This was especially true since engineers, supervisors, and managers were consistent in agreeing that the KMS made them more productive and effective. It was decided that what was important was that engineers use the system when appropriate. To show this would be the case, an instrument from Thompson, Higgins, and Howell (1991) was adopted to measure engineer intent to use the KMS. The Thompson, Higgins, and Howell (1991) instrument, called the Perceived Benefit Model, was based on a study of workers' attitudes and behaviors with respect to optional computer usage. This work was based on Triandis' theory that the perception of future consequences predicts future actions. The implication was that the utilization of a PC in an optional use environment would be influenced by the individual's feelings, habits, and expected consequences of using PCs; and the social norms and environment governing PC use. They developed an instrument that was adapted to measure the relationships between social factors concerning KM use; perceived KMS complexity; perceived KM job fit; and perceived long-term consequences of KM use with respect to the utilization of KM. An additional factor, fear of job loss, was added to determine if fear affected an engineer's willingness to contribute to the KM. Table 3 reflects measurements of the engineers with respect to their perceptions affecting future use of the KMS and shows that the engineers will use the KMS when appropriate.

Finally, before it could be determined that the KMS had an impact on productivity, it had to be shown that the KMS was effective in performing its KM functions of

Table 3. Perceptions affecting usage

Perceived Benefit Factor	Score	Result
Social factors	4.08	Organizational culture encourages use of the KMS
Complexity (inverse scored)	2.38	Not complex, supports use of the KMS
Job fit, near-term consequences	4.56	Fits job well, supports use of the KMS
Job fit, long-term consequences	3.36	Neutral
Fear of job loss	2.32	No support, no fear found

Note: score is based on a 5-point scale where 5 is "strongly agree."

capturing, storing, searching, and retrieving knowledge. This was done by using Stein and Zwass' (1995) adaptation of Quinn and Rhorbaugh's (1983) Competing Values Model to assess KMS effectiveness. Table 4 summarizes these findings. Data were collected via 20 interviews that were coded and analyzed using a 5-point Likert scale (1 is strongly agree). The scores lead to the conclusion that the KMS was considered to be effective.

Further qualitative analysis of effectiveness utilized structured interviews that asked for opinions and examples on the effectiveness of the KMS. A consensus was found that the KMS made the subject audience more effective. Nearly all agreed that most past decision information could be retrieved within a couple of hours and usually within minutes. However, nearly all agreed that the KMS could be better. Elements of these interviews were used in stages 2 and 3 and found the same results. Examples of comments include the following:

It [the KMS] helps us to keep from reinventing the wheel. Every decision we make is not a new decision. Our systems help us to do this.

We have much more capability now than we did. As a Shift Technical Advisor (STA), we can do so much more than we could 10 years ago. There is almost too much data.

The information is there but the tools are slow, systems crash, and the information and tools are unreliable.

Table 4. Results of effectiveness functions

Factor	**Score**	**Result**
Integration	2	Good time/spatial integration, support effective KMS
Adaptation	2	Boundary spanning done, outside information brought in, supports effective KMS
Goal Attainment	1	Goals/performance tracked, support effective KMS
Pattern Maintenance	1.5	Procedures/revisions, individual skills tracked, supports effective KMS

Note: score is based on a 5-point scale where 1 is "strongly agree."

The last comment demonstrates that while the KMS was considered effective, it was found wanting in the areas of hardware performance and overall integration. Users who had a PC with less than a Pentium processor (during the case study) or a lower-level Pentium (during the latter two stages) found the systems slow and cumbersome. Lack of adequate RAM was a common issue (initially 32 MB were needed, expanding to 128 MB for the final stage — in each study, over half the subjects had PCs with half or less of the necessary RAM). Also, users noted that there were many tools and sources but no observed intentional cohesion between them. It was noted that all the systems are on Windows so that data could be copied/cut and pasted, thus providing a basic level of integration. However, no master plan for developing or maintaining the KMS was developed during the period of the research and no evidence was found suggesting this would ever be done. This indicates that the KMS will continue to lack cohesion and will not improve in effectiveness. The two observed changes in the KMS, noted above, actually reduced effectiveness by increasing access times. Also, reducing dependence on e-mail, while better for reliability, accuracy, and security, reduced individual effectiveness by removing an easy-to-use, readily accessible repository.

CASE DESCRIPTION

The key research question for this case was whether engineer use of the KMS results in improved productivity. Two areas of productivity were defined and examined. The first was individual engineer productivity as it was assumed that for engineers to continue to use the KMS, there must be a perceived benefit. The second was organizational productivity as it was assumed that for organizations to continue to support a KMS, there must be a benefit at the organizational level. This is consistent with the individual and organizational impact outcomes of DeLone and McLean's (1991) IS Success Model. The following paragraphs report the characterization of both forms of productivity.

Engineer Productivity

The standard measure for productivity is the ratio of resources used to products generated. This does not readily apply to most engineers. Instead, effectiveness was used as a measure of engineer productivity where effectiveness is a function of quantity and quality of engineering work accomplished. Engineering work in the context of the nuclear power facility was found to be related to decision support. Engineers performed evaluations and made recommendations to resolve plant issues, usually under time or resource pressure. Sometimes the work involved making and implementing the decision. In all cases, the engineer was measured on the timeliness, correctness, and quality of the decision support as determined by the supporting documentation and the satisfaction of the client. The case study explored engineering productivity and determined a model for it. Interviews were used to outline what measures the managers used to evaluate their engineers and to identify what measures the engineers' thought should be used. While no unique set of measures was identified, several factors together could be used for this measure. Figure 2 illustrates the personal productivity model derived for the subject organization.

Figure 2. Engineer Productivity Model

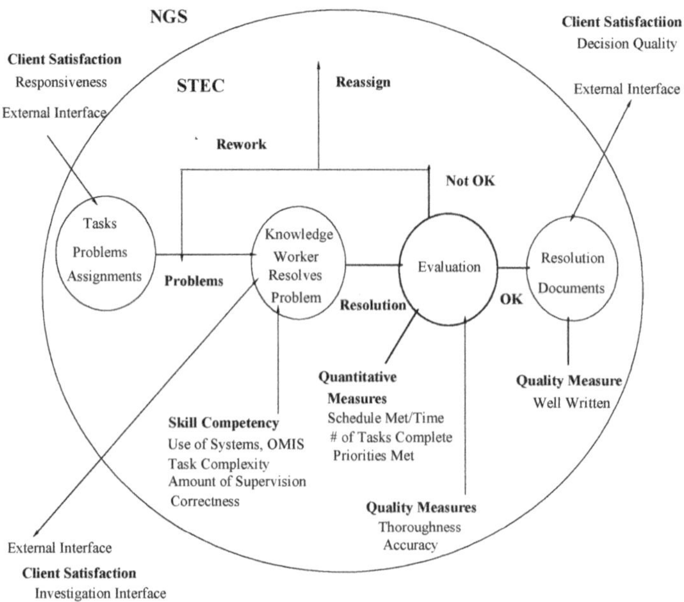

The Engineer Productivity Model has several quantitative, qualitative, and competency measures that are directly impacted by the use of the KMS. These measures are as follows:

- Timeliness in completing assignments
- Number of assignments completed
- Identifying and completing high-priority assignments
- Completeness of solutions (all the bases are covered)
- Quality of solutions (well written with complete documentation)
- Solving problems the first time
- Amount of work that has to be repeated
- Complexity of work that can be assigned to a worker
- Amount of backlog

Using this characterization of productivity, it was found that use of the KMS was considered a basic skill that each engineer was expected to possess. Use of the KMS was expected to improve the ability of the engineer to find and retrieve key information and knowledge that would aid the engineer in meeting deadlines and completing assigned work. As a result, the work would include all available knowledge and be complete and accurate. Managers and supervisors rated the best engineers as those who used the KMS most effectively as manifested by timeliness and completeness of work and with sufficient quality such that little to no rework was required and the clients (i.e., those who had the problem the engineer was resolving) were satisfied with the recommendations and/or decisions. Engineers who met these expectations were rewarded with pay increases, promotions, and more interesting assignments, providing additional extrinsic motivation for the engineer to use the KMS.

Organizational Productivity

Identifying productivity measures for the organization was more difficult than identifying them for the engineers. Three approaches were used. The first looked at the performance assessments done by external organizations. These provide an effectiveness assessment of productivity. The second looked at performance relative to the goals in the business plan. The third looked at performance relative to preset key performance indicators. The second and third approaches are more traditional in their representation of productivity.

Approach #1

The first measure was based on the SALP (Systematic Assessment of Licensee Performance) Reports issued by the NRC. Review of scores issued since 1988 showed an increase from a rating of 2 to a rating of 1 in 1996, the time of the first stage of this research (Table 5). Observed strengths in 1996 included the depth of component failure analysis; timely and thorough support for operations and maintenance activities; excellent diagnoses of equipment failures and investigation and resolution of emerging issues; operability determinations were well written and reflected conservative engineering judgment; and engineering self-assessments and resultant corrective actions were determined to be superior.

This rating dropped to a 2 in 1997 due to inconsistencies in management oversight and the quality in provision of engineering support to a few activities. However, it was noted that engineering had strong performance in resolving issues and determining corrective actions, self-assessment, and outage support (NRC News, 1997). The SALP program was suspended in 1998, as it was perceived that local government, insurance carriers, and others used ratings as objective measures of performance and not as self-assessment indicators. The SALP program was replaced by periodic plant performance reviews (NRC News, 1998). The plant performance review is a comprehensive review of plant processes with just the overall assessment released to the public; particular findings are given to the plant as guides for improvement but are not made public. The subject site was given acceptable ratings for the remainder of the study period.

The other part of the external evaluation process is the site evaluation performed by the Institute of Nuclear Power Operations (INPO). An evaluation was conducted during the spring of 1996 and resulted in a 1 rating. This rating was maintained throughout the 5 years of the study. A history of these ratings is not included, as the organization did not grant permission to publish it.

The external assessments identified several strengths directly related to engineer effectiveness. These include decision making, root cause analysis, problem resolution, timeliness, and operability assessment documentation. This indicates a direct link between engineer productivity and organization productivity. Also, since internal engineering effectiveness assessments were positive and organization effectiveness is rated highly, it can be inferred that engineer effectiveness does directly impact organizational effectiveness.

Table 5. SALP ratings

Year	Engineering Rating	Overall Rating
1997	2	1.5
1996	1	1.5
1994	2	1.5
1993	2	1.43
1991	2	1.57
1990	2	1.43
1989	3	1.71
1988	2	1.82

Approach #2

The second measure was how well the organization's performance matched the expectations of its business plan. The first stage found only a few goals related to the subject organization and few performance indicators and goals that could be used to determine productivity. Two indicators were linked to knowledge use: unit capacity and unplanned automatic scrams. Unit capacity and unplanned scrams are influenced by how well the engineers evaluate and correct problems. Both factors improved over time. These two factors plus unplanned outages and duration of outages became the standard measure within the organization and throughout the industry during this study. Reporting and monitoring of these factors significantly improved during the course of the study. Originally, information on how the site was performing was distributed infrequently with little attention paid to it. During the last 2 years, as management became more aware of KM and the need for measuring their own effectiveness, the process was changed. Currently, performance information is available on the site's intranet. Also a quarterly report is produced that discusses how the site is performing and pays particular attention to lessons learned, what is working well, what is not working well, and where there are problems.

Originally, this approach was not considered valuable as a measure of effectiveness. However, it is now considered to be a very effective measure and has replaced the first SALP approach as the method of choice for assessing organizational effectiveness. Table 6 lists the capacity factors for the units of the site. The table also lists the cumulative capacity factor because refueling outages cause lower capacity factors in the year they occur and the cumulative tends to show the overall impact of improvements in performance. Table 6 shows generally improving performance for both units during the period of the study (1996-2002). The dip in 1997 is due to special, first-time cleaning activities that caused refueling outages to be extended and is considered an anomaly in the generally improving trend. The dip for Unit 3 in 2001 is due to time needed to repair the turbine following an accident during start-up following completion of the refueling outage. This accident was not due to activities performed by the subject-engineering group and therefore was not considered a failure in KM.

Table 6. Capacity factors, actual and cumulative (PRIS, 2003)

Year	U2 Capacity Factor %	U2 Cumulative %	U3 Capacity Factor %	U3 Cumulative %
1990	88.65	69.47	69.78	69.75
1991	61.55	68.48	91.89	72.91
1992	93.58	71.27	72.00	72.79
1993	81.67	72.31	75.34	73.08
1994	99.32	74.77	96.69	75.44
1995	69.3	74.31	79.29	75.79
1996	90.97	75.59	93.17	77.24
1997	71.01	75.27	72.33	76.86
1998	89.94	76.24	95.75	78.21
1999	87.95	76.98	88.96	78.93
2000	90.69	77.78	101.55	80.34
2001	101.27	79.09	60.03	79.15
2002	90.80	79.70	100.92	80.36

Note: A capacity factor greater than 100% is possible because capacity factor calculations are based on the original reactor rating of 1,070 MW but the reactors are approved for operation at 1,105 MW.

Approach #3

The third productivity measure used performance indicators selected by the subject organization. These indicators are monitored monthly and graphs illustrating performance are printed and posted. This method provided less-than-useful results. It does tie in well with the organization's goals as defined in the second approach, but only addresses the quantifiable measures of the engineer productivity model. Since KM primarily affects the qualitative and competency skills of engineer productivity, this method does not provide any insight into whether KM improves productivity. However, as the organization progressed in its understanding of KM, this method was rolled into the second approach and is now used to report quantifiable results as well as to report on qualitative measures such as lessons learned. Combining of the second and third approaches, first observed during the third stage, has provided an acceptable measure of organizational effectiveness. This approach consists of a digital dashboard of key performance indicators along with a summary of issues needing improvement and lessons learned that is available to all employees on the site intranet. This measure indicated satisfactory performance during the data collection period with respect to quantifiable measures such as capacity factor (the unit 3 turbine accident occurred after the data collection period) as indicated in Table 6. It also provided focus on what employees needed to focus on and improve to ensure continued acceptable capacity factor performance.

CURRENT CHALLENGES FACING THE ORGANIZATION

Deregulation cost the organization dearly due the ensuing energy crisis that caused many western utilities to suffer huge losses due to the difference between the cost of power and what they were allowed to charge for it. This utility was forced to reduce staff and cut significant budget. The result of this was that the subject organization developed an even finer appreciation for the impact of the KM on productivity as well as the limitations of their KMS. The main challenge will be in improving the KMS while creating formal measures of KMS success and impacts on productivity and effectiveness. The organization has made a start in this direction by appointing a responsible manager for KM and by beginning to develop a formal KM strategy. This will be a challenge given the demand for resources from everyday operations.

LESSONS LEARNED

Many organizations have reported difficulty in measuring the impact of KM on organizational productivity/effectiveness. This case shows that an organization can find these measures if it looks deep into the organization. The following reflect the lessons learned from this case:

- Measures reflecting the impact of knowledge use can be found both for individuals and the organization.
- Formal management of KM is needed to guide the development of KM and the KMS. Without this oversight, the KMS tends to not be as integrated or usable as it could be. Additionally, the KMS may lack the capacity or processing power needed to transfer and use knowledge.
- A KM strategy is needed to guide management in identifying and measuring the impacts of KM on the organization.
- Amount of use is not a good measure for KM or KMS success or effectiveness. However, intent to use is a good measure.

REFERENCES

Alavi, M., & Leidner, D. (2001). Review: Knowledge management and knowledge management systems: Conceptual foundations and research issues. *MIS Quarterly, 25*(1), 107-136.

Davenport, T.H., & Prusak, L. (1998). *Working knowledge*. Boston: Harvard Business School Press.

DeLone, W.H., & McLean, E.R. (1992). Information systems success: The quest for the dependent variable. *Information Systems Research*, (3), 60-95.

Huber, G.P. (1991). Organizational learning: The contributing processes and the literatures. *Organization Science*, *2*, 88-115.

Huysman, M.H., Fischer, S.J., & Heng, M.S. (1994). An organizational learning perspective on information systems planning. *Journal of Strategic Information Systems*, *3*(3), 165-177.

Jennex, M.E., & Olfman, L. (2002, January). Organizational memory/knowledge effects on productivity, a longitudinal study. *Proceedings of the 35th Hawaii International Conference on System Sciences.*

Kaplan, R.S., & Norton, D.P. (1992). The Balanced Scorecard, the measures that drive performance. *Harvard Business Review.*

Malhotra, Y. (1998). Knowledge management for the new world of business. Retrieved October 18, 2003, from *www.brint.com/km/whatis.htm*

Nuclear Regulatory Commission (NRC). (1998, October 2). *NRC administrative letter 98-07, interim suspension of the Systematic Assessment of Licensee Performance (SALP) program.* Washington, DC: United States Nuclear Regulatory Commission.

Nuclear Regulatory Commission News (NRC News). (1997, April 8). *RIV-99-18, NRC finds performance "acceptable" at San Onofre in latest review.* Washington, DC: United States Nuclear Regulatory Commission.

Nuclear Regulatory Commission New (NRC News). (1997, August 1). *RIV-4497, NRC rates San Onofre Nuclear Plant "good" and "superior" in SALP report.* Washington, DC: United States Nuclear Regulatory Commission.

Power Reactor Information System (PRIS). (2003). Power reactor details. Retrieved July 31, 2003, from *www.iaea.org/programmes/a2/*

Quinn, R.E., & Rhorbaugh, J. (1983). A spatial model of effectiveness criteria: Towards a competing values approach to organizational analysis. *Management Science, 29*(3), 363-377.

Rubin, H.A. (1994). In search of the business value of information technology. *Application Development Trends, 1*(12), 23-27.

Stein, E.W., & Zwass, V. (1995). Actualizing organizational memory with information systems. *Information Systems Research, 6*(2), 85-117.

Strassmann, P.A. (1990). *The business value of computers* : The Information Economics Press.

Thompson, R.L., Higgins, C.A., & Howell, J.M. (1991). Personal computing: Toward a conceptual model of utilization. *MIS Quarterly, March,* 125-143.

Walsh, J.P., & Ungson, G.R. (1991). Organizational memory. *Academy of Management Review, 16*(1), 57-91.

About the Authors

Murray E. Jennex is an assistant professor at San Diego State University and president of the Foundation for Knowledge Management (LLC). Dr. Jennex specializes in knowledge management, system analysis and design, IS security, and organizational effectiveness; and is the editor-in-chief of the *International Journal of Knowledge Management* and the knowledge management systems track cochair at the Hawaii International Conference on System Sciences. He has managed projects in applied engineering and business and information systems development and implementation. His industrial and consulting experience includes nuclear generation, electrical utilities, communications, health services, and governmental agencies. Dr. Jennex is the author of numerous publications on knowledge management, end-user computing, international information systems, organizational memory systems, and software outsourcing. He holds a BA in chemistry and physics from William Jewell College, an MBA and an MS in software engineering from National University, and an MS in telecommunications management and PhD in information systems from the Claremont Graduate University. Dr. Jennex is also a certified information systems security professional (CISSP) and a California registered professional mechanical engineer (PE).

* * *

Hani Abdel-Aziz obtained his Bachelor of Science in communications engineering from Cairo University in 1989. In 1991, he joined Alcatel as a digital telecommunications engineer. In 1993, he moved to Triangle Information Systems as a network engineer. Two years later, he moved to IBM–Egypt also as a systems engineer, and in 1996 he joined Sun Microsystems–Egypt as a systems engineering manager. He obtained his Master of Science in communications engineering from Cairo University in 1997. In 2002, he was promoted to sales manager, and remains in this position to date.

Minwir Al-Shammari is a professor of operations management and technology in the Department of Management and Marketing in the College of Business Administration at the University of Bahrain. Professor Al-Shammari earned his PhD in industrial management from the University of Glasgow, UK (1990). He has been involved in teaching, research, training, and consultancy in the areas of knowledge management, operations and information management, business process reengineering (BPR), decision making with computers, project evaluation and management, management science, and research methodology. He is a member of several national, regional, and international professional associations. He has received a number of research awards. Professor Al-Shammari has authored/coauthored more than 25 research papers and served as a reviewer for several regional and international research journals. His publications have appeared in such refereed international publications as *Logistics Information Management, International Journal of Information Management, Knowledge Management Research and Practice, European Journal of Operational Research, Expert Systems with Applications: International Journals, Journal of Computer Information Systems, International Journal of Operations and Production Management, Production and Inventory Management Journal, International Journal of Commerce and Management, International Journal of Computer Applications in Technology, Cross-Cultural Management, International Journal of Management, Leadership and Organization Development Journal,* and *Creativity and Innovation Management.*

Yogesh Anand joined the Reserve Bank in April 2000 as chief information officer of knowledge services. Prior to this, he was information systems manager with the New Zealand Health Information Service for four years. In that role, he developed and implemented an e-business vision and strategy for the health sector in New Zealand. This resulted in the implementation of a sophisticated, secure, and user-friendly communications infrastructure for the health industry. His focus during that time was to work with the health sector to develop an information culture that would improve health care delivery in New Zealand. Between 1990 and 1996, Yogesh was project director at the New Zealand Dairy Board. He has also held positions at Databank in Wellington, Royal Globe Insurance in New York, Royal Saudi Naval Forces in Saudi Arabia, and Westpac in Wellington. Yogesh was a finalist in Computerworld IS Manager of the Year, 1999.

Teresa R. Bailey has been a Jet Propulsion Lab (JPL) technical librarian for more than 22 years. In addition to performing typical library functions such as cataloging and reference work, she is the program development coordinator for the Library, Archives, and Records Section, which allows her to use her creative and leadership talents in activities that include networking, marketing, outreach, and community building. She has an MLS from the University of Southern California and is currently a doctoral student at the Fielding Institute where she is researching the contribution of storytelling to organizational learning and knowledge sharing.

Rajeev K. Bali currently lectures and conducts research at Coventry University, UK. He is an invited contributor and reviewer for various international journals and conferences. His involvement with the IEEE resulted in an appointment as publications chair for the Information Technology Applications in Biomedicine Conference in 2003. He was the invited guest editor of the *Special Issue on Knowledge Management and IT in Healthcare* for the IEEE Transactions on Information Technology in Biomedicine in 2004. He is the founder and head of the Knowledge Management for Healthcare (KMH) research subgroup and has a biographical entry in *Who's Who in the World.*

Lieutenant Colonel Summer E. Bartczak is an assistant professor of information resource management at the Air Force Institute of Technology (AFIT) in Dayton, Ohio. In this position, she is responsible for the graduate education of officer and enlisted candidates selected from across the Department of Defense. She currently acts as program manager of the Information Resource Management Program. Lt. Col. Bartczak holds a BS from the United States Air Force Academy (1986), an MS in information resource management from the Air Force Institute of Technology (1990), a Master's of Military Operational Art and Science from the Air University Air Command and Staff College (1998), and a PhD in management information systems from Auburn University (2002). Her primary research interests include information and knowledge management, strategy, and implementation.

Florian Bayer studied economics at the University of Regensburg (Germany). Since 2003, he is research assistant and PhD student at the Department of Management Information Systems at the Martin Luther University Halle-Wittenberg. His research interests include knowledge management, strategic alliances, and risk management.

Anton Bradburn holds a PhD in management. He is currently a research fellow in the Department of Business Information Management and Operations at Westminster Business School (WBS). Anton is a member of the Business Information and Communications Technology research group within WBS where he is conducting a research programme into intellectual capital, knowledge management, and information strategies. Prior to taking up his research fellowship at the University of Westminster, Anton had been a senior manager with London Fire Brigade and a visiting lecturer in strategic management at other London-based universities.

Frada Burstein is associate professor at Monash University. She obtained her PhD in decision support systems in 1984 from the Soviet Academy of Sciences. At Monash University, Professor Burstein initiated and continues to lead the Knowledge Management research group, which comprises a virtual knowledge management laboratory. She has been a chief investigator for a number of research projects supported by grants and scholarships from the Australian Research Council and industry. Frada's research interests include intelligent decision support, knowledge management technologies, organizational memory, and knowledge reuse. Professor Burstein has published extensively in scientific journals and collections of papers, including *IT & People, European Journal of Operations Research,* and *Journal of Decision Systems*. She was an editor for special issues of international and Australian journals in knowledge management and decision support. She is a member of the editorial board of the *Journal of Information and Knowledge Management, Decision Support Systems*, and *International Journal of Knowledge Management*.

Ivy Chan is an instructor at the Chinese University of Hong Kong. She received her PhD in business administration from the School of Business at the University of Hong Kong. Her research interests include knowledge management, information systems planning, and organizational learning.

Patrick Y.K. Chau is a professor of information systems at the University of Hong Kong. He received his PhD in business administration from the Richard Ivey School of Business at the University of Western Ontario, Canada. His research interests include IS/IT adoption and implementation, decision support systems, and information presentation and model visualization. He has published in journals such as *MIS Quarterly, Communications of the ACM, Journal of Management Information Systems, Decision Sciences, Information and Management,* and *Journal of Organizational Computing and Electronic Commerce.*

Elayne Coakes is senior lecturer in Business Information Management at the Westminster Business School, University of Westminster (UK), teaching Strategies for Information Management and Knowledge Management as well as e-Business Strategies. Her research interests relate to the sociotechnical aspects of information systems especially knowledge management systems and at Westminster she is the co-ordinator of a research cluster, looking at Information and Knowledge Management. She is a member of the British Computer Society's Sociotechnical Specialist Group and active in promoting this view of information systems strategy and development. She has co-edited a number of books in this, and in the knowledge management field, as well as writing conference papers, articles in journals and several chapters in books. Elayne is also an Associate Editor of *OR Insight* with special responsibility for knowledge management and recently edited a special edition of the journal *JORS* on knowledge management and intellectual capital. Her PhD (Brunel Univesrity, UK) relates to a sociotechnical view of the insufficiencies of boundaries and stakeholders in the strategic planning of information systems.

Lynne P. Cooper is a senior engineer at the Jet Propulsion Laboratory (JPL) where she divides her time between developing Mars science instruments and knowledge management to support JPL proposal development and flight projects. She received her BS in electrical and computer engineering from Lehigh University and MS in computer engineering from USC. Her work has been published in *Management Science* and the *Journal of Engineering and Technology Management*. She is currently a PhD candidate in industrial and systems engineering at the University of Southern California investigating how risk operates within project teams. Her awards include the NASA Exceptional Service Medal for her work in automation, and the Best Paper, Academy of Management Organizational Communication and Information Systems Division (2001).

Gail Corbitt is a full professor at California State University where she is currently the department chair of accounting and MIS. Her teaching specialty is software development and ERP systems. Her teaching experience includes 18 years in the California State University system. Her PhD in management information systems is from the University of Colorado at Boulder. She also has more than 15 years of experience working in systems environments plus several consulting engagements that have offered students real-world experience or research opportunities. Areas of research and/or consulting include SAP/ERP implementation, business process redesign, and collaborative group technology. Gail has worked with several organizations including Hewlett Packard, Chevron, U.S. Navy, Intel, BASF, Simpson Paper Company, California Prison Authority, and the Huber Company. She had faculty internships at both Chevron (1997, 2002) and Hewlett Packard (10 months in 1999–2000) where she worked on SAP implementation projects. She was an SAP Distinguished Scholar for three years and currently serves on the Advisory Boards for the SAP Academic Alliance in the Americas and for International Programs.

David T. Croasdell is on the information systems faculty in the Accounting and Computer Information Systems Department at the University of Nevada, Reno. Dr. Croasdell's research interests include distributed knowledge systems, knowledge networks, knowledge management, organizational memory, and inquiring organizations. Dave has published in outlets such as the *Information Systems Management Journal, Communications of the Association of Information Systems, IS Frontiers, Australian Journal of Information Systems,* and *Annals of Cases on Information Technology*. He cochairs the knowledge management research track at HICSS.

Sally Dexter is currently completing a doctoral thesis exploring knowledge sharing among informal networks in a collaborative multiagency project within the public sector. Sally brings to the research field experience gained over a 15-year career spanning business operations, communications, and information systems. Her research interests include public and private sector knowledge management, cross-cultural knowledge management, and gender issues in information systems.

Peter Duchessi is an associate professor in the Department of Information Technology Management, School of Business, University at Albany. His areas of expertise include business planning and transformation, service management, operations management, information technology management, and e-commerce. He also lectures at the Graduate School of Business Administration, Switzerland, and the Universidad del Salvador, Argentina, and provides consulting and management education services to a number of international companies, including GE, Siemens AG, and Arthur D. Little. He publishes regularly in leading business journals, including *California Management Review, Management Science, Journal of Management Information Systems*, and *European Journal of Operational Research.*

Ashish Dwivedi is currently a senior lecturer at Hull University Business School, UK. His primary research interest is in the application of information and communication technologies (ICT) and knowledge management (KM) paradigms on organizational decision making, which was also his PhD research topic, received in 2004. One of the main areas of concern in KM is that there are no commonly accepted methodologies and a standard framework, despite the fact that the KM paradigm is recognised as an area of significant importance. He has additional interests in the use of ICT, data warehousing, decision support systems, and intelligent data mining.

Lieutenant Colonel Ellen C. England is an assistant professor of engineering and environmental management at the Air Force Institute of Technology in Dayton, Ohio, and has served as an Air Force bioenvironmental engineer for 18 years. She currently acts as program manager for the Environmental Engineering and Science Program and director of the Environmental Health and Safety Committee. She holds a BS, industrial engineering, University of Iowa, 1986; MS, general administration, Central Michigan University, 1991; MS, environmental health, University of Minnesota, 1996; and PhD, environmental engineering, University of Missouri-Rolla, 2003. Her primary research interests include occupational exposure assessment, air pollution control using bioreactors, and environmentally sustainable design. Lt. Col. England has coauthored 25 manuscripts in these areas and others.

Rafael Enparantza is an industrial engineer and holds a PhD in mechanical engineering (1992) and an MSc in advanced manufacturing technology (1988) from the University of Manchester, UK. His research experience began in 1986 at Tekniker (Spain) in the Department of Applied Mechanics. In 1992, he joined the Production Engineering Department where he took part in international projects related to cost estimation and computer-aided systems integration. From 1995 onward, he worked in different mechanical manufacturing companies and he rejoined Tekniker in 2002 in the area of product development technologies.

Robert D. Galliers is currently the provost and VP for academic affairs at Bentley College in Boston, Massachusetts. He has been a professor of information systems and research director in the Department of Information Systems at the London School of Economics (LSE). Prior to his positions at LSE, he served as Lucas professor of management and dean of the Warwick Business School, and earlier as foundation professor and head of the School of Information Systems at Curtin University in Australia. A leader in the field of management information systems, Galliers is editor-in-chief of the *Journal of Strategic Information Systems*, and a fellow of both the British Computer Society and the Royal Society of Arts. Galliers is a Harvard University graduate, with a master's in management systems from Lancaster University, UK, and a doctorate in information systems from LSE. He is past president of the Association for Information Systems, and was co-chair of the 2002 International Conference of Information Systems.

From 1988 to 1994, **Thomas Hahn** completed professional training to become a locksmith. Afterwards, he studied business and informatics at the University of Linz, Austria. The focus of his studies was on workflow management, process management, and in particular, knowledge management. He finished his study in November 2000. In 2001, he began working at Profactor Production Research GmbH where he was responsible for processing several projects in the area of process and knowledge management. He managed and coordinated projects on national and European level. In May 2004, he took over as the scientific head of the organizational development department at Profactor.

Afsoun Hatami is a PhD candidate in information systems at the London School of Economics (LSE). Her doctoral thesis is on the role of information and knowledge in decision making and strategizing. She examines the alignment of information infrastructure and strategizing processes in global organizations through a socio-technical lens.

Professor Robert D. Galliers and Dr. Edgar Whitley supervise her work. She earned her MSc in analysis, design, and management of information systems (ADMIS) in 2001 at LSE. Her master's dissertation was on exploring the influencing factors of a knowledge-sharing context, focusing on a knowledge management case at McKinsey & Co., where she worked closely with IMD and the University of St. Gallen in Switzerland. Her future research will expand into strategic organizational design and development in the global context. She resides in Hamburg, Germany.

Li Ping is a lecturer of business administration at the School of Management of Harbin Institute of Technology. She specializes in human resource management and manufacturing strategy. She focuses on the graduate program and undergraduate program, where she teaches human resource management and business plan. She is the author of book chapters and international conference proceedings on production and operation management.

Ronald Maier holds a PhD in management information systems from The Koblenz School of Corporate Management–Otto Beisheim Graduate School of Management (WHU) and a habilitation degree from the University of Regensburg. He worked as a visiting assistant professor at the Terry College of Business, University of Georgia in Athens, Georgia, (1998-1999). Since 2002, he has been with the School of Business and Economics, Martin Luther University Halle-Wittenberg and holds a chair in MIS, Information Systems Leadership. He has published articles on knowledge management (systems) in a number of research journals, books, and conference proceedings. His research interests include data management and business intelligence, business process management, and knowledge management.

Brigette McGregor-Macdonald is a learning and development consultant based in London. For the past four years, her work has taken her across Europe supporting financial services businesses in project management, leadership development, and coaching. She designs and implements leadership programmes, facilitates learning events, and has a keen interest in sustaining learning. Prior to her current role, Brigette worked in Japan managing a private school. Brigette graduated from Victoria University of Wellington with a Bachelor's in Commerce majoring in management.

Judy McKay is an associate professor and information systems discipline leader in the Faculty of Information and Communication Technologies at Swinburne University of Technology, Melbourne. She has a Bachelor of Arts from the University of Queensland, postgraduate qualifications in business and business systems from Curtin University, and has completed a PhD from the University of Queensland, studying the provision of information needs for managers. She teaches a number of master's- and MBA-level units, specializing in information systems planning and management, IS governance, and the delivery of business value from IT. Her areas of interest from both a teaching and research perspective are in the fields of information systems management, IS/IT strategy and alignment, IS governance, e-Business, and IT evaluation and benefits realisation. She is a regular presenter at international conferences and has published numerous journal articles and book chapters. In 2004, she coauthored a book with Associate Professor Peter Marshall entitled, *Strategic Management of e-Business* (Wiley). In addition, she is very interested in the practice of action research, and has written and published extensively on this particular subject. Her research interests frequently find her undertaking action research projects in government and industry.

Anju Mehta is currently pursuing her PhD in organizational analysis and change at Auburn University. She has a Masters degree in international business from Kurukshetra University, and a Masters degree in psychology from Maharshi Dayanand University, both in India.

Nikhil Mehta is currently completing his PhD in management information systems at Auburn University. His research and teaching interests include knowledge management, IT strategy, and analysis and design of information systems. He has a Masters degree in business administration from Kurukshetra University in India.

Raouf Naguib is head of the Biomedical Computing Research Group (BIOCORE) and professor of biomedical computing at Coventry University, UK. He has published over 180 journal and conference papers and reports in many aspects of biomedical and digital signal processing, biomedical image processing, and the applications of artificial intelligence and evolutionary computation in cancer research. He has also published a book on digital filtering, and coedited a second book on the applications of artificial neural networks in cancer diagnosis, prognosis, and patient management, which is his main area of research interest. Professor Naguib is a member of several national and international research committees and boards, and recently served on the administrative committee of the IEEE Engineering in Medicine and Biology Society (EMBS). He is actively taking part in a number of collaborative research projects with various partners and consortia in the UK (breast, colon, ovarian, and urological cancers, and Hodgkin's disease), the EU (prostate and colorectal cancers), the United States (breast cancer and cancers of the oesophago-gastric junction), and Egypt (bladder cancer).

Rebecca L. Nash is a senior software engineer devoted to technical communications and institutional computing at the Jet Propulsion Laboratory. She received her BS in biological sciences from California State University at Los Angeles, and her MS in interactive telecommunications from the University of Redlands. Rebecca designs interfaces from Web sites to applications, and helps organizations improve the usability of their products.

Franz Obermair studied automation technology in Wels (Austria). He worked seven years at a supplier for car manufacturers and one year in the area of die and mould engineering for TCG Unitech AG. For the last five years, he has been a research assistant at the Department of High-Speed Cutting and Manufacturing Engineering at Profactor Production Research GmbH.

Jill Owen is a PhD candidate in the Knowledge Management Research Group in the School of Information Management and Systems (SIMS) at Monash University. She has worked with some of Australia's major corporate companies in the airline, financial services, health, credit card, and information technology industries specialising in both business and IT project and program management, including at a senior management level. Jill's research interests are in the area of how knowledge management integrates with project, program, and portfolio management.

David J. Pauleen (PhD) is senior lecturer at the School of Information Management at Victoria University of Wellington, New Zealand. Current research interests include knowledge management in the private and public sector, cross-cultural factors in information and knowledge management, and virtual team leadership, dynamics, communication, and technology. His work has appeared in the *Journal of Management Information Systems* (2003–2004), *Journal of Global Information Management, Leadership and Organizational Development Journal, Journal of Knowledge Management, Journal of Information Technology*, and *Internet Research–Electronic Networking Applications and Policy*. He is also editor of the book, *Virtual Teams: Projects, Protocols and Processes* (2004).

Tu-Anh T. Phan is a senior software engineer at the Jet Propulsion Laboratory (JPL) where she is responsible for the implementation of many Web-enabled database systems, such as those that support JPL flight projects and proposal activities. Currently, she is leading the development of the NASA Program and Project Management Support System. She received her Bachelor of Science in mathematics from the University of California, Los Angeles, and has been with JPL since 1994.

Eliot Rich is an assistant professor in the Department of Information Technology Management, School of Business, University at Albany. His research and teaching focus on the interplay between software systems, knowledge management, and technology implementation. His approach combines computer simulation with the techniques of organizational analysis to identify and analyze complex business and governmental problems. Prior to receiving his PhD from the University at Albany, he worked for 13 years as a software designer, business analyst, and development manager in the financial, health care, and public sectors. He also holds degrees from Harvard University and Brooklyn College.

Bernhard Schmiedinger studied computer science in Linz, Austria, and during his study he was responsible for ICT and knowledge management at the VA TECH International GmbH. Currently, he is research assistant in the department of organizational development at Profactor Production Research GmbH. As project manager at Profactor, he is responsible for the EU Project Know-CoM (Knowledge and Cooperation-Based Engineering in Die and Mould making SMEs), and is also involved in several national and international projects such as the EU Project PLEXUS.

Elisabeth Stephan is a student at the University of Applied Science (College for Information and Knowledge Management) in Eisenstadt, Austria. She worked as an intern at Profactor Production Research GmbH in the Department of Organizational Development and Management Systems. Her main task was assisting in a research project about evaluation and development of organizational competencies in small and medium-sized enterprises.

Tian Yezhuang is a professor at the School of Management of Harbin Institute of Technology and the director of the Department of Business Administration. He specializes in human resource management, organizational theory, and manufacturing strategy. Professor Tian focuses on the postgraduate program and the MBA program where he teaches human resource management and management innovation. He is the author of over 30 journal articles, book chapters, and international conference proceedings on organizational theory. He holds a BA in psychology sciences from Hangzhou University, and an MS in management engineering and a PhD in management from Harbin Institute of Technology.

Khaled Wahba is an assistant professor in the Department of Systems and Biomedical Engineering at Cairo University. Dr. Wahba is also the academic adviser at the Regional IT Institute (RITI) in Cairo. He graduated with a Bachelor of Science from the Department of Systems and Biomedical Engineering at Cairo University in 1985. He continued on to a master-level program in the same department from which he received his MSc in 1989. Dr. Wahba later studied at Aachen University of Technology in Germany where he received his PhD in 1996. Wahba's fields of interest are system/business dynamics, Web-based applications, information systems, distance education, e-learning, simulation and modeling, control of dynamic systems, and knowledge management. Dr. Wahba has supervised more than 150 theses in business administration, computer science, and business information technology, as well as more than 20 senior projects in systems and biomedical engineering. Dr. Wahba is an active member in various associations including the Information Resources Management Association (IRMA) since June 1999 and the Systems Dynamic Society since June 2001 where he also acts as president of its Egypt chapter. He has participated in various conferences and workshops in the fields of system dynamics, software engineering, biomedical engineering, information technology and knowledge management, entrepreneurship, and distance education among others.

Colin White is systems analyst at Deloitte Consulting. His consulting practices focus on ERP implementations, specifically those involving SAP applications. Prior to his work at Deloitte, Mr. White was an Information Technology Application Specialist for the State of Washington. Notable projects involved project management, systems integration, and knowledge management. Mr. White has a bachelor's degree (Honors) in management information systems and electronic commerce from Washington State University in Pullman, Washington.

Zhang Li is an associate professor of business administration at the School of Management of Harbin Institute of Technology. She specializes in knowledge management, organizational memory, organizational learning, organizational communication, and manufacturing strategy. Professor Zhang focuses on the graduate program and the MBA program for which she teaches management, management communication, and knowledge management. She is the author of over 10 journal articles, book chapters, and international conference proceedings on knowledge management. She also conducts some research on knowledge management in manufacturing enterprises in China.

Suzanne Zyngier is a doctoral candidate at Monash University. Her research interests include intelligent decision support, evaluation, and obstacles to knowledge management. Her current research centres on the governance of knowledge management strategies. Her master's dissertation was concerned with knowledge management understandings and practices amongst Australia's top 1,000 companies by survey research and case studies in various contexts. Prior to joining academia, she was an experienced knowledge management and information services analyst who had her own business as a consultant to the professional, corporate, and not-for profit sectors. Suzanne has published in journal articles, a technical report, and book chapters, and has presented papers at international conferences and at presentations to industry groups.

Index

D

E

F

G

H

I

J

CPSIA information can be obtained at www.ICGtesting.com
Printed in the USA
LVOW03*1738230714

395707LV00014B/365/P

9 781591 403517